THE OLD REGIME IN FRANCE

THE OLD REGIME IN FRANCE

BY

FRANTZ FUNCK-BRENTANO

TRANSLATED BY HERBERT WILSON

NEW YORK

Howard Fertig

1970

First published in English in 1929
by Edward Arnold, London

HOWARD FERTIG, INC. EDITION 1970
Reprinted by permission of Edward Arnold, London

Library of Congress Catalog Card Number: 68:9656

PRINTED IN THE UNITED STATES OF AMERICA
BY NOBLE OFFSET PRINTERS, INC.

FOREWORD TO THE ENGLISH EDITION

WHEN an English translation of M. Funck-Brentano's *L'Ancien Régime* was first suggested to Messrs. Edward Arnold & Co., they consulted the late Professor H. W. C. Davis and asked his opinion of the work. His report encouraged them to proceed, and they think it may be of interest to reproduce the following extracts :

" The author is well known as a student of the social history of France. His books on *The Legends and Archives of the Bastille*, on *L'affaire du Collier* and on *The Middle Ages* have been extremely successful. No doubt you have noticed that the first and third of these works have been ' crowned ' by the French Academy. The value of *L'Ancien Régime* to English readers is that it explains the social institutions and traditions of the eighteenth century, with copious illustrations from the Memoirs of that period. . . . A book of this kind has been needed for a long time past in England, as a sort of introduction to the works of the great French Memoir writers. Chapter II (the Family), Chapter III (The Seigneurie), Chapter VI (Lettres de Cachet) and Chapter VIII (The Village) contain much that will be new to the best-informed English readers. . . . It may interest you to know that, quite ten years ago, Mr. H. A. L. Fisher said to me that there was a crying need for a book which would explain the fundamental ideas of the old social system in France and their influence on the government of the Monarchy. M. Funck-Brentano seems to have written this very book."

Professor Davis recommended us to print the verse quotations in the original French, on the ground that they would lose all their flavour in a translation, and to reproduce the bibliographies, which are attached to each chapter. His advice has been followed in both respects.

CONTENTS

THE OLD REGIME IN FRANCE

CHAPTER I

THE FEUDAL STATE AND TRADITION

I. Meaning of the term " Ancien Régime."—II. The Aims we have in View.—
III. Origins.—IV. The Mesnie and the Fief.—V. Tradition.—VI. The
Need for Unity.

I.—*Meaning of the term " Ancien Régime "*

BY Ancien Régime is commonly denoted that social and political
régime which was destroyed by the French Revolution. In
order to define the period of its duration it has been customary
to place its beginnings at the advent to power of the Bourbons
at the end of the sixteenth century—the period comprised between
the termination of the wars of Religion and the beginning of the
Revolutionary era. But during that long space of time France
was far from presenting a picture of unchanging immobility. Quite
the contrary ; as different periods succeeded each other she underwent numerous and profound modifications. Society at the time
of Louis XIII presented still greater differences between it and the
conditions prevailing at the end of the seventeenth century than
the latter showed when contrasted with the society which followed
the Revolution. On the other hand, we can hardly any longer
say that the reign of Louis XVI still formed part and parcel of
the Ancien Régime, so important and swift had been the political
and social transformations therein.

We should rather be tempted to say that the French Revolution
began with the coming of Louis XVI to the throne ; still more
must we bear in mind the Parliamentary reforms instituted between 1770 and 1771 by Maupeou, the Chancellor—a revolutionary
procedure and one of a very comprehensive nature. What we
term the " Ancien Régime " is most truly represented by the
social and political conditions of the reign of Louis XV, a fine and
glorious epoch during which France was famous, not only for the

1

brilliance of her literature and art, the high efficiency of her industries, and the widespread diffusion of her influence and her language, but also because it was a period during which her armies and her diplomacy did not fail to do her honour. " These French, these Romans of modern times," as Frederick II admiringly exclaimed.

It formed the period of the Ancien Régime in its full maturity, a picture of which will be more specially presented in the following pages, without neglecting the reigns of Louis XIV, Louis XIII and Henri IV, which taken together may be considered as forming the adolescence of the institutions in question, sound and vigorous in the first portion of the seventeenth century, spacious and brilliant during the second. As regards the reign of Louis XVI, a special chapter will be devoted at the end of this study to the transition between the Ancien Régime and the France of to-day.

II.—*The Aims we have in View*

If these pages possess any special quality it is that they are written from an independent point of view, with no other idea than to present an accurate picture of the France of the great grandparents of our own grandparents. I have kept before my mind what my master, H. Taine, said to me more than once :

" I admire those men who had such clear political opinions ; in spite of the efforts of my whole life I have never been able to reach a similar result."

Taine begins his *France Contemporaine* with the following words : " I am going to endeavour to give an accurate description of these three states, the Ancien Régime, the Revolution and the new Régime, and beg leave to declare that I have no other end in view."

I am thinking also of the remark made by Benjamin Guérard, one of the greatest historians of the nineteenth century—*the* greatest, perhaps, certainly in my opinion the greatest—in his immortal *Prolégomènes au Polyptique de l'Abbé Irminon* : " Let us have greater confidence in the reason and justice of our fathers, and not be so ready to correct their judgments."

And I take this salutary and true reflection made by that charming, simple-minded, upright, modest and refined man, Albert Babeau, from one of his admirably expressed and succinct monographs on old France : " It is by knowing how to respect the past that one merits the respect of the future."

" One cannot really love one's country unless one loves her entirely, and under every régime," wrote Albert Duruy.

Let me end by quoting the remark of Henri de Boulainvilliers, the writer on feudal customs : " Every period has its own special merits which do not pass to succeeding generations."

Will the reader kindly follow us in the spirit of the above remarks ? We are not seeking to convince, to prove, or to make proselytes. Here we are before the documents we have collected, like an artist who has set up his easel facing a country scene, of which he is endeavouring to paint a faithful representation.

III.—*Origins*

The Ancien Régime sprang from society in a state of feudalism. No one can gainsay this. The state of feudalism was the issue, in that marvellous period extending from the middle of the tenth century to the middle of the eleventh century, of the old French *familia* in process of transforming its private into public institutions.

During the ninth and tenth centuries the successive invasions of barbarians, Normans, Hungarians and Saracens had plunged the country into a state of anarchy in which all its institutions had foundered. The peasant abandoned his fields to flee from violence ; the people huddled crouching in the depths of the forests or on inaccessible heaths, or took refuge on the mountain heights. The links uniting the inhabitants of the country were shattered ; the governing rules derived from custom or legislation were broken up ; society was no longer kept together by any guiding principles.

In this state of anarchy the work of reconstructing society took place under the influence of the only organized force which had remained intact, under the one shelter that nothing could overthrow, for its foundations rest on the heart of man—that of the family.

When faced with imminent danger the family resisted and held together more strongly, thereby acquiring greater cohesion. Obliged to satisfy its needs it created the appliances necessary for agricultural and mechanical labour, and weapons for self-defence. As the State no longer existed, the family took its place. Social life concentrated round the family hearth ; the life of the community was confined to the precincts of the dwelling and the jurisdiction of the family ; it was limited to the walls of the house and surrounding enclosure.

It formed a society to itself on a small scale, neighbour to, but isolated from, similar small societies constituted on the same model.

At the beginnings of our history the head of the family recalled the *pater-familias* of classic times. He commanded the group surrounding him and bearing his name, organized their common defence, and distributed the work to be done according to the capacity and needs of each. He *reigned*—this is the word to be found in documents of the period—as absolute master. He was called " Sire " ; his wife, the mother of the family, was called " dame," *domina.*

The family lived in its fortified residence. Men toiled, loved, and died in the same spot where they had been born. The head of the family was by turns a fighting man and agricultural worker, like the heroes in Homer. The lands he cultivated lay around his dwelling.

Under the direction of its chief the family became skilful in building its shelter, and in making hooks and ploughs. In the inner courtyard glowed the fire of the forge in which weapons were fashioned on the resounding anvil. The women dyed and wove fabrics.

The family became a fatherland, and the Latin writings of the period designated it by the word *patria*, and it was loved with all the more affection because it was a concrete and living fact under the eyes of every one. It made its compelling power directly felt, as well as its gentle influence. It became a solid and well-loved defence, an indispensable protection. Without the family, man could not maintain his existence.

In this way were formed those sentiments of solidarity uniting the members of the family to each other, which continued to develop and become more and more definite under the influence of a powerful tradition. A man's prosperity contributed to that of his relatives, the honour of the one became that of the other, and, as a consequence, the shame of the one was reflected upon all the members of his kin :

> La honte d'une hore (heure) del jour
> Tolt (enlève) bien de quarante ans l'onour . . .
> Li (les) parent qui corpe (faute) n'i ont
> Longtans après hontous en sont. . . .
> > Robert de Blois.

At the end of the eighteenth century, when Retif de la Bretonne composed his moving drama *Les Fautes sont personnelles*, he was writing at a period when, even after such a long span of years, these sentiments had not yet disappeared.

We shall see them becoming strengthened and developed, and assuming greater importance as the family developed, and as the work accomplished by it shone forth in a clearer light. The House had been built up, and its lineage—the *geste* as it was called in the Middle Ages—had been extended. The Bailli de Mirabeau rightly interpreted the opinion prevailing in the eighteenth century when he wrote : " To bring honour or advantage to the family is the sole ruling sentiment."

IV.—*The Mesnie and the Fief*

The family, constituted in this way, did not remain limited to the father, mother, children and servants. From the commencement of the tenth century it became enlarged. The sense of solidarity uniting its different members, strengthened by the necessities of the times, held the various branches firmly united to the trunk. The younger members and their offshoots remained grouped around the eldest, and continued to receive at his hands a superintendence in common. This enlarged family, which embraced the younger sons and their children, their cousins, the servants and workmen attached to the house, took the name of mesnie—from the Latin *mansionata*, or House.

The mesnie comprised the family, the relations assembled around the head of the principal branch, the servants and all of those living round, maintained for the service of the House, and supported by it. At the head of the mesnie was the seigneur, invested with a patronal and paternal character in accordance with the authority he exercised. There was an old saying, " *tel seigneur, telle mesnie,*" just as we say, " like father, like son."

Kinsmen and their most faithful allies were grouped together in the mesnie. They were fed, brought up and instructed in the cultivation of the land and the calling of arms, together with the nephews, descendants and other relatives. The spirit ruling the mesnie remained strictly on family, patronal and *feudal* lines, for out of the mesnie arose the fief.

The family, now grown larger and organized into a mesnie, had its artisans and farm labourers, who, when occasion arose, became fighting men under the leadership of the chief ; it possessed a moral organization, again under the direction of the head of the family. The members of this enlarged family were united like a corporation ; they gave each other mutual assistance ; they possessed their tribunal, the tribunal of the seigneur, that is, of the head of the family ; they had their own customs, manners and traditions ; they had their standard and their battle cry ; they had their banner on its staff with gilded point.

In this way the family, by perpetuating itself through successive generations, strengthened its traditions and the special characteristics of heroism and honour in which it took pride.

This was the living cell from which France issued. For the

mesnie produced the fief, as we have just said, and the feudal
state engendered society as it is to-day.

The fief made its appearance in the eleventh century in the
form of a greatly enlarged family over which the father was suzerain,
and so, in order to designate the entire agglomeration of persons
united under the governance of a feudal chief, contemporary
writers made use of the word *familia*. The Baron—this word
means " master "—at the head of a fief, was in reality the *chef
de famille*. This comprised all his faithful following, his *subjects*,
and it would be a good thing to go back to this term. The Baron
called his subjects his kinsmen. They were closely united to each
other, like members of the same family, whether on questions of
good or evil. " The fault will be yours," said a vassal to his lord,
" but mine is the hurt ; and in this you will share, for the hurt
falls upon him who holds the Lordship, and you must make it
good to me."

In return, the vassal was bound to his suzerain by the sentiments
and duties of a son towards his father. He must serve him with
loyal affection, follow him to battle, take his advice on important
matters, obtain his consent to marry or when he was making a
match for his children ; he owed him affection, aid, and fidelity ;
and these sentiments, engendered by the fictitious relationship
created by the feudal bond, but also inspired by the ties and sentiments proper to a real family, were so strong that they carried
greater weight than the obligations of real relationships.

Such was the soul of feudalism, and upon it France built up her
organization, and, need we say, all that is great and glorious in
her history.

The eleventh, twelfth and thirteenth centuries in France formed
the greatest epoch in the history of the world. After that, when
feudal institutions no longer corresponded to changed social conditions, the term " feudalism " assumed a more unfavourable
sense ; but the greatest minds from Frédéric Le Play, the economist
and sociologist, to Viollet-le-Duc, the architect and archæologist,
have done justice to it.

Feudalism, which ensured the protection of the weak by the
strong, combined with the reciprocal duty of devotion on the part
of the *protégé* to his *patron*—the latter word was thus early the
term applied—not only gave rise to fiefs properly so called, domains
grouped round a château ; it also produced the towns, and urban
conditions ; it formed corporations and guilds, and even gave to
the clergy the impregnable position they held.

The mesnie sprang from the family, the fief from the mesnie ;
the small fiefs produced the large fiefs, and from the latter the royal

power took its rise, carrying to the highest point in a great nation the character and traditions of one large family.

Like the authority of the feudal Baron, the royal power sprang from paternal authority. " The King," said Hugue de Fleury, " is in the likeness of the father." And let us beware of only see-ing in this some abstract relationship, some remote origin merely outlined by external forms, words or formulæ ; we shall discover a direct origin, established by precise facts, the consequences of which we shall see following each other in the clearest manner down through the centuries. This paternal, family, and patronal character—*feudal* let us call it, using the word in its true sense—was to constitute the greatness of the French Monarchy ; it formed its beauty and power for good, and after it had gloriously accom-plished its task, and, with the change in ideas and customs, had become out of harmony with new social conditions, this same feudal, patronal, family and paternal character—these words are here synonymous—was to bring in its train destruction and death. The two grandest figures in our history, those of Joan of Arc and Napoleon, were to end as martyrs to it, and such likewise was to be the end of the greatest and most glorious of our institutions—the monarchy.

V.—*Tradition*

These facts will remain present in the mind of anyone who will take the trouble to read the following pages. From age to age our institutions, practices, customs, way of looking at things, and usages, have remained profoundly impregnated with them by the force of tradition. This is the second of the two great permanent facts which dominate and regulate the history of France from the coming of the Capets right down to the Revolution.

First comes " Family," or to speak more exactly, Feudalism : for in defining as accurately as possible the real meaning of this word and giving to it its historical sense, we should call it the develop-ment, the extension of the family ; and secondly " Tradition." For do not " family " and " tradition " live by each other ?

The France of old knew nothing of any legislative system which traced out, by the decisions of a deliberative assembly, or an established authority, the paths it should follow. People lived after the manner of their ancestors : " Our forefathers acted thus." Custom was the law, firm and undisputed. And if one considers the matter in this light one will understand that it could not be otherwise.

VI.—*The Need for Unity*

But what happened ? What was bound to happen ; and all
the more pronounced because, as was said above, men's deliberating
reason had little scope for action in those days. The thousands
and thousands of diverse groups, assembled around the family
cell, developed, and as they developed they clashed with neighbouring groups. From the very fact of the progress they had
accomplished intercourse became necessary, not only with the
surrounding neighbourhood, but with distant settlements. The
birth of trade and the extension of industry ; common views and
aspirations, the necessity of defence against common enemies :
from all these points of contact disputes arose, which were the
more animated and frequent because each of these local and feudal
groups—and in the feudal system, we must repeat, were included
the bishoprics, monasteries, towns, corporations and guilds, all
organized on a feudal basis—had been built up on original and
independent lines, possessing its special features, personal character and particular interests. Cannot one imagine what a swarm
of ants this became ?

The seigneurs within the limits of their jurisdiction, the important
Barons throughout the extent of their great fiefs, and the King
at the head of the country, each strove to co-ordinate, reconcile,
and appease the incessant and innumerable quarrels. We may
say that the securing of interior peace and harmony was the great
and almost sole task of the Kings of France. But all these " peace-
makers," to use the expression of St. Louis, acted as feudal lords,
that is, as *pères de famille*, striving unremittingly, right down to
the eighteenth century, to bring about harmony between diverse
interests. In the case of Louis XV, Voltaire showed this wonderfully well ; but they did not use their efforts in making laws, for
such an idea had not occurred to them—no one in those days
would have thought of such a thing. In this way the French
nation unfolded her history naturally and spontaneously ; she
wrought it out vigorously, and realized her dazzling destiny by
the energy of her living forces. But the further she advanced
the greater became the need for unification and legislation, for a
system of order common to, and in harmony with all.

The essential elements of her social life which we have sketched
above—that of the family, feudal and local on the one hand, the
powerful sentiment of tradition on the other—out of which the
nation took her rise and guiding principles, were opposed, by an
infinity of active forces, to this work of nationalization. Instinctively they were antagonistic, owing to thousands of active energies

which drew their sap from roots deep-buried in the minds of the people right down to that day in 1789, when this antagonism became so pronounced that the explosion occurred.

Augustin Thierry has drawn the following sketch :

" Perpetual lack of order in the public finances, chaos in the Assemblies, the pretensions of the Parliaments, lack of any rule and proper authority in the Administration, a kaleidoscopic France with no uniformity of laws and administration, more a conglomeration of twenty kingdoms than one State—so that one looks back to the period when one enjoyed the benefits of union between laws, administration, and territory."

Augustin Thierry possessed a brain modelled by the nineteenth century ; had he lived in the old days he would have wished to escape from this uniformity he vaunts so greatly. However this may be, we have just seen at a glance that it was impossible that the people of France could have worked out their history in any other way, when the origins from whence they sprang are taken into consideration ; and these origins could have been none other than what they were. So much so that we might be tempted to repeat with our friend, Candide, " that all was for the best in the best of all possible worlds."

We might conceive of a France at the beginning of the nineteenth century without the Empire, for Napoleon might have died when seventeen years old from an accident or illness. We cannot picture a France in the tenth century extricating herself from a condition of anarchy by any other forces than those of the family, since these were the only forces in existence ; and it is impossible to imagine this social organization maintaining and developing itself on any other line than that of tradition.

At the end of a very interesting book on the condition of France as recorded in the State Registers of 1789, Edme Champion gives it as his opinion that a society organized in a more absurd, incoherent, and extravagant manner than that of the Ancien Régime could not be imagined. That excellent historian judges it in accordance with the ideas of his own times. If he had thought fit to base his judgment on the conceptions in which men of the seventeenth and eighteenth centuries were steeped, everything would have seemed to his mind co-ordinated and duly explained. This is the result at which we shall endeavour to arrive by keeping constantly present before our minds the two great facts which dominate and rule our history ; namely, the feudal spirit and tradition.

BIBLIOGRAPHY

Avenel (Vicomte d'), *La Noblesse Française sous Richelieu*, 1901.—Babeau (Albert), *Le Village sous l'Ancien Régime*, 1891.—Babeau (Albert), *La Ville sous l'Ancien Régime*, 1880.—Boulainvilliers (Henri de), *État de la France*, 1727.—Duruy (Albert), *L'Armée Royale en 1789*, 1888.—Guérard (Benjamin), *Prolégomènes au Polyptique de l'Abbé Irminon*, 1844.—Retif de la Bretonne, *Les Fautes sont personnelles.*—Taine (H.), *Les Origines de la France contemporaine, l'Ancien Régime.*

CHAPTER II

THE FAMILY

I. The State is an Agglomeration of Families.—II. The Father of the Family.—III. Marriage.—IV. Integrity of the Patrimony.—V. The *Maisons de Village*.—VI. Family Solidity.—VII. Honour is the Foundation Stone of Monarchies.—VIII. Hereditary Capacities and Callings.

I.—*The State is an Agglomeration of Families*

WE can still say of French society in the seventeenth and eighteenth centuries what was applicable to the time of Philip-Augustus and St. Louis ; it was composed of an agglomeration of families, and not of individuals. "The partition of the republic (State)," wrote Bodin, "is regulated by descent and not by brains." This point of view is of preponderating importance. By relegating it to the background we lose all possibility of understanding this society, so different from our own, in which the life of our ancestors was unfolded.

Bodin begins his celebrated *Livres de la République* with these lines : "A Republic (State) is the just direction with sovereign power of several households, and of what is theirs in common." And what is a household ? "It is the just direction of several subjects under the obedience of the head of the family."

Bodin keeps on returning to this : "Just as the well-conducted family is the true image of the Republic, and authority in the home is like to the authority of the sovereign, so is the just direction of the house the true model for the direction of the Republic. And just as when each member in particular is doing its duty the entire body is healthy, so when families are being well governed the Republic will go smoothly."

Retif de la Bretonne, a singular and possibly the most interesting writer of the eighteenth century, so little known, so adversely known and so misunderstood—from whom we shall often have occasion to quote—he too writes : "The State is a large family, composed of all the private families, and the Prince is the father of all the fathers." It is a precise and the truest definition that has been given of the France of former days ; moreover, it is

11

identical with what we find in Diderot's *Encyclopédie* : " The family is a society which serves as the foundation of the society of the nation ; for a people, a nation, is nothing but a compound of several families."

II.—*The Father of the Family*

Let us picture to ourselves the family of former days living in the paternal house which successive generations have been enlarging and transforming as fresh requirements have arisen. Around it lies the heritage of their ancestors, preserving the traces of each one's toil, a heritage which each and all strain to preserve in its integrity. The Father, the head of the family, maintains his authority, not only over his wife and children, but also over his younger brothers who will one day found new families. He keeps up the tradition of the convictions, ideas, manners, and calling left to him as the patrimony of his ancestors, and he too will bequeath them to his descendants.

The authority of the head of the family over his children remained absolute throughout their lives, and it was stretched to even greater lengths in those districts living under written laws [1] and following the Roman laws—the Provinces of the Midi, generally speaking—than in the districts where the laws of custom held sway. The son living in the paternal dwelling remained a minor throughout his entire life, even though he married and became the father of a family of his own. Everything he possessed, everything his energy and industry produced, were the property of his father. " And the reason is," says Bodin, " because the household can only tolerate one head, one master, one seigneur ; otherwise, if there be several heads the orders given would be contradictory, and the family would be in perpetual confusion."

The exercise of the highest functions in the magistracy, or important military or administrative positions emancipated the son from paternal authority, " as it is not reasonable," observes La Roche-Flavin, " that those who have under their authority the honour and possessions of all those within their jurisdiction should be under the power of another," but this did not hold good in the case of positions of secondary importance. With the exception of Bishops, the exercise of ecclesiastical functions did not emancipate a son, neither those of an Abbot, a Prior, or Parish priest. But marriage released the son of the family on condition that he set up an independent home, and left to establish himself away from the

[1] Described as *pays de droit écrit*, in contradistinction to *pays de droit coutumier*. (H. W.)

paternal dwelling ; though again this did not hold good in the case of *pays de droit écrit*, but only for those living within the jurisdiction of the Paris Parliament, and for the town of Toulouse, where children, married and dowered by the father, were held to be emancipated.

The father, it is true, could emancipate one of his sons ; it was a solemn ceremony :

" The father, seated on a chair, with his son kneeling before him on both knees, placed his son's hands between his own, and then, yielding to the prayer and request of the latter, emancipated him of his own free will, placing him outside paternal authority, save only, of course, as regards the demands of honour, respect and affection owed him by his son who humbly thanks him. In token of which, his said father, taking his hands away released those of his son, and placed him at full liberty, making him a *père de famille* with the right now and henceforth to traffic, contract, engage his person and goods, and acquire profit unto himself, either by the liberality of others, by good luck, or by the exercise of his toil and industry."

When the head of the family—*le cap d'hostal*, as he is called in the texts of the Midi, *le chef du feu* in Lorraine—when the *chef de la maison* died, the eldest son carried on the work, succeeding his father in his rights and duties. He gave his sisters in marriage, and settled his brothers in the spirit of the House. One sees cases of large families entirely reduced to confusion on being accidentally deprived of the effective control of their elder brother on his succeeding his father. These features are noticeable in bourgeois and simple peasant families as much as, and perhaps more than in the great aristocratic houses.

Naturally the family, in the light in which we have been considering it, kept to its traditions more strongly in the country than in the towns. In the country the *finage*, that is, the confines of the paternal dwelling, by isolating the family from contact with their neighbours, contributed to preserving it in its integrity.

Nevertheless, even in Paris, the old French family, such as we have been describing, held together right down to the eve of the Revolution in a way that amazed foreigners. The English writer, Arthur Young, expresses his surprise at this in his celebrated *Travels in France*.

" Some of the hotels in Paris are immense in size, from a circumstance which would give me a good opinion of the people, if nothing else did, which is the great mixture of families. When the eldest son marries he brings his wife home to the house of his father where an apartment is provided for them ; and if a daughter does not wed an eldest son, her husband is also received into the family, in the same way, which makes a joyous number at every table. This cannot altogether be attributed to economical motives, though they certainly influence in many cases, because it is found in families possessing the first properties in the kingdom. It does with French manners and customs, but in England it is sure to fail and equally so amongst all ranks of people."

We have spoken of the sentiments which arose in the family thus constituted, the family which for centuries past had made up the State, and had perpetuated itself while becoming greater and stronger. "It was the family, one liked much more than the individual, whom so far one had not yet got to know," remarked Talleyrand; a characteristic remark which should be borne in mind.

Documents portraying the special characteristics of the father, the *chef de famille*, who *reigned over* his household, are numerous, and applied to all classes of society. Etienne Pasquier, a lawyer who weighed his expressions, wrote in his treatise : " The true representations of God on earth are fathers and mothers in regard to their children." Edmond Retif, a peasant of Lower Burgundy, expressed himself at the beginning of the eighteenth century in the following terms : " I obeyed my visible God, my father."

Bodin would have liked a father to possess the right of life and death over his household, " otherwise we must never hope to see good manners, honour and virtue flourish."

The eminent jurist was not followed to that extent, but we shall see later on with what singular prerogatives the public powers strengthened paternal authority. On a question of extradition they did not admit judgments pronounced by foreign tribunals ; but they gave way to the *chef de famille* in his capacity as ruler over his own people :

" Sovereigns hold in their hands a superior authority independent of the laws, which it is right they should exercise for the greater good of their subjects. When a son betakes himself to a foreign country in order to escape from the authority of his parents the King reclaims the fugitive." [1]

In his *Mémoires*, Chateaubriand depicted one of these *chefs de famille*, saturated through and through with the dignity of his position, with no thought in life other than for the honour of the name he bore :

" M. de Chateaubriand was tall and lean ; he had an aquiline nose,

[1] Memorandum from Séchelles, Controller of Finance to Rouillé, Minister of Foreign Affairs, August 30, 1755. *Archives du Ministère des Affaires étrangères*, Turin 225, ff. 210–13.

thin and colourless lips ; his eyes were deep set, of a bluish or bluish-green colour, like those of a lion, or the barbarians of old. I never saw anyone with a glance like his. When he was angry his sparkling eye-balls seemed to detach themselves and strike you like a bullet.

One sole passion dominated my father, that for the name he bore. His habitual mood was one of profound melancholy, increasing with age, and of taciturnity from which he emerged only in spasms of anger. Parsimonious from the desire to restore to his family its former splendour, haughty towards the gentlemen at the meetings of the States Assembly in Brittany, harsh to his vassals at Combourg, taciturn, despotic and threatening towards those in his own household, he inspired nothing but fear when one looked at him."

How like a hard steel instrument ! We could give twenty similar *silhouettes* in a less harsh and rugged setting. The charming little Marquise de Villeneuve-Arifat presents us with the following picture of her grandfather :

" My grandmother had the deepest attachment to him ; she called him ' master ' ; when she won a smile from him she was very happy."

Elsewhere she says : " The fatherly kindness of this imposing old man presented no weakness. He scarcely ever addressed his children otherwise than ' Monsieur,' uttered with a chilling gravity and serious-ness. When my uncle one day was called ' my son ' his eyes filled with tears. Such were the manners of many fathers at that time ; they did not, however, prevent the father of whom I am speaking from always striving after the welfare of his family."

And it is just the portrait which Retif de la Bretonne also draws of his grandfather, a farm labourer in the little village of Nitry in Burgundy.

Retif de la Bretonne worked at the plough until he was twenty years of age, and always remained in contact with his native village. When he describes the life of the peasants among whom he lived, these are not artistically drawn sketches, or the work of a literary imagination : they are men of flesh and bone placed exactly in their own surroundings which the author faithfully describes. His most characteristic work, *Vie de mon Père*, is of incomparable value from this point of view, and is unique in the literature of the eighteenth century, and of the very greatest importance to the historian.[1]

" This father (Pierre Retif, grandfather of Retif de la Bretonne), so amiable when among strangers, was terrible in his own family. He ruled by a glance, the meaning of which had to be divined. Even his daughters received scant indulgence at his hands. I am not

[1] An edition of this work, illustrated from contemporary documents, has been published under the title of *Le Village*, by Messrs. Arthème Fayard in their collection of *Mémoires Illustrés*.

speaking of his wife ; deeply penetrated with respect for her husband, she only saw in him an adored master. Although she came of a superior family to his, for she was connected with the Cœurderoys who still number Presidents in the Parliaments of Burgundy, she rushed to fulfil his least wishes, and after having done everything that was required, a word from her imperious husband overwhelmed her with gratitude :

' Wife, go and rest yourself.'

A courtier could not have been more flattered on receiving the accolade at the hands of his sovereign."

This terrible Pierre Retif was still only a young man, for he died at the age of forty-one.

When Pierre Retif and his son, Edmond, went to the market together the latter would never have dared to ride abreast of his father's horse. Pierre Retif ambled along in front, and Edmond respectfully made his horse keep behind. During the journey it would not have entered his head to address his father, and he would confine himself to answering with deference only after he had been first spoken to.

"There was at Nitry," continues Retif de la Bretonne, "a young girl named Catherine Gautherin ; she was a good, hard-working girl with a face that seemed to ask for nothing better than to laugh.

Edmond (the father of Retif de la Bretonne) noticed her. The custom in the country, which still exists, was to snatch something from the girls who were pleasing. The youths would take away from them anything they could, their nosegays, rings or needle cases. . . . One Sunday, as he was coming out of Church after High Mass, Edmond caught sight of one of his rivals snatching away Catherine's nosegay. He went up to the young girl and taking his own from his buttonhole offered it to her. Catherine blushed.

' Let us at least share it,' she said.

The nosegay was composed of red and white roses. She kept the white ones.

The scene had been witnessed by the terrible Pierre. He was surprised that his son had dared to cast his eyes on a young girl without his permission. He said nothing, however, at dinner. Next morning, just as Edmond, in his shirt sleeves and already mounted on his horse, was starting for his ploughing, his father came up.

' Give me your whip.'

' Here it is, father.'

Three vigorously applied lashes cut through his shirt in three places, staining it with blood. Edmond merely groaned. Pierre phlegmatically gave him back his whip with the remark :

' Now let that stick in your mind ! '

Edmond was unaware of the cause of this rigorous correction. He went off and worked all day just as usual. On his return, Anne, his mother, noticed his shirt, and thought he had met with some accident. She questioned the plough boys and learnt what had happened, but not the cause. Anne came back to her son and dressed his wounds, which required attention owing to the linen having penetrated into the skin. Her husband came on the scene. She looked at him with tears in her eyes.

'You *have* given him a dressing down!'

'That's how I treat lovers.'

But this man, outwardly so harsh, possessed a tender heart—no one could have suspected it! He went out into the garden. Edmond, after his wounds had been dressed by his mother, had gone to the end of the garden and finding there was a bed that wanted digging, had set to work at it.

His father heard him. He went up, and taking his spade from him, said:

'My son, you have worked enough for to-day; go and rest, I will finish it.'

'The words, "my son," had never before come from the lips of Pierre,' remarks Retif de la Bretonne.

Palpitating with joy, Edmond went and told his mother what had just happened. A day of rejoicing for the family. Edmond was petted by his sisters, and from time to time the good Anne half-opened the window and, watching her husband at his digging, said:

'He is finishing it, my children, he is finishing Edmond's bed! I tell you he has a father's heart. It is because he does not wish his son to have the labour of finishing it. Oh! what a good father he is!'

And the children repeated:

'What a good father he is!'"

We are dealing now with peasants in Burgundy in the first half of the eighteenth century.

This Edmond Retif, so roughly corrected by his father, became in his turn the father of a family, and the following is the picture of him as sketched by his own son:

"If he had been on a journey and arrived home in the evening a little later than the hour for supper, all the family, children and domestics, would be seen waiting with an air of uneasiness and gloom. Should he knock at the door, the blow of the door-knocker would be answered by a shout of joy from the whole household. I never heard this sound of the door-knocker without seeing my mother tremble with joy. She would rise with alacrity and give the order to go and open the door, although five or six persons were already there. She would bustle about and fetch his night cap and sabots herself. She would put fresh wood on the embers of the fire, although her daughters had offered to spare her the trouble, place his chair on the spot where he liked to sit and pour out a glass of warm wine which she would present to him on entering, before addressing a single word to him.

The patriarch drank it with a satisfied air. After that he would salute her, and then all of us, down to the boy who minded the sheep, enquiring after each one in a pleasant and kindly manner."

These were patriarchal figures which, in many provinces, existed till after the Revolution. Mistral found them again in Provence, " Magnificent, *tel qu'un roi dans son royaume*, he sowed his holding and ruled it."

Maître Ramon says :

" A father is a father ; his wishes must be carried out. . . .   When families were like that we saw them strong, sound, and able to resist the tempest. Doubtless they had their quarrels, but when Christmas evening brought together the grandfather and his descendants around the hallowed table over which he presided, the grandfather would wipe out all that kind of thing with the blessing that he gave with his wrinkled hand."

III.—*Marriage*

" That's how I treat lovers," exclaimed Pierre Retif when lashing his son with blows from his whip, like a vicious horse. *Mésalliances* —or more accurately speaking *désalliances*, to use the neologism coined by the Marquis de Mirabeau—were the chief danger which families, constituted as we have described, had to fear. Every one of these families possessed its own usages, sentiments and social position, all clearly defined by heredity. The introduction of a disparate element would have introduced customs, ideas, sentiments and usages of a too different complexion, and this would have threatened the ruin of the organism for which, from time immemorial, succeeding generations had made every sacrifice, and on which rested the very structure of society.

The individual counted for nothing ; it was the family that came first, and that by a long way. When preaching before the Court at Versailles, Bourdaloue expresses indignant surprise at this : " Out of so many marriages that are contracted every day, how many do we see wherein any mutual affection may be found ? " When we come to study society as it existed under the Ancien Régime we shall find less cause for surprise. Can we say of present times that marriages contracted between sovereign Houses are love matches ? I think not. The marriage of Louis XII brought Brittany to the French Crown. Would his contemporaries have admitted, should we admit it in our own time, that the successor of Charles VIII married in accordance with the dictates of his heart ? At the age of twenty, Louis XIV was infatuated with Marie Mancini, the niece of Mazarin, who was the first to oppose the marriage. The young king married the Infanta of Spain ; she brought to him rights over Franche Comté and French-speaking Flanders which were thereby effectively restored to France.

What we are saying about the ruling families applies to the great Princely, or Seigneurial Houses, which were identical in their essence, their structure, their interests and their aspirations, although on a lower scale. Consider the Houses of Savoy, Mantua, Nemours, Condé, Montmorency, Guise and Vendôme, under Henri IV and Louis XIII. The coming of the Bourbons to the throne did not allay the jealousy of the Guises. When, in 1611, the Comte de Soissons saw the Duc de Guise, followed by a numerous escort, passing by under his windows, he felt the hatred of the Bourbons for the Lorraine family boiling up within him. He dared to say to Marie de Médicis, then Regent during the minority of Louis XIII, that either the Guises or the Bourbons must get out of France. " The quarrels between the Houses of Guise and Bourbon go on increasing in violence day by day," wrote the Venetian Ambassador. " If no means are found to allay them, they may create great difficulties ; at the slightest provocative word they muster their armed following."

It was a case of two powers existing in the State, each strongly constituted. Under these conditions, can we imagine a young lady, embodying in herself an endless chain of consequences, marrying according to the dictates of her heart ? Consider the disturbance to vast interests the fascinations of a gallant young cavalier might introduce.

A similar rivalry existed between the Houses of Vendôme and Condé, families enjoying less importance, although they were eminent in the realm. It was a case of real powers at strife with each other, for whom the question of matrimonial alliances, with all the consequences they entailed, played a preponderating part. One degree lower we find the Rohans, the Lesdiguières, the Chevreuses, the Epernons, and the Longuevilles, families still wearing the outward trappings associated with the sovereign. They possessed huge domains wherein they ruled, and a numerous following, amongst whom were sometimes people of the highest distinction, a civil and military household, guards, carabineers, men-at-arms, drummers and trumpeters, forming an escort for their chief several hundred strong. They occupied a whole street in the town. The domestic household contained a variety : gate-keepers, gentlemen-in-waiting, dwarfs, pages, and muleteers, all wearing a livery of which they were proud, the colours of their lord borne as a trophy. Also among the household a number of gentle-men were maintained by the seigneur, some of them being distinguished men-of-letters. Richelieu maintained a *joueur de vielle*,[1] like the feudal chiefs sung in epic songs : he only admitted to the higher ranks of his retinue the sons of Counts and Marquises. Even the young ladies had their " household " attached to their small persons, with pages and equerries, like the Princesses of the Royal Blood.

Let us descend a further stage. The model is on a reduced scale, but it is always the same. It embraced all the nobility of France ; then came the Parliamentary families, after them the great bourgeois houses, then the middle-class bourgeoisie, artisan families and even the peasants themselves. Some great controlling influence had struck the same imprint on all alike.

The humble cluster of young elms on the plain resembles the forest in its luxurious foliage. " On the question of *mésalliances*," writes M. Dupuy in his studies on Lower Brittany, " the bourgeoisie, and even the peasants in easy circumstances, are just as susceptible as gentlemen " ; and M. Joly in his monograph on Caen writes, " On this point the humblest families are no less exacting."

The Parisians of 1747 sang the ditty :

> Dès qu'on s'lie, il faut s'lier
> Avec gens du même méquier. . . .

In his *Ecole des Pères*, Retif de la Bretonne gives some striking examples when dealing with the rustic families of peasants. The best looking youth in the village of Nitry in Burgundy was the son of the public baker,[2] the man who farmed out the seigneurial bakery. " He was a tall fellow, 5 ft. 6 in. in height, well turned out and possessed of a certain manner, from his having been in service in towns." The question arose of a marriage between him and the daughter of Thomas, a farm labourer ; but the young man did not suit the latter. " He was the son of the public baker, who is like a farmer working under a farmer, from whom he receives commission and orders to hew his wood, and he has been a lackey in town. . . . Now we peasants," continues Retif, " who work in with each other, have no liking for livery, and have great contempt for it ; we leave the honour of having a relation who has been a lackey to the lowest drunken brawler."

Thomas set his face against the marriage of his daughter.

The traditional organization of the family, handed down and strengthened by succeeding generations, had given great stability and definition to the constitution and character, not only of the different classes of society, but to the families themselves, each one

---

[1] The original of the barrel organ. (H. W.)

[2] *Four banal*, the public bakery rented from the seigneur under certain conditions of service for the benefit of the village. (H. W.)

of which had reached the point of having its own customs, ideas
and sentiments peculiar to it—customs, ideas and sentiments which
had been transmitted from age to age, gathering greater strength
and activity with each succeeding generation. The special distinction of the Guise family was an extreme affability. They
saluted all and sundry with an *empressement* and ostentation inherited from the days of the League, from the illustrious François
de Guise and from the Cardinal de Lorraine in quest of popularity.
The de Retz family was noted for its quarrelsome spirit, and the
turbulent Coadjutor [1] was the natural outcome of it. " Probe
comme d'Ormesson " passed into a common proverb.[2] Several
families, just like the Greek γενος or the Roman *gens,* possessed
their own Saints and recognized protectors.

The following are very important facts : " Outside the general
laws common to every subject," state the authors of the *Encyclopédie Méthodique,* " each family could have its own particular laws
peculiar to itself ; this is what the Romans termed the *jus familiare.*"
Thus the House of Laval possessed its own customary rights, confirmed by the Paris Parliament, which were contrary to those
current in Anjou, Brittany and Maine where the estates of the
House were situated ; the Houses of Baume, d'Albret and Rodez
had like privileges. These were " family laws, made by the *chefs
de famille* for the preservation of their possessions, names and
distinguishing marks," wrote Bodin. The same thing applied to the
Counts of Sancerre and the Barons de Montfort [3] in the Province
of Berry.

These details might be multiplied and applied to the most diverse
facts.

We need hardly add that the traditions forming the spirit of a
family varied in different classes, and created marked differences
between them. The sudden vicissitudes afforded by chance circumstances in our days were then unknown, so that wealth was
handed on among the ranks of the bourgeoisie, thereby creating a
way of looking at things and a manner of life special to them. Even
among the bourgeoisie itself, Marivaux notes profound differences
in their habit of mind and their traditions, according to whether
they belonged to the class of shop-keepers or to the merchant
bourgeoisie, " and between these two sections there is still a somewhat marked difference."

[1] Cardinal de Retz, Coadjutor Archbishop of Paris (1613–1679). (H. W.)
[2] A family holding magisterial appointments, of whom the most celebrated
was Olivier III (1610–1688). (H. W.)
[3] This would form an extremely interesting subject for a thesis for the
Doctorate of Law.

What shall we say about the families who followed the practice of the law ? They came to form a distinct class within the State, proud of their importance. Even within the law itself different degrees decided the exact proportion of respect accorded to each other. The Portail family was descended from a mere surgeon to Louis XIII. Important appointments and distinguished alliances had succeeded each other since then, but had not effaced the very humble origin of the family. The daughter of Rose, the right-hand man of Louis XIV, married a Portail. Despite her modest dot, this lady turned up her nose. " I have to live with these Portails," she would keep on saying, and a hundred other disdainful things. The Portails complained to Rose ; at last, being annoyed with her, he said:

" You are quite right ; she is an impertinent thing; if I hear any further complaints about her, I shall disinherit her." There were no more complaints, says Saint Simon.

The aristocratic Houses had their traditions of haughty aloofness and refined distinction. It was not therefore, as in our days, merely a case of family vanity being wounded by a *mésalliance* ; it was not only a question of material interests that might in a certain measure be compromised ; it meant, by the introduction of a foreign body into an organism unsuited to receive it, the destruction of a family formed by the centuries, and constituting the basis of the State.

The Marquis de Mirabeau, in his interesting work, *L'Ami des Hommes*, gave more solemn expression to this point : " *Mélanger les états par les mariages, c'est tout détruire, tout avilir.*" And this brilliant economist, dipping his pen in Saint Simon's ink-pot, gives a picture of these *désalliances* in the highest ranks of society. He begins by sketching a portrait of a magistrate who chose a wife from among the nobility at the Court :

" Your Magistrate," writes Mirabeau, " who marries a young lady of the Court, makes a *désalliance*—if one does not care to call it a *mésalliance*—as disadvantageous as his neighbour who becomes son-in-law to a financier. The young lady overlays her outer varnish of inherited impertinence—her aristocratic disdain—with a mixture of magisterial formality, and soon looks down upon the house she has entered because her credentials now no longer permit her to go to Court (where her own family is firmly established) ; she transplants her grand airs, shows special favour to her titled cousins, and her children curse the magisterial gown which matches ill with ' red heels ' ; [1] the title of President gives offence to them, although they would by no means wish to lose the emoluments attaching thereto

---

[1] The nobility at Court wore red-heeled shoes in compliment to the fashion set by Louis XIV. (H. W.)

—oh, no !—they would act the part of ' my lord Marquis,' and if they cannot display the trappings pertaining thereto, except in the country, they exhibit at least all the puppyish conceit and paraphernalia attending that condition. All that kind of thing is destructive, for the old gravity of the law loses itself in the effort, and the Justice's room of the father is no longer frequented, except by creditors and musicians."

The second panel of the diptych painted by the Marquis de Mirabeau, is a worthy fellow to the former.

Near neighbour to the Magistrate who has made a *désalliance* by taking to wife the daughter of a Court nobleman, is the gentleman who has married for money in order to re-gild his escutcheon, as we say nowadays.

This man, authentically descended from the Knights of St. Louis in Tunis, going as far back as the companions of Godfrey de Bouillon in the Holy Land,

" took to himself a little gem who had retained nothing of the Gascony or Picardy accent characterizing ' Monsieur, her father '—the convent and masters had put all that right; she was very talented, accustomed to the obsequiousness of valets, and crammed full of high axioms of munificence, such as that one must not wear the same dresses—always of course of new designs—for more than one season, that one must always give away everything to one's ladies' maids, that one must keep a *perruquier* for one's attendants so that they may be fit to appear in one's apartments, that one must have feathered plumes, coloured reins and harness, new horses, Martin's varnish and all the rest. The mother-in-law, who had made the calculation that 400,000 francs produce an income of 20,000 francs, and that a wife in a well-regulated house should cost 6,000 francs a year, and that the other fourteen thousand would accumulate to establish in life the children to come whom she already saw in their dozens around her armchair, patiently waited for the end of the entrancing days following the marriage, tossed her head when theatres, balls, the Opera, etc., were mentioned, but hoped there would be an end of all such talk. However, all these gaieties followed ; she became uneasy, hazarded some advice, and the little bride yawned ! . . . Alterations in the furniture began to take place in the lower part of the house. The economic lamps which lighted her ante-chamber were replaced by gilded branches ; porcelains and varnish dazzled her everywhere ; the careful woman cook was replaced by a chef who took off three days a week for himself and on the other four days made his assistant do the work ; at last the trusty retainers of the old days took to their heels on seeing such waste. Soon after the mother-in-law of the young bride followed suit and went to live apart in separate apartments. The first *accouchement* called her back ; they announced a daughter.

' Another time we shall have a boy,' said the old mother.

' Oh ! as to that I beg to be excused,' replied the daughter-in-law.
' I am in no mood to sacrifice myself for posterity. I already love
this little one to distraction, and I wish her to be my heir.' And
there we have a House, whose flag had brilliantly flown for centuries,
in danger of breaking up in ruins."

The Bouillon family had made an alliance with that of Crozat,
the enormously wealthy financier, in view of a fine dowry of
1,600,000 francs, worth fifteen or twenty million at the present
day. D'Alainville wrote a comedy on it, *l'Ecole des Bourgeois*
(1728). Crozat's daughter was as nice as could be wished, but her
mother-in-law did not forgive her for having entered the family,
though she regarded with satisfaction her well-filled money bags.
She called her " my little ingot of gold," an impertinence without
vulgarity coming from the lips of this high-born lady who amiably
described her moneyed daughter-in-law as " dung to manure our
lands."

On the other hand, consider the alliances made between families
of equal degree, among the nobility, the magisterial class, the
bourgeoisie, and peasants. Their traditions acquired thereby still
greater strength and power. By allying themselves with each
other their foundations became firmer. Being well acquainted
with the identity of their family and professional customs, and the
similarity of their tastes and aspirations, the heads of families
married off their children without taking much thought for the
material advantages they would bring, the importance of which
became a secondary consideration in their eyes. Robert Arnaud
d'Andilly married Mlle. de la Borderie ; the marriage contracts
were signed in blank ; each party was left to add the settlements
it thought fit.

Every historian who has made a study of the Ancien Régime
from the point of view of its private customs, has arrived at this
conclusion : " A matrimonial union appears to-day as the joining
together of two individuals ; in the seventeenth century it was
above all the alliance between two Houses. From that fact it
necessarily follows that to-day the interests of the married couple
are placed first, whereas formerly those of the family were the
chief concern," (Vicomte d'Avenel).

" It was understood," writes Arvède Barine, " that one belonged
to the family before belonging to oneself ; marriage did not escape
falling under this rule or, if you prefer, this social tyranny." In
his writings on the country gentry, Baudrillart notes the general
principle " that when a young girl of the plebeian class marries a
nobleman she marks him with a kind of infamy." The same thing
applied to a farm lad marrying the farmer's daughter. We find

cases of young peasant girls being imprisoned at the request of their parents because they wanted to marry respectable young men who happened to be only day-labourers. Very many examples of this kind could be given. It is the story of Mireille [1] over and over again. In a ruling on conjugal unions the Government drew attention to the " disorder which disturbs the tranquillity of so many families and tarnishes their honour by unequal alliances." As a consequence, what appeared in those days to be reprehensible were not irregular love affairs, provided they did not cause too great a stir, but love matches, considered in the light of the danger they brought. Mademoiselle de Montpensier turned a young woman of her suite out of the house because she had just made a love match. La Grande Mademoiselle felt she could not tolerate such a pernicious example in her servant. This point has been brought out very clearly by Balzac in his marvellous portrayal of the family of olden days. " Mad courtesan ! " said the Vicomtesse de Lestorade in a letter to her friend, Louise de Chaulieu, who had just made a love match.

Let us consider the alliances made between families of princely rank. The son of Charles III, Duc de Lorraine, had only two daughters. The elder was not three years old when Henry IV requested her for his eldest son, and then afterwards demanded the younger for his second son. He wished to assure for himself the possession of the fine province on the frontier. Who, even in our own days, would not consider this policy, not only astute, but justifiable ? It was just the same in the case of members of the great Houses ; the important thing was to make safe their possession of Duchies, fertile meadow lands, fine properties, important appointments and honours. The second daughter of Anne de Gonzaga married the son of the great Condé ; " Happy marriage ! " exclaimed Bossuet. He was by no means unaware of the kind of person this Henri de Bourbon, Prince de Condé, whom the young woman had been so " happy " as to marry, really was. Of him Saint Simon wrote, " unnatural son, cruel father, detestable tyrant, he brought misfortune to all who had any relations with him," and more especially to his wife whose existence was that of a martyr.

Traditional feuds raged between many of these Houses ; the initial causes had often been forgotten, but the hatred was kept up and handed on from one generation to another. Of such a kind was the ancient hostility existing, at the end of the seventeenth century, between the Houses of Joyeuse and Vervin, which led to

[1] A Provençal poem by Mistral (1859) dealing with rustic family life in Provence. (H. W.)

the assassination of the Marquis de Vervin by one of the Joyeuse family and the Abbé Grandpré.[1]

Matrimonial alliances provided the means to put an end to these rivalries, just as the marriage of Marie Antoinette to the Dauphin had in view to terminate the differences which had existed for centuries between the Houses of France and Austria.

A violent difference of opinion arose between the Duc de Saint Simon and the Duc de Noailles. The former talked of it with his usual fury. He said to the Regent :

" I do not conceal from you, nor from anybody, not even from him (the Duc de Noailles) that the finest and most gratifying day of my life would be that on which it should be granted to me by Divine Justice to beat him into a pulp, and to step on his stomach with my two feet, for the satisfaction of which there is no sacrifice of fortune I would not make." Now the niece of the Duc de Noailles was in a position to bring great possessions and powerful alliances to M. de Ruffec, Saint Simon's son. The " House " before everything ! The enmity was hushed, and the marriage took place (1727).

The Comtesse de la Roche-Guyon, who had married according to the wishes of her father, became a widow, and desired to marry a second time according to the dictates of her own heart. She had fixed her choice on the most charming swain in the world, the young Marquis de Vardes. The Comtesse knew that her father would not consent to this marriage, and so it was arranged that the Marquis de Vardes should come and carry her off from Liancourt, where she had made her home. Everything was well planned and the day fixed, but the father of the fair one was beforehand with the young lover, and it was he who carried off his daughter whom he destined for the Prince d'Harcourt. The Marquis de Vardes was furious and sent to his rival the letters which Madame de la Roche-Guyon had written to him. Prince d'Harcourt coldly declared that the letters were forgeries, and then married the charming widow.

Marriages decided upon for family reasons were often drawn up without the couple having the opportunity of becoming acquainted with each other. Sometimes at the tumultuous ceremony, at which a very great throng of people were assembled together, there was such a racket that the future bride and bridegroom had no suspicion that all this to-do concerned their marriage.

" It was a brilliant gathering," wrote Mme. de Sévigné : " there was Mme. la Duchesse de la Ferté holding the hand of her daughter, who looked very pretty, and her little sister, resembling her in colour-

[1] Bibl. Nat. MS. Français 8125, ff. 10–12.

ing ; Mme. la Duchesse d'Aumont, and M. de Mirepoix, who made a wonderful contrast. What a din ! And what compliments on all sides ! . . . Mme. d'Olonne has given a fine *coulant* ; [1] Mme. la Maréchale de la Ferté was dazzling ; every one is pleased at this marriage. They could not hear each other speak. The young man had never seen his mistress ; he does not know what it is all about."

One might almost say it was an assembly of mad people. Two great families were linking their destinies together.

So much for the nobility ; the same thing happened among the bourgeoisie.

A Counsellor of the Parliament of Dijon decided upon a marriage for his son. He came to an agreement upon all points with the father of the future bride. The young man learnt of his father's designs from the rumours going about the town. Much disturbed, he took upon himself to knock timidly at the door of his father's office. It was the first time he had presented himself in this dreaded spot without having been summoned there.

" They assure me, father, that you have decided to marry me to a person whose name has been mentioned to me. Might I be permitted to ask you what foundation there is in this proposition ? "

The Counsellor of the Dijon Parliament was very surprised at this unexpected question. He looked at his son with severity and said gravely :

" Sir, mind your own business."

A month had not passed before the young man was married to the lady destined for him by the paternal will.

Sébastien Mercier presents to us a father and daughter. The latter is engaged at her toilette. She had learnt from her maid that she was to be married. The father enters, and steps forward :

" Mademoiselle, I see from your eyes that you have not slept."

" No, father, I have not."

" So much the worse for you, my daughter ; one ought to be beautiful when one marries, and one is ugly when one does not sleep."

"'I am not beautiful enough," she replied with a sigh.

" Is it then with a view to being more beautiful that you assume the melancholy and cross expression that I see . . . I command you to look smiling."

" You are commanding what is impossible."

" Impossible ? And why, if you please ? What harm is being done to you by marrying you to a man who is well born, very amiable, and very rich ? "

[1] A diamond ornament for the neck, which could be raised or lowered. (H. W.)

" It is always a very cruel thing to be handed over to a man
one does not know."

" Very good ! Does one ever know the man or woman one
marries ? Believe me, my dear child, the only bad marriages I
see in the world are love marriages ; the dice are far less blind
than love."

Let us now come back to the peasant families to whom we are
introduced by Retif de la Bretonne. There existed between two
families of market gardeners at Nitry a feud similar to that dividing
the de Noailles and the Saint Simons, or the Joyeuses and the
Marquis de Vervin.

" For long years," said a peasant of the village who was known
by the nick-name of " Tous-les-jours," " the Léonard family and
our own have hated each other on account of a remark made by
my father's grandfather, on whom he wished to foist a grand-
daughter of Léonard's grandfather. The old man Léonard had
said that he hoped to see my great-grandfather taking thought for
his granddaughter, who was an orphan, and that he himself would
keep her for him. This was repeated to my great-grandfather who
replied, ' In that case let father Léonard *keep her pickled in a barrel
of salt.*'

" This expression so shocked old Léonard that a week after he
married his granddaughter to some one else, and ever since he and
his children have borne a grudge against our family."

There was only one way of putting an end to this feud—to
unite the two families by a marriage.

One day " Tous-les-jours " announced to his son, Georges, that
he had decided to marry him to Perrette Léonard. Georges was
in love with a young girl named Jannette. His father said to him :

" I am your father, and one day you will be a father too. If you
disobey me, neither will your children obey you."

Georges held back from doing violence to his heart ; but in the
end, one evening, after the reading of the Holy Scriptures had
concluded, he said :

" Father, you know better than I do. I have come to tell you
that I am ready to do your bidding. Pray for me, my dear father,
for I had a deep attachment of the heart."

" Yes, my poor boy," answered " Tous-les-jours," " God knows
that you are submitting yourself to your father's wishes, and He
will ratify my blessing."

In a family diary kept by Jeanne du Laurens, niece of the
Physician to Henri IV, we read :

" Having come back to Arles, my mother thought of making a
marriage for me, saying that when girls reached the age of eighteen

one must think of making a home for them. She therefore married me
to a very honourable man, named M. Achard. My marriage only
lasted for four years, four months, and four days, which I thought
was singular. When I became a widow, and had spent my year of
widowhood with my mother-in-law, my mother took me back to her
house, saying that a young widow has as much need to be looked
after carefully as a girl, and that I would obey her more readily than
I should a mother-in-law ; she then married me very honourably,
a second time, to M. Gleyze."

These things happened, as we see, in the most natural manner.

So much for the part played by the ladies ; we will now turn to
the gentlemen's side of the matter. The Marquis d'Argenson, the
future Minister for Foreign Affairs, wrote to his aunt, Mme. de
Balleroy, as follows :

"I have just come back from the country. During my absence
they have disposed of my hand. On my return I found the articles
already signed. I am entering a very respectable family. The
daughter is well educated, she knows how to dance, sing, and play
the spinet ; in addition, she is fair."

Doubtless these were weighty reasons to make the Marquis
d'Argenson decide on marrying a young person he had never seen.
The letter is dated 31st October ; the first meeting between the
future husband and wife took place on 19th November at the
convent of the Filles-Sainte-Marie, where Mlle. Mélian had been
placed. The young lady had learnt on the 18th that she was to
marry M. d'Argenson on the 22nd. Mlle. Mélian was not fifteen
years old.

It is interesting to note to what extent the general feeling was
in harmony with social exigencies. As we know, Corneille in his
comedies depicted very accurately the ideas of his contemporaries,
and their manner of looking at things. Note the following dialogue
between two young girls in the *Menteur* :

Clarisse.

Mon père a sur mes vœux une entière puissance.

Lucrèce.

Le devoir d'une fille est dans l'obéissance.

And these two lines so well express the ideas held by young people
at that period, that Corneille makes an identical repetition of them,
placing them this time in a tragedy instead of in a comedy. His
tragedy *Horace* contains these very same two lines, uttered by
Camille and Curiace.

In the *Veuve*, Doris replies to her mother, who thinks she is in love with Alcidon: " Appearances might perhaps lead you to think so,

> Mais mon cœur se conserve au point où je le veux,
> Toujours libre et qui garde une amitié sincère
> A celui que voudra me prescrire une mère . . .
> Votre vouloir du mien dispose absolument."

A still better example is the dialogue between Pleirante and his daughter, Célidée, in the *Galerie du Palais*. The worthy Pleirante has noticed that his daughter has a liking for Lysandre. He lets her see that he has guessed it, and that he approves of her choice : but Célidée, like a well brought up girl, proudly replies :

> Monsieur, il est tout vrai, son ardeur légitime,
> A tant gagné sur moi que j'en fais de l'estime . . .
> J'aime son entretien, je chéris sa présence,
> Mais cela n'est enfin qu'un peu de complaisance,
> Qu'un mouvement léger qui passe au moindre jour. . . .

And this last line, which is altogether amazing :

> Vos seuls commandements produisent mon amour.

The romances of the period were written in the same vein as the comedies. Turn over the leaves of *Grand Cyrus*, by Madeleine de Scudéry who described the *Pays du Tendre*. A *précieuse* tells her aspirant that she has no authority to lay bare her heart. For that the mandate of her parents is necessary. Only in that case can she dare to tell him that her inclination accords with their choice.

The picture has not changed in the eighteenth century. In Ardène's *Nouvelliste* Félicie replies as follows to the swain who is courting her :

> Soyez juste, Olibar, une fille bien née
> Pourrait-elle à son gré régler sa destinée
> Ce droit n'est dévolu qu'aux auteurs de nos jours.
> A leur autorité laissant un libre cours
> Nous ne devons porter dans le nœud qui nous lie
> Qu'une flamme à leur choix vraiment assujettie.
> Voyez donc, Olibar, si ce juste devoir. . . .

In his *Tableau de Paris* Sébastien Mercier observes :

" There is nothing more false in our comedies than where young men are represented as declaring their sentiments to young ladies. Our theatre is not true to life on this point. People do not make professions of love to young girls. The latter are kept shut up in convents until the day of their marriage. It is morally impossible to make a declaration to them. They are never seen. The daughters of the upper bourgeoisie are also kept in convents. Those belonging to the lower middle class never leave their mothers. Young girls receive their husbands at the hands of their parents. The marriage contract is nothing more than a bargain and the young people are never consulted."

And so, as the children were not consulted, it was not considered necessary to wait until they were of an age to be consulted.

Here are some cases of fathers who settled the matrimonial fate of their children at their birth. At the time when he was a counsellor, Chamillart, the celebrated favourite of Louis XIV, had as a colleague a man of the name of Dreux, whom he particularly liked. Their wives, in due course, gave birth to a daughter and a son respectively. Dreux, who was very rich, pressed Chamillart to have them affianced to each other. But Chamillart, an upright man, refused from motives of delicacy.

Finally he gave his consent. The children grew up, and in the meantime Chamillart made a conspicuous fortune. When the time had come to marry the young people, it fell to Dreux, from the same sentiments of delicacy, to offer to release Chamillart from the promise he had given ; but the latter, who could have made his daughter a Duchess, was faithful to his engagement, and kept to his word. And the young people, who had been betrothed in their cradle, became man and wife with the approval of the King, who, on the occasion of the marriage, presented the young man, now in the army, with the command of the fine regiment of Burgundy.

We find cases of this practice going to still greater lengths. Not content with betrothing their children before they were yet weaned, they even decided on the careers of those yet to be born, at the time of making the marriage contract between the future husband and wife. A lawyer gave the hand of his daughter to Counsellor Simon de Tributiis, on the express condition, drawn up before a notary, that the future sons of the marriage should study law.

The legal age of puberty was generally fixed at the age of fourteen for boys and thirteen for girls. On arriving at that age the young *fiancés* gave consent, which was held to be valid, to their marriage, and from the time of their attaining the age of reason, that is, seven years old, the parents could betroth them ; and if the little *fiancés* of seven years old had lived for a short time under the same roof—which depended, as we can quite imagine, solely on the wishes of their parents—the marriage was regarded as having taken place. The son of Bautru, the Academician, married Mlle. du Plessis-Chivray when she was twelve years old ; Chazeau, Governor of the Bourbonnais, married Mlle. de la Guiche, who was likewise twelve years old. When Henri de Rohan, in 1605, married

Sully's daughter, she was such a tiny little lady that Dumoulin, the pastor, on seeing her arriving at the church clothed in white, asked the parents :

" Are you bringing this child to be baptized ? "

It is true that this little person was of marvellous precocity. They separated the young husband and wife after the marriage, but they soon had to bring them together again. Mme. Henri de Rohan made her husband a happy father, much to the astonishment of everyone, and to that of her husband in particular.

But why quote facts and names ? One could fill pages of them. Dangeau relates in pathetic terms the sumptuous marriage cere-monies which united the young Duc de Luynes, then fourteen years old, with Mlle. de Neufchatel, aged thirteen. As they were both extremely young they were only left for a quarter of an hour to-gether in bed, with the curtains drawn back and all the company present in the room. Mlle. de Mailly was also married at the age of thirteen ; but the marriage ceremony lasted more than a quarter of an hour ; she was a mother at fourteen ! Mlle. de Bourbonne was married when twelve years old to M. d'Avaux. She was then at the Abbaye-au-Bois in the Rue de Sèvres. Her playmates in the Abbaye said to her :

" What an ugly man this M. d'Avaux is ! If I were in your place I would not marry him."

" I shall marry him because Papa wishes it ; but I shall not love him, that's quite certain."

One of my best friends, a gentleman of good family, living in the Department of the Orne in a country manor after the fashion of old times, was talking to me about the marriage of his great-grand-parents as recorded in the family documents. A sumptuous banquet was spread out after the ceremony in the church. As it lasted a very long time the young couple rose from the table. They seemed very quiet when suddenly cries from the bride were heard. Her husband was exercising his conjugal authority by slapping her face. They had had a tiff while catching flies. . . .

One should read the contemporary accounts of the marriage of Mlle. de Blois, the daughter of Louis XIV and Mme. de Montespan, to the Duc de Chartres, the son of the Duc d'Orléans, written by Saint Simon, Dangeau, Bussy-Rabutin and Mme. de Sévigné. Mlle. de Blois was sent for into the King's private room together with her parents, the Duc de Chartres, and the Duc and Duchesse d'Orléans. The poor little mite, in whom the royal majesty of her father inspired a terrified awe, was trembling like a leaf. She thought she was going to be scolded. Mme. de Maintenon had to take her on her knees in an endeavour to reassure her that it was not a question of reprimanding, but of marrying her. The child had difficulty in understanding what it meant.

Mlle. de Montbarrey, the daughter of the Minister for War, married in 1779 the Prince of Nassau-Sarrebrück, who was twelve years old. Some verses, of which the family were very proud and took care to spread abroad, were addressed to Mlle. de Montbarrey on the occasion :

> Vous partez, vous allez loin de votre patrie
> Passer des tendres mains d'une mère chérie
> Dans les avides bras d'un époux enchanté. . . .

This enchanted husband, aged twelve, was furious at the rôle he was to play. On the wedding day he repulsed his bride with the roughness of a badly brought up brat ; in other respects the marriage ceremonies were magnificent, but the bridegroom would not talk to his bride, and had to be threatened with a whipping, and then stuffed with burnt almonds and nuts before he would consent to take her hand for just a moment. But—faithless even before the consummation of the marriage—he displayed the keenest interest in a fair little girl, Louise de Dietrich, to whom he ran off whenever he was left free for an instant.

The daughter of Mme. de Genlis was married at the age of fourteen in the chapel of the Palais Royal. " In the evening," writes Mme. de Genlis, " I gave at Bellechasse a little cold supper to my intimate friends ; after which the doors of Bellechasse were closed, and the husband left his bride in my hands ; she remained with me for another two years."

Convents in the days of the Ancien Régime were full of little girls who were taking lessons in dancing while awaiting the age when they could go and live with their husbands.

One can imagine the sort of married life that resulted. Some turned out well, some moderately well, some badly, and some were poignantly tragic. To one instance in the last category the Comte de Montlosier devotes a striking page :

" My mother was good, she possessed an intelligent mind, and was well educated ; she had a lofty and sensitive soul, a quick imagination, and she was beautiful. . . . She had not known the gentle side of domestic life. Her most tender heart had had no experience of the sweetness of love. She had had for my father no attachment when she married him. That would be putting it too lightly. Twelve children resulted from the marriage, and we had not only been brought forth in suffering, like the rest of mankind, but had been conceived in repulsion. We had enjoyed none of the sweetness of childhood."

It was only as time went on and her memories softened down that the Comtesse de Montlosier began to know the beauty of mother-hood.

But cases like the above were exceptional. Contrary to what we might think would be the case in marriages of the Ancien Régime, they usually lived happily together, because these marriages were in conformity with the constitution and manners of the period, and because they were the sole guarantee possible for maintaining intact those family traditions on which society had been built up. More-over, as Nivelle de la Chaussée puts it in the mouth of one of his characters :

. . . Sans amour on peut très bien aimer sa femme.

And then there was the antidote, which we can guess.

Here again we must rid ourselves of our modern notions if we would place ourselves in imagination among the conditions obtain-ing in the days of our forefathers. " To bring honour and profit to the family is the only thing that matters " (The Bailli de Mirabeau). " Individuals did not exist then " (Talleyrand). Bourdaloue from his pulpit thundered " as though he were deaf " before Louis XIV and his Court against loveless unions and their consequences—love affairs without marriage, or rather in contravention of the marriage bond. His hearers only smiled.

La Grande Mademoiselle (Montpensier) tolerated love affairs indulged in outside the married state, although her own conduct was irreproachable ; but, as we said above, she would not suffer love matches. She saw the ravages that the shafts of the little god of love were capable of producing on the old family scutcheon. Bussy-Rabutin frankly confesses it. He would prefer the miscon-duct of his daughter to the thought of a regular union with a man not of her own rank. An anecdote related by Tallemand brings out this feeling in a whimsical manner :

Mme. de Termes, who had become a widow, set her heart on a leading member of the Parliament of Metz, named Vigni.

A young lady, Mlle. Du Tillet, came to see her.

" What do your people mean, my dear Madame ? They call you Madame Vigni. You bear a fine and good name, why do they not call you Madame de Termes ? "

" Well, Mademoiselle, it is because I have married Monsieur le President Vigni."

" Good heavens ! my dear friend, what is it you are saying ! If you love this young man could you not have satisfied your passion ? God forgives, my dearest Madame, but man never ! "

Is Montesquieu exaggerating in his *Lettres Persanes* ? " A man who would keep his wife all to himself would be regarded as a disturber of public happiness, and as bereft of his senses as a man who would enjoy the light of the sun to the exclusion of other men."

And this brings us to those marriages in the Ancien Régime in which the married pair were on their guard as to loving each other, or at least of appearing to do so. To appear a happily united couple was regarded as showing bad taste.

Rose de Launay shows us a piquant little scene :

"*La Comtesse, to her brother the Chevalier.*
So you thought, like every one else, that I detested my husband ? . . .

The Chevalier.
I thought so on good proofs.

The Comtesse.
All that was only a ruse, and it cost me pretty dearly ; but one must save appearances, at least, and fortunately I was paired with one who had just as much horror of anything that looked out of place as I had. We had agreed to take wise measures so as not even to be suspected. His death looked as if everything might be discovered. As you know, he was killed in the army. It was an accident that took me unprepared. I was unable to restrain my first emotion. However, I had the consolation of hearing some one at my bedside whisper quite low, 'Her way of behaving is overdone.'"

On this subject Nivelle de la Chaussée, of the French Academy— one of those rare Academicians who made their *discours de réception* in verse—wrote a very amusing comedy which the King's Censor considered " a clever criticism of a very common fault " :

> Je remarque aujourd'hui qu'il n'est plus du bon air
> D'aimer une compagne à qui l'on s'associe :
> Cet usage n'est plus que dans la bourgeoisie ;
> Mais ailleurs on a fait de l'amour conjugal
> Un parfait ridicule, un travers sans égal.
> Un époux à présent n'ose plus le paraître :
> On lui reprocherait tout ce qu'il voudrait être.
> Il faut qu'il sacrifie au préjugé cruel
> Les plaisirs d'un amour permis et mutuel.
> En vain il est épris d'une épouse qu'il aime,
> La mode le subjugue en dépit de lui-même
> Et le réduit bientôt à la nécessité
> De passer de la honte à l'infidélité. . . .

And d'Allainville, in his *l'Ecole des Bourgeois*, causes his heroine to be asked :
" Is there any harm in loving one's husband ? "
" At least there is something ridiculous . . ."

This prejudice existed down to the end of the Ancien Régime, just about the time when men's ideas and customs had come to undergo a great transformation.

At the one o'clock Mass, the fashionable Mass at the Church des Feuillants, husband and wife sat apart, each on their own side; good form forbade them to come in together. The same custom prevailed in fashionable drawing-rooms. Only in the boxes at the Comedy Theatre, or at the Opera, were husband and wife allowed to be seen together, and even there they might not come in together. The husband had to take a turn round the *foyer* while his wife was settling herself in her box; after that he could enter the box as a visitor.

A lady in high society had her own separate establishment in the house, distinct from that of her husband; they had separate quarters and each their own servants; their receptions and the society they frequented were distinct from each other. They paid visits to one another like strangers, and a footman would announce: Monsieur! . . . Madame! . . .

Again we must be careful not to take too general a view of these matters. The feelings of the parents and their children were often in harmony with each other. How often did the secret choice of the young people, when revealed to their parents, fill the latter with joy because it responded to their own desires.

Moreover, as M. Gustave Fagniez observes, a *mariage de raison* was often considered to be the most suitable in the opinion of both daughter and parents.

And then we should remember the remarkable facilities that existed for a clandestine marriage celebrated before a priest, and often without witnesses. If the marriage was consummated, it was regarded as a legitimate one, and no one could dissolve it. On this point the civil authorities, who would have liked that a marriage contracted without the consent of the parents should be declared null and void by the Church, always encountered the firm resistance of the clergy.

Following the decrees of the Council of Trent, the Church consistently refused to make the consent of the parents a condition of validity, much to the despair of the genial Rabelais, Curé of Meudon, whom one would have expected to be in the lovers' camp. The Church remained faithful to her traditions, in accordance with which she did not marry them, but only acted as witness to the union of the consenting pair. Dom Martène expressly draws attention to the fact that the old Rituals do not give the words *vos conjungo* uttered by the priest; but only the words of the couple declaring that they are married before the Church.

In some Provinces, Normandy, and even in Paris, the custom came in of contracting the marriage merely before a notary, who would draw up the act of ratification " by these presents " before witnesses. Then came the turn of the ecclesiastical authorities to protest, but with no more success. This form of marriage by the simple act of a notary had a great vogue at the theatre, where it provided plays with a definite ending, for custom forbade the representation of the clergy on the stage.

Once the marriage had been consummated it was indissoluble. The young Baron de Survilliers, son of President [1] de Brion, first met Mlle. de la Force at a ball, then at the Comedy and the Opera, following which their marriage was celebrated in her bedroom between midnight and one o'clock, on the 7th June, 1718, by a priest in the presence of a few friends. The priest appeared in a short coat and short cassock. The banns had been duly published in the churches of St. Sulpice and Notre-Dame-des-Champs, as the young man was absent in the country. A contract had even been executed before a notary, but the whole matter had been kept from the knowledge of the father and the family.

The Chief of Police took a note of these different circumstances and added : " M. de Brion desired me to interrogate his son at his own home, and I did so, but I do not think he will get much out of this enquiry." [2]

Clandestine marriages increased in spite of injunctions, royal rescripts, and Acts of Parliament. In 1623, Omer Talon, the Advocate General, followed in 1637 by Bignon, also Advocate General, protested against these clandestine marriages which were increasing in number ; a simple declaration before a priest, followed by an act executed before a notary, constituted these marriages, which were called " à la Gaulmine," from the name of a *Maître des Requêtes*,[3] who had been married in this manner in the middle of the seventeenth century.

Some Parliaments, like that of Paris, endeavoured to oppose this practice, and to proclaim the nullity of marriages à la Gaulmine ; but when once they had been consummated, the parents found themselves faced with a difficult position.

In Provence, on the other hand, the Parliament of Aix, and

---

[1] The title President is partly honorific and partly a definite title borne by a judge, a member of one of the different Parliaments, or of some local legislative Assembly, of which there were many performing different functions in France. (H. W.)

[2] Bibl. Nat. MS. Franc. 8119, ff. 76–85.

[3] A Magistrate who drew up reports to be submitted to the Council of State. (H. W.)

all the authorities, both civil and religious, declared these marriages to be valid, and in conformity with the doctrine of the Church. Throughout the entire Archdiocese of Bourges nullity could only be pronounced at the request of one of the married couple.

Seduction was punished with death. The Royal Decree of 1730 confirmed all the previous rescripts relating to this matter, and made them still more stringent. Judges were forbidden to allow any mitigating circumstances, even in cases where the parents of the victim of the seduction, reverting to more indulgent sentiments, might have specially pleaded for a reparation by marriage.

The preamble of this decree should be underlined in all its details :

" The Decrees which have been made by the Kings, our Predecessors," states Louis XV, " with a view to the prevention of seduction, had in mind to strengthen the authority of fathers over their children, and to act as a restraint on unworthy alliances which, through the inequality in their condition, and by smirching the honour of many families, might become the cause of their ruin."

The commentator on this decree adds " Since seduction might as equally come from one side as from the other, and since, when coming from the weaker side, it is often the more dangerous," the decrees condemned to death in like manner the gentleman or the lady.

And then there were abductions, and these were frequent. Men would break through the walls of convents wherein the young ladies were shut up. Montlosier gives an account of his grandfather's marriage. He lived under Louis XIV in that rough and rugged Auvergne, at the time when Fléchier's [1] *Grands Jours* made people acquainted with its high-handed methods. With the assistance of five or six comrades, Montlosier, after a regular assault like on some fortified place, carried off the young lady from the convent in which she had been shut up in order to secure her against his pursuit. " For a long time this practice had been an established custom in Auvergne and in several other provinces," writes Montlosier. " I know of few marriages among gentle people at that time which were not brought off in this way." Against this practice, as in the case of so many others, this brilliant historian adds that Louis XIV fulminated in vain : " In the morning a judge would condemn the gentleman ravisher to be hanged, in accordance with the decree, which procedure was carried out in effigy ; and in the evening both judge and condemned would sup together." A similar adventure happened in 1739. The Comte de Courbon-

---

[1] Bishop of Nîmes, a celebrated preacher, who wrote many funeral orations, the most celebrated of which is that on Turenne, also *Mémoires sur les Grands Jours tenus à Clermont en* 1665, etc. (1632–1710). (H. W.)

Blénac, a captain in the Clermont regiment, carried off Mlle. de
Moras, aged fourteen. Her mother, Mme. de Moras, died of grief,
so it was said. Courbon-Blénac was condemned in March, 1739,
and in like manner had his head cut off . . . in effigy.

One finds cases of the abduction of minors for the advantage
and "honour" of the family, and not under the influence of the
god of love. Mayenne carried off Anne de Caumont-La Force, who
was then twelve years old. The child was a very rich heiress.
Mayenne destined her for his son, then aged ten. He gave the
child to his wife to keep. "Once the words of consent had been
duly pronounced before witnesses ' by these presents,' the consummation of the marriage, which made annulment difficult, was
enforced." (G. Fagniez.)

There were also cases of children themselves having recourse to
the intervention of authority superior to that of their parents, to
Parliaments, official powers, and, in the last resort, to the King,
the head of all families. Henri IV and Louis XIV showed themselves great protectors of young lovers. Thus the former took
away Jeanne de la Roche-Fatou from her parents who opposed her
marriage to the Baron de la Force. He entrusted the child to
Saint-Georges de Vérac and Parabère, and charged a *Maître des
Requêtes* to ascertain her real feelings. When the *Maître des
Requêtes* was convinced of the love of Mlle. de la Roche-Fatou for
Baron de la Force, and Henri IV had duly received his report, the
marriage was celebrated (1608). Decrees issued by a Parliament,
or by official notification, annulling a promise of marriage imposed
by parents on their children, were not rare. We find an order
issued by the Parliament of Toulouse removing Mlle. Claude Roger
de Commenge from the convent wherein her father had confined
her, and giving her permission to marry in accordance with the
dictates of her heart ; in 1641, the same Court placed Mlle. Claire
de Bernard under the protection of the Criminal Judge of the
Seneschalty of Armagnac, with a view to removing her from the
authority of her parents who wished to marry her against her
wishes. And this intervention was not exercised among the aristocratic families alone ; we also find records of daughters of the
humble bourgeoisie asking for, and obtaining the same protection.

IV.—*Integrity of the Patrimony*

Together with its customs, traditions, and social rank, it was
incumbent on the family to preserve itself intact in the hands of
its head, and strong in its patrimony to be handed on in its integrity to the next heir. The patrimony by which the family

maintained its existence was sacred. " He who dissipates his patrimony commits a frightful robbery," wrote Antoine de Courtois in his journal ; " it would have been better for him and for all his race if he had never been born."

The lands belonging to the family must be preserved intact. It was considered blameworthy, not only to sell them, but even to exchange them. " So long as this domain shall remain in my family," we read in the above journal, " it will have an honourable existence. I pay no attention to the consideration that my descendants may be placed under the necessity of selling it. To sell their inherited lands would be to disavow my name. It is no good thinking it might be possible to replace them by others ; it is enough to see how all those who have exchanged the patrimony of their ancestors have ruined themselves."

These lines written by a modest country gentleman are characteristic, and cannot be considered with too great attention. Here we have the very pith of the Ancien Régime. We may apply these sentiments to the various classes and conditions of society, but we shall always find ourselves faced by the same three constituent elements—family, tradition, stability. The preservation of their patrimony, and attachment to the ancestral hearth were the ruling preoccupations, and among the bourgeoisie and rural classes these sentiments were handed on perhaps still more jealously than in the case of the aristocracy. " All my ancestors worked to acquire the small patches of land making up this property," wrote a farm labourer of Ollioules in 1750, " and I will not destroy the fruits of their toil."

The right of primogeniture, and the right of the father freely to dispose of his property came to be recognized. The rights of succession were of infinite variety in old France ; they differed not only between one province and another, but between one district and the neighbouring district, between one town and the next. This was carried to such an extent that we meet with families provided with special laws of succession, duly recognized by the Parliaments. But the general tendency was to leave the patrimony intact in the hands of the head of the family who disposed of it in the best interests of his house. The maintenance of the splendour of his name and the integrity of his domain formed his constant preoccupation.

To satisfy this aspiration the practice of creating entailed life interests in the hereditary inalienable portion, and in the owner's own " personal " property, co-operated with the right of primogeniture and the faculty of devising. The holding of a life interest meant that it was impossible for the holder of certain possessions to alienate them under any pretext whatsoever, the succession thereto devolving in a pre-determined order. Among the nobility these entailed life-interests bore the name of *majorats*. They acted, as we can understand, as a restraining power on the rights pertaining to primogeniture. The owner merely enjoyed the usufruct of a property which belonged to the family. Customs which gave to the eldest son the larger portion stipulated that the entail should cover the widest range and be most rigorously enforced.

" Personal Property " consisted of bequests limited to a special tenure which made them family endowments far more than individual benefits. These were called by different names—ancient property, " avitins," patrimonial, or some other term, often of a strange character. They consisted of houses, and often of profitable rights, such as seigneurial dues, income from invested monies and perquisites from the exercise of judicial authority. One finds even herds of cattle included in the " personal property " of a family. The head himself only had the right of enjoyment over his " personal property " ; and however powerful he might be he could not alienate it. To do this he would require the consent of his heirs. Is it not remarkable that these family traditions which had come down to the Ancien Régime—and we shall notice them many times as we proceed—are to be found in their first forms under the Capet Monarchy ?

The right of primogeniture, which, as we have seen, had been established to safeguard the integrity of the family, was not uniform throughout France. In Champagne the customs of succession among the nobility were of one kind, and those of the lowly cultivators of the soil were of another. The custom in Paris, on the contrary, extending to a large portion of France, gave the right of primogeniture to the humblest and the nobility alike. In conformity with this custom the eldest son took as his own privileged inheritance the principal dwelling, the château or manor house, together with the cattle yard, the common quarters of the labourers and dependants, and all the outbuildings within the flight of a *chapon*,[1] which as a rule comprised the extent of one acre ; he received in addition " la part avantageuse," that is, two-thirds of the property if there were only two children, and a half if more children had been left by the father. In Lorraine the eldest son's right included the château, cattle yard, the walled-in park, garden and enclosed land, together with the seigneurial rights, the right of appointing the priest to serve the castle chapel, and the Curé of the village. This portion of the eldest son could not be taken from him even in cases where his father had wished to do so.

[1] *Le vol du chapon*, equivalent to the extent of a manorial right. (H. W.)

On the other hand, in those parts of France *de droit écrit*, the father had entire liberty in the matter of his testamentary dispositions. The following is an instance of a will made at Aix on the 12th February, 1622 : the father disinherited his eldest son because he had made a marriage which he considered unsuitable ; he reminds his eldest son " that he had expressly forbidden him either to be constantly near the young lady or to frequent her society . . . "; he will therefore receive only an annuity for life, and the inheritance will go to the youngest son ; but, contrary to what one might have supposed, the latter refused to accept an inheritance which he considered to be a heavy burden ; for the possession of an inheritance by an eldest son entailed obligations considered by many to be a burden under which any advantages accruing therefrom disappeared. These obligations consisted in having to work for the common welfare of all, in sacrificing his own tastes and independence, in looking after old and infirm relations, in directing and establishing in life the younger brothers, as well as the sisters, and in managing the estates. An eldest son might have a taste for a more adventurous career ; a military life might attract him, or he might desire to explore the unknown seas, or trade in the Indies or the Levant ; [1] in another case he might be attracted to one of the liberal careers ; he would be an artist, or a poet attached to one of the companies of travelling play-actors whose roving life may have filled him with enthusiasm—the life of which Scarron has given such a picturesque account. He might not care about seeing himself strictly bound down to the life of exploiting his domain, with all the accompanying duties which would devolve upon him.

The father who had decided to disinherit his son in order to mark his reprobation of a marriage of which he disapproved, was aware that his younger son had no desire for the succession, and inserted in his will binding clauses which would compel his obedience. He reminded him of " all he had spent on his son's studies in becoming a doctor." This amount would have to be paid back if he should refuse to succeed as " head of the house " and undertake the care of his property.

As to younger sons who had only a small portion of the family patrimony divided between them, they would in their turn perhaps have younger sons of their own ; these younger sons might find themselves in the position of having to divide up a windmill, a stack of corn, a sporting gun, a chicken or duck. Moreover in certain

[1] The term *Echelles du Levant* (from the Turkish word *iskele*, jetty) was the name given to those Mediterranean ports under Turkish domination, Constantinople, Salonica, Beyrouth, Smyrna, Alexandria, Tripoli, etc. (H. W.)

districts, as in Brittany, this small portion left to the younger sons entailed only a life-interest, and at their death what had been derived from the family patrimony went back to the principal branch.

The lot of the girls was likewise subject to great variations in matters connected with the succession. In Anjou and Maine, should the occasion arise, they were allowed to enjoy the rights of the first born, which were forbidden by Paris custom. In Artois custom went so far as to deny them all right to inherit ; in fact they did not count.

It would be almost superfluous to remark that these prescriptions, which were often so rigorous, had in view the sole end of maintaining the integrity and perpetuity of the family. Among the rural classes in Brittany the right of succession was in favour of the youngest instead of the eldest. It was a *droit de jeunesse*, if we may be permitted to use the expression. If the house possessed no son the youngest daughter inherited. The youngest, *le juveigneur*, alone entered into possession of the family inheritance. He or she divided between the brothers and sisters only the furniture that had been left by the father, but a fact to be noted is that he or she could only receive the inheritance on condition of having been living for one year and a day, uninterruptedly, beneath the family roof before the right to succeed arose. We can understand the reason for this : there was the necessity of continuing the cultivation of the domain under the same traditional conditions, of retaining the same *personnel* and perpetuating the general appearance of the holding. An eldest son who had been married for a long time and had perhaps set up a separate home elsewhere and worked a farm at some distance from his father's house, might have introduced a spirit that was too new and too different.

We saw above that a son remained a minor throughout his life. Marriage emancipated him, but only on condition that he went away and lived far from his father, and set up a separate home of his own. If he lived under his father's roof with his wife and children he could call nothing his own. Anything he might be in a position to possess, anything he earned, any gifts and legacies he might receive, became the property of his father, and in most provinces the son could only inherit from his father as eldest son— we are speaking now of the peasant class—on condition that he was living with him under his roof. In that case only, on becoming the head of the family at the death of his father, did he take over the management of the patrimony, which in many cases had been increased through his own toil and care. We can always feel this same preoccupation dominating the most deeply rooted customs in the soul of the people, that of making secure the integrity, stability and perpetuity of the family in its manners, usages and traditions. An eldest son who had been living and working far away from his father would bring the risk of introducing ideas, habits, and ways of doing things of a different character, were he called upon to carry on the family patrimony; he would not have known the servants of the estate, nor appreciated them at their true value; it was to be feared that he would introduce too great changes.

Champagne, Lorraine, and Alsace were provinces in which the right of the eldest to inherit was less strongly embedded. It did not exist in the case of collateral branches, and did not apply to daughters. In the case of peasant families the property was equally divided between the children, but the same sentiment animated all classes; it reserved to the principal beneficiary the family home, the house—making him the head of the fief, as it was called in the Middle Ages, the chief of the patrimony, as the Ancien Régime termed him, in order that each family should continue to possess its central point, its pivot, its "retirance" as the peasants called it, using a very characteristic expression. Pierre Joseph de Colonia writing in his journal, in 1807, expresses himself as follows:

"Provence, like several other districts in southern France, was administered under Roman laws. . . . In every province living under this legislation there existed in the different families the most affectionate unity. The heir regarded himself as the father of all the younger brothers and sisters, who, more often than not, were fed and housed under his roof, sometimes without paying anything for their board and lodging. This in very truth made one family of them."

These customs therefore justified themselves; they contributed to the happiness and prosperity of France, and were beneficial in so far as they were practised not only in the letter but also in the spirit.

In our own times every subject of a State has a direct interest in seeing it strong, prosperous and united. The fiefs and seigneuries were real States in themselves whose subjects likewise had a direct interest in seeing their chief powerful, rich and respected; the different families were States, like the fiefs, and similarly their members had a like interest in seeing their head enjoying a brilliant position, which was reflected back upon them in every incident of their lives. By living on the family domain the eldest son held it together in all its integrity, and maintained the name, honour and importance of the House; he took pains to fit the younger members for the careers that were open to them, supporting them by his influence, and helping them to make their way in the army, or in diplomacy, often in distant regions overseas where in the seventeenth century the sons of good families played such a brilliant and sometimes such a useful part. Let us always bear in mind the family sentiments animating the men of those days with a force and energy which we can hardly now conceive, causing an elder brother to devote himself to the younger members of the family not only from natural affection, but also in that spirit of solidarity and corporate family oneness of which we have been speaking. The honour and brilliancy of a younger brother's career reflected its rays directly upon the elder, just in the same way as did his poverty, or dishonour, should the path along which he was to support him be cut short by a disastrous issue.

It is true to say that though the majority of those who became the mainstay of the family understood the duty that was expected of them, and practised it towards their relations, it happened that sometimes one or other was neglectful in this respect. In his *Avis sur le Partage des Nobles*, d'Argentré writes, " The elder brother proves to be hard and cross-grained, and shuts his ears. He does not show the affection of a father in the matter of contributing from his means ; seated by his fireside he hears his younger brother asking for bread outside the door." The sentiments which had acted like cement in binding the family together were to lose their force in the eighteenth century ; we shall see them deteriorating. We shall see the elder brother, far from keeping up with dignity— often with his personal toil—the ancestral manor—the *hôtel*, as the bourgeois called it, the *retirance* of the peasants—far from making the lands, constituting its wealth, bear fruit ; far from fulfilling his obligations to the entire family of which he was the head, we shall see him profiting by his privileged position to thrust himself into the world of honours and pleasures, cutting a figure and amusing himself at Court, while his younger brothers, left to their feeble resources, were no longer able, from lack of means, to make a career for themselves worthy of their name. What had been a great benefit became a cruel abuse. But cases like these, for the reasons we have shown, were exceptional so long as the sentiments on which the Ancien Régime rested still remained whole and entire.

We must once more bear in mind that the above remarks applied equally to every class of society.

Districts enjoying the *droit écrit* divided the inheritance in equal portions among the children. Generally speaking these districts comprised the south of France. The dividing line was approximately the southern frontier of the following provinces : Saintonge, Angoumois, Marche, Auvergne, Bourbonnais and Burgundy. The *droit coutumier* (custom) ruled north of this line, the *droit écrit* in the regions south of it, with the exception of Alsace which lived under the latter. But as we have seen, in the provinces of *droit écrit* the liberty of the head of the family to make provisions in his will of almost unlimited application was recognized, but in practice the wishes of the father represented a division which was in conformity with the feelings and ideas of the times. In a number of towns, such as Arles, Toulouse and Montpellier, and throughout Provence, daughters who had received a dowry were considered as having already partaken of their share of the inheritance. This was likewise the custom among the peasants as well as the nobility. Moreover there was the practice of life-interests.

On this point the customs of the Ancien Régime were so strongly held, and the interests attaching to them were considered to be so important by those living in those days that it was by no means rare, in cases where the father had died intestate, for the younger children to give up to the elder brother of their own free will that portion which their father could have left to him, in order to place him in a position to fulfil his duties as the prop and mainstay of the house.

Many examples could be given to demonstrate the prosperity and advancement these practices were able to afford to those " houses " which conformed most closely to them. I will give one, out of a hundred that could be cited, to be found in the *Mémoires* of the Marquis d'Argenson. His grandfather had had seven or eight children of whom five had done well : two daughters, one of whom had been made a Carmelite nun, the other had married with a small *dot*, " but M. de Valori d'Etilly held himself greatly honoured in marrying her " ; of the three sons, one became a Knight of Malta, vowed to celibacy ; another entered the ranks of the clergy —the eldest, " the support and mainstay of the family," pushed him forward till he became Archbishop of Bordeaux ; we now come to Marc Réné d'Argenson, the head of the family. We mentioned above the sacrifices which had been made in order to enable him to occupy the position in the world which his family wished. One of his uncles, the Abbé d'Argenson, had likewise given up his share to him ; another uncle too, a younger son who had become Governor of Canada, gave up a portion of what was his, " and through the assistance of all these gifts," writes the Marquis d'Argenson, " my father set himself up, took a wife and assumed his charge." We see him becoming Lieutenant[1] General of Police, *Garde des Sceaux,*[2]

[1] *Lieutenant général de Police*, now *Préfet de police*, the head of the police in Paris. (H. W.)

[2] Roughly corresponding to the functions of Lord Privy Seal. (H. W.)

President of the Finance Council, Minister of State, and member
of the Académie Française. Of his two sons one became Minister
for War, and the other Minister for Foreign Affairs. Facts like
these should be borne in mind. When we see a family consenting
to such sacrifices, and showing such a spirit of solidarity in advancing one of their members to an eminent position, we shall be less
astonished at finding the head of the house profiting by his position
in order to extend to his family and relatives the favours, even the
State appointments, which might be at his disposal.

It may be objected that the personal worth of the Argensons was
the cause of the rise of their house ; certainly this fact must not
be scouted ; but, as Duclos, permanent Secretary of the French
Academy, remarked at the time : when a family was placed con-
spicuously before the public view its personal worth was only
accessory. We come back again and again to this essential fact :
society in the Ancien Régime rested on the family much more
than on individuals.

V.—*The Maisons de Village*

For the maintenance of the family patrimony or *retirance* which
gave protection and support, the Ancien Régime had developed
many particular customs apart from the advantages accorded to
the eldest son and the testamentary liberties permitted to the head
of the house.

The aristocracy had certain communal usages which grouped
together the different branches of the family, maintaining control
over the possessions they held in common. The manor of Château
Létard, where Noël du Fail dwelt, was a buzzing hive under the
control of the eldest son. Brothers and sisters and their households
lived there together. When the time came to make a division of
the paternal inheritance, houses and properties were left undivided,
and only the *revenue* from the domain was divided up amongst
those who were entitled to it.

At the end of the eighteenth century, Comte de Montlosier broke
away from this state of joint-possession by getting married. " I
was going to have a house and servants of my own. What had
belonged to me up till then had been merged in the joint-possession
of all the property by my other brothers, and this we had had to
cultivate in common so as not to bring prejudice to any one of us."

These customs were held in honour with much greater force among
the rural classes than among the aristocracy. The association of
many relatives in the common development of the patrimony went
by the name of *frérage* or *fraresche*, the members forming which

were called *frarescheux*. The *frarescheux* were those possessing property in common, co-heirs who kept the patrimony undivided among themselves.

The *frérages* played a prominent part in rural life in olden times, and more than one charming picture of them has been preserved. Montlosier takes us to a gentleman's country estate in Auvergne, and we are introduced into the circle of a family of peasants by the steward Chazerat, at about the time when the Ancien Régime was coming to an end. In the neighbourhood of Thiers, not far from his own lands, Chazerat was in the habit of frequently visiting the Guittard family consisting of four sets of married couples, whose households altogether numbered nineteen persons. The buildings of the homestead were situated on a narrow piece of level ground on the lower range of the mountains of Thiers, above a valley where an old forest of lofty trees alternated with green meadows. The Guittards had organized a *fête* at their large farm in honour of the steward, and Chazerat had accepted the invitation. He came with his wife and several of their friends. The ground beneath the vast open barn was strewn with grass and flowers, and the walls and framework were decked with green. A rustic feast took place, after which they danced till nightfall. Merriment shone in every eye. Shortly afterwards the steward gave a magnificent feast to the Guittards. The head of the Guittard house received a distinction from the Royal Government, which had been requested for him by the steward, in the shape of a sash denoting the head of an Auvergne family. It was of blue velvet embroidered with red, and in front there was a silver plate bearing the blazon of France on which had been engraved four lines celebrating in rustic doggrel the virtues of the Guittards.

Communities called *taisibles* (meaning those established by a tacit convention without any contract, or public act) were associations of peasant families under the leadership of an elected head. This head " ruled the other members, sat down first at table, went to the fairs and markets, and was the only one whose name figured on the list of taxes to be collected " (Guy Coquille). The personal and real estate of the community stood in his name, and it was he who drove the oxen. Any action he took bound the whole community of several families grouped together, issue of the same stock. The *communautés taisibles* were also called *communautés coutumières*, *communautés convenues*, or *Maisons de village*. The head went by the name of the *Maître*, and the members were called *parsonniers*. Coquille speaks of them at some length in his *Coutumes du Nivernais* : " The head of the community is commonly called the *Maître*, and in the *maisons de village* belonging to this district it is usual to appoint one, but in the *maisons de ville* this practice is seldom observed." In Auvergne the *Mouistre* (Maître) alone had the right to wear leather shoes ; the *parsonniers* wore sabots, and the children went barefoot. The *Maître*, in addition, carried a silver watch, and tied a sash of red and green wool round his waist.

The *Maître* exercised sovereign authority over his own people, but in matters of important business, such as engaging in a lawsuit or acquiring a piece of land, he would call together a council of the *parsonniers*. He was elected and chosen out of the principal family, almost always on lines of primogeniture. However, this was only a traditional attribution, and it might not be ratified by the assembled council. It is very interesting to note that we still find in these *maisons de village* in the eighteenth century the same constitution and manner of succession which characterized royalty at the time when these communities had been formed.

In the case of the Pinon family in Auvergne, the election took place under a great oak tree, several centuries old, in the midst of a huge field separated from the farm road by a line of beehives, on the other side of which rose the farm buildings. From this spot could be seen looking eastwards, " *à jour*," the mountains of the Forez ; to the south, " *à midi*," the district of Limagne, the fields and meadows of which were interspersed with vineyards ; to the west, " *à nuit*," the rounded humps of the Auvergne heights, and to the north, " *à bise*," the forest of Saint Rémy lying in an amphitheatre. The *parsonniers* took counsel together, and the election was held gravely without any noise. After the elected member had given his consent to take over his functions, an Act bearing the signatures of the chief members of the community was handed to him ; it contained the clauses embodying the terms of his headship, together with an acknowledgment of the submission of the members of the community. The new *Maître* promised faithfully to fulfil his duty, and then related what he knew about the history of the great family and spoke of any changes he thought it might be advisable to introduce into the life and work of each member. The day ended with a family feast.

By the side of the *Maître* was the *Maîtresse*. She was not the wife of the *Maître*, but like him was chosen by election. She presided over the women ; her department comprised the *basse-cour*,[1] the kitchen, the laundry, the spinning and weaving, the linen and clothes ; she also looked after the children who went to work in the fields.

Thus ruled under one head, these communities of families, by combining together all their possessions, reached the stage of forming

[1] The part where the cattle and poultry were reared. (H. W.)

one single " house " ; they called themselves by the same name, that of the chief of the family, which they made into a plural— they talked of the Jaults, the Pinons, the Pannés, the Pélignats, to take illustrations from the names of a few celebrated communities.

The *maisons de village* had customs peculiar to themselves which enabled them to preserve unity, since the patrimonies of several families were grouped together in one common stock. The girls as a rule married within the community ; those who married outside it received a dowry of a few hundred francs, in return for which they renounced their portion of the common heritage. Those who remained single also gave up their portion of the inheritance in return for a few hundred francs ; but for the greater part they lived simply together in the community, asking for nothing but their keep.

These communities grouped all they had under the leadership of the *Maître*. There were some numbering as many as thirty-two married couples, as, for instance, the community of the Mesles in the parish of Saint Ennemond, in Allier. They had a large dwelling, the " house," in which each couple occupied a room communicating with the outside ; these rooms were sometimes joined up by large corridors. Michelet calls these *communautés taisibles*, " convents of married labourers." The furniture consisted of chairs with straw bottoms ; the beds, chests and cupboards were made of pine. The *Maître* alone had a cupboard of oak and walnut. Often each couple had their own private dwelling, but they always met together in one common house in which there was a large stove, forming the family hearth, where they could warm themselves.

The warm living room (*chauffoir*) was characterized by an enormous hearth in the centre, under a lofty conical chimney. Thirty or forty people could easily dispose themselves around the huge fire of broom bushes the flames from which mounted to the ceiling. The children sat on little benches, and the old occupied arm chairs of rustic woodwork in the forefront.

This room served as the kitchen ; the *parsonniers* ate their meals there, sitting round an enormous patriarchal table. When the Pinon community was broken up in the nineteenth century, their table was sold, and two huge doors were made from it. The men took their meal first, seated round the table, and waited on by the women ; the latter followed, but they stood while eating. At the end of the room was a niche with a statue of the Virgin, and a Crucifix. Sometimes this room served as both the bedroom of the *Maître*, who slept there, and that of the little children.

The room contained beds ranged round the wall, end to end, and closed in by curtains of yellow serge ; there were also cupboards, arranged in a row like the beds ; there was a cupboard common to the whole community, and each branch, that is each separate family forming the community, had also one to itself. Then there was a cupboard for the plates and dishes, a clock, a kneading trough, and a stone trough in which the potatoes were mashed up when cooked. Lastly, from the low ceiling blackened by smoke, one could see hanging from the beams picturesque bunches of lime and elderberry, dried herbs and clusters of fruit, and from the chimney in the centre dangled smoked hams and salt meat on skewers.

During the winter evenings the old people would tell stories connected with the history of the family, or the exploits of the *Maître* who could pacify a mad dog by his voice alone ; their life-like narratives unfolded the legends of the country, and the hearers shuddered when they listened to the details of crimes that had remained notorious. At nine o'clock, at a sign from the *Maître*, all would become silent. " Children, it is time for prayers ! ", and every one, including any wandering beggars met with during the day and who had taken their places at the meal at the common table, fell on their knees and recited in unison the evening prayers. The girls then retired to one side of the room, the boys to the other, each to their beds shut off by their yellow serge curtains.

Many of these *maisons de village* had established on their domain a hospital, or lazar-house as it was called, in which the sick and wounded, even though they were strangers to the community, were tended and fed. For poor people passing through, and tramps, a special room was set apart, and in the winter these were lodged in the bakehouse where it was " good and warm."

A writer of the time shows us the community of the Jaults in Nivernais coming out from Mass under the leadership of their chief on their way back to the huge patriarchal farm which, during the service, had been guarded by an old woman all by herself. And here is another picture of the Pinon family in Auvergne, like-wise coming out from Mass one Easter Sunday, preceded by their banner. The men were wearing white waistcoats, and large straw hats decorated by their women folk with sprigs of the Auvergne box-tree.

A number of these communities gave their name to the village where they lived and which had been built up by them. Are there not many localities in France still called to this day by the names of families, such as those of Pinon, Dameriot, Ferrier, etc. ? We may be quite certain that such names owe their origin to *maisons de village,* for most of these went back to a remote period, sometimes to the beginning of the Middle Ages, to the ninth century, and even to the eighth, as in the case of the Pinons. What ducal house—Montmorency, La Rochefoucauld, Saint Simon, or Choiseul—could have rivalled in the nobility of their antiquity the Pinons of Auvergne, who went back authentically to Carlovingian times, that is, as far back as the period when feudal France took shape ?

Everything that the inhabitants of the house used was made by themselves ; the women spun the thread and wove the materials ; the skins of animals which had been killed were tanned. The furniture, linen, sabots, socks and implements of labour, were all made in the community. The *parsonniers* had no need to employ any outside assistance in putting up their buildings. They lived on the produce of their holding, and employed no outside servants. They bought nothing from without except iron and salt. It was rare to find among these happy and prosperous communities a single man who could read and write.

Village communities were very numerous in Auvergne, Nivernais, le Morvan and Bourbonnais. Around Saint Léon, in Allier, they numbered one to the square kilometre. When a community became prosperous it swarmed, as it were, and set up another from its own offshoots either near or at a distance, and this too might swarm in its turn and produce others.

Many of these *maisons de village*, thanks to their labour and good mutual understanding, attained a position of great prosperity. There were some possessing as many as seven domains. The communities, so numerous in the seventeenth century in the Department of Allier, worked the land each with a team of eight oxen. On the eve of the Revolution the fortune of the Pinons was valued at 600,000 francs, which to-day would correspond to six millions. It numbered forty members.

Some of these *maisons de village*, such as that of the Pinons, had had an historic past, and were possessed of ancestral legends which were carefully handed down ; trophies of war hung on their walls. In 1740, the Pélignats stirred up the region of the Jura, where they were established, to revolt against their suzerain, the Prince Bishop of Bâle. They appealed to the States of Berne to make an alliance with them against the Bishop, who called for the support of the King of France. They were a peasant family, presenting all the attributes of a great seigneurial house. The Pélignats lost their cause, and their *Maître* was executed at Porentruy. Here we have, in the middle of the eighteenth century, a living image—without the grim setting of iron and stone, for social conditions had by then changed—of the feudal baronies of the time of Louis le Gros.

We said above that marriages frequently took place between young people belonging to families forming the same community. If the young man chose a wife from outside, the *Maître* saw to it that she belonged to a neighbouring community. Our peasants were extremely particular on this point, far more so than the aristocratic families. The subject to be admitted to the " house " was carefully looked over. He must be possessed of good health, and be a good worker, and our *parsonniers* laid special stress on the antiquity of his family—just like gentlefolk. It was a guarantee to them of good traditions valiantly upheld. Ah ! your Graces, Dukes of Montmorency, La Rochefoucauld, Saint Simon, Choiseul, Croÿ and others, which of you would have been considered worthy on account of the antiquity of your race, to enter the family of *Maître* Pinon, which went back authentically to the days of Charlemagne ?

And so when marriages were to be made our peasants displayed great circumspection. The *Maître* indicated the girl, chosen from among the community, whom the *parsonnier* was to take as his wife—like the Counsellor in the Parliament of Dijon whom we saw dictating his choice to his son.[1]

In the case of a refusal the community was convened to the field, where the election of the *Maître* had taken place beneath the old elm, or ancestral oak. The youthful rebel was solemnly called upon to conform to the wishes of his kinsmen. Should he still persist in his refusal, the *Maître* would remind him of the origin and importance of his house :

" It is a long time ago, more than a thousand years, that a man, the father of a large family, counselled his children not to separate from each other so that their possessions in like manner should not also become separated ; that they would become stronger and richer if, instead of one taking his blade of grass and another his faggot of wood, they would sit down and eat together and in like manner burn their faggots together. Since then their children's children have joined hands to defend themselves and to work, with their sheaves in the same granary and their wood in the same shed. . . ."

The awakening of these memories, together with the pressing words of counsel, sometimes had their effect on the young *parsonnier*. If he still persisted in his resolve, the *Maître*, after breaking a piece of bread, would put into his hands a parcel containing his best belongings, a purse holding the sum of money given him to set himself up with outside, to which was added a gnarled staff newly cut in the forest near by, and would then conduct him to the gates of the enclosure. The young *parsonnier* was thenceforth an exile.

[1] Page 27.

We have likened these old peasant families to the aristocratic houses. The similarity might be pressed still farther. As was the case with the nobility, a hierarchy existed among these communities. Thus a difference in social rank and position existed between the community of the Jaults and that of the Pannés, the latter representing a house of secondary rank. The *Maître* of the Jaults was a great personage in the district, but the Pannés too, from a social point of view, were on a very much higher level than the simple peasant families who did not plough with several oxen, and whose children consented to serve outside. We should add that a number of these communities used their savings to acquire other properties on which they placed men to farm them, *métayers*,[1] and cultivators on whom they levied dues which scarcely differed from those exacted on the seigneuries.

The scarcity and difficulty of communications, combined with the spirit of tradition, contributed to the maintenance of ancestral customs in these *maisons de village*. With the advent of the eighteenth century roads were multiplied through the assiduity of the Intendants. Up till that time mere footpaths served as the means of communication between one homestead and another. There were no bridges. Rivers were crossed by a ferry or on planks of wood.

It is very noteworthy that from the commencement of the reign of Louis XVI, when new ideas were coming into play, ideas already those of the coming Revolution, the *communautés taisibles* —held in such great honour by writers of the preceding generation, Voltaire, Retif de la Bretonne, and the authors of the *Encyclopédie* —were losing popular favour. The Provincial Assembly of Berry decided, in 1783, upon the breaking up of *communautés taisibles* as being "injurious to agriculture."

Their social sway was, however, so strong that many of them lasted through the Revolution and, in opposition to the new laws with which they had to contend, persisted as late as the middle, and even to the end of the nineteenth century. The Ferrier community was not only still in existence at Escoutoux (Puy-de-Dôme) in 1858, but in that very year the marriages of five young men, all named Ferrier-Ferrier, to five girls likewise all named Ferrier-Ferrier, were celebrated, and a contract was drawn up placing them all in one community. This *maison de village* was still in existence in 1898, and possibly may be still existing. In 1898 the community numbered twenty-three members ; the *Maître*, elected in 1897, was thirty-five years old. He administered the property and held authority over all the members of the group,

[1] The *métayer* worked on a system of profit-sharing. (H. W.)

whatever their age might be. A marvellous example of the social power of the institutions of ancient France! Would that our own might have a like fate!

We have thought it well to speak in some detail of the village communities. Nothing can give us a better understanding of the Ancien Régime. They are a living example of that family activity which extricated France from the appalling anarchy of the ninth century, and formed the source from which sprang her institutions lasting right down to 1789.

VI.—*Family Solidity*

The family, like its patrimony, formed a solid block, whose several constituent parts were held closely together. " I am merely a morsel of the family," wrote the Bailli de Mirabeau to his elder brother, the Marquis. The honour of the relative was reflected back upon all of them, in the same way as the errors he might commit, and the shame which thereby might fall upon him. As with the constitution of the family, so the origin of these sentiments went back to the first beginnings of the Middle Ages. When Olivier, under the menace of the innumerable Saracen host at Roncevaux, asked Roland to sound his horn to recall Charlemagne and the bulk of the French army, Roland refused, from fear lest his kinsmen should incur dishonour thereby: God forbid " *que mes parens pur mei seient blasmés !* . . . " and with the same thought in his mind the poet who wrote the *Miserere* of the Recluse of Molliens-Vidame, exclaimed in the thirteenth century, " *Las ! autrui pekié nous assome* . . . " " the fault of another is going to overwhelm us."

Men of the Ancien Régime spoke of " families of merit " and " families worthy of punishment " just as often as of individuals meet to be punished or rewarded. The Abbé de La Feuillée writes to the Subdelegate of Douai in connection with a young relative who threatened to turn out badly : " It would be very distressing if, for the sake of a person whose utility is very uncertain, we were to expose ourselves to the possibility of seeing the downfall of a large body of people who are working with so much courage." [1] A Parisian lady of modest condition draws the attention of her uncle, named Randon, to the behaviour of a female cousin, " a hussy who is dishonouring our family, a rotten member for whom we have done all we could to make her sound and good." [2] An

---

[1] Letter dated 26th July, 1760. *Archives du Pas-de-Calais*, C. 709, f. 57.
[2] Written in 1789. Bibl. de l'Arsenal, *Archives de la Bastille*, 11763, doss. Randon.

officer in the Beauvais regiment begs the Lieutenant of Police to give him permission to take away one of his relatives from the hospice at Bicêtre, where he is being detained, with a view to enlisting him in his regiment where he will be able to look after him " so that he may not conduct himself in a manner prejudicial to his family." [1] Just as the discreditable behaviour of one member tarnished the reputation of the entire family, so did his worth and the distinction he won, in whatever capacity it might be, shed its rays over the whole house. In his very interesting historical romance, *Le Bon Plaisir*, Henri de Régnier gives the following sketch, somewhat ironical but very true to life :

" M. de Collarceaux was not interested in these subjects (stories of military life), not having served in the army on account of a difficulty he had in breathing, as he alleged, which, however, was no hindrance to his talking. To those who showed astonishment at his having done nothing he would boast about the services rendered by his uncle, M. de Chamissy. Was it not a kind of gallantry to be the nephew of such a brave officer, and especially since his uncle had perished at Dortmude he had something whereby to shut the mouth of the most troublesome people ? "

The honour, as well as the fortune and integrity of the patrimony belonged to the entire house as an undivided possession, which it was the duty of each member to help in maintaining and defending, for in this each one personally was interested. When Concini, the Maréchal d'Ancre, was assassinated on the drawbridge of the Louvre on the 24th February, 1617, on a sign given by the King, all the members of his family were affected ; his brother-in-law, the Abbot of Marmoutier and Archbishop of Tours, had to resign all his dignities and leave the kingdom. When Fouquet, the chief Administrator of Finance under Louis XIV, was arrested, his relatives were exiled.

During the Regency,[2] Bernard Girardin was compromised in matters of finance ; his son, Girardin de Vauvray, *Maître des Requêtes*, received orders to resign his appointment. After the death of Louis XV, the Comtesse du Barry was sent to the convent of Pont-aux-Dames, and every one bearing her name was driven from the Court. When the Maréchal de Luxembourg and Cardinal Louis de Rohan became implicated in law proceedings, their relatives, among them the greatest names in France—the Condés and Montmorencys—might have been seen drawn up by the gate

---

[1] Letter of 15th March, 1745, *ibid.*, 11544, ff. 482–83.

[2] Unless otherwise stated the Regency, where mentioned in this book, refers to that exercised by Philippe d'Orléans during the minority of Louis XV, 1715–1723. (H. W.)

of the Bastille, or at the entrance to the Houses of Parliament, in order to testify to the solidarity of the family. *"Messieurs,"* said the Comtesse de Marsan to the magistrates as they passed in, " you are now going to pass judgment on us all."

From this principle arose the practice of confiscation which has not been sufficiently understood. When the head of a family had judgment passed upon him, the confiscation of his possessions was pronounced, not only of his own personal property, but that of the family patrimony as well; it was the family that was punished. In his enactments directed against the Ancien Régime in 1771, Maupeou, the Chancellor, endeavoured to suppress "this odious law which for the fault of one man incriminated a whole family."

This principle permeated the social ladder from the top to the bottom. After the assassination of Henri IV the kinsfolk of Ravaillac were threatened with death. Cartouche's [1] family learnt to their cost that justice was not squeamish in regard to the relatives of criminals, however innocent they might have been. After the execution of Mandrin, the youngest of his brothers, then aged fourteen, was arrested and put in prison at Grenoble where he remained for two years, that is, until he should be old enough to undertake to serve in the colonies for the rest of his life. [2]

The attempt made by Damiens (on the life of Louis XV) entailed the condemnation of his father, by decree of the 27th March, 1757, to quit the realm. [3] " Vengeance pursued his entire family, father, children, wife, relatives and connections." [4]

By a logical sequence, the fortunes of one member of a family, especially those of the head, flowed forth over all. Madame de Maintenon, after she had become all powerful, showed extreme circumspection and discretion. She requested no Court favours on behalf of her relatives, or only to a very modest extent. To-day we should accord her merit for this, but her contemporaries blamed her.

The family had contributed to the rise of one of its members : its moral and material progress had been attained by degrees, from generation to generation, through their joint virtues, efforts and sacrifices ; it seemed to be only just that the day of glory should be spread over the entire house.

[1] Cartouche, the notorious chief of a band of robbers, was broken on the wheel (1693–1721). (H. W.)

[2] Letter from the Chief Administrator of Dauphiné, 8th December, 1756. *Archives de l'Isère.*

[3] Damiens struck Louis XV with a penknife. After being tortured he was bound to two horses and torn asunder. (H. W.)

[4] Bibl. de l'Arsenal, *Archives de la Bastille*, doss. Gautier, 11998, f. 7.

These facts had the greatest consequences. They brought in their train the manners and most important institutions of the old days, from the rights pertaining to primogeniture, to *lettres de cachet* which we shall consider later on. It is not our place to examine in this book whether the principle was good or bad ; the fact existed, not through the will of a man, of a Prince, of a despot, of a Court of Justice, or of a deliberative assembly, but through the powerful influence of custom, and the social urge of a whole nation of one mind.

Many sociologists and great minds, from Balzac to Le Play, taking into consideration the general advantages to the progress and prosperity of society that accrued from the rights of primogeniture and free testamentary dispositions, have desired the restoration of these old customs ; but would they be able also to restore those sentiments of family solidarity we are here explaining ? One is the consequence—and the condition—of the other. One is the *raison d'être* of the other, and its justification. The head of the family was permeated with the feeling that he was directly responsible, not only for his own destiny, but also for that of all his kinsfolk. M. Dupuy draws attention to this fact in his interesting studies on Breton society under the Ancien Régime :

" When an individual falls upon evil times it is not a rare thing to see all those bearing his name joining together to help him. The same thing occurs at every moment in every class of society —a close solidarity and a jealous regard for their joint honour."

VII.—*Honour is the Foundation Stone of Monarchies*

We now come to one of the most important principles which dominated social life under the Ancien Régime—the sentiment of honour.

In his *Cabinet des Antiques*, Balzac says, " Honour was set up in men's hearts like a lighthouse ; it lighted their most insignificant actions, and animated their most trivial thoughts."

" To soil the honour of the house in this world and to be damned in the next, were the only dangers known to a French gentleman, the only things he took care to avoid " (Vicomte d'Avenel). And not only the gentleman by birth, but the Frenchman in every class of society, right down to the end of the Ancien Régime.

" In our family we have good hearts, and pardon everything except dishonour. Thanks be to God, this has not touched us. Good-bye Pierrot. I embrace the little Retifs ; we must live for honour." This letter was from a lawyer in a small way in Burgundy to his cousin, Pierre Retif, a farm labourer in Nitry.[1] Retif de la Bretonne, whose writings are of priceless value in the study of the most humble classes of society in the eighteenth century, described in his *Paysan Perverti* the life of one of his relatives, of peasant origin, like himself, who went to Paris and became corrupted by the evil society he frequented. He was condemned to the galleys. The news of this reached the modest hamlet in Burgundy where his family lived. The despair of these good folk presented a harrowing spectacle. His brother became a pariah in the village.

" The other little children will no longer play with mine," he wrote ; " our neighbours shun my wife, and the men no longer greet me on coming from church, or in the fields. I always greet them, and they do not return my greeting ; but I continue to greet them, and am covered with my shame. And I speak to my wife of this precept of the Gospel, ' If we greet only those who greet us, what praise shall we have ? '

She answers me with a sigh which goes through my heart ; and every evening we go together to the graves of my father and mother, and of his father and his mother, and cry aloud to God, ' Have pity.' "

The condemned man, through the exercise of some outside influence, was allowed to come back from the galleys. " A wretched looking man was seen in the outskirts of the village. His beard was unkempt, and his clothes were torn and in holes ; he had lost an arm and did not emerge from the woods until the approach of nightfall. . . . "

This was the *paysan perverti*.

Next day his brother received the following letter :

" The day before yesterday I kissed the threshold of your door ; I prostrated myself before the home of our venerated parents. I caught sight of you and your sobs choked me. Your dog came at me to bite me ; he fell back with a yelp the moment he sniffed at me, as if I had been a fierce wild beast. You thought so too, doubtless, for you threw a stone ; it hit me. That was my first torment. . . . Your wife called to you ; you went out together to go to the graves. But I got there before you. You prayed, and said to your wife, as you noticed that the gravestones were moist as though from drops of water :

' There is a heavy dew, the stone is all wet ; the evening damp might do you harm ; let us go away.'

The dew was my tears."

The public authorities took into consideration the honour and

---

[1] Dated 10th March, 1710, and published in Retif de la Bretonne's *Village. Collection des Mémoires Illustrés* (Fayard, Paris).

integrity of families. The Provincial Superintendants note " that a family cannot take too many precautions to ward off dishonour," and in the towns the local authorities, mayors, consuls and magistrates were equally concerned over the question. " The judge who is about to issue a warrant against a criminal," notes Sebastien Mercier, " sometimes holds back at the thought of seeing a family shortly brought to dishonour." At the time when Law's [1] system was in force, the young Comte de Horn, aged twenty-two, assassinated in a cabaret in the Rue de Venice a dealer in public securities in order to rob him. He was condemned to be publicly broken on the wheel. His cousins implored the Regent to pardon him, representing that if their kinsman suffered this infamous punishment " no daughter of the house of Horn would be able to enter any Religious House down to the third generation."

These sentiments were still stronger among the popular classes than among the aristocracy. The latter relaxed their stringency towards the end of the eighteenth century, under the freer scope of new ideas, but in the minds of the people they still continued to have full weight. On this subject Mercier writes a particularly interesting page :

" The ruling opinion is clearly unreasonable and unjust. It might have been equitable when families were in a patriarchal state and when the heads were punished, so to speak, for not having looked after their members. But at this time of day . . . ? "

We are now on the eve of the Revolution. Mercier goes on to note that a Montmorency, a Biron, or a Marillac, does not feel himself dishonoured by ancestors whose heads have fallen on the scaffold, " while a cloth merchant is rendered unable to aspire to the petty little offices distinguishing his petty little village because his brother-in-law, whom he never saw, went and hanged himself."

Thus the celebrated remark of Montesquieu, " *l'honneur est le fondement des Monarchies*," is most illuminating, but again this expression must be taken in the sense intended by the author of *l'Esprit des Lois*, and in the sense given to it by his contemporaries, which was more comprehensive than it would be to-day.

" Honour : a testimony of esteem or submission given by word or action to anyone ; an external mark by which is shown the veneration and respect a man has for the dignity or merit of anyone. One must give honour to God, to kings, magistrates, and to one's parents . . . " [1] (Dictionnaire de Trévoux.)

And if you understand the word in its full meaning as given in the lines quoted above, in its meaning as we understand it to-day,

---

[1] John Law, a famous financier, was born in Edinburgh in 1671, and became Comptroller-General of the Finances in France. (H. W.)

and as it was understood in the eighteenth century, you will see Montesquieu's dictum in all its amplitude characterizing the Ancien Régime in its living image, its active vigour, and its fruitful originality.

At the end of the reign of Louis XVI the sentiments on which the society of other days had been based were undergoing a change ; it had been a gradual change which had begun some time before ; and now we see it openly recognized. The Metz Academy crowned Robespierre's discourse, *Contre le préjugé qui déverse sur la famille entière l'infamie d'une condamnation.* Retif de la Bretonne had written his great play, *Les Fautes sont personnelles* ; in the fourth act there comes on the stage the old man, whom the reproach with which his son's crime had covered him, had caused to lose his reason. He is led on by one of his daughters, and can only utter these words :

" Tell me, have I still any honour ? "

Advanced minds were proclaiming that society must not make any difference between the family of du Guesclin and that of Cartouche. Finally, on the 25th January, 1790, the Constituent Assembly abolished the " prejudice " attached to a criminal's family.

Prejudice it doubtless was : all the conventions which make up any society become " prejudices " when they are no longer in accordance with the manners and customs of the day.

VIII.—*Hereditary Capacities and Callings*

With the hereditary preservation and transmission of the family patrimony were closely combined the preservation and transmission of the father's profession, from the *métier de roi* (Louis XIV's expression) in the reigning family, to that of farm labourer in the most modest peasant family. The father had exercised such and such a profession, and the son must follow it. Among labouring or artisan families this transmission seemed clearly marked out for them, but the practice is to be found among the most diverse callings, wherein we should least expect to find it.

Louis XIV has been warmly reproached for having entrusted the Ministry of War to Barbezieux on the death of his father, Louvois. Barbezieux was twenty-three years old, a very intelligent young man, but idle and dissipated. The King's action looks like a mark of pride, evidence of his self-sufficiency, and an abuse of power ; now it should be judged from quite the contrary point of view.

Barbezieux succeeded his father at the Ministry of War because he had a right to it, as being the son of the deceased Minister. Louvois himself had received the reversion from his father, Le Tellier, at the age of thirteen and not even at that of twenty-three, and was authorized on the 24th February, 1662, to sign as a Secretary of State; he was then twenty-one years old. The practice of making the highest positions in the State into family obligations dated back to the most distant period, as was the case with most of the customs of the Ancien Régime. In this way were built up those great ministerial families, the best known example of which is that of the Phélypeaux. For the space of one hundred and fifty years the Phélypeaux family occupied well-nigh continuously one or several ministries. "The counter-signature of a Phélypeaux fits in with the royal signature just as the adjective does with the substantive," remarked Marius Sépet.

Paul de Phélypeaux had been provided with a Secretaryship of State shortly before the death of Henri IV. On Paul's death in 1621, his son, aged eight, succeeded him. As a little boy of eight years old could not carry on a Ministry, one of his uncles took his place by commission; but he turned out a false guardian and appropriated to himself his ward's property.

The Phélypeaux were divided into two branches—the Phély-peaux de Pontchartrain, the elder branch, and the Phélypeaux de la Vrillière, the younger. The latter ended by supplanting their cousins. The Marquis d'Argenson speaks of this in his *Mémoires* as a usurpation of the patrimony. Thus Maurepas—Jean Frédéric Phélypeaux de Maurepas—became Minister of Marine in 1715, replacing his father, Jérôme Phélypeaux de Pontchartrain, whose incapacity had caused howls of disapproval. "All he did was to snuff the candles at the meetings of the Council," said Saint Simon. He had himself succeeded, in 1693, to the reversion of the Ministry which had been directed by his father, Louis Phélypeaux de Pontchartrain.

Maurepas, the new Minister, was barely fourteen years old. The business was transacted in his name by his guardian, the Duc de la Vrilliére, whose daughter he married, and at whose house he went to live till the year 1718, when, being seventeen years old, he was authorized to take charge of his Ministry himself. He did not prove a bad Minister of Marine, and introduced some useful reforms.

Positions of State Secretaryships were given as a dowry to young girls. Thus, in 1617, Mlle. d'Alincourt, according to the testimony of Richelieu, brought to her husband a State Secretaryship which had been filled by her grandfather. These ministerial functions could be possessed and exercised as a right held in common, like a landed property. A noteworthy instance of this practice was the Ministry directed in this same year, 1617, by Villeroy and d'Alincourt (*Mém. de Richelieu*, ad ann. 1617). A ministerial portfolio might figure in a marriage contract. In 1700, the Marquis Louis de la Vrillière was appointed a Secretary of State on the condition that he should marry Mlle. de Mailly. He had as his son and successor the celebrated Comte de Saint-Florentin " destined to sign and despatch throughout his life, as his father and grandfather had done," wrote Saint Simon.

One and the same family even succeeded in occupying nearly the entire functions of a Ministry. Maurepas again became a Secretary of State under Louis XVI. He was the son, grandson, and great-grandson of Secretaries of State ; he was the cousin and son-in-law of de la Vrillière, another Minister ; his wife was by birth a Phélypeaux de la Vrillière ; a third Minister, the Duc d'Aiguillon, was his nephew, and lastly, he was connected with the Chancellor Maupeou.

Governorships and military commands were devised by will. Richelieu bequeathed to his nephew, Armand de Vignerot, the dukedom and territorial peerage of Vignerot, together with the title of General of the Galleys and Governorship of Havre.

Colbert appointed his brother, Colbert de Croissy, to be Minister for Foreign Affairs, with the reversion thereof to his nephew, Torcy. When Croissy died, in 1689, Torcy was considered too young to take charge of this department which, at that time, was regarded as the most important of all. He was placed under the guardianship of his father-in-law, Arnaud de Pomponne, who had been Minister for Foreign Affairs and had fallen into disgrace in 1679 after the failure of his negotiations with Count Mattioli (the man with the Iron Mask). Pomponne gave audience to the representatives of Foreign Powers in the presence of Torcy, whom he was moulding and who afterwards occupied with distinction this difficult Ministry. All these men, Colbert, Croissy, Torcy, Pomponne and Seignelay, were Ministers of great value.

We know, moreover, how Colbert, who made his brother Minister for Foreign Affairs, placed his son, Seignelay, in the Ministry of Marine, and entrusted the superintendence of public buildings to Ormoy-Blainville, another son. Examples like these could be multiplied. When the daughter of a Secretary of State married, the King gave her a dowry. It was a family matter.

Hugue de Lionne, the most remarkable Secretary for Foreign Affairs we ever had, was brought to this position by his uncle, Abel Servien, the famous negotiator of the Treaty of Westphalia.

For the proper conduct of these different departments, an education for the post, carried out at home, and from earliest childhood, was a useful preparation. At the period when he was French Minister in Sweden, Arnaud de Pomponne recalls the education he had received at the hands of his Pomponne uncle : " The things he related to me have not been effaced from my memory ; they formed my first introduction to a knowledge of Courts, countries, and foreign affairs and customs, together with a thousand historical matters which I have always retained in my memory." [1]

Just as there were ministerial, so there were also diplomatic families. Jean de Selves, French Ambassador at the Court of Charles V, in 1625, had six sons : Lazare was Ambassador in the Swiss Cantons ; Jean-Francisque, Ambassador in Turkey ; Jean-Paul, Bishop of Saint-Flour, was charged with missions at Rome and Venice ; Odet was Ambassador in Rome and in England ; and Georges, Bishop of Lavaur, was Ambassador in Italy, Spain and Germany.

Naturally the same thing happened in regard to more humble offices, and with greater reason. The Italian master of the Dauphin, son of Louis XIV, was just dead. His post was solicited by Sebastian Locatelli, who had influential friends at Court and left behind him an account of his sojourn in France full of a lively interest. Louis XIV in his reply begged to be excused : the former master had died without any fault being found with him ; it would be unjust not to give the post to his son as his successor. We have just spoken of Ministries being directed by guardians during the minority of the real holders. Mme. de Brionne administered the royal stables during the minority of her son, for whom the post was held in reserve.

We will now take a similar bird's-eye view of careers in the Church. It was a tradition that the family of Clermont-Tonnerre should always have among their members three ecclesiastical Peers at the same time. The Archbishopric of Lyons hereditarily belonged to the Villeroy family—which does not mean that it descended from father to son ! The Rohans succeeded each other in the Episcopal See of Strasbourg, and the Gondis in that of Paris. The future Cardinal de Retz (a Gondi) was distinguished in his youth by his duels and gallantries. The soul which vibrated in him was the least ecclesiastical soul in the world, but as a younger son he could only be destined by his father for the Archbishopric of Paris. The clerical life was, as we know, the career

[1] Letter from Pomponne, 10th September, 1667, Bibl. de l'Arsenal, MS. 6626, ff. 189–90.

of the youngest members of titled families. From his earliest
infancy, from the age of four or five, the youngest son was familiarly
called " Monsieur l'Abbé." Of her two youngest sons the Marquise
de Mailly made one a priest and the other a monk, " *à coups de
bâton*," as it was said.

Bourdaloue, who was decidedly in opposition with his times,
continued to thunder forth as though he were deaf. He railed
against these obligatory vocations. Talleyrand, the future Bishop
of Autun, spoke of them sadly. He had had a fall which broke
his foot : " As this accident had persuaded my parents that I
could not enter a military career they were led to design another
calling for me, which appeared to be favourable for the advancement of the *family* (underlined in the text). I do not like falling
in with this idea. . . . I am giving it up."

The same traditions of continuity of profession are to be found
among legal families. There are innumerable examples of this.
From the reign of Charles VIII, the Nicolai had succeeded each
other as Presidents of the Chambre des Comptes [1] right down to
Aymar Charles Marie, who died on the scaffold in 1794.

Notary chambers which had remained in the same house for
centuries could be quoted in great numbers. A modest bourgeois
begins his journal with the following lines :

" In putting together the genealogy of my family I have nothing else in view than to be of service to it by placing before its
eyes the examples of probity, decency and good conduct, which
our fathers gave in handing down to us, from father to son, through
the space of more than four centuries, the same possessions, the
same status. . . ."

In the eighteenth century we find bourgeois families in possession
of municipal functions which had been exercised uninterruptedly
by their forerunners since the reign of Philippe le Bel.

Professional aptitudes were thus acquired naturally and familiarly
in great perfection. Not only were their minds and acquirements
turned in that direction, but their very characters and manners
were modelled on it from their infancy. And what a support in
life was this long line of ancestors all exercising the same profession and holding the same position with honour and
dignity !

What surprises us still more is that this same family tradition
which imposed the continuation of the father's calling, is found
among the liberal professions, wherein, one would think, personal
talent, natural dispositions and individual tastes would have
served as guides. We see families of doctors, families of learned

[1] Court of the Exchequer. (H. W.)

men—the Emerys, the Geoffroys, the Sainte-Marthes—families of artists, and families of comedians. . . .

"It is not the same with genius as with commerce," observed Emile Faguet ; "the public does not admit that the family continues the business." Under the Ancien Régime it was quite the contrary : the public insisted on "the family continuing the business."

To be the son, grandson, or nephew of an Academician became not only a distinction, but a distinction sufficient to win entry into the French Academy. That the Academy should have elected a Richelieu at the age of seventeen, on account of the name he bore—even if Cardinal de Richelieu had not founded the Academy —we may pass over ; but when the Academy, on the death of the Duc de Coislin (1702), unanimously elected his eldest son, because he was the son of his father, and when, on the death of this eldest son, it elected his younger brother, again unanimously, because he was the brother of his brother, this might possibly seem to be pushing concern for family tradition to too great lengths.

A father might be a musician, painter, sculptor, or a famous architect : whether he liked it or not the son must be a musician, painter, sculptor or architect, in his turn. This hereditary obligation clearly became a rather serious drawback when the son showed neither taste nor disposition for the career wherein his father had made himself famous ; but this point of view appeared to be of secondary importance : the essential thing was that the son should do what his father had done. Moreover there was a way of arranging this. Lulli's sons succeeded their father in the office of musicians to the King. They understood nothing about music. They had their ballets and operas composed for them by skilled *artistes* whom they paid—and this was well-known to everybody ; the music was very good, and was signed "Lulli"—what could be better ? [1] From this practice arose those families of musicians who fill the eighteenth century—a dozen Couperins, one of whom, François, was one of the greatest musicians that ever existed ; a like number of Philidors ; the little Philidors were eleven years old when, as in the case of Lulli's sons, the reversion of the musical functions of their father was given to them ; then there were the Auberts, Rebels and Francœurs. . . .

If we go among the painters we shall come upon a similar spectacle. At the end of the sixteenth century, in the reign of Henri III, we find two painters, Beaubrun by name, attached, in accordance with the mediæval custom, to the Royal Court in the capacity of

[1] *Archives Nationales,* 0^1, 842.

valets de chambre, in the same way as Jean Foucquet, the brothers
Van Eyck, the brothers Maelewel, and Roger de la Pâture. The
dynasty of the Beaubruns, painters to the Crown, was continued
under Henri IV by Louis Beaubrun, and under Louis XIII and
Louis XIV by Henri and Charles Beaubrun. Louis Boulogne,
who died in Paris in 1674, left two sons and two daughters who
all painted, the two sons, Bon and Louis, being painters to the
King. The Audrans formed a great family of artists who won
the greatest renown as painters, engravers, and decorators. The
same thing happened in the eighteenth century in the case of the
Cochin, Drouais, Tardieu, Belle, Oudry, Parrocel and Saint-Aubin
families.

We have before us a list of the best painters in the Academy in
1737. Out of eight names we find : De Troy, *pupil of his father*,
Coypel, *pupil of his father*, Van Loo, *pupil of his father*.[1] The
family Van Loo may be compared as regards painting to that of
Couperin and Philidor in music. Jean Van Loo was painting in
1585. He instructed in the art of painting his son Jacob, who
made his son Louis a painter ; Louis made painters of his sons,
Jean Baptiste, Carle and Joseph. Jean Baptiste made painters
of his sons, Louis Michel, François and Charles Amédée Philippe ;
and Carle Van Loo made his son, Jules César, a painter. Here
we have ten Van Loos in succession cultivating with talent the
family art ; seven of them were Academicians and painters to the
King. And the artistic activity of the family was not confined
to those examples. Carle Van Loo had a brother-in-law, Lebrun,
a miniature painter, whose son likewise became a miniature painter.
The same thing occurred in the case of the Parrocel family.
Barthélemy Parrocel was painting at Montbrizon at the beginning
of the seventeenth century ; he had three sons, Jean, Louis and
Joseph, who all three became painters. Joseph became celebrated
as "*Parrocel des Batailles.*" Louis had two sons, Ignace and
Pierre, both of them painters. Ignace was the father of the
renowned painter "*Parrocel le Romain.*" Pierre Parrocel had
two sons who were artists, Pierre Ignace, the engraver, and Joseph
François, the painter, who had three daughters, all of them painters.
"Parrocel-des-Batailles" was the father of the painter Charles
Parrocel.

Noel Coypel, the painter, had two sons, Antoine and Nicolas ;
both followed painting, Antoine with great success. He was
made a noble, and his son, Charles, became chief painter to the
Duke of Orleans.

François Boucher was the son of a sign-painter ; his wife painted

[1] Bibliothèque de l'Arsenal, MS. 4041, f. 320.

and engraved, his two daughters married two painters, Deshayes and Baudouin, and François Boucher's son became an artist.

The dynasty of the Vernet family has remained famous. At the end of the seventeenth century Antoine Vernet, the painter, had four sons, Joseph, Ignace, Gabriel and François, who all became painters. Joseph was the celebrated painter of marine subjects. He was the brother-in-law of Guilbert, the sculptor. Joseph's son, Carle Vernet, the painter, married the daughter of the younger Moreau, and was the father of Horace Vernet who married the daughter of Paul Delaroche. The Petitot family produced a dynasty of portrait painters on enamel.

Amongst the sculptors the same family traditions formed off-shoots of artists in the same branch of art—the Dupré, Boudin, Bourdin, Coysevox, Coustou, Adam and Slodtz families. Bachaumont writes : " The family of M. Slodtz has for long been prolific of skilful artists. To-day there are several brothers skilled in architecture, painting, sculpture and decoration. They are the sons of a very good sculptor who was employed by the late King (Louis XIV)." [1] The Caffiéri enriched French art for the space of a century and a half with sculptors, draughtsmen, and workers in copper, from the first, Philippe, whom Colbert appointed to be sculptor and designer of the King's ships, down to Jean-Jacques Caffiéri, the creator of the wonderful busts in the Comédie Française. Among architects too there were the families of Chambige, Guillain, du Cerceau, Debrosse and Gabriel. The great André Lenôtre, who designed the most beautiful gardens and most celebrated vistas was himself the son and grandson of a designer of gardens. He was ennobled by Louis XIV. When he was asked what figures he would choose for his coat-of-arms, he replied :

" A cabbage, charged with three snails ! "

When announcing the death of Charles Boulle, the famous cabinet-maker to Louis XIV, the *Mercure* informed the public that his sons "were heirs to his talents "—a succession which could not be passed over.

In 1755 the question arose of appointing an inspector of the Gobelins tapestry establishment. Cochin, secretary of the Académie des Beaux Arts, proposed the painter François Parrocel, and wrote about him to Marigny, the superintendent of the Beaux Arts :

" I am certain that the greater part of the Academy would be of my opinion. It is true that Parrocel is not quite a first-class man, but he belongs to a family very well thought of, he is the son of a painter who was in the Academy, and cousin to the famous Parrocel, one of the greatest painters of the French School "—

[1] Bibliothèque de l'Arsenal, MS. 4041, f. 340, on the back.

reasons which would appear rather singular under similar circumstances to-day.

It was the same in the realm of art as in politics : the family overruled every consideration. We may laugh at this perhaps, but not so much after a little reflection. In a study on the " gardening " dynasty of the Lenôtres, M. Gascoin wrote :

" In our century people neglect the laws of heredity. It is from having understood them that the Ancien Régime came to know those families which gradually rose to the front by adapting themselves to this slow evolution, reaching the highest places in the State ; it is from having respected them that our Kings possessed those dynasties of incomparable collaborators, in which the fathers, whatever their special functions might be, instructed their sons to do good service and to continue their work."

It was a broad current of custom, irresistible and life-giving. There were families of the nobility of the sword, families of the nobility of the law, families of bourgeois, petty magistrates, artisan families, each one of them firmly entrenched in their calling from father to son, families of peasants attached by heredity to the little morsel of ground which they cultivated, families of ministers, families of painters, sculptors, architects, musicians. . . .

We find families of dramatic artistes whose heads watched over the tradition of the family calling with surprising vigilance. At the Bibliothèque de l'Arsenal, among the archives of the Bastille, is preserved the petition of a humble comedian begging the Minister of the Royal Household to lock up his son with a view to his being subsequently transported to the American colonies because, inasmuch as he refused to take up the same calling as his father, he could not fail to bring shame upon his family. We find families of smugglers who courageously went to the galleys from father to son, and families of sorceresses who still more courageously continued from mother to daughter to be burnt alive. The grandmother had been a sorceress, and had perished in the flames ; the mother was a sorceress, and knew that the same fate would be reserved for her ; yet she did not hesitate to bring up a daughter, whom she tenderly loved, in the same dreadful profession.

From the preceding facts each one may draw the conclusions that seem best to him. We are concerned with placing on view the facts as they are revealed by the documents. We may criticize the Constitutions of the Revolution and the Civil Code, because they are the duly intended, well pondered, and deliberate work of a certain number of persons : the institutions and manners of the Ancien Régime emerged spontaneously from the social conditions on which the entire nation was modelled. We cannot

blame the apple-tree for producing apples, nor the hazel for producing hazel nuts, nor can we make it a merit in them.   Here we
have the fruits of the great national tree.   The industrial arts,
by preserving the family tradition in the practice of each calling,
drew therefrom great advantages.   The children were moulded
under the eyes of the father, and profited by all the experience
and practice their forefathers had acquired.   The son became as
proud of his calling as of his name ; he had it at heart to preserve
the honour—we always come back to that—of the house, and we
must likewise always come back to the house, too.   Progress and
changes came about harmoniously and by degrees, in an atmosphere of respect for the work accomplished by the family, under
the influence of the taste and genius peculiar to the individual
and to the new generation.

At the present day there is not an artist who does not try to
create a completely new art, style or new method.   Man's genius
is ransacked through and through.   While I am writing, the
Exhibition of Decorative Arts is being held.   It reminds me a
little of the cabinet maker, put on the stage by René Benjamin.
He had made a table which looked like a bed, and he was dreaming
of making a bed that should look like a table !   There's originality
for you !   In our art there is not a detail out of harmony with its
surroundings.   The designer of an arm-chair must suit it to the
stuff which the upholsterer will put on it; he must adapt it to the
room in which it will be placed, if he would not turn out " bric-à-
brac."   See how harmoniously the style of Louis XIII, with its
robust detail, emerged from that of the Renaissance, and the
style of Louis XIV from the preceding period—a spacious and
profound evolution, unconstrained and natural, which was to
lead to the majesty of that of Louis XIV, and becoming more
elegant and delicate under the Regency emerged dainty and
hyper-decorative in the style of Louis XV.   In striving after straight
lines it was to assume greater sobriety under Louis XVI, when
already there were indications of a preference for that taste for
antiquity which characterized the Empire style.

Under the First Empire there were still remaining artisans who
had been brought up in the habits and traditions of the Ancien
Régime.   The Restoration was to look on, a mere woeful spectator
of these lost traditions.   Where are now the silks of Lyons which
fairy fingers seemed to have woven ?   Where are the wainscottings
designed by artists like Boffrand, De Cotte, Lassurance, of whose
work we preserve such beautiful examples at the Arsenal, the
Archives, the Bank of France, and in the Director's offices of the
Beaux Arts ?   Where can we find now carvings like those on the

little cabinets at Versailles ? What has become of the art of furniture designing which from Boulle down to Oeben and Riesener produced thousands and thousands of masterpieces which we cannot even cherish the hope of ever seeing equalled again ? In what corner now hides the art of those Parisian goldsmiths which was unrivalled throughout the world ? What has become of our graceful and productive china ware—Nevers, Rouen, Moustier, Strasbourg, Sinceny, Quimper, Sceaux, Saint Cloud, Marseille, Saint Armand, Lunéville, and so many other kinds, the remaining examples of which are now jealously guarded under glass cases ? Where are now the dances and songs of old France ? But where are " les neiges d'antan ? " [1]

BIBLIOGRAPHY

Argou (Gabriel), *Institution au droit Français*, ed. Boucher d'Argis, 1771.—Audiger, *La Maison réglee*, 1700.—Avenel (Vicomte d'), *La Noblesse Française sous Richelieu.*—Balzac (Honoré de), *Mémoires de deux jeunes mariées.*—Barine (Arvède), *La Jeunesse de la Grande Mademoiselle*, 1901.— Baudrillart (H.), *J. Bodin et son temps*, 1853.—Bayard, *Histoire du bon chevalier sans peur et sans reproche*, ed. Hachette, 1872.—Beaucaron (Regnault de), *Donations . . . de famille dans l'ancienne Bourgogne*, 1908.— Bellecombe (Mlle. H. de), *Les Denis, une famille bourgeoise de l'Agenais du dix-septième et du dix-huitième siècle*, 1894.—Bodin, *Les Six livres de la République*, ed. of 1583.—Bonnefon (Paul), *La Société Française au dix-septième siècle*, 1903.—Bonnefon (Paul), *La Société Française au dix-huitième siècle*, 1903.—Bouchot (Henri), *La Famille d'autrefois*, 1887.—Boulainvilliers, *Etat de la France*, 1727.—Broc (Vicomte de), *La France sous l'Ancien Régime*, 1887.—Burgat (G.), *De la dévolution héréditaire dans la coutume de Bretagne*, 1905.—Charlot, *Le Droit d'aînesse dans la France coutumière*, 1901.—Chateaubriand, *Mémoires d'outre-tombe.*—Corneille (P.), *Théâtre.*—Coulon (H.), *Principes généraux sur la dévolution héréditaire*, 1889.—Coquille (Guy), *Œuvres*, ed. of 1646 and 1665.—Croy (Duc de), *Mémoires*, ed. Cottin et de Grouchy, 1905–1908.—Du Broc de Segange, *Les Anciennes communautés de cultivateurs*, 1898.—Du Fail (Noel), *Propos rustiques*, 1547.—Du Fail (Noel), *Baliverneries*, 1548.—Dumoulin (Maurice), *Les Livres de raison*, Rev. de Paris, 15 May, 1901.—Dupuy (Ant.), *Histoire des lettres de cachet en Bretagne.*— *Encyclopédie méthodique* called *Encyclopédie de Diderot*, Part : *Jurisprudence*, 1786.—Escard (François), *Les Communautés de famille en France*, undated.— Fagniez (Gustave), *La Femme et la Société Française dans la première moitié du dix-septième siècle*, Revue des Deux Mondes, 15 Jan. 1909 and 1 Jan. 1911. —Fagniez (Gustave), *Livre de raison de N. Versoris, avocat au Parlement de Paris, 1519–1530*, Soc. de l'hist de Paris, v. XII, 1885.—Goncourt (Edm. et T. de), *La Femme au dix-huitième siècle*, 1862.—Joly (A.), *Les Lettres de cachet dans la généralité de Caen*, 1864.—La Roche-Flavin, *Treize livres des Parlements*, 1617.—Loménie (L. de), *Les Mirabeau*, 1889.—Maron (Albert), *La Communauté des Jault*, 1890.—Mirabeau (Marquis de), *l'Ami des hommes*,

---

[1] A literary phrase of Villon, the French poet born in 1431, which has become a proverb : " Where are now the snows of a former day ? " (H. W.)

1756–1760.—Mireur (F.), *Le Tiers Etat à Draguignan*, 1910.—Mistral (Fréd-éric), *Les Iles d'or*, 1876.—Montlosier, *Mémoires*, 1829.—Pasquier (Etienne), *Œuvres*, 1723.—H. de Régnier, *Le Bon plaisir*, 1902.—Retif de la Bretonne (N.), *La Vie de mon pére*, published under the title of *Le Village*, Fayard, *Coll. des Mémoires illustrés.*—Retif de la Bretonne (N.), *Les Fautes sont per-sonnelles*, ap. *Théâtre*, 1784–93.—Retif de la Bretonne (N.), *l'Ecole des pères*, 1776.—Ribbe (Ch. de), *La Société Provençale à la fin du Moyen Age*, 1897.— Talleyrand, *Mémoires*, published by the Duc de Broglie, 1891–1892.—Teissier (O.), *Histoire d'une ancienne famille de Provence*, 1862.—Thiébault (Lucien), *Le Privilège de la masculinité et le droit d'aînesse en Lorraine et Barrois*, 1904.— Tocqueville (Alexis de), *l'Ancien Régime et la Révolution*, 5th ed., 1866.— Vachez (A.), *Les Livres de raison Lyonnais*, undated.—Young (Arthur), *Travels in France*, 1794.

CHAPTER III

THE SEIGNEURIE

I.—*The Feudal Nobility*

IN his admirable book on the country gentlemen of noble family (*Gentilshommes campagnards*), M. Pierre de Vaissière writes very discriminatingly as follows :

" According to the view of many people the French nobility was represented by two types—the supreme and powerful feudal baron of the Middle Ages, and the brilliant and refined courtier of the last years of the Monarchy ; on the one hand they reflected the abuses of feudal days, and on the other the corruption of the Court of Louis XV. And this summary judgment sufficed ! "

During the appalling disorder characterizing the ninth and tenth centuries, the family, as we saw, was the sole social active force that remained, the sole element of organization and progress. As it grew larger the family grew into the mesnie, and the mesnie developed into the fief. Feudalism was the issue of the organization of the family and continued to embody its special characteristics. Jacques Flach says very justly, " What constituted the foundation of feudal society was the principle of protecting the family."

The feudal baron was a *chef de famille* ; therefore the whole group of his vassals and tenants was called in the documents of the time, his family, his *familia*.

It was a large family, which the baron protected with his sword, and it was enabled to live and prosper under the shadow of his

73

donjon.[1] " In those days," says the author of the *Chroniques d'Espagne,* " in order to be in readiness at any moment the barons kept their horses in the great hall where they slept with their wives."

In case of danger the people of the surrounding district took refuge within the castle enclosure, where they found shelter for themselves, their families, their cattle and booty. They were called *retrahants de la chatellenie,* that is, refugees in the castle, from the Latin *retrahere,* to withdraw. In this connection we should note that our peasants of the Ancien Régime called their family dwelling the *retirance,* like the baron's castle in the beginnings of feudalism.

Vassals and tenants provided the armed force for their common protection. Many castles only held one fighting man by profession who collected around him the *retrahants* of the district.

The seigneurs were feudal lords recalling the kings of primitive Greece sung by Homer, and resembled those Epic warriors who fought under the walls of Troy ; they were soldiers and agriculturists, like Ulysses, King of Ithaca, skilled in ploughing the furrow in the fields. They were vigilant farmers, superintending the labours of the farm, going the rounds of their stables and cattle sheds, and riding over their lands to see whether the work was being well carried out. The feudal castle included agricultural industry in its embrace. Our forefathers showed wonderful skill in building those feudal, patriarchal, and defensive abodes which formed the centre around which gravitated the thousands of little autonomous groups in the immediate neighbourhood, forming the society of the Middle Ages. Viollet-le-Duc even placed the civil and military architecture of the Middle Ages above that of its religious architecture. And we must not think that there was any antagonism, or any opposition of interests or sentiments existing between the vassals and tenants and their baron, who was the lord of the feudal manor. The protection afforded by their lord was, in the eleventh century, a necessity for the peasant, artisan or merchant. " *Gent sans seigneur sunt malement bailli,*" we read in Guillaume d'Orange's ballad.

The feudal lord lived by the prosperity of his lands, but this prosperity was due in a large measure to himself. He made his domain safe ; his sword enabled the merchants to traffic on it, and his labourers to work ; he added useful improvements. Through his instrumentality the village was often surrounded by ditches and palisades in order that the cultivators of the soil might keep their cattle in security ; he would maintain a force

---

[1] *Donjon :* the old term for the baronial stronghold. (H. W.)

of armed men in any spot infested by robbers; he would build a church, found a hospital, and set up a place for fairs and markets to be held. He built mills, public bakehouses and wine presses which the peasants, if left solely to their own resources, would have been powerless to acquire for themselves. In return for the use made of these by his tenants he would receive dues.

When a vassal died, his lord extended his protection to the widow, and cared for the children; in him the widows and orphans found a guardian.

In his life-like chronicle Lambert d'Ardres relates a curious anecdote, which gives a picture of the kind of relations existing in the twelfth century between lord and vassal; it shows too the origin of manorial dues and the way in which they were capable of degenerating into abuses in the course of time.

Arnoul, lord of Ardres, came back from England with an enormous bear, which the King of England had given to him as a present. The inhabitants of his small manor found amusement in the spectacle of this bear being baited by the dogs, which threw themselves upon it barking and tearing out its coat. The lord of Ardres decided to keep this bear in an outbuilding of the castle, where he appointed a keeper to have charge of it. His vassals were enjoying a sport which greatly amused them. But, in return for this, Arnoul d'Ardres demanded one loaf of bread per annum from each family for the upkeep of the bear and his keeper. It was a small contribution but sufficient, and thus everything seemed satisfactory all round—at least so long as the bear was alive and gave amusement to them. But the bear died, whereas the levying of the loaf of bread from each family on the manor continued.

"And thus," ends our chronicler, "on account of a bear the people of Ardres were penalized in an unjust exaction."

Thanks to their lord, fairs and markets were able to be held in the district; he gave safe-conduct to the merchants who repaired thither, and guaranteed their safety within his domain; he guarded the merchandise offered for sale or brought to the fair, and undertook responsibility for any loss that might occur.

Lord and vassal were thus united to each other by close bonds; they felt themselves indispensable to each other. The *seigneurie*, its spirit beating within the stone-built donjon, became a fatherland which was loved with a blind instinct and devotion. It was bound up with the lord and his family, and the people took a pride in him, and told stories of the heavy might of his sword;

they greeted him with acclamations when his cavalcade passed by, its banner floating in the breeze.

But the twelfth century rolled by, and the greater part of the thirteenth—the finest epoch in our history.

The feudal lordship enclosed within its donjon had accomplished the work for which it had been constituted. Beneath the shadow of its massive towers, and under the protection afforded by the strong hand in its iron gauntlet, society had become organized and prosperous. The donjons were losing their usefulness. The lord and his *retrahants* had no longer a common interest in remaining closely united. Very much the opposite, for the feudal baron had now accomplished his work, and his interests and those of his vassals were in process of taking diverging directions : an opposition between the lord of the castle on the one hand, and the dweller on his lands on the other, which was to become more violent from day to day. The baron no longer rendered to his tenants those services which erstwhile had constituted his *raison d'être*, and this fact arose from the very security and prosperity he had helped to give to the district ; but he wished to continue to enjoy the rights and dues which the services he had rendered in former days had justified—the story on a larger scale of the loaves of bread levied annually for the upkeep of the great bear of the manor of Ardres.

After having been places of safe retreat the donjons were entering on a fatal course, and were becoming places for offensive operations. In his lofty fortress, vibrating with the clang of steel accoutrements, their lord, a falcon in this eyrie, was busy keeping in subjection his vassals, to whom it was now no advantage to be vassals.

Under the gentle suzerainty of St. Louis, feudal society shed forth a last gleam of splendour. It was the " golden age," as both noble and peasant called it fifty years later. Under St. Louis the relationship of affection and devotion between lord and vassal still showed some vitality. The prosperity which this vast organization, characterized by the armed patronage exercised by the ruling class over the interests of the toilers, had been capable of, was now an accomplished fact, and in accordance with the usual trend of human institutions, once the summit had been attained, decadence set in. Decadence and disorganization, having as their first cause that very progress which had been engendered by feudal institutions.

Agriculture had prospered, industry had begun to develop, and trade had expanded ; peace, relatively speaking, reigned over the country ; but the feudal barons continued to levy, both in the country districts and even in the towns, tolls and dues as numerous as they were varied : *droits de justice*,[1] *cens et dîmes, péages et tonlieux, lods et ventes, droits de relief et de mutation, meilleur catel, corvées,* and *banalités.* The walls of the crenelated keep had offered protecting ramparts, when feudalism was in process of formation, for the serfs whose hands had helped to build them, but now served only to defend the unjustifiable exploitation of the labouring classes by armed men, and the peasant now only thought how he could demolish them. The merchant carrying his merchandise from one part of the country to another found himself faced with similar demands. At cross roads, when passing over bridges and the river fords, at locks, at the entry into canals, on the borders of forests, at every corner and turning and cross-road he was confronted with a collector of some local tax supported by armed men who fell upon his baggage and would not let go until they had levied their ransom on it.

It was owing to these various causes that the great mass of the nation came to rise in rebellion against the governing class ; they formed the deep-seated reason for that long and bloody social conflict which is called in history the Hundred Years War, in the course of which mediæval feudalism was to founder.

II.—*A Rural Nobility*

Frightful popular risings, like the Jacqueries and Maillotins, lighted up the country with their sinister glare. The feudal nobility fell beneath their violence ; they were massacred, either in their castles, or on the battle-field. During this crisis, which lasted a hundred years, France was transformed. A new aristocracy entered on the scene to take up the rôle of its predecessors, making it fit in with a world into which the invention of printing, the discovery of America, the development of artillery, and the general use of fire-arms, were introducing elements unknown to the days of feudalism.

This return of spring to France after the Hundred Years War,

---

[1] *Droits de justice :* the right to hold a court of justice and to levy the fees ; *cens et dîmes :* quit-rents and tithes ; *péages et tonlieux :* toll-gates and market dues ; *lods et ventes :* the tax levied on the sale of any property within the lord's domain ; *droits de relief et de mutation :* the fee payable to the lord of the manor when any property on his manor passed by succession to a collateral branch, and not in direct succession, or by sale ; *meilleur catel :* falling under " personal property," including cattle, trees, etc. ; *corvées :* contributions either in service or goods due to the lord of the manor ; *banalités :* dues levied on the public and obligatory use by the vassals of certain public conveniences erected by and belonging to the lord of the manor, such as public ovens, mills, etc. (H. W.)

making us in very truth think of the clear blue sky seen after a
severe storm, has been more than once described, in very masterly
fashion by Gustave Fagniez, Vicomte d'Avenel and Pierre de
Vaissière. The first cause was the re-birth of agriculture in the
country, and this was due to the country nobility getting into
closer touch with the people during the years of storm and
tempest, thereby exercising a guiding, profound and salutary
influence over them. It will be useful to study this process
during the sixteenth and the first portion of the seventeenth
centuries.

The French aristocracy of the Renaissance was a rural nobility.
It lived on the land, and on the produce of the land. In his castle
of the Pradel, which still preserved its towers and ramparts, one
of these country gentlemen of noble family—*gentilshommes champêtres* as they were called—Olivier de Serres, the illustrious author
of the *Théâtre d'Agriculture*, may be taken as an example.

Rustic as it might be, the French nobility of the Renaissance
was none the less a warrior class, like its elder brother the Feudal
nobility. As agriculturists and soldiers, our country nobility
suggest a comparison with those Roman patricians who left their
fields for the camp, and then, when the war was finished, returned
to their fields. Even writers in the sixteenth century made the
comparison, recalling " the example of those staid Roman fathers
of old, like Cincinnatus, Attilius Collatinus, Scipio Africanus and
other great men of like calibre, who were called from the plough
to take up arms, and then, laying these aside, returned again to
the plough."

How did our *gentilhomme champêtre* pass his time ? Noel du
Fail, one of the most charming and best among them, has drawn
for us a picture.

An honest-spoken product of the good land of Brittany, Du Fail
was born about the year 1520. He was a councillor in the Parliament of Rennes, and divided his time between it and his country
house where he wrote with a simplicity, which is entirely French,
his *Propos Rustiques* (1548), and towards the end of his life, his
Baliverneries (1585).

" You will find me among the orchards working with my pruning
hook and sickle, my sleeves turned up to the elbows, you will see me
cutting, lopping and pruning my young trees ; or else you may find
me in the gardens putting my cuttings in order, squaring the edges
of the paths, drawing water or letting it run, adjusting my hives, or
perhaps getting into a rage as with one foot raised I make a watchful
search for moles and field mice which do me so much harm ; or I may
be sowing different kinds of seed or watering the dry portions of the

ground so as to push on the fruit that is late to ripen ; then there are the woods where there may be dykes to make higher, and drives to straighten out."

These gentlemen had no hesitation in going themselves to sell the produce of their estate at the market in the neighbouring town, where they might be seen with their sword hanging at their side and a basket on their arms, at sight of which the peasants were not long in trying to put obstacles in their way, contending that the nobility had no licence to traffic. Our country squires would make their purchases in the markets for the requirements of their household, after acquainting themselves with the current prices, and would then sell their own produce on that footing.

When the well-filled day was drawing to a close, after taking their meal in the great kitchen of the manor in common with their family and dependants, they would once more go the round of their fields and meadow lands to see if any of their cattle had suffered harm. Even after dark they would go through the vines and orchards firing off their haquebuts to frighten off any depredating animals, marauders or mischievous boys. And after Vespers on Sundays they might be seen walking over their property carrying a stout staff, and a gun hung from the shoulder, to enjoy the spectacle of the good order they had established and to reckon up the prospects of the next harvest.

" Soldier-husbandmen " we have called them, for they did not neglect their military functions. Jacques de Pontbriand, standard bearer to the Comte de Sancerre, with an appointment in the Artillery in 1530, once recounted to the King that at Paignon, his home in the Seneschalty of Angoulême, he bred oxen, sheep and " much other cattle " which he afterwards sold in person at the market of Confolens, " which brings in money," added the loyal gentleman, " to maintain myself in the service of the King." It is a wonderful little sketch depicting in a few lines our rustic country gentlemen in their true colours. They made agriculture prolific of results and progress, and by their proud eagerness to bear arms they released their tenants from service in the wars. It would be difficult to imagine how prodigal this rural nobility was in shedding its blood on the battlefield ; one could not mention a single family of these *gentilshommes champêtres* in the seventeenth century which had not had several of their members killed while fighting at the front, and out of some houses as many as twelve or thirteen brothers are found to have fallen in battle.

Their status as nobles obliged them to serve the State both in their own person and with their resources ; it was a duty incumbent upon our rural aristocracy ; to these obligations should be added those entailed by their being the patrons, protectors and supporters of their subordinates, the functions of a real local government, and the complete renunciation of any desire to grow rich. " In a state constituted as France is," we read in the *Ami des hommes*,[1] " the nobility must be proud and courageous, and must pride themselves on being poor."

The country seigneur was a valuable auxiliary of the royal justice which he represented, while trying to keep its royal exercise as far as possible from his fief ; he would protect his tenants against the agents of the Treasury and would endeavour to maintain good feeling between them all ; he would place himself at their head in driving off roving bands of malefactors and in preventing them from being pillaged by the soldiery.

His home was the manor, a half-way house between the feudal castle with its towers and keep, and the peasant's home. It was made up of an agglomeration of buildings, with a principal house where the owner lived, and outhouses for the purposes of the farm. It was provided with courtyards and orchards, and was surrounded by gardens and walls, for if the manor no longer had the important defensive surroundings of a fortified castle it was not devoid of the means to repel a band of pillagers.

After the pacification of the kingdom in the sixteenth century, the manor underwent still further changes ; it shed its defensive characteristics ; the outer walls were pierced to make windows, and the moats were transformed into terraces or made into fish-ponds ; there was no longer any tower to be seen, save that for the pigeons, and the thick walls were used principally for training espaliers of fruit trees. The manor houses then assumed the name of " *gentilhommières* " and " *noblesses*."

The interior arrangements were almost always the same. There was an avenue leading to the entrance gate, and a large courtyard the origin of which went back to remote antiquity ; within the courtyard (*curtis*) were Gallo-Roman living-quarters ; at the far end was the seigneur's house ; to left and right, backing on to the outside walls, were the servants' quarters, and behind the seigneur's house were the cattle sheds, stables and garden.

In the time of Henri IV the custom was introduced of building the barns and stables at a certain distance from the seigneur's house. Possibly some of our *gentilshommes champêtres* began to find the smells therefrom a little strong, but Olivier de Serres considered this new custom a regrettable one :

[1] *Ami des Hommes :* written by the Marquis Riquetti de Mirabeau, the father of the celebrated orator. (H. W.)

" To move the barns, stables, and sheds for the cattle away from the house is a sorry matter, for when the quarters for the animals are put farther back the seigneur is unable conveniently to keep a watch over his stock and manage it in a fitting manner."

The most important room in these manors was the kitchen. It was the largest room of all and the best furnished. Placed, in the best houses, on the first storey, it gave on the one side on to the *salle*—we should call it to-day the *salon*—and on the other, on the *chambre* or sleeping quarters.

" Your kitchen," says Olivier de Serres, " should be situated on the first storey of the house, near your living room and bed-room. In this wise those in the kitchen are able to be controlled by access from the *salle* and the *chambre*, where one often happens to be, and the idleness, clamour and blasphemy of the servants can thus be reprimanded."

In the kitchen both master and servants had their own customs. The seigneur took his meals there with his household, and if any peasant, a tenant in the neighbourhood, happened to come when they were at table the diners would squeeze up to make a place for him.

The meals were of patriarchal simplicity. There would be a huge dish piled up with beef, mutton, veal and bacon, and a large bowl filled with broth made of cooked herbs, like a vegetable soup. Each one helped himself as he wished in accordance with his appetite. " Everything proceeded good-naturedly and with no formality," observes Noel du Fail. Before sitting down to table they would go and wash their hands at the well and sharpen their knives " in order the better to cut off long broad slices of the fat ham, or the huge and quivering piece of salt beef, and spread them on the good brown bread."

In his *gentilhommière* of Mesnil-au-Val, the Sire of Gouberville dined and supped in the kitchen where he passed his evenings, made up his accounts and wrote his letters. This room was called the " *chauffoir* " in more than one province—which appella-tion we have already met with when treating of the peasant com-munities ; the furniture too of these manorial " *chauffoirs* " was very like what we have described in the *maisons de village*—the great chimney, table, sideboard and huge cooking pot, also the beds similarly ranged against the wall, and two or three chairs with backs to them, generally of wood, like those reserved for the old people in the rural communities.

As regards ornaments there were pewter or earthenware dishes on the dresser or on the ledge of the projecting hood of the chimney, and there would be family portraits on the wall. Seated by this huge chimney, where faggots of broom or vine crackled under the

iron or shining copper cauldron, the seigneur and his wife would
pass the winter evenings surrounded by their servants. It was
very comfortable in the " *chauffoir* " seated there with the household, everyone at their ease and conversation interspersed with
old songs—those good wholesome songs of the land of France in
which each province would echo its customs, traditions, and rustic
Christmas glees. And then there would be different games, or
one of the party would start telling some pretty legend or fairy
tale from which the son of Charles Perrault drew his immortal
little stories—stories of brigands and family legends the entrancing
veracity of which no one doubted ; the seigneur would recount
his military exploits under the King's standard, and sometimes
he would read aloud to his people to rest them after their rough
toil on the farm. " That day my people were in the fields, but
the rain drove them in," notes Gouberville in an entry dated
6th February, 1555, " and throughout the whole evening we read
aloud *Amadis in Gaul* and how he overcame Dardan."

In the course of the sixteenth century the good old custom of
French seigneurs taking their meals in the kitchen together with
their household was tending to die out. Olivier de Serres notes
this with regret, also the Constable de Montmorency whose statue
now stands on the terrace at Chantilly. The latter remarks :
" A gentleman who has arrived at an income of 500 *livres* no longer
knows how to observe good cheer because in his desire to cut a
great figure he now dines in his *salle*, subject to his cook's inclinations, whereas formerly, when he took his meals in the kitchen,
he had himself served to his own liking." Nevertheless the old
custom continued in many respects right down to the end of the
Ancien Régime. Retif de la Bretonne was yet to show us the
country gentleman eating in the same roof with his household.
He took his seat at a round table with his wife, his three daughters
and four sons. Hung on the wall in a conspicuous position was the
portrait of an ancestor ; close by there was another very long
rectangular table over which hung the portrait of the seigneur's
father. At this second table the servants took their places, farm
hands and day labourers on the one side, the women on the other ;
there were six plough boys, eight vine-dressers, the cow-herd, the
shepherd, the goat-herd and swine-herd. The women servants
and farm girls sat opposite the men, occupying the same side as
the mistress of the household at her round table. One of them
served the meal.

The *salle*, as compared with the *chauffoir* and bed-chamber, was
a state-room. It was a chamber of honour containing a bedstead
with columns and canopy, and served as a dining-room where the

tables were spread for guests of high descent ; it was the chamber
where animated conversation took place when everyone was
dressed in their Sunday best in honour of select company. High
up on the wall was a stag's head used for hanging up bonnets
and hats, hunting horns and leads for the hounds. A collection
of picturesque arms reminded those present of old traditions, and
showed the tastes of the seigneur. There were bows and quivers
of arrows, haquebuts or arquebuses, and ash-stemmed lances
measuring no less than seven yards long, inherited from the
tourneys of their ancestors ; huge formidable-looking swords,
halberds and cross-bows with their strings and wooden finger
pieces fastened through the cord.[1] Shirts or coats of mail were
kept in chests filled with bran. At a little distance off on the
wall might be seen large hawking nets, hunting implements, and
the shining armour worn by the horses on ceremonial occasions.
Standing on the shelves of a primitive bookcase were the Bible,
and a few books for amusement, such as *Les Quatres Fils Aymon,
Ogier le Danois, Mélusine, Le Calendrier des Bergers, Le Roman
de la Rose* and the beautiful stories in the *Légende Dorée*.

You need not expect to find in this chamber any soft, rich
bright-coloured carpets, but herbs would be scattered on the
floor and these were often renewed giving an agreeable scent to
the room. It was the *jonchée* of the old manors, for it often consisted of rushes (*joncs*) ; at the foot of the long benches and
chests, which latter also served as seats ranged round the walls,
was a layer of straw which kept the feet warm in winter and was
used to wipe them on at all seasons of the year. It also provided
litter for the dogs, " for they are all the better and more vigorous
when they hear and scent their masters near them," as Noel du
Fail remarks. In the fire-place " great big green logs, with one
or two dry faggots, gave a fire which lasted a long time." The
chests along the walls continued to serve as seats just as in the
Middle Ages, hence the expression "*piquer le coffre*" when one
has a long wait. With what care did the mistress of the house
lay her well-arranged linen therein, perfuming it with lavender
for her daughters, and the baron's apparel ! The chests closed
down with huge wrought iron locks, and what a collection of things
issued therefrom when it was unpacked—*Tournois*[2] *écus* and

---

[1] *Garrot :* a small piece of wood passed through the bow-string at right
angles for the fingers to grasp when drawing the bow. (H. W.)

[2] *Tournois :* the coins struck in France down to the thirteenth century
were called *tournois* from having been minted at Tours. The *livre* (franc)
Tournois was worth 20 *Tournois sous,* and the *Tournois sou* twelve *deniers.*
(H. W.)

livres, jewels, rare weapons, bed-warmers, crockery and harness! In a coffer painted with flowers lay the trousseau for the bride to be. It sometimes happened that the bride was not very beautiful. " Elle est belle au coffre " (she has gold in her coffers), would murmur the friends of the bridegroom. Enormous beds, sometimes several in the same room, would be arranged end to end, in which several people would sleep; the girls were in one room and the boys in the other, for it was a well-known custom in the old days for several people to sleep in the same bed, often with complete strangers at inns.

Our sturdy *gentilshommes* exuded from their persons a rustic scent, a faint smell of goats, which passed into a proverb. One could sniff our country gentleman from some way off. The cleanliness of newer times was in a backward state in the Middle Ages. Such pleasures of the intellect as the schools could offer were not held in honour. At the end of the eighteenth century it could still be said that " a washerwoman in Paris wrote more correctly than a gentleman in Poitiers." Many a country nobleman could neither read nor write. When he did write it was for the purpose of compiling one of those admirable *livres de raison*, or family histories drawn up for his descendants. There is no finer characteristic of these heads of old French families in all classes of society, or one that does them greater honour. They loved to read over and over again the acts and heroic deeds of their great-great-grandfathers, and to study their genealogical tree, although the pleasure derived from this could not have been too absorbing, if we may judge from the following statement of this country gentleman, " who, being seated in the chimney corner, after reading the old script relating the good acts and deeds of his late father, by chance fell asleep, and while slumbering let fall by misadventure the said old script into the fire which was completely charred and spoilt to the great regret and hurt of the said seigneur."

As regards their apparel it was in keeping with the wholesome rusticity of their dwellings. César de Cadenet de Charleval writes of it in his family journal in 1728 :

" My great-grandfather never wore anything but homespun material and woven linen, and had straps to his shoes. People had no acquaintance with wigs, nor any such like contraptions on which one now spends more money than was disbursed on all the household expenses in his time. Meals were taken in the kitchen which was lighted by lamps; there was only one fire; they baked their own bread. The mistress of the house herself tidied up the sleeping sacks of her menservants and made them start off on their work at the appointed hour.

It was the accepted custom then; if any one should wish to behave like this at the present time people would point at them. The beds knew no tapestries nor silk stuffs; no chair was stuffed with anything but straw. I saw the winter dining-room again with its stone paving two huge walnut chests in front of the windows, an olive-wood wardrobe and a bed with print cover, upholstered in gilded leather."

In the eighteenth century the Marquis de Mirabeau recalls to mind the solid rural manor of a former day:

" The country nobility of the previous age used to drink too much, went to sleep in their old arm-chairs, or on miserable pallet beds, and mounted horse and went out hunting at a very early hour; this kind of life produced few geometricians, poets or showy actors; but the nobility were not required for that kind of thing. The nobility of those days led a gay and hardy life, costing the State little, and producing more for it by living on their estates and on dunghills on their own lands than we are worth to it nowadays with our tastes, our researches, colics and vapours. They knew nothing in comparison with ourselves, for we understand the canons of the theatre and the essential differences between Italian and French music; we are connoisseurs of carriages, lacquered work, snuff boxes and porcelain; we are not ignorant of the art of doing business, nor how to solicit alms in ' red heels,' and, above all, of the value of money and moneyed people. . . ."

It was a country nobility possessing at least three great qualities :

It was rooted to the soil, like the homes they had themselves built; it assured the defence of the country; it was careful to afford protection to its tenants, among whom it strove to maintain order and mutual understanding.

This nobility lived on familiar terms alike with their vassals and the humblest. With wife and children they took part in *fêtes* of the people at which the seigneur, his wife and daughters danced with the peasants. At *fêtes* commemorated by a general banquet, held on the green sward under the great elms in the village square, the seigneur would sit at table with his tenants, bringing with him wine, game and sweetmeats to brighten up the *ménu*.

The seigneur would play bowls and skittles with the young lads and clink glasses with them; he would intervene in their quarrels and smooth out differences in a friendly manner; he preserved them from blood-sucking lawyers and all their gibberish. Even at the taverns he would not mind putting his own legs under the same white wooden table with his vassals.

Our country gentlemen made the country safe against marauders and vagabonds. As at the best period of the Middle Ages their castles served as a safe shelter in the event of danger. At the

head of their peasants they would drive off the incursions of bands
of pillagers.

" If any dispute between the peasants arose," writes Michel de
l'Hospital, " the seigneur of the village would generally appease
them.   The peasant was never taken from his plough to go to
the justice's court."

Moreover the seigneur in person was vested with magisterial
rights.   Some of those good country squires, it is true, interpreted
their judicial functions very summarily, like the Sire de Gouberville.   With a few peasants whom he had armed he set off one day
to remove certain boundary landmarks which had been placed
too far back, and uproot some pear trees which had been planted
in the public road of the *commune*, thus regulating the questions at issue in the most efficacious manner, according to his
own good judgment.   These expeditions generally took place by
night :

" After supper we went to Tourlaville with Symonnet, Lajoie, Pierrot
Diédoyt, Giret Maillart and Hubert Charleville in order to break down
the dam which had been placed in the old course of the river so as
to let the water flow to the cloth mill which Ferrant Pastel de Cherbourg had constructed.   Jehan Lesaulvage and Guillaume Groult also
accompanied us.   It was midnight when we arrived at the spot."

We can see how very practical such a procedure was, even
though certain of these honest dispensers of justice sometimes
pronounced strange judgments.   Thus one worthy seigneur condemned a sow to the gallows for having devoured a little child ;
another issued a sentence on grounds duly set forth against some
mice which were eating up the crops ; a third boldly rendered
null and void, on his authority as a magistrate, the decrees issued
by the Paris Parliament.

As supporters of that clear-sighted and practical justice which
caused harmony to reign among those good people without any
jargon of written complaints and underhand dealing, our *gentilshommes champêtres* had a horror of lawyers.   One of them used
to drive off with his stick any myrmidon of the legal fraternity
who was so imprudent as to venture upon his domain.   The Sire
de Verdas used to say that " when he heard any one mention a
notary his bowels turned in his stomach," adding that " some
day or other the time will surely come when I shall eat the liver
of one of those animals ! "

With a view to bettering the lot of the people in their neighbourhood some of these country noblemen would undertake the
most useful offices.   Some would give a dowry to the young girls,

others would see that the sick and ailing were looked after. As regards the dues they levied on their tenants, some of these represented rents of farms, and others feudal rights which were justified in their origin and by services rendered. In any case these dues were not high ; they had originally been established at a time when the value of money was far greater than it was to become in subsequent centuries. This progressive depreciation in the value of money, from age to age, from the time of St. Louis, is one of the important facts in our history and was productive of unforeseen consequences. People have not sufficiently taken it into account.

To these beneficial rights must be added those which were merely honorific and it was on these that the country baron set the greatest store.

He had the right of presentation to the Bishop of the new *Curé* ; his pew was set apart in the choir of the church, and the priest had to wait for his arrival before saying Mass ; he was the first to be incensed, the first to make his offering at the collection, and he walked at the head of the processions. " It is one of the misfortunes of our century " (the reign of Henri IV), wrote Loyseau in his *Traité des Seigneuries*, " that the privileges of rank are in no place whatsoever more stubbornly sought after than in the House of God wherein humility is most specially commanded." Among these honorific rights are some singular examples : A decree of Parliament (1st August, 1620) maintained the Seigneur de Turbilly in his right " to receive every year on the day of Pentecost a key and a ball of wool from recently married bridegrooms ; and a slipper from the brides, unless the newly married couples preferred to pay four *deniers*."

In words that have become famous Montaigne depicted the independence of our rural *seigneuries* in regard to the royal authority :

" There is nothing more royal than the suite, the subjects, the officers, the occupations, the attendance and ceremony of a retired seigneur living in his own home among his serving-men ; he hears mention of his master once a year, just as he might of the King of Persia, and only recognizes him on account of some old distant cousinship which his secretary keeps in his register. In truth our laws are fairly liberal, and the weight of sovereignty barely touches a French gentleman twice in his life. Essential and effective subjection is of no concern to us except for those who care to obtain honour and riches for themselves by such service ; for the man who likes to sit crouched by his own hearth and knows how to rule his house without disputes and lawsuits is as free as the Duke of Venice."

III.—*Trade and Commerce forbidden to the Nobility*

As we have seen, the fortune possessed by the nobility remained still essentially a territorial one in the sixteenth century; now the period following the Hundred Years War was a time of prosperity in agriculture. The value of land and the revenue arising therefrom continued to increase, and our *gentilshommes champêtres* enjoyed times of happy and abundant ease; but from the middle of the sixteenth century the consequences of an event which was to overthrow the social and economic conditions of Western Europe began to be felt—the discovery of America. The treasures of Mexico and Peru were flowing into Europe, producing a depreciation in the value of money which went on becoming more accentuated and thereby affecting the country nobility whose revenues from land were for the most part fixed on an immutable basis. In one generation the value of money was seen to fall by one-half. We have now reached the time of the great trade and industrial movement of the Renaissance from which the nobility, from their very constitution, had to keep aloof. This is a fact that had important consequences. People talk of the privileges of the nobility, but they paid a heavy ransom for them in being forbidden to engage in commerce and industry.

We must always bear in mind the traditional character of the Ancien Régime. The family continued under the traditions and customs of the house; the father's calling was transmitted to the son, together with the usages and sentiments belonging to it. The same thing happened as regards the different classes of society. The nobility were hereditarily constituted for military service and for the care and promotion of agriculture. That is what it existed for. Any other functions, including those bringing wealth and the power of money, were forbidden. On the other hand the bourgeoisie, amongst its other privileges, possessed hereditarily the right to engage in commerce and industry.

It was a very fine conception, simple and productive of results. On it France was built up, and it was moreover a natural growth.

The English nobility engaged in trade; this difference was due to differences in origin. The English nobility had not taken its rise on the basis of the family, feudally; it was a nobility of conquerors imported from abroad.

The French nobility arose for the purpose of fighting, while under the shadow of its protecting valour the peasant was working the land, and the merchant was trading. This was its special form of work—the exercise of an armed patronage; but, inasmuch as this work was not rewarded, it was fair not only that the nobility should be exempt from certain taxes, such as the poll-tax, but also that it should exact its dues, since other sources of wealth were excluded.

We are now touching on one of the points in the history of the Ancien Régime on which imperfect ideas are often entertained. When our ancient aristocracy systematically abstained from engaging in trade and industry, why is this attributed to sentiments of vanity and pride ? Trading and industry were forbidden to the nobility at the express request of the Third Estate, which emphasized its own special rights and privileges in a very strenuous manner. Look at the formal injunctions enumerated by the representatives of the people at the last meetings of the States General in the sixteenth century. The bourgeoisie would have no competition : it upheld its monopoly, in return for which it left to the nobility their exemption from the poll-tax, and abandoned to them military rank and functions at the Court. The Third Estate retained the best part, and therefore it was considered that they had no grounds for coming forward with complaints at being excluded from taking rank in the army, from diplomatic appointments, and high Court functions.

The penetrating mind of the Comte de Montlosier has well analysed the structure of this social condition in which the privileged class was not the nobility, but the bourgeoisie. The nobility were going inevitably to their ruin while the lower classes were growing rich.

" One cannot say," writes Montlosier, " that the condition of the nobility was as fair as that of the lowest classes. The latter had open access to wealth by all paths of commerce, and were able on that account to reach as high a position as they wished. The classes above them, next to the nobility, had in their turn the full disposal of all the avenues of finance, administration, and magisterial appointments. The nobility, excluded from all these careers, were also in the position of not being really called to any of them. Their condition in fact increased the opportunities of dissipating their fortune without offering them the means to acquire one. One saw them falling everywhere into extreme poverty."

IV.—*The Wars of Religion*

One consequence of this great crisis was the breaking out of the Wars of Religion. Every religious war springs from the social condition of the nations or classes engaging in it. Brantôme relates a conversation between two important personages at the Louvre in the chamber of Catherine de Médicis. These two notabilities were remarking on the great benefits which the Wars of

Religion had brought to the nobility in the shape of Church treasure which the wars had enabled them to pillage. We must remember all those petty Huguenot gentlemen who showed such great ardour in asserting their new faith. Théodore de Bèze depicted to Calvin the army assembled at Orleans under command of the Prince de Condé in April, 1563—two thousand noblemen, embittered by straitened circumstances, taking up arms from necessity and in the hope of " fishing in troubled waters." Our two high personages in the Queen's chamber quoted the Prince de Condé who had laid hands on the magnificent treasure of St. Martin of Tours, bars of silver given by King Louis XI, from which were struck and taken away round barrels full of fine coins, " and many other seigneurs too who had done the same thing with other treasures and relics, and all these were forged coins notwithstanding they bore the image of our little King Charles IX who was reigning at the time."

And the rich merchants, usurers, bankers and other extortioners, who kept their money locked up in their coffers—ah ! How well those worthy country gentlemen, who had impoverished them-selves in the foreign wars, even to mortgaging their properties, knew how to redeem them ! With what complacent good humour does Sully, in his *Œconomies Royales*, recall how he obtained in 1580 " by the greatest good luck in the world " an iron box which contained 40,000 gold *écus*. " So much so," concludes Brantôme, " that I have seen such and such a gentleman who formerly would go about the country with only two horses and the little stable boy, now so well mounted that he might be seen during and after the civil wars travelling in the country with six and seven horses, and fine ones too, like the Bastard de Lupé, and many others in like manner up and down the land."

V.—*Decline of the Country Nobility*

Such then was the first of the great factors which changed the position of the nobility in the sixteenth century : the lowering of the value of money brought about by the treasure of the New World, combined with the commercial and industrial movement of the Renaissance which was concentrated in the hands of the bourgeoisie.

Another factor entailing important consequences was the develop-ment of artillery and fire-arms. Montaigne and Brantôme both note it. The bourgeois, the artisan, and even the peasant who had learnt how to handle the haquebut, musket, *ribeaudequin*,[1]

---

[1] *Ribeaudequin :* an engine of war in the form of a chariot mounted with one or two pieces of artillery of small calibre.- (H. W.)

or culverin, felt themselves the equal in strength and power of the noblest knight, hampered as he was by his shell of iron.

A third cause of the changing position of the French nobility was the development of the royal authority—a development which was inevitable, being due to the very progress the country had made. The thousands of diverse groups of which France was composed, and which had had their origin in the formation of independent family organizations in the first centuries of the Middle Ages, in course of time became more closely associated, and this wast he consequence of that commercial and industrial movement, and of the wars waged in common against the foreigner —the war against the English helped this on in large measure. In proportion as this great movement was in process of accomplishment, and was gaining in extent and depth, a common directing force, that of the royal power, became more and more necessary. And thus we see the local seigneur gradually losing his active authority over his tenants from the very fact that France was shaping herself. No longer did he lead his men to fight in the wars ; they were taken there by the King's representatives ; he no longer sat as a sovereign judge ; the Parliaments now issued decrees in conformity with mandates partaking the character of general laws ; it was no longer his place to take in hand important undertakings of public interest : these public works, such as canals, connecting roads, and the draining of marsh land, became the province of the royal power which alone was in a position to carry them out on a large scale because they concerned a great number of *seigneuries* at the same time.

The country nobleman was deprived of his useful activity which had been the justification of his feudal rights ; simultaneously the value of his revenues fell in alarming proportions ; arquebuses and mortars had transformed the least of his men into warriors as formidable as himself. In fact as he became more and more poverty stricken, and increasingly less useful on his own lands, he was driven to absent himself in order to seek honour and subsistence at the Court.

From the beginning of the eighteenth century a large number of gentlemen could no longer find subsistence save on the favours of the King. MM. d'Avenel, Pierre de Vaissière and Montlosier have demonstrated this admirably :

" People often complain," writes Montlosier, " of the multiplicity of royal favours : one should complain that they had become necessary." That is a far-reaching remark, a remark of a real historian ; let us engrave it on our mind.

VI.—*Ecclesiastical Benefices*

Among the favours distributed by the King upon the members of the nobility the bestowal of Ecclesiastical Benefices was one of those which, in our days, arouses the strongest criticism. It seems to us to be a surprising and iniquitous thing that a gentleman of noble birth should hold an Abbey *in commendam*, should receive the greater part of its revenue ; and that often the greater part of the tithes given to the Curé for the exercise of his functions and the upkeep of his church should go to personages who were strangers to the parish. People in those days thought differently. Let us listen to charming Pierre de Bourdeilles (Brantôme) who has made famous the name of the Abbey of Brantôme in Périgord, of which he was the lay Abbot :

"May God give long life and happiness to our King who, by such good ordering, bestows favours on his nobility, who through this good countenance are bound to spare neither their goods nor their life in his service ! " And Brantôme relates how his good Abbey had been bestowed on him :

"I have an Abbey—Brantôme—which that great King, Henri II, gave me in recompense for Captain Bourdeilles, my second brother, who was killed in his service at the top of the breach, and his head was carried away into the air in a cannonade at the siege of Hesdin." And Brantôme recalls, "for I must needs pride myself on that," how he had always well kept, maintained and ruled his Abbey, "although the repairs which I effected each year were considerable and cost me a good sum, all the more because it is one of the finest and most superb Abbeys existing in France." In his pleasant style the good seigneur adds, "the armies of Messires the Princes (Condé) and of Messire l'Admiral (Coligny) have passed by and lodged there twice, once when I was present. They never wrought any havoc nor ruin in the Abbey to the value of a single doit, nor pulled down a single statue in the church, nor touched any of the monks. . . . Come now, find me or imagine any big fat Abbot who could have made such a skilful pass."

The movement which was to cause the nobility to desert their lands and drive them to take shelter under the wings of the royal power became noticeable in the time of Francis I. The Court, in the modern sense of the term, dates from him. Admission to the royal palaces, to draw the attention of the Sovereign and to partake of his favours, grew to be the leading ambition of the great families. With the same eagerness with which they sought after pensions and appointments they vied with each other for

the honour of being included in the hunting parties, in the company on a journey, in the *gala* performances, and in the *livrées*
(gifts made by the King) which at this period were still an accompaniment of these amusements. The liberality of Francis I in
the matter of distributing wearing apparel went far beyond anything that had been seen up to his time.

Bernard Palissy sharply takes to task those who were eating
up their revenues in the suite of the Prince " in swagger, unneces-
sary expenditure and extravagant dress." " It would be more
useful for them to eat onions with their tenants, instruct them
how to lead good lives, show a good example, reconcile their
differences, prevent them from ruining themselves over law-suits,
and plant, build and ditch. . . ."

Even at that time we see courtiers, and even Prelates buying,
renting and building houses in the neighbourhood of the royal
residences.

And as early as the reign of Francis I the existence of the
nobility at the Court seems to have been a fairly destitute one.
Driven from their lands by need, they continued to be in want
in spite of princely charities and what they won by gambling as
their last resource. Being thus deprived of their usefulness the
nobility continued to lose the favour of the Third Estate which
they had formerly enjoyed. In the fifteenth century the records
of the States General were still proclaiming the beneficent rôle
of the nobility, and the lawfulness of their privileges : in the
records of 1485 we read, " The nobility is necessary for the
guardianship and safety of the Republic ; it forms the sinews of
the Kingdom." In the eighteenth century will it be still necessary
for the safety of the Kingdom, and will it be still its indispensable
support ? " Everything went on without them," says Montlosier.
" People were obliged to accord them advantages, no longer as
in former days because they were useful, but in order that they
might be made of some use ; no longer because they formed the
sinews and strength of the State, but in order that they might
continue to serve it by way of ornament."

In many places, however, the worthy country nobility maintained their position and by a new form of patronage accom-
modated to new circumstances, continued to render service to
their tenants.

VII.—*The Provincial Nobility in the Eighteenth Century*

During the course of the seventeenth century the manor shed
its defences. In the eighteenth century it no longer possessed
any tower that was of practical use except that of the pigeon house ;

the moats had been converted into fish ponds, and the surrounding walls were only a protection against the hoar frost, and a shelter for the espaliers. The essential feature of the seigneurial residence was now the square weather vane, recalling the form of the feudal banner. Sometimes the gibbet and the pillory placed in front of the château still proclaimed the rights of supreme justice which in former days had been exercised to their full extent and rigour.

The old hefty, well-tempered sword, with its strong hilt set with relics, had given place to an elegant and light rapier hanging at the side of the nobleman. In many districts the familiar relationship between lord and country vassal was still maintained. On the coasts of Brittany the Staff of the coastguards was composed exclusively of members of the old nobility. "I have not yet seen one of these *gentilshommes* showing any quarrelsome disposition towards a peasant soldier," writes the Bailli de Mirabeau, "and I have noticed an air of filial respect on the part of the latter. . . . It was a terrestrial paradise of good manners, simplicity, and true patriarchal grandeur."

How many country districts were still lacking in roads ? The different localities were connected to each other by paths only, a fact which contributed to the maintenance of patriarchal manners and traditions. The ladies of the manor rode on horseback or in conveyances drawn by oxen. Should there be a ball at a house in the neighbourhood they would go there astride of a horse, with their legs in baskets hanging to the sides of their mount, whereby their dress was well covered and protected from the mud which did not fail to splash up from their horse's shoes. The village dances were led off by the seigneur, his sons and daughters. Wolf hunts were organized, with the baron at their head ; the company sang songs together and drank at the same table after the game bag had been well filled.

The sons of the seigneurs were brought up among the peasants of the village ; Montaigne " was reared in the lowest and most common manner of living " in the house of one of his father's farmers.

Evidences marking the good relations which prevailed between the country baron and his tenants are numerous. He was their counsellor ; he assisted them in improving their land, instructed them how to perfect their methods of cultivation, and protected them against the fiscal agents. He was often their doctor and veterinary surgeon, and at the manor a room was set apart as a store for drugs.

It was his duty to contribute to the upkeep and education of all natural children left destitute within the bounds of his territory, and to provide for their necessities until they reached an age fixed in accordance with varying customs.

Our country gentry preserved the tradition constituting them Justices of the Peace in their district. The following sketch by the Marquis de Mirabeau has remained famous :

"I knew an old gentleman who was never quite sober, but he nevertheless regulated all matters for twenty leagues around. He used to have the documents and papers brought to him and would consult the lawyer folk in due form, and then form his decision in accordance with his own good judgment. This done, he convoked the parties to his castle. At dessert, he reminded them, glass in hand, of the matters to be decided. He enumerated the points and considered them. The first one who was tempted to interrupt him was pulled up short by what was a positive order : ' A glass of wine for Monsieur.'

The order was carried out and the glass of wine drunk ; the new Rhadamanthus looked at him with that fatherly and conciliatory manner which comes naturally from long habit.

' Is Monsieur still aggrieved ? ' he would ask.

If the indignant plaintiff wished to finish the sentence he had begun he was quietly listened to and was subjected to a second glass of wine in return for his frankness."

At last, when the wine and din of conversation had produced a friendly feeling and general good humour, the worthy judge would deliver his definite pronouncement to hearts that by now were softened.

When travelling in the Quercy, "*l'Ami des Hommes*" stopped on the edge of a stream, surprised at the large number of crayfish he saw swarming there. At the inn Mirabeau made the observation that such a well-preserved fishery must cost the seigneur of the place a numerous staff of water bailiffs :

"Ah ! Monsieur, M. le Marquis and Mme. la Marquise are the best seigneurs in the world. Far from taking anything from them there is not one of us who would not be the first to denounce his neighbour were such a thing to happen."

"I have seen cases," continues the Marquis de Mirabeau, "of communities buying themselves back from their lord, when he wished to sell them, in order to return to him." But the old customs were to continue their process of modification.

"We know to what extent," the Marquis proceeds, "was practised the custom—we might call it the mania—of peasants giving continual presents to their lords. I have seen this custom being discontinued nearly everywhere in my time, and with good cause : the seigneurs are no longer good for anything, and it is quite natural that they should be forgotten as they too forget ; and don't let any one call it the old attitude of servitude. In places where the practice still obtains these good people, even the poorest, would be very mortified if their presents were refused, and still more so if any attempt to indemnify them by a present of equal or higher value were made to them : I have seen it a hundred times."

The life of these country notabilities at the close of the Ancien Régime has been wonderfully described by Talleyrand and Chateaubriand at the beginning of their Memoirs, and also by Balzac in his two romances, *Cabinet des Antiques* and *Béatrix*.

Talleyrand depicted the peaceful and benevolent life of his grandmother at the Château de Chalais lès Barbezieux. An apothecary's store was kept at the manor, and on Sundays after Mass she would distribute remedies made up from recipes of the time, lint and bandages of fine linen for making compresses, and prepared by her own hands.

A layer of old dust had gathered over the manors ; a good deal of tapestry was made in those days, even by the old gentlemen who had come back from the wars ; they spun silk on the humming spinning wheel ; they played piquet, *la mouche* and *trictrac* (backgammon), and went to bed early. Meals were the principal preoccupation ; these were very long, generally well served, and abundant. The produce from the domain was practically all the outlay requisite—vegetables and fruit from the garden ; leverets, quails and partridges from the preserves, chickens and pigeons from the poultry yard, fish from the pond and streams near-by.

And they were very economical at the château, dividing a *liard* [1] into four. Look at Balzac's picture given in the first chapter of *Béatrix*. On this point (economy) our country gentry were very like the peasant class among whom they lived. The seigneur kept a tight hand over his day labourers, superintended their work and the gathering in of the crops ; the mistress of the house would chide her domestic servants over expense : money was scarce, and one must be content with the produce of the seigneurial domain as far as possible.

One can imagine the contrast soon to arise between this rural nobility, with its garb and language of olden times, and the highly polished nobility of the Court. And so those writers, whose *clientèle* were at Versailles, with La Bruyère and Molière at their head, loaded our poor rustics with disdain : " The provincial

[1] *Liard :* a copper coin of former days of the value of a quarter of a *sou*. (H. W.)

nobleman," writes La Bruyère, "often without a roof to his head, with no clothes and no merit, is a nuisance to his country, his family and himself."

The title of "*gentilhomme de campagne*," notes the Marquis de Mirabeau, "is regarded almost as an insult." People jeer at your country nobleman with his gold ear-rings, leather gaiters, clouted shoes, and sword-belt embroidered in wool, "a bragging chatterbox of a hunting man." They laugh at his pride in his genealogical tree of which he boasts in his drawing-room and even in his kitchen. He is a "peacock" on the subject of his ancestors' prowess. In his eyes his kinship owes its importance to the remote date in which its representatives lived. He decorates the walls of his manor with portraits of his ancestors in armour, plumed and scarred with wounds to his heart's content, and "these fine captains couldn't even read."

Marivaux himself silences his customary benevolence where our rustics are concerned. He does not even spare their wives :

"Take away from the country lady the mask she wears when she goes from one château to another mounted on her hackney ; take away her vanity over the antiquity of her family, her loud tone, the positive embarrassment of her countenance and the uniform movement of her walk—all this goes to the make-up of the figure she presents—take away her sons, the Marquis and the Chevalier, little chits whom she draws up in front of you, after the manner of a village salute, who are always dribbling at the nose on their arrival, in order to have their noses wiped by their mother's handkerchief ; take away all these things and there is nothing in particular left to her. . . ."

And this is the heir :

Un fort aimable enfant : il garnit bien sa panse
Et toujours dans la main il tient quelque morceau
De flan ou de pâté, de tourte ou de gâteau ;
Il a sur son jupon cent taches bien écrites . . .
Il se mouche en sa manche et porte des sabots.
Maucroix, le Baron de la Vespière.

VIII.—*The Country Squires*

It is true that in comparison with those good seigneurs who, down to the close of the Ancien Régime, endeavoured to fulfil their rôle to the best of their ability in spite of opposing circumstances, there were many who abused their position by arbitrarily levying on their subjects new contributions, or increasing the old ones. The King had to forbid the forcing of tenants "to give their daughters, nieces or wards in marriage, against their will, to the seigneur's servants or others." The *Grands Jours d'Auvergne*, described so amusingly by Fléchier, have become celebrated.

"*Grands Jours*" was the name given to the sessions of special tribunals invested with a jurisdiction from which there was no appeal; they were established by the King in the provinces for the purpose of checking the acts of oppression of which the local seigneurs might have rendered themselves guilty, of punishing their acts of violence and of putting an end to the practice which many of them wished to introduce of making the different *corvées* payable in kind, and of creating unlawful tolls. During the seventeenth century *Grands Jours* were held in Auvergne, Vivarais, Velay, Gévaudan, upper and lower Languedoc, Quercy, Rouergue, Aunis, Saintonge, Angoumois, Périgord, Limousin and Poitou. "There is nothing more important," wrote Colbert, "than to punish severely the crimes committed by petty provincial tyrants."

A popular Christmas song described the exactions of these country squires in Auvergne :

> L'homme du château
> Au métayer arrache
>   Ce qui le soutient,
>   Et sans droit retient
>   Son lard, son chanteau,
>   Le cochon ;
> Il prend avec l'oison
> Le cabri, l'agneau et la vache ;
> Il prend la charrue et le bœuf,
> Le coq, la poule et l'œuf,
> Et puis il lui donne sur la joue
>   Et les coups lui restent . . .

Fléchier wrote, "Auvergne was a very disorderly province ; the distance separating it from the King's jurisdiction, the weakness of subordinate judges, the easiness of taking refuge in the mountains, and possibly the example and bad dispositions of a few others encouraged the majority of *gentilshommes* to play the tyrant and oppress the people."

The magistrates presiding over the *Grands Jours* proceeded with great activity. A large number of representatives of the nobility, some of them belonging to the foremost families in the district, were seized and beheaded. Those who had taken flight were executed in effigy, thirty at a time on some days.

"It was a fine sight," wrote Fléchier, "to see so many pictures exhibited on the place of execution, on each of which the executioner was shown to have cut off the head. These bloodless executions were all the more pleasing as a spectacle, because justice was done without any blood flowing. These pictures remained on exhibition the whole day, and all the people came from curiosity to see this collection of criminals who were dying incessantly, and yet did not die."

Very many seigneurial residences were razed to the ground. The outer defences of feudal castles, with their deep moats and crenelated towers, were demolished, in spite of any protests that might be raised, such as that of the Marquis de Saint Floret, " a person of quality," to quote Fléchier, " the most learned and the most peaceful nobleman in Auvergne," who protested before the Court against the demolition of' a tower near-by " to the top of which he had the right to send every year a trumpeter to play a few gladsome airs " in proof of his own suzerainty over the château in question.

Under Louis XIV the Government more especially endeavoured to protect the field labourers against the misdeeds or usurpations of their lords. " At this day," we read in a document of 1689, " a seigneur must have right on his side, and one half over, in order to win his suit against a peasant."

IX.—*The Poverty of the Country Nobility*

In the eighteenth century the " rustic dwellings " of our country squires had for the most part greatly fallen away from their original condition. Hidden in the fold of a valley or perched upon a small cultivated scrap of land, a small tower, often in no very good repair, looked like some old abandoned relic of defence hard by the residence, at the top of which grated the banner-shaped weather-cock. Here too stood the barn, with its white walls weathered by time. A few greyhounds or bassets would lift their noses at the approach of a passer by ; there might be a huge ditch for manure, where chickens, ducks and geese were pecking for food, a garden surrounded by hedges containing bluey green cabbages, or a few fruit trees—the peaceful dwelling, crumbling with age, of the petty country lordling.

Notwithstanding their spirit of economy our worthy rural nobility, deeply attached to their lands and to the service of the King whence they would return home with the cross of St. Louis, with wounds and debts, continued to grow poorer and poorer. The château of the Du Gage Berthelot family was only kept standing by means of props. Madame du Gage wrote in 1782 that in a short time the rupture of a beam might bring down the building. M. Pradines de Laurabue, living in the neighbourhood of Castel-naudary, made light of his poverty. It was a cold winter, and he kept himself warm with the planks and girders of the ancestral manor as they fell down from the ceiling.

The following story is only one example out of many. M. de Parigny owned thirty-six acres in Touraine, which he cultivated *en métairie* (sharing the profits with the farmer who cultivated it). He had four sons, all of whom like himself, were in the service of the King. He was killed with three of his sons while serving the King. At the conclusion of the war the fourth son returned to the home of his fathers—a dilapidated farm-house with the roof and windows fallen in and the doors down. The barn and stables were in ruins, and the fruit trees had been cut down to the roots.

After three years spent in making petitions and representations he obtained from the Comptroller-General a grant of a thousand *livres*.[1] He set to work bravely, and we find him now with ten acres ready for sowing; but he must needs live. Shylock lent him a hundred *écus*,[2] and the poor gallant gentleman wrote to the Comptroller of Finances saying that he was done for, failing another grant in aid. We could mention a number of Lieutenants, Captains, and Lieut.-Colonels who, on their return from serving in the wars, and generally bearing wounds, found themselves in such a wretched condition in their homes that they literally had to become a burden on public charity.

" A gentleman in reduced circumstances," wrote a cultivator of Poitiers in 1764, " is often a neighbour very much on our hands." We find cases of some who had sunk down lamentably to the workhouse.

The reason of this was that in the course of the eighteenth century the depreciation in the value of money had been still going on, although the fall was less sharp and rapid than at the time of the Renaissance. From the end of the reign of Louis XIV to that of Louis XVI money had again lost more than half its value, while the fixed rate of seigneurial rents, and the dues they received on their lands continued to remain immutably fixed by force of custom. Add also to this the prodigious swelling of the size of the families of this robust and healthy rural nobility, who had no mind to stand in the way of a rapid increase in the number of their heirs.

Piece by piece the lands surrounding the family manor had been sold to peasants and farmers of old standing, with reservation

[1] *Livre :* not of the value of a pound, but the name formerly given to the standard coin which gradually depreciated in value, and is now represented by the *franc*.
[2] *Ecu :* represented formerly 3 *livres*. There was also an *écu* of 6 *livres*. St. Louis struck the first *écu*. (H. W.)

of the seigneurial rights which were attached to them inalienably. Thus gentlemen of noble birth and their families were to be seen subsisting merely on the revenue derived from these dues, and we can imagine what these now amounted to with the declining value of money. They were accounted for in *livres*, *sous* and *deniers* ; in the time of Saint Louis the *livre* was a gold coin, in that of Louis XV it was only a silver coin ; under Saint Louis the *sou* was a silver coin, under Louis XV only copper ; but the figure representing the amount of the dues, which had been originally based on *livres* and *sous* of Tours,[1] had not changed. Add to this the great depreciation in even the value of silver and one can understand how the *livre*, which in the thirteenth century was a considerable sum representing nearly 500 francs at the present value, was no longer anything but an insignificant trifle.

To-day the law allows the rent to be doubled in comparison with that paid before the war ; through all those centuries no law had ever changed the rate of the dues payable to the seigneur.

Writers are unanimous in stating the poverty of the rural nobility. A great number of them had become simple peasants ; their daughters would look after the cattle and take the geese and sheep into the fields ; in Brittany their fathers, wearing their old hats of shiny felt, might have been seen on their way to market to sell the most modest produce of their cultivation, carrying a basket on their arm and a sword at their side. The fine titles of their house, inscribed on parchment, would serve to cover the pots of butter.

In the neighbourhood of Auch, observes Arthur Young, the nobles ploughed their own fields. " And these may possibly be much more estimable members of society than the fools and knaves that laugh at them."

Some among them even worked on neighbouring farms as day labourers, and did the roughest kinds of work.

The dilapidated manor offered a contrast to the good appearance of thriving *maisons de village*. Pierre Retif, a cultivator at Nitry in Burgundy, said to his son Edmond, " You saw those gentlemen huntsmen from la Puisaye, in gaiters and nailed shoes, carrying an old rusty sword under their arm and dying of hunger. . . . Would you like to be in their place ? "

We know the proverb :

Gentilhomme de Beauce
Se tient au lit quand on refait ses chausses.

" In Boulonnais," wrote Smollett, "the country gentry have

[1] *Tours :* see p. 83.

given up shooting from lack of money to buy themselves a gun." Cardinal de Fleury, when Prime Minister, discovered one of his relations at Pérignan, in Languedoc ; his name was Hercule de Rosset, Marquis de Rocosel, " of ruddy brown face, and ruddy brown coat and wig." His chief occupation was to drink with the local blacksmith. Fleury made him a Duke and a Territorial Peer. In Rouergue many noble families lived in the fields on an income of fifty, even twenty-five *louis*. In Berry " three-quarters of the nobility were dying of hunger " (1754). Turgot states that the same conditions obtained in Limousin.

In 1750 the Intendant of Besançon left to his successor a sketch of the rural nobility in Franche-Comté :

" The nobility in this district is of fairly good stock, but very poor, and as proud as it is poor. It is in a very humiliating position compared with what it was in former times. It is not a bad policy to keep them in this state of poverty in order to oblige them to serve, and to have need of us. They form a close brotherhood among themselves and will only admit to their caste persons who can show proof of four quarterings. This confraternity has no legal standing, but is merely tolerated, and meets only once a year in the presence of the Intendant. After partaking of a meal together, and hearing Mass, these nobles return home, some on their miserable hacks, others on foot. You will see what a comical affair this assembly is."

These unfortunate gentlemen of noble birth, fathers of large families, no longer knew where to turn to provide for their children. As for putting their sons in the army, and their daughters in convents—an allowance of 600 *livres* at the very least was necessary in the case of a *gendarme* or guardsman. Where was this to be found ? Colas de la Baronnais had eleven sons and eight daughters. The future of the latter made him tremble. " What am I to do with them ? " he wrote despairingly. " The Abbesses demand dowries of 900, 1600 and 3000 *livres* to admit them into their convents ! "

Paris-Duverney, the financier, states in 1753 that in order to place their daughters at Saint-Cyr the provincial nobility had to come down to furnishing " proofs of poverty " far oftener than proofs of nobility.

How many of these impoverished small noblemen were in a position to provide the expenses of the education of their sons at college ? They would enter them as ships' boys in merchant ships, and even in " privateers " as early as eleven years old.

That happened to Chateaubriand's father. When he was fifteen years old he guessed his mother's anxieties. He went to her one day when she was in bed.

" I do not wish to be a burden to you any longer."

" René, cultivate your fields," said his poor mother, bursting into tears.

" They are not capable of feeding us ; let me go away."

" Very well, go then whither God may wish."

" That same evening my father left the ancestral farm and arrived at Dinan where one of our relatives gave him a letter of recommendation to an inhabitant of Saint Malo ! "

And the boy, entering as a volunteer, went on board an armed schooner which lifted her anchor a few days later.

In the course of his travels in France, Arthur Young writes, on 1st September, 1788, of the Comte de Chateaubriand and his Château of Combourg :

" The country has a savage aspect; husbandry not much further advanced, at least in skill, than among the Hurons ; the people almost as wild as their country, and their town of Combourg one of the most brutal filthy places that can be seen ; mud houses, no windows, and a pavement so broken as to impede all passengers, but ease none— yet here is a château, and inhabited ; who is this Monsieur de Chateaubriand, the owner, that has nerves strung for a residence amidst such filth and poverty ? Below this hideous heap of wretchedness is a fine lake, surrounded by well-wooded enclosures."

Chateaubriand spoke later of this lake and the woods in phrases which complete the picture.

" The fair, which was called the Angevine Fair, was held every year on the 4th September in the meadow by the lake. The vassals were obliged to carry arms, and came to the château to raise the banner of their seigneur ; thence they proceeded to the fair to maintain order and enforce the payment of the toll due to the Comtes de Combourg on every head of cattle. My father kept an open table on these occasions and dancing was kept up for three days, the masters in the great *salle* to the squeaking of a fiddle, the vassals in the green court-yard to the musette.[1] They sang, cheered, and fired off their old arquebuses. These noises were mingled with the bellowing of the cattle at the fair ; the crowd wandered freely over the gardens and woods, and thus at least once a year something that resembled light-heartedness was seen at Combourg."

We have seen above the causes of the distressed circumstances of the French gentry ; to these should be added the increasing hostility shown by the peasant class, from the beginning of the eighteenth century, at least in certain provinces. The peasants began to bring lawsuits against their seigneurs, contested their privileges, the dues they claimed, and the landmarks and marches which were everlasting matters for dispute. Advocates and lawyers

---

[1] *Musette :* a kind of bag-pipe, used in the country. (H. W.)

would uphold them, and among the peasant families were many advocates who had been educated in the law, thanks to the easy circumstances of many of them. Towards the middle of the eighteenth century France was shaken, as it were, by the first movement of revolt which presaged the Revolution.

Gentlemen of noble birth were sometimes attacked by the peasants in their own village with pitchforks ; poachers would come and kill their game at the very doors of the manor. Those liable to pay dues to the Seigneur de Gramont Pioger in Poitou threatened to break down the doors of the château. They shouted out " that they would cut off the head of their lord with their sickles, or would kill him with their shot guns." These movements were premature, but they indicated thus early the feelings which were smouldering in the minds of the people.

The Marquis de Mirabeau notes one of the resources of the country nobility in earlier times—the noble-born domestic servants living in the great seigneurial houses.

" The low-born domestic servants," writes *l'Ami des Hommes*, " consumed less then than they do to-day when they now dress them up like actors, feed and bed them like masters ; but the great houses were full of mess-mates of another order ; the ladies had demoiselles to wait on them, the seigneurs had gentlemen belonging to families as good as their own, and the others had pages and equerries. It was an outlet for the poor nobility which no longer exists."

The lustre that used to emanate from the great houses had paled before the brilliance of the Roi-Soleil—feudal hearths the fires of which were continually dwindling down like other more modest hearths which they were keeping alive.

There remained to our country *gentilshommes* a career in the army, but it could not be any source of wealth to them. At any rate the preceding pages will have helped us to understand the decision come to at the close of the Ancien Régime by the Maréchal de Ségur, one of the best and most generous spirits that had ever been seen at the Ministry of War. He decided that all the commissioned ranks in the army should henceforth be reserved for gentlemen of noble family. In order to become a captain a gentleman would have to be in a position to prove four degrees of nobility. After this the King's Council declared that a man must also be of noble family in order to be eligible as a *Maître des Requêtes*, and that henceforth " all ecclesiastical property, from the most modest Priory to the richest Abbey, would be reserved to the nobility." These decisions were made at a time when public opinion, even including the ranks of the nobility, " befriended " the Third Estate. The bourgeoisie were in a position to live, and in an increasingly splendid manner ; the rural nobility were not.

In 1790, Brissot, with his republican pen, dared to render justice to the old, poverty-stricken and brave rural nobility. The *Patriote Français* was to celebrate the services it had rendered to the army, for which it had only been rewarded with poverty. " If there is one order of citizens," he exclaimed, " which is the victim of the aristocracy of the great and rich, it is the poverty-stricken nobility, that numerous class of agricultural gentlemen of noble family, who have been limited to one single profession by gothic prejudice. . . . The picture of the annoyances to which it has been exposed is one of the most revolting to be seen. . . ."

X.—*The Gilded Nobility*

In the course of the centuries forming the Middle Ages the aristocracy deriving from the family grew to be organized into hierarchies one above the other. Above simple knights came the possessors of strongly organized fiefs ; above them, the great feudal Houses, such as the Sires of Coucy and Montlhéry ; above these the heads of the great fiefs, such as the Counts of Flanders, Champagne, Brittany, Poitiers and Toulouse, and the Dukes of Burgundy and of Normandy, who were sovereign Princes ; crowning the edifice was the King.

The process of drawing closer together and levelling down, to which we have already drawn attention, tending from age to age to unite social conditions more closely with administrative uniformity, produced their effect in the corps of the nobility just as in all the other parties of the country. In the eighteenth century the French nobility formed one compact body. It is true that the *noblesse présentée*, that is those noblemen whose wives had been presented personally to the King and Queen at a stately ceremony, and thus enjoyed honorific distinctions, regarded as inferior to themselves the greater portion who had not been admitted to this distinction, those whose wives had not been honoured with the King's kiss and did not ride in his carriages ; it is also true that the Dukes and Peers of the Realm would have liked to embody a distinct corps of nobility under the name of *noblesse titrée*, and that above them ranked the Princes of the Blood, members of the Royal Family, and above them the " enfants de France "—the King's children ; it is again true that in the eighteenth century a distinction was made between the nobility of ancient lineage who derived their illustrious position from their antiquity, and the nobility by creation, newly created by letters royal—an official nobility arising from the four thousand different functions connected with those not of noble birth ; a nobility of the army ; a nobility of the law or of Parliamentary functions ; a nobility, called " *de cloche*," of municipal office holders, deriving from high urban functions which, like certain offices of the Court or of the Administration, permitted the holders to possess a coat-of-arms ; a " *noblesse de ventre*," which in certain cases might be given to wives of noble birth married to bourgeois husbands ; and a foreign nobility conceded to gentlemen of noble birth and of foreign origin who had settled in France—yet, in reality, the sole distinction separating them, and this moreover in the most modern, crude and brutal manner, felt even in the eighteenth century amongst French gentlemen, was—wealth.

Turgot stated in 1776 that the nobles exempt from the *taille* (poll-tax) and other burdens borne by those not of noble birth, comprised "the whole body of the rich." In the struggle for political reform which was taking place, the cause of these privileged ones had become " the cause of the rich against the poor."

On leaving the soil to which the country seigneur, bound down by the weight of traditions, remained attached, the nobility endeavoured to put their fortunes on a level with their rank by a display they considered to be their duty to themselves. Although excluded from trading and industry they managed to make good by other channels. First of all there was the nobility of very high rank, possessing domains which from their extent and importance gave them large incomes ; then there were the pensions and profitable positions at Court, lucrative posts, wealthy benefices, Bishoprics and Abbeys, the revenue from which might amount to hundreds of thousands of *livres ;* there was also the booty taken on foreign territory when serving under the King's standard ; in this way the Connétable de Lesdiguières amassed a royal fortune, and the Maréchal de Richelieu a scarcely lesser one.

A nobleman would lower himself by engaging in trade and industry, and thereby lost his privileges ; but an edict of Louis XIV, of August, 1669, confirmed on the 8th September, 1701, and the 11th January, 1724, permitted trading on the grand scale and traffic beyond the seas—an illusory benefit for our *gentilshommes champêtres*, but one which opened out vast horizons to members of the great families. Marquises and noble ladies might have been seen freighting ships, and commissioning privateers and filibusters. When the enterprise was successfully accomplished, pirates and aristocrats would divide up the booty like good comrades, share and share alike. Speculation was lawful, such as on army equipment and victualling, for a sum down to the contractor. The

Comtesse d'Argenson, wife of the Minister for War, " did business in enormous sums," as her brother-in law, the Marquis, used to say. Under Law's system Princes of the Blood, such as Condé and Conti, gathered in gold by the cart-load ; the Marquis de la Faye made a profit of twenty million *livres* (two hundred million francs of the present day) ; Saint-Fargeau made seventeen millions ; the Maréchal d'Estrée speculated in tea and *eau-de-vie*. Louis de Gesvres, a Duke and Peer of the Realm, and Governor of the Ile de France, held the privilege of conducting games of chance, and the Duc de Carignan had a similar one ; the town houses of de Gesvres and de Carignan were gaming houses. Cocks no longer found pearls in the dung heap, but the first families of France found ingots of gold in them, to refer again to the noble ladies mentioned before. The daughter of a gentleman of noble family might not marry a financier ; she would have compromised the name of her family, and her relations would have had her shut up in a convent ; but a nobleman of ancient lineage was very willing to marry a sack of *écus*. *Noblesse dorée !*

XI.—*The Court Nobility*

Among the questions addressed to the Intendants[1] by the Government of Louis XIV was the following : " Do the *gentilshommes* in your province like to stay at home or to leave ? "

Tocqueville quotes the reply of an Intendant. As a faithful servant of the King he (the Intendant) complained that the noblemen in his province preferred living among their peasants to fulfilling the duty which should call them to live near the Prince. " These *gentilshommes*," adds Tocqueville, " who had refused to do their duty by the King were the only ones, who with sword in hand defended the Monarchy in France, and died fighting for it . . . because they knew how to retain round them those very peasants for living with whom they have been harshly judged."

The years went by. At the spectacle of the country districts becoming abandoned by the aristocracy their eyes were opened, and at the end of the eighteenth century the Intendants replied to the same questionnaire :

" The nobility are giving the regrettable example of deserting the country districts."

How many of them could not make up their minds to lead the mean existence of a *gentilhomme champêtre* which we have described ! And on the other hand at Versailles, Paris, and even in their neigh-

---

[1] The Intendants under the Ancien Régime were Inspectors-General acting on behalf of the King. They controlled the administration in the provinces, and held great authority. (H. W.)

bouring town, the sources of wealth were pouring out only too abundantly. The Chevalier d'Arc, descendant of the family of the sublime Maid of Orleans, was anxious to check the movement :

" If you would be rich," he exclaimed to the noblemen who were deserting their fields, " give up the luxury which is degrading you ! " But what luxury was there for our poor country nobility to give up ?

No longer able to live on their lands, writes the Vicomte d'Avenel, they could not lay out money on their properties, the revenue from which was ludicrously small. " The nobility, to whom trade and industry were forbidden, had no other means of living than to buy appointments at Court, out of which they could at least draw the bare necessities of existence and still find some outlet for their activity."

Their horizon moreover was widened by this movement, this drawing closer together, and this fusion towards a national unity which we have mentioned. Their outlook was no longer shut in by the boundaries of the manor. Before them lay the capital of their province, Bordeaux, Toulouse, Rennes, Rouen, Dijon . . . and further off, Versailles and Paris ! The *gentilhomme* was growing weary of his rustic domain. Why should not he too become a man of consideration, and shine in the world, and make his way at Court ?

Add to this the infiltration of the royal power, steadily following this same movement of unification of the country, and similarly making itself felt in Lorraine and Savoy under the influence of the Dukes of those provinces before they were restored to France. The royal power was penetrating more and more into the different *seigneuries*, and was developing therein on a larger scale, weakening the *raisons d'être* of the local authority, and thereby taking away from the man to whom it belonged any interest in exercising his functions.

When the peasant had any claim to put forward, or any petition to make, he now knew that henceforth he would obtain it by making his request to the Intendant or to his sub-delegate, rather than by applying to his seigneur. The apportioning of the payment of the poll-tax and other taxes, and exemption from serving in the militia, were now in the hands of the Intendant and his sub-delegate.

What a fairy-like existence, on the other hand, followed in the brilliant wake of the Court.

We spoke on a former page [1] of the Marquis de Rocosel, cousin of Cardinal de Fleury, whom the latter took away from his

[1] Page 102.

village and made into a Duke and Peer of the Realm. In addition
to this he made a gift to his son, now promoted to be Marquis de
Fleury, of lands estimated at the value of 400,000 *livres* (4
million francs at the present day), and married him to a young
lady who brought as her marriage portion an income of 30,000
livres with expectations of shortly succeeding to revenues amounting to an additional 80,000 *livres*—totalling in all an income of
1,100,000 francs at present value, in addition to lands worth 4
million francs. Moreover, since the Cardinal, then Prime Minister,
considered that the father, M. le Duc de Fleury, was too poorly
provided for with an annual income amounting to 1,800,000 francs
of our day, he had allotted to him an annual grant of the value
of 12,000 *livres* (120,000 francs present value) out of the revenues
from the Crown property.

We could go on for pages citing similar instances, which would
open before the eyes of the reader a flowing stream of wealth as
enchanting as it was scandalous. All the figures which follow
should be multiplied by ten so as to bring them up to their present
day value.

The Comte de Toulouse, the natural son of Louis XIV, had an
income of 1,700,000 *livres* (17 million francs) and a Prince could
not be expected to live upon that ! So Louis XV added another
million francs. His widow was left with an income of 80,000
livres a year (800,000 francs) which the King further increased by
another 50,000 *livres*.

On the death of her husband, the Duchesse du Maine secured
for herself an annual pension of 100,000 *livres* (one million francs) ;
the Duchesse d'Orléans had as her dowry an income of 6,500,000
francs, of which the Royal Treasury provided more than two-
thirds. When Prince Louis Henri de Condé, who had dabbled so
profitably in Law's schemes, by which so many unfortunate people
were ruined, died on the 27th January, 1740, at Chantilly, he left
behind him an annual revenue of 17 million francs (present value)
—mere beggary ! and so the King augmented it at the expense
of the tax-payer with a pension of 2,600,000 francs (present value).

These figures take one's breath away, and the list might be
prolonged indefinitely.

In 1780, Louis XVI had it at heart to lighten the expenses of
the Treasury which a universal outburst of feeling declared to be
intolerable. He instituted a great cutting down of the expenses
of the Court, after which economies his aunts—three in number :
they were Madame Adélaide, aged forty-eight, Madame Victoire,
aged forty-seven, and Madame Sophie, aged forty-six—received
no more than 600,000 *livres* annually (6 million francs, present

value) . . . for the expenses of their table. That is what three old maiden ladies were costing the public annually—solely for their table !—and were not finding it enough !

M. de Sartine, as Lieutenant of Police, received 200,000 *livres* (2 million francs) to help him pay his debts. Lamoignon, Keeper of the Seals, also received a little present of a like amount, and he was really satisfied with quite a little, for Miromesnil, his successor, received 600,000 *livres* (6 million francs) " as an aid to settling himself in his post." The Duc d'Aiguillon, discharged from the Ministry in 1774, obtained as " consolation money " 500,000 *livres* (5 million francs). The widow of the Maréchal de Muy, Minister for War, secured for herself a pension of 30,000 *livres*, and the Comte de Saint Germain, who had been discharged from the War Secretariat, a pension of 40,000 *livres*, plus 150,000 *livres* as " consolation money."

Marie Antoinette obtained the grant of 1,200,000 *livres* (12 million francs) for the Duc de Polignac ; the Prince de Salm received 500,000 *livres* (5 million francs). During his short term as Comptroller of the Finances (1785–1787) Calonne paid to the Comte de Provence 56,000,000 *livres* (560 million francs), and to the Comte d'Artois—he was only the younger brother—25,000,000 *livres* (250 million francs). It is enough to make one howl ! The Prince de Condé—yet again—received 12,000,000 *livres* (120 million francs) in one lump sum, as well as an annual income of 600,000 *livres* (6 million francs). Ah ! the Duc d'Aumale was well inspired when he left his domain of Chantilly to the nation ; in truth the nation paid dearly for it.

Money was given away—and in what huge amounts—to anybody, provided that they belonged to the *haute noblesse*, or enjoyed the favour of the Secretaries of State. Representation was made to His Majesty of the bad state of affairs that M. the Prince de Pons found himself in. Just as if such a thing could be possible ! The Chevalier Camille thereupon received an annual pension of 15,000 *livres*, and his daughter, Mlle. de Marsan, " Canoness of Remiremont," one of 16,000 *livres*. It became necessary to console M. Rouillé for not having taken part in the Treaty of Vienna : a pension of 6,000 *livres* allotted to his niece, Mme. de Castellau, and another 10,000 *livres* to his daughter, Mme. de Beuvron, already very rich, was to soften down his disappointment. Rouillé's " consolation money " was to cost the taxpayer in the course of years a sum equivalent to 260 million francs. Puisieux owned considerable properties ; but the greater portion consisted of vineyards " which yield only an uncertain revenue " ; frost and hail must be taken into account. The King's Treasury compensated for this "uncertainty" with a handsome annual grant of 77,000 *livres* (770,000 francs) at the taxpayer's cost. Out of such a huge sum relief could have been given to forty families of country *gentils-hommes* who had ruined themselves and had had their bodies riddled in the King's service.

The House of Polignac alone managed to secure for themselves pensions amounting to 700,000 *livres* (7 million francs) out of the public Treasury, and that of de Noailles to 2 million *livres* (20 million francs !).

And the Ecclesiastical Benefices ! Fifteen hundred sinecures, prebends, tenures *in commendam*, canonries and abbeys, some of them yielding enormous revenues which fell like a golden rain upon the favoured aristocracy ! Then too there were the high positions at the Court or in the Government. Let us put aside the Ministries, military appointments, and the office of Intendants, the holders of which gave some return for the money they received ; but we must take into consideration that there were forty depart-mental governments, seventy Lieutenants-General of Division with their establishments, four hundred and seven special government departments, and thirteen government departments connected with the royal residences—all sinecures, and all remunerated on a magnificent scale. And the unofficial appointments, which did not mean, as they would to-day, that they were unpaid—alas ! no—but that their holders had nothing to do for them ! M. de Machault's son received 18,000 *livres* per annum (180,000 francs) for signing his name twice a year. These absorbing duties were held by the Intendant *des classes*. Mme. de La Borde was appointed Lady of the Bed-chamber to the Queen with a salary of 120,000 *livres*, in which capacity neither the Queen, nor she herself, nor anybody else knew what there was for her to do. There were also the honorariums granted to the holders of decorations : a pension of 4,000 *livres* was attached to every holder of the *cordon rouge*. There were also the "commissions" given and received. The Duc de Penthièvre drew his pay as Grand Admiral, in addition to which he received anchorage fees on every ship entering French ports, which amounted to another 90,000 *livres* (900,000 francs) per annum. The salary paid to the Princesse de Lamballe, mistress of the Queen's Household, was only 6,000 *livres*, plus a pension of 6,000 *livres* and 3,000 *livres* for personal expenses ; but the profits arising from her functions amounted to 150,000 *livres* (1,500,000 francs, present value !) The Duc de Gesvres was the Governor of Paris, where his town house was a gambling establish-ment, as we said above,—think of Monte Carlo ! He also held the right to sell at his own profit the erections put up for fireworks, from which source he drew in one year 50,000 *écus* (1,500,000 francs).

And the gentlemen of noble family who trafficked in anything that offered itself in the offices of Ministers! They swarmed therein, a frantic and flourishing crowd. The *noblesse dorée* were to be found there like carp in a pond. We all know how keenly sought after were the posts of Contractors of Finance. In the words of Voltaire the farming out of the taxes was an organized system of robbery, legalized on the most vast scale. Each time a vacancy arose there was a throng of importunate persons, each one striving his utmost to obtain the coveted post. The nobility did not canvass for these scandalously lucrative posts—fie! that would have been derogatory—but they were not above greasing palms in pushing forward the interests of their favourites. In 1738 a rich partisan promised to pay the Duc de la Trémoïlle 150,000 *livres* for having undertaken to push forward his claims, and a further annual sum of 20,000 *livres* if his efforts met with success; but they ended in failure, and the brother of the Farmer-General of Taxes, Lallemand de Betz, carried off the prize. Great was the Duc's discomfiture. The Prime Minister, Cardinal de Fleury, came to hear of it. What would have happened in our time? M. le Duc de la Trémoïlle would probably have been summoned before a Court of Justice; at the very least he would have been dishonoured. But Cardinal de Fleury did not see the matter in that light. He decided that the newly appointed Contractor-General must pay him 120,000 *livres* (1,200,000 francs) to console him for his discomfiture. It is true that the Duc de la Trémoïlle owed this sum to the Duc de Richelieu, who had won it from him at cards. A year after, la Trémoïlle was appointed Governor of the Ile de France.

The Abbé de Vermond, who had charge of the education of Marie Antoinette, wrote in frigid terms to the Empress Maria Theresa as follows:

"Your Majesty knows better than myself that by immemorial custom three-quarters of the appointments, honours, and pensions are awarded, not for services rendered, but by favour and outward repute. The motive animating this favour is that of birth, alliances and wealth; in almost every case it has no real foundation saving that of patronage and intrigue. This method of procedure is so firmly established that it is respected as some sort of justice, even by those who suffer from it the most; a worthy *gentilhomme* who is not in a position to shine by his alliances at the Court, nor by a profuse expenditure, would not dare to aspire to the command of a regiment, of whatever long date and distinction his services and his birth may have been. Twenty years ago the sons of Dukes, Ministers, people attached to the Court, relatives and *protégés* of mistresses, became Colonels at sixteen years of age ; M. de Choiseul caused a loud outcry by making the eligible age twenty-three ; but, in order to afford some compensation to favour and arbitrary choice, he handed over to the mere grace of the King, or rather to that of the Ministers, the appointment of Lieut.-Colonels and Majors which hitherto had been regulated by length of service, and also the Governorships and Commands of provinces and towns. You are aware that these posts have been greatly multiplied, and that they are awarded by interest and favour, like the regiments. The *cordon bleu* and the *cordon rouge*, sometimes even the Cross of St. Louis, are in a like case. Episcopal Sees and Abbeys continue still more under the rule of influence. Of the appointments connected with finance I dare not speak. Judicial posts are those most regulated by services rendered ; yet, notwithstanding, how greatly do interest and patronage influence the appointment of Intendants, Chief Presidents," and others!

Later on, in the time of the *émigrés*, a portion of this fine *noblesse dorée*, who had escaped the knife of the guillotine by flight, were to recall the great days now past. They were talking of the abuses that existed in former times. " Abuses ! " exclaimed Mme. de Monregard, " but that was the best part of those days ! " " Very good, Madame, but do not wonder that those who profited by them had their heads cut off."

As appointments, favours, pensions, benefices and sinecures were not enough for their needs, the *haute noblesse* plunged into mercenary alliances. They sold themselves, in spite of the cutting and cruel words thrust at them as usual by the Marquis de Mirabeau : " Nobles and financiers : two orders of men whom it is all the more difficult to bring into harmony inasmuch as the profession of the one (the nobility) when carefully analysed, is to ask for all it can get, and that of the other (finance) to take all it can." An *alliance de raison* was forged by the cupidity of one side and the vanity of the other.

It would be a lengthy and irksome task to give a list of the marriages made between noble houses and financiers in the eighteenth century. The prejudice against *mésalliances*, so firmly anchored in the aristocratic traditions of the seventeenth century, had disappeared, at any rate from among the ranks of the highest nobility. As M. Carré observes, " Very few people would have been able to gain entry for their sons into the Order of Malta, if proofs of nobility in the eight quarterings on the maternal side had been strictly required." In the time of Louis XIV, Champfort could write, " Almost all the women of any position, either in Versailles or Paris, are only *bourgeoises de qualité*." Hardly any members of the highest nobility living in Paris and frequenting Versailles any longer married except for money ; birth and lineage were becoming a second consideration.

This movement was very marked under the Regency, at the time when the frenzied finance of Law was to give it a disastrous impulse. The Marquis de Prié, a cousin of Louis XV, married the daughter of a tax-gatherer, Berthelot de Pléneuf, who was also the father-in-law of MM. de Matignon and de Nouvion ; moreover these noble alliances did not prevent our financier from being condemned in a court of law. The Marquis de la Fare became the son-in-law of Paparel who was condemned to death for breach of trust. La Fare inherited 4 million *livres* (40 million francs) with which he consoled himself for the disgrace to his family.

The eighteenth century, with no acquaintance with industrial manufacturing on a large scale, was built up chiefly on the wealth of financiers—this was the most distressing side of that great period—on wealth amassed by speculating on the toil of honest men, and passing into the hands of the nobility by marriage. And then, by means of their money, the tax-collectors raised themselves in the social scale by buying one of the numerous appointments open to those not belonging to the nobility. This had its repercussion on the general public. In their capacity as tax-contractors —the *nouveaux riches* in the highest ranks of the nobility—our *gentilshommes*, now become wealthy again, scattered money wholesale, and with incomes amounting to millions the first families in the land were no longer in a position to honour their commitments. The Prince de Guéménée failed for 35 millions ; the Prince de Soubise was head over ears in debt ; the Duke of Orléans, the wealthiest landholder in France, died owing 740 million francs.

If only this wealth, dissipated with such mad frenzy, had been used to good purposes ! Arthur Young bears sorrowful testimony in this respect :

" Thus it is whenever you stumble on a Grand Seigneur, even one that was worth millions, you are sure to find his property desert. The Duke of Bouillon's and the Prince of Soubise's are two of the greatest properties in France, and all the signs I have yet seen of their greatness are wastes, *landes*, deserts, fern, ling. Go to their residence, wherever it may be, and you would probably find them in the midst of a forest, very well peopled with deer, wild boars, and wolves."

Governor Morris, the celebrated United States Ambassador to France, was inspired with the same feelings when he wrote the following passage full of poignant truth :

" It would appear that at a certain period of their development there exists in human societies a natural tendency towards the rule of money, and where this comes uppermost it ruins and destroys the aristocracy. This takes the form of diminishing respect for virtue, because in reality, whatever may have been the origin of the great families, certain of their members have shed over each one of them a splendour which makes virtue an imperative duty. Moreover, I think that this assertion is justified by experience, and that such families are generally more distinguished and lofty in their conduct than the others. It matters little whether this is the fruit of education, or the example and respect for their ancestors, or whether it results from the affluence of wealth which places them above temptation ; conduct such as this should inspire a feeling of respect in others. But when the influence of wealth becomes great, the maxim ' Be rich, honestly if you can ; but be rich,' becomes a general one. From that moment I think we may date the decline."

XII.—*Life in the Château*

The bad state of the landed properties in the provinces, left to themselves by their wealthy owners, was remarked upon by foreigners :

" The fields are scenes of pitiable management, as the houses are of misery," writes Arthur Young. " Yet all this country highly improvable, if they knew what to do with it (he was speaking of Sologne) : the property, perhaps, of some of those glittering beings who figured in the procession the other day at Versailles. Heaven grant me patience while I see a country thus neglected—and forgive me the oaths I swear at the absence and ignorance of the possessors ! "

However, a return to country life began to set in. This became the fashion in high society about the middle of the eighteenth century. Famous writers—Rousseau, with his sentimental imagery, *l'Ami des Hommes*, with his picturesque and incisive pen, and Retif de la Bretonne, in vigorous and realistic portraiture—were celebrating the benefits arising from agricultural life. Voltaire, ennobled by his office as Gentleman-in-Waiting to the King, wished to offer an example of the *noblesse dorée* to his fellows. In 1759 he took possession of the Seigneurie of Tourney which the charming President de Brosses had given up to him. A contemporary writes about this as follows :

" All possible honours were paid him ; cannons, bombs and grenades were discharged ; he was received with drums and fifes, and all the peasantry assembled with their arms. The Curé made a speech. M. de Voltaire told him, ' Ask for anything you would like to put your parish in repair, and I will do it.' The girls of the parish presented him with flowers . . . and the health of the new seigneur was drunk, to the accompaniment of the firing of cannons. Voltaire was radiant."

At Ferney the illustrious philosopher had the soil dug, introduced the planting of root crops, and grew wheat and lucerne ; he planted vines and made wine ; his cattle sheds sheltered twenty choice oxen and fifty cows ; his sheep-yards were quoted as models ; like a real country gentleman he desired his house to be supplied exclusively from the produce of his property ; like a real village seigneur he had his own reserved pew in the church ; he was the first to be sprinkled with holy water and incensed, and he handed round the blessed bread.[1] At his orders poachers and marauders were energetically dealt with, even including the worthy old women who thought they might come and pick up sticks in his seigneurial woods. He wished to put into a state of cultivation the land held in common by the people, that is common land belonging to the inhabitants of the parish of Magny-lès-Ferney, but at this they protested ; finally they came to an understanding on this point ; the marshy commons were to be drained, the inhabitants of the village doing the work and Voltaire providing the necessary money, and as seigneur of the village he was to receive the proceeds of this land during the space of eighteen years, when it had been made suitable for cultivation.

"*Aimez vos champs et vos châteaux*" became a fashionable saying, but this return of the nobles to their country homes was not always to the advantage of the district. Display, and a life of luxury and pleasure formed their chief concern. *L'ami des Hommes* boldly tells them with sparkling frankness : " The land on a good *métairie* becomes an avenue and its produce zero ; the park, the rows of elms, the quincunx, labyrinth, and trees cropped into a round ball produce zero likewise."

Arthur Young reproaches them for thinking only of hunting : " Great lords love too much an environ of forest, boars, and huntsmen, instead of marking their residence by the accompaniment of neat and well-cultivated farms, clean cottages, and happy peasants." And when they did give a glance to agriculture, sometimes, as in Voltaire's case, it was only to make incursions into common lands, heaths and moors used by the villagers to pasture their cattle, and this was done without coming to any good understanding with them such as Voltaire reached from a sentiment of fellow-feeling and friendly relationship.

[1] *Pain bénit* in French churches is sometimes offered to the congregation cut up into little morsels of which they take one from a basket as it is handed round during the celebration of Mass. It is quite distinct, of course, from the Host, and bears the same character as holy water. (H. W.)

The ostentatious and brilliant life, of which we have a hundred descriptions, continued at the Château. Wealth and the refined manners of the Court, the grace and charming wit of that period, its *savoir vivre*, its gaiety and good taste made it a delightful place to stay at. It is at the château, more than anywhere else, that Talleyrand's remark finds its fitting place : " Whoever did not live before 1789 did not know the real charm of life."

The Maréchal de Saxe, crowned with laurels, retired to his château of Chambord and thither he brought a hundred pretty women to partake of his venison and wild boars, the spoils of his hunting, and to act plays. He went to the Court in quest of them, and wrote to his brother, Auguste III, the King of Poland :

" I count on their having a very amusing time. I have a gathering of very select and good-looking officers shut up in the château like monks. . . . Your Majesty will find me playing a rôle conformable with the life I have led. It is the lot of old waggoners to like still to hear the crack of the whip."

One great pastime was acting. There were few of these châteaux without its stage for performances. The caste was filled by noble ladies and actresses, young lords and actors. The stage manager was sometimes a retired actor. Fashionable poets, like Collé, were specially attached. At Sceaux, the Duchesse du Maine, the daughter-in-law of Louis XIV, and grand-daughter of the great Condé, trod the boards with Le Kain and Voltaire, the latter of whom took the part of Cicero in *Rome Sauvée*. He was excellent in it. Le Kain wrote in his *Mémoires :* " It was in very truth Cicero himself thundering from the tribune."

In his château of Chanteloup, Choiseul displayed a royal magnificence—acting, concerts, suppers, and an open table. The house-steward would reckon how many places at table he would have to provide by the number of people present in the *salon*. Marquises and Marchionesses would take their part in the orchestra, together with professionals, just as they did on the boards ; the Duc de Gesvres played the flute, and over the strings of a harp, plated with gold, ran lightly the fingers of the Duchesse de Castries.

This does not mean that agriculture was neglected. Enormous fortunes, such as that of Choiseul—an income of eight million francs at present value—could be put to many uses. Arthur Young admires his stables, which were magnificent buildings and very commodious. The noble lord had imported from Switzerland live-stock of exceptional excellence which he visited every day. The sheep folds of Chanteloup were the best constructed that Young had seen. When he fell from office Choiseul was exiled to his country property. Arthur Young adds : " The work of

Choiseul has merit in it, but it was all the merit of banishment. Chanteloup would neither have been built, nor decorated, nor furnished if the duke had not been exiled. It was the same with the Duke d'Aiguillon," and was the case with the Duchesse du Maine, the Comte de Maurepas, and Comte d'Argenson at Ormes where Beaumarchais made him the model of Comte Almaviva in his *Mariage de Figaro.*

XIII.—*Public Benefactors*

De Tocqueville quotes the letter written by a large landed proprietor in 1774 to the Intendant of his province ; he talks to him of opening up roads, instituting fairs, organizing a school for the study of manufacturing, and shows him how these things might be brought about. " This worthy citizen had not hitherto thought of these useful improvements for contributing to the well-being and prosperity of the inhabitants of his *seigneurie* ; but a *lettre de cachet* had banished him to his lands." Notwithstanding its efficaciousness on this occasion *lettres de cachet* were not always necessary, for many a seigneur in former days understood and carried out his duties without their brutal intervention. Some protected their tenants against the licence of troops passing through, others improved the means of communication and built hospitals at their own expense.

Saint-Simon speaks of the good works of Mme. de Pontchartrain. All that was to be seen was the Pontchartrain hospital and her community at Versailles, " which could not be hidden." " Everything else was buried in the most profound secrecy ; but the year 1709 betrayed it. Want and high prices had produced a kind of famine. She redoubled her almsgiving, and as everyone was dying of hunger in the country districts she opened bakehouses at Pontchartrain, instituted soup kitchens and collected people to distribute loaves of bread and soup to all comers, and cooked meat to the majority of them, so long as the sun was above the horizon." *L'Ami des Hommes* gives a hundred similar examples.

In how many parishes was the parish priest without any means to distribute to the poor, except what was placed at his disposal by the local seigneur ; how many rural districts had no other schools than those maintained by him !

The influence the nobility could exercise over the welfare of their tenants, and the progress of agriculture and local industries became more marked in the second half of the eighteenth century. The Maréchal de Belle-Isle took in hand the planting of mulberry trees at Bissy, near Vernon. The Baron de Dion introduced at Wandomme the system of irrigation recently introduced in England. "His flowing meadows," writes M. de Calonne, "are the finest in Artois." At Malesherbes, M. de Malesherbes had fine rows of trees planted along the roads ; over a distance of more than two miles they were all mulberry trees.

The Comte de Mailly established an expert and skilful doctor in his château of Louvrechy. He lodged him in the house, and allowed him 400 *livres* a year, over five *setiers* [1] of wheat, four cords of wood, four hundred faggots, two barrels of cider and a barrel of wine ; in return for this the doctor was to be at the disposal of all the sick in the district. The King became interested in this initiative, and authorized the doctor to wear the uniform of a military surgeon, which was a very fine one, and added considerably to his *prestige* among the country folk ; the King also sent boxes of medical stores to the Château of Louvrechy. The Marquis de Caulaincourt endeavoured to supplement the earnings of the peasants by industrial work ; and had them instructed in the making of muslin and *tulle* "after the Dutch manner." At Longpré, in Picardy, a cloth-weaving factory was established in 1778 by the Marquis de Louvancourt, and another by the Marquis d'Hervilly on his own property for weaving what went by the name of Courtrai cloth. The Marquise de Choiseul-Gouffier established a paper-making factory, for the ladies of the manor also did not wish to be behindhand in their efforts.

The Duchesse d'Anville opened up communications at her own expense to connect the village with the high roads, and distributed manuals on potato cultivation. This industry spread through the efforts of Parmentier and Marie Antoinette, but it was already known in France in the seventeenth century. The Duchesse d'Anville had silk workers brought from Languedoc to show people how to rear those precious little creatures which produce the silk, and how to deal with the silk thread they gave. The Comtesse de Lameth distributed spinning wheels by the hundred among the women and girls working in the fields.

In his interesting study on agricultural life in Picardy and Artois under the Ancien Régime, M. de Calonne mentions by name a large number of *gentilshommes* belonging to the district he was dealing with, who were living on their lands and occupying themselves in the most useful manner. Some of these gentlemen farmers have remained famous, such as the Duc de Rochefoucauld-Liancourt and the Duc de Charost, the Comte de Montyon and the Marquis de Turbilly.

The Duc de La Rochefoucauld, created a Field Marshal in 1788, liked country life. His estate of Liancourt in Beauvais became

_____
[1] *Setier :* 34 gallons. (H. W.)

an example to all. The noble Duke had established there a model farm, and a cloth factory where twenty-five looms were buzzing. " As the spinning of the thread for these looms had also been set on foot," notes Arthur Young, " this gives employment at home to many who had nothing to do." Girls of humble condition were received at the factory where they were taught, not only to spin cotton, but to read and write. When they married they received as a dowry a portion of their earnings which the Duke had had put by for them. The Prince de Croy and the Duc de La Rochefoucauld imported sheep and cattle of the finest pedigree from Lincolnshire, giving the highest price for them. We can imagine the trouble he was put to in doing this when we remember that the English, now great free-traders, at that time forbade under pain of death the export of their finest specimens of breeding stock. The Duke imported bulls and cows from Switzerland, and from Spain the famous merino sheep with their thick and valuable wool, and their general introduction, combined with that of potato growing and the sowing of foodstuffs for cattle, was one of the most important acquisitions of French agriculture in the eighteenth century. The Duchess busied herself over a dairy, less gracefully conceived than that at the Trianon, but on a larger and more practical scale. The Vicomtesse de Pons, the sister of the Duchesse de Liancourt, was a " great farmer." She was young and beautiful, and, as Arthur Young noted, " had more lucerne than anyone else in Europe." " She gave me some information on lucerne and the soil."

On his estate at Montyon, M. de Montyon offered prizes to those who were breaking up or draining the land. He initiated an admirable idea, then still too far in advance of the times, in his endeavour to found an agricultural system of credit, promising a prize of 5,000 francs to any association which would lend money to artisans and field-workers without interest.

Then there was the Duc de Charost. Twenty years before the Revolution he abolished statute labour due to the lord-of-the-manor throughout his vast domains. He founded a hospital on his property at Meillant, and at the Academy at Amiens he founded a prize of 600 *livres* for the best memorandum " touching matters relating to agriculture." ¦He was an all-round good little man. In speaking of him Louis XV said : " He is not much to look at, but he is keeping three of my provinces alive."

Many similar examples might be quoted. The Marquis de Mirabeau, who describes so well the duties incumbent on the country gentleman, added example to precept : he set up on his estates in Limousin an office for smoothing over disputes ; at Fleury he had nine hundred pounds of cheap bread baked daily for the benefit " of poor people, who fight among themselves to get it."

We come to the Marquis de Turbilly, born in 1717 of an ancient Angevin family at the château de Fontenailles, on the borders of Anjou. His enterprise in preparing his land for cultivation at Turbilly, not far from La Flèche, and his book, *Mémoires Originaux sur les Défrichements*, became famous even in England. His intelligent activity extended to all domains of agriculture. He set up pens for sheep in the district, introduced everywhere the best agricultural implements and artificial manures, and imported the best seeds from distant countries, especially cabbage seed to produce the largest kinds. He invented special implements for breaking up the soil, weed extractors and grub-hoes, which he let out on hire for the public benefit. The population on his large estates, running to over 3,000 acres, doubled in one generation. In 1763 the King's Council granted him common lands to break up. The Government thought it wise to encourage his useful initiatives, but it was the downfall of this noble and benevolent gentleman ; the people having the right to use these common lands brought him before the courts of justice, and law-suits followed without end. We well know the long-drawn-out complications and entanglements of matters of this kind at that period. Turbilly was ruined.

None the less, cordial good fellowship in the relations between seigneur and vassal was still maintained in many districts of the country. The Bailli de Mirabeau writes on the 25th September, 1760 :

" I am at Harcourt. What a joy it is on *fête* days to see all the people everywhere about the château and nice little peasant boys and girls coming up to stare at their good patron right under his nose, and almost taking his watch out of his pocket to see the trinkets on his chain—and all this with an air of fraternity having no familiarity about it. The good Duke does not allow his vassals to go to law ; he listens to them and then gives his judgment, bringing them into agreement with each other with admirable patience."

Admiral Comte du Chaffault, one of the best officers in the French navy, went to his property in La Vendée as soon as he came ashore, and passed his time in the midst of his peasants. He would go and find them in the fields, take off his coat, and hanging it on a bush would handle the plough himself. So great was the veneration in which he was held that the country folk would never pass his uniform coat, hanging on the hedges of the field, without saluting it. A descendant of his, the Comte du

Chaffault, has been kind enough to confirm this detail : " The
men uncovered and the women dropped a curtsey as they passed
the gold-braided coat of the Admiral where, between two battles,
it hung on a bush by the road."

XIV.—Seigneurial Rights and Privileges

The nobility possessed rights and privileges, and these aroused
violent protests at the end of the eighteenth century, especially
from the pen of men of letters and from the lips of lawyers.

The records of the Lorraine peasantry, drawn up for the States
General of 1789, embody a short historical study, of a nice accuracy,
on the origin of the feudal dues exacted on their *seigneuries*.

" Our community," wrote the good people of Sommerviller, " is
surcharged in many things which the seigneurs allege are their due
by right, things which our ancestors promised them in order to have
their protection in time of war ; but the ruined castle of to-day has
no defensive use for us. Besides, we are under the rule of a very
puissant King. We hope that these alleged rights will be abolished."

History can find no word to modify in this little statement,
neither can it in one formulated on the same occasion by the people
belonging to Lignéville. In the latter case the question concerned
more particularly the right to have night watchmen, an obligation
imposed on the tenants to come on certain occasions and provide
a watch for the seigneur's castle :

" The former Dukes of Burgundy often tried to take possession of
the estates of the Dukes of Lorraine. They employed armed forces :
the troops always began their ravages on the borders of each estate,
and their unfortunate subjects living there were the first victims
sacrificed to the fury of the conquerors. The only remedy was to
oppose force by force. Nearly all the seigneurs exalted themselves
into sovereigns, and kept troops in their pay in order to defend their
possessions and those of their subjects ; but the latter were only
protected in so far as they indemnified their protector, either by
providing food for his troops or by recognizing themselves as his debtors
in the form of certain services consisting of the payment in kind of
several days of obligatory labour (*corvée*), of quit-rent and annual
fees. At the present day this protection and defence are a dead letter.
. . . Notwithstanding this, none of the rights and dues which the
seigneurs obtained have been suppressed. . . ."

A large number of writers, both under the Ancien Régime and
under modern conditions—the Marquis de Mirabeau, Comte Beugnot, Tocqueville, H. Taine, the Vicomte de Broc, have stated that
in the neighbouring countries to France feudal rights were exercised

much more harshly in the eighteenth century than in France, and that, in spite of this, the people made no protest. In Germany the people were still real serfs ; but as a set-off to this the seigneur was a real feudal lord bound by the very rigorous duties which linked the mediæval baron with his vassals, providing them with a safe asylum in case of necessity, feeding them in times of want, making provision for widows, and acting as guardian to orphans under very strictly defined obligations. It was a system of inter-change of rights and duties. All was for the best, in the words of Candide.

People—among them very great minds like Le Play and his disciples—have reproached the royal Government with having progressively despoiled the provincial seigneurs of their authority. This evolution was imposed by the transformation taking place in the life of the nation, by the relationships existing between neighbouring *seigneuries* and the different provinces, by the multi-plication of means of communication, by the expansion of trade and industry, and, in a word, by the constituent character of the nation which was demanding greater uniformity in its customs and in the policy of its rulers. And this same movement con-verging to one centre, which preluded and prepared the way for the royal policy, came about in the different provinces, and even in the *seigneuries*, at the hands of the local authorities. Take Lorraine, for example, before its restoration to France. " The Dukes of Lorraine," writes Cardinal Mathieu, " had little by little taken all political, juridical and military authority from their nobles, but they had not at the same time despoiled them of the honorific and pecuniary privileges which were their reward. People were asking, therefore, why they were paying for two budgets, while they had only one government, and why there should be such a shocking disproportion between privileged rights and services rendered." That is exactly what we see happening in France.

Seigneurial rights were divided into three categories—honorific, productive and judicial.

Honorific rights in the eighteenth century were confined to questions of precedence in church and in processions ; we should add the right possessed by the seigneur to be saluted by his tenants with bared head, or by a curtsey. This salute was obligatory on the part of those paying him dues, and a failure in this respect might lead to punishment by the King's officials. Finally only gentlemen of noble birth had the right to surmount the tower, or gable-end of their manors, with a weather-cock of square shape, a symbol of the feudal banner.

The dues paid in money were very numerous, extremely varied, and of very diverse nomenclature, a fact which exaggerated their importance in the eyes of historians. A first group comprised dues directly exacted in money or kind ; land taxes, *lods et ventes*, dues receivable on the price realized on the sale of any heritable property on his domain, succession rights, and *terrage* or *champart*, called *carpot* in the case of vineyards (the toll of vegetables or wheat sheaves), formed the principal. Then there were tonnage dues and tolls on roads and fords. A third group consisted of *banalités* (dues receivable for the obligatory use of the seigneur's public bakery, etc.), a fourth of *corvées* (a toll of a certain number of days of obligatory service), and a fifth of hunting rights.

The *cens* (quit-rent) represented the chief seigneurial right, and was the one which stamped, as with a trade-mark, land occupied by the peasants. The man who paid this quit-rent belonged to the seigneur. The rent was exacted annually, was immutable, indivisible, and could not be seized, but it had become a very light charge with the depreciation in the value of money.

The feudal rights, therefore, which took the shape of money, represented in the time of Louis XV only a trifling amount, with the exception of those like the *lods et ventes* which were in proportion to the amount realized by the sale, a price nominally higher, of course, as the value of money fell. The *lods et ventes* levied on properties sold generally came to a twelfth part of the price realized.

The *terrage* or *champart* was of all the feudal dues the one which seemed to press most heavily. It took every twelfth sheaf of corn. When it was a question of vineyards it might even go so far as to take a quarter of the vintage crop.

The *banalités*, together with the hunting rights, were the most contested feudal dues. The former imposed an obligation on the tenants, at the cost of paying a due therefor, to use the public bakery, mill, wine-press and breeding sires of the seigneur. The origin is easy to disentangle. The seigneur alone was in a position to build a mill, bakery, wine-press, and to procure breeding sires, and these he placed at the disposal of his vassals in return for a contribution.

There are still in existence a few public bakeries in France, which naturally are no longer subject to any seigneurial dues. That standing at Savigny-lès-Beaune is in perfect condition. The people of the district are right in saying that it used to be the seigneur's bakery, since become public after the Revolution. Each person may bring their loaf to be baked in it. The street, " Rue du Four," found in so many localities, has no other origin for its name.

The establishing of *banalités* was not left to the Seigneur's caprice.

The King forbade the exaction, without a well-founded title, of any dues whatsoever, for the public use of a mill, bakery, wine-press or breeding sire.

One vexatious consequence of these *banalités* was that the seigneurs of the eighteenth century, too large a number of whom were non-resident, farmed them out to contractors who, to the detriment of the peasant, did their best to squeeze out for themselves the greatest profit they could wring from them.

The public bakery was no longer properly heated, the miller was of questionable honesty, and the breeding sire was not an animal of the first quality. Tenants complained of the insufficient number of public wine-presses. The people of Blainville wrote in their report for 1789 :

" The baneful experience we have undergone in different years, and particularly in this last year (1788), through the deficiency in adequate numbers of wine-presses, has caused us the loss of a great quantity of our wine, to such an extent that more than four hundred measures have turned sour and have been completely spoilt through over-fermentation of the grape juice. The contractor does not fail, however, to exact a considerable fee, every eleventh measure for pressing, and, not content with that, he requires in addition that private individuals should provide men to assist in the pressing, and board him and his assistants at their expense."

A large number of *banalités* had been redeemed at the time of the Revolution. Turgot would have liked to apply this to all.

What we have said about the *banalités* applied also to the tolls, that is, dues exacted by authority of the lord-of-the-manor at the cross-roads, the passage of water-courses, and on tow-paths. Some of these were very lucrative. In times past they were justifiable ; the bridges had been built and the banks kept in repair by the seigneur. He had made secure the transit of merchandise over his lands. The archives of the thirteenth century have handed down to us more than one decree pronounced by the royal judges condemning the feudal lord to indemnify the merchant robbed of his goods on lands belonging to his fief. The following is an amusing story dating from that period which depicts the customs of those times :

A poor mercer on a journey had tethered his horse in a field belonging to the seigneurial fief. The beast would be able to browse there, for he had no oats to give him, and so the mercer left his nag to the safe keeping of the seigneur and of God. Now during the night the nag was devoured by a she-wolf. The mercer therefore betook himself to the Baron's seat of justice :

" I placed my beast under your protection and under that of God."

" How much was the animal worth ? "

" Sixty *sous*."

" Here then are thirty for you ; for the remainder you must make application to God."

Conditions were no longer the same in the eighteenth century, and these numerous tolls had become a hindrance to commerce. On several occasions the royal administration suppressed a large number of them, twelve hundred in one year, and among them were tolls belonging to the highest personages in the kingdom.

We have drawn attention to only a portion of these seigneurial rights which the landed nobility exacted under the most various forms. A complete enumeration of them, with explanations, would take too long. We must, however, make special mention of the succession dues, and dues exacted when a vassal died intestate. In certain provinces this right went to the extent of giving the entire inheritance to the seigneur in cases where the children were not living with their father at his decease ; there were also the dues called by the name of *nouvel entrant*, that is, those levied on every new-comer who established himself on the lands of the *seigneurie*, those on property left vacant, the tax on strayed animals, treasure trove, of which a portion went to the seigneur, fees payable on corkage and cabarets, the gauging of casks at the wine-sellers, etc.

By the side of these dues claimed by the nobility, their exemption from taxes seemed to the people to be still more iniquitous and vexatious. The nobility were free of the poll-tax, which was a direct contribution. Oh ! that poll-tax, that execrated and terrible tax, become still more burdensome owing to the manner in which it was levied rather than by the amount demanded from those liable to it ! The nobles did not pay this tax. This privilege was justifiable in its origin at a time when the noble undertook military service and the defence of the country almost exclusively ; but since the establishment of a standing army and its development under Louis XIV, the people also became liable for this. In addition, as already mentioned, by fresh admissions into the ranks of the nobility and by the purchase for money of posts belonging, strictly speaking, to the middle and lower classes, most of the wealth was in the hands of the nobility, and they were exempted from paying the chief impost, the poll-tax. In practice, however, and especially since the coming of Louis XVI to the throne, this inequitable grievance had been lessened to some extent. In this connection Sénac de Meilhan writes :

" The exemption from the *taille* (poll-tax) brought with it the privilege of having three ploughs for one's own use and profit; but in order to avail himself of this privilege a nobleman had to improve his land himself; this privilege ceased if the land was let out. If we take into consideration how very few *gentilshommes* were in a position to profit by this exemption it will appear to have been of little value. The large landed proprietors, all the noblemen who were occupied at the Court or in the army, and all those who lived in the capital or held positions in the provincial towns, let out their lands, and thus only a portion of the nobility enjoyed this advantage."

We have seen how greatly the poor nobility were worthy of consideration, but it was just that section which lived in contact with the peasantry. The country nobleman was almost a peasant himself, and the privilege he possessed (exemption from the *taille*) was bound to strike his fellow labourer as all the more revolting on that account.

XV.—*The Corvée and Hunting Rights*

Much has been said about the *corvées seigneuriales*, and the unfortunate peasants who were obliged to go out during the night and scour the ponds and ditches round the château, the haunts of frogs, lest their incessant croaking should disturb their lord's slumber. This matter lent itself to exaggeration. The *corvées seigneuriales* did exist—that is compulsory work for the lord-of-the-manor—but, relatively speaking, they were not of great importance. Hardly ever did they arouse complaints, and they were not of the ridiculous nature often attributed to them. The *corvée* which *did* however press very heavily on dwellers in country districts was the royal *corvée* for the upkeep of the high-roads.

We now come to those seigneurial rights which down to the end of the Ancien Régime provoked the most indignant complaints—namely, hunting and shooting rights.

Hunting has been man's great passion from the earliest times and the most remote ages—it is the heritage of the cave-dwellers. From the time of Charlemagne down to that of Louis XVI it was the special distraction of kings. The feudal barons and the nobility of the Ancien Régime were addicted to it almost to the exclusion of anything else. Le *droit de chasse* was reserved to the *seigneur justicier*, one endowed with magisterial authority, and was forbidden under severe penalties to all others. The punishment for a man who dared to trespass on the privileges of the nobility in this respect went as far, in the middle of the seventeenth century, as condemnation to the galleys, confiscation of his goods and the penalty of death. It required the passing of the *Eaux et Forêts* decree in 1669 before the penalty of capital punishment disappeared from the hunting laws, but the prohibition to kill game continued to be rigorously enforced upon all persons not of noble blood.

" We forbid merchants, artisans, bourgeois and inhabitants of towns, boroughs, parishes, villages and hamlets, peasants and all persons of humble birth of whatever condition and quality, not being in possession of fiefs, *seigneuries* and high magisterial functions, in any place, form or manner, to hunt any fur or feathered game whatsoever."

The *capitaineries* were portions of land subject to special jurisdiction and restrictions as regards hunting rights; of these the most important were the royal *capitaineries*, those of Vincennes, Fontainebleau, Meudon, Compiègne and Sénart. . . . There were also *seigneurial capitaineries*.

Throughout the extent of a *capitainerie* it was forbidden to enclose a property with walls, hedges or ditches, which would have interfered with hunting; a man was forbidden to keep arms in his house and to walk abroad with a dog, unless it had a billet of wood hanging from its neck; he was forbidden to reap before the end of June, and to enter his own fields between the 1st May and the Feast of St. John—by the Feast of St. John the partridges are fledged, and neither my lady partridge, nor sitting pheasant must be disturbed. It has been very justly remarked that no such consideration was given to women in childbirth. The Duke of Orleans re-established the *capitainerie* of Villers-Cotterets, the hunting rights of which had been allowed to lapse; within a few days sixty farmsteads and properties were put up for sale on account of the vexations to which the proprietors would find themselves exposed.

In these *capitaineries* the King's Lieutenants acted with extreme rigour. Beaumarchais in his *Mariage de Figaro* thunders forth in immortal eloquence against the prerogatives of the nobility; but in his capacity as Lieutenant-General of Preserves in the warren at the Louvre, he condemned an honest woman to a fine of one hundred *livres* and ordered her to demolish the walls of her enclosure, and her barn, as they might prove a hindrance to Louis XV when hunting with his pack of courtiers. The game-keepers of a Marquis, Prelate or General would quite callously shoot any private individual caught hunting game, and such murders went unpunished.

The preserves were so jealously guarded that we come across idyllic scenes, and only a Virgil is wanted to put them into dactyl and spondee. For ten leagues all round Paris the prohibition to fire a gun was so well ensured that partridges could have been seen walking familiarly along the roads in the company of man. Stags and hinds wandered around man's dwellings in the full light of day—in graceful contradiction of the old adage that man is the only animal before whom all others flee. That was all very well, but the hares, rabbits and partridges devoured the crops, and the inhabitants were no longer able to sow. They were obliged to stay up watching at night in order to preserve their harvests, and were not even permitted to kill the game which came to eat up what they had gathered for their own use. Disturbances took place. In 1754 the peasants in the environs of Mantes and Meudon, armed with cudgels, assembled by hundreds under the leadership of their parish priests. It was a *Jacquerie*,[1] but one directed against the hares and partridges, several thousands of which were killed. The gendarmerie were called out against these worthy people who had a mind to preserve their crops.

Prohibitions in favour of the pleasures of the chase went to still greater lengths : it was forbidden to remove the thistles and dandelions from the fields without the presence of watchful keepers, and we can well imagine that the latter were not always ready to give their time to this task of supervision ; it was forbidden to cut sainfoin before the Feast of St. John, to extract weeds from the growing crop after the 1st May, and added to all these prohibitions there was the obligation to plant out the fields immediately after the harvest, that is to plant thorn bushes to form a cover for the game. We can picture to ourselves the multiplicity and violence of the complaints in the reports for the year 1789. We will quote those brought forward by the good people of Bettoncourt (Lorraine) :

" That the seigneurs may be forbidden to hunt among the standing crops and vines, which often happens, even at the height of the harvest and at the gathering in of the grapes ; it would be dangerous to remonstrate with them." One's heart is wrung at such things.

To their hunting privileges, entailing the destruction of crops, may be added that of the seigneur's pigeon-house. Formerly of slight importance, these privileged pigeon-houses assumed formidable proportions. There were some containing ten thousand pigeons. We read in the report presented by Thiaucourt (Lorraine) : " The pernicious custom of having pigeon-houses often puts private individuals to the necessity of resowing their land " on account of all the seed devoured.

---

[1] *Jacquerie :* a murderous rising of the people : the origin of the word dates from the rising of the peasants or Jacques in the Ile de France against the nobility which broke out on the 28th May, 1358. (H. W.)

At any rate these aristocratic hunting parties, however injurious to humble folk, and humiliating to all not of noble birth, offered a brilliant spectacle to the happy participators therein. Watch them in their bustling brilliancy in the forests of Villers-Cotterets or Compiègne, Amboise or Montmorency. Horses and hounds by the hundred, lords and ladies in scarlet coats ornamented with gold and silver lace, and sky-blue facings, the correct costume for stag hunting ; for the *vautrait*, or hunting the wolf, wild boar or roebuck, the dress was of dark green with silver lace and crimson facings. The prettiest and most elegant women followed in open carriages from which would burst forth peals of laughter mingled with little exclamations of joy ; the forest resounded with the sonorous " hallali " of the huntsmen ; and a repast, graced with a golden flood of champagne, was served on the grass in a clearing ; in the evening they danced beneath the crystal lustres in the large halls of the château.

What is there to complain of ? You do not hear the weeping in the cottages. . . .

XVI.—*The Seigneurial Courts of Justice*

The Kings of France were often reproached, and still are, for having brought into being a central authority which deprived the local *seigneuries* of their sovereign rights. Monarchical government, as we have said, was only obeying a necessity. The more one studies the Ancien Régime the more one has to realize this. Provincial administrations like those of Lorraine and Savoy, which had not yet in the eighteenth century returned to France, had to submit to the same obligation. Under the government of their dukes these provinces experienced exactly the same phenomenon ; it was unavoidable as soon as the people of France were constituted a nation.

It is a remarkable thing that the suzerain right which the *seigneuries* retained the longest was that appertaining to the administration of justice, and naturally it preserved greater vitality in the country than in the towns ; but it was still maintained in the towns, and in the larger ones to a surprising extent. It was a relic of the formation of French towns out of the family, each of which was made up of a collection of several *seigneuries* existing close to each other. Is it not astonishing to be able to state that in the year 1674, in the middle of the reign of Louis XIV, Paris was still divided into thirty-four different seigneurial jurisdictions, including that belonging to the King which, it is true, was the most important, but did not extend over half the town ? There were sixteen seigneurial courts at Angers, nine at Troyes, and in proportion elsewhere. M. Marcel Marion estimates these courts of justice existing in France at the end of the seventeenth century at the number of sixty or eighty thousand, four hundred and sixty of which were within the electorate of Paris.

These jurisdictions were divided into *haute, basse* and *moyenne.* The *haute justice* gave the right to pronounce sentence of death, and of this the gallows, decorated with the arms of the lord-of-the-manor, was the outward sign. The bodies of those condemned to death were hung on this gibbet. François Villon's wonderful ballad is well-known. The gibbet was made of wooden posts bound to each other by transverse beams ; the number of these posts signified the rank the judge held in the hierarchy of the nobility : a mere squire set up a gallows with two posts ; a baron had four, a count six, and a duke as many as ten. The royal gibbet at Montfaucon reared sixteen posts on the famous mound where crows came to peck the bodies of criminals swinging to and fro in the wind, " plus becquetés que dés a coudre," more rent by pecks than a thimble. But this *haute justice* possessed by the nobility had lost much of its former authority in the seventeenth and eighteenth centuries. It was not allowed to take cognizance of cases reserved to the King, which included rebellion, false money, heresy, abduction, incendiarism and parricide. The sentences they passed were subject to the right of appeal. Nevertheless we still find cases of such seigneurial justice being exercised in the seventeenth century, as for example, the sentence passed at Dampierre on the 13th June, 1679, condemning an individual who had " homicided " another " to be decapitated until death shall ensue."

The *moyenne justice* took cognizance of weights and measures, and condemned in fines amounting to sixty *sous Parisis*. These *sous*, like the *sous Tournois*, were silver coins ; the *sous Parisis* were of 25 per cent. higher value than the *sous* struck at Tours.

The *basse justice* only took account of trivial disputes in everyday life.

The sentences passed by these seigneurial tribunals were subject to the right of appeal, and with the multiplicity of different ranks in the feudal hierarchy, these appeals might involve endless complications. M. Marion quotes the following example : " In the county of Dunois, Rameau was subordinated to Prépalteau, itself subordinate to Montigny, which in its turn was subordinate to the Royal Bailiwick of Blois, from which appeals might be made to Parliament." Here we have four different stages of appeal. The reports drawn up by the Third Estate in Rennes in 1789 lay stress on the " multiplicity of the stages of appeal which sometimes reach seven in number." The lines written by Loyseau, the writer on feudalism, are absolutely true : " What poor peasant suing for his sheep or cows would not rather abandon them to the man unjustly retaining them than be compelled to pass through five or six different tribunals before obtaining a verdict ? And, if he makes up his mind to go on with the case to the end, is there a sheep or a cow which can live all that time ? Even its owner will die before his case is finally judged." Domains elevated to the rank of territorial dukedoms had the privilege of appealing direct to Parliament. We can imagine the value attaching to this privilege and how greatly these promotions were sought after. This is a testimony, among a hundred others, of the usefulness and the necessity of that work of centralization which became incumbent on the King.

The seigneur owning judicial rights took possession of his domain with solemn pomp. He was received with honours by the local authorities, with whom he visited the manorial gaol, the keys of which were presented to him ; if any prisoner were being detained there, which in truth was rather rare, he set him at liberty in token of the joyful event ; he was installed with much ceremony in the church with all the honours he had the right to therein. Voltaire did not fail to be intoxicated with all these fine ceremonies when he became the lord of Tourney ; but his *seigneurie*, which carried judicial rights, was not without its inconveniences, and Voltaire was less flattered by them than by the homage rendered to him. The *seigneurie*, issuing from the development of the family, had preserved right down to the eighteenth century many surprising traces of family solidarity, or solidity as it was called under the Ancien Régime. The seigneur had still to take charge of all children found within his boundaries. He was still responsible for those who paid dues to him, like a father responsible for his children. The high and *puissant* lord of Ferney and Tourney was quite amazed at it, and we find *Messire* Voltaire summoned by the judicial authorities of Gex because one of his " subjects " was unable to pay the costs of a judgment.

"I am persecuted by the Council," writes Voltaire. " They would have me believe that there is no finer thing than to pay other people's costs, and they are going to seize my oxen to do me honour." (Letter of the 17th March, 1760.)

In a number of *seigneuries*—the lesser ones as a matter of fact —the lord-of-the-manor would sit in person at his tribunal, and pronounce sentence in a fatherly manner more from the point of view of equity rather than that of strict law. In the sixteenth, and especially in the seventeenth centuries, our Rhadamanthus took his seat under the big trees in the village square, whence arose the term "*juges dessous l'orme*"; or else he would hear the litigants while sitting on his lawn, or at the door of the manor, like Saint Louis under the oaks at Vincennes, under the arbours in his garden in Paris, or on the doorstep of his royal palace.

They would explain the law to them, perhaps not always in a very legal fashion, but in terms that could be understood; they would smooth over disputes, often going themselves to the houses where the disputants lived, settling the matter without expense, and without all the trouble of lawyers and quill pens. Even in 1789 a certain number of the reports drawn up by the Third Estate asked that the seigneurial courts might be retained, averring that there was not much to be altered. This happened in the case of Champs, in the Bailiwick of Auxerre, and at Vaux-sur-Yonne which demanded an extension of their jurisdiction " so that the inhabitants in the districts may have the advantage of being judged by them in the last resort for a very small cost." We read in the report sent in by Beauvais : " As regards seigneurial courts, the communities of some districts solicit their being maintained, and even request that they should pronounce final judgments on sums up to a certain amount, without the right of appeal."

But the greater number of seigneurs exercised justice through the intermediary of officials appointed by themselves, the chief of which was the Bailli ; next came the Procurator Fiscal, corresponding to our modern Procureur de la République, then notaries, clerks of the court, sergeants and sheriff's officers. The *gruyer* judged offences against the forest laws.

These agents of seigneurial justice were, as one might suppose, very small fry. The important *seigneuries* chose their Bailli from among the advocates living in the neighbouring town. In order to augment their earnings many of these petty magistrates exercised their functions in several localities, in as many as ten, and even more, at one and the same time. Cardinal Mathieu gives an instance of an advocate in Lorraine who, in the year 1778, was a judge in twenty-eight villages. These judges, acting for the *seigneuries* in so many different places, took the course of exercising their functions more comfortably in their own homes, to which they made the litigants come " by a change of venue." Grosley, the Academician, exercised the functions of *mayeur* (judge) in an Abbey, and of judge in two villages ; but our Baillies were very rarely men of any education. They were more often only beadles of the village churches. From a thatched barn, their seat of justice, they would repair to the sacristy where they would busy themselves with the vestments and sacred vessels, and then ring the bell for the service.   In many districts, as in that of Beauce, the seigneur's judge was paid in kind—a ham from each pig killed in the village, the first pint of wine from the grape harvest, and the right to a seat at wedding feasts. A number of seigneurs chose one of their farmers to be their Bailli, sometimes one of their servants.

It is true domestic conditions under the Ancien Régime differed from our own. Figaro is an accurate portrait. Body servants wore a sword in conformity with their origin, which formed one of the grades of chivalry.   The secretary of the editorial staff of the *Mercure* was a *valet-de-chambre*. Dangeau had part of his famous journal written out by a domestic servant. The Baillies often added more humble callings to their magisterial functions, but they were forbidden to keep a tavern. They were also forbidden to hold their courts for administering justice in cabarets or in cemeteries. As we said above, their tribunals were generally installed in various little barns. The Bailli, as sovereign judge, pronounced his judgments seated on a large truss of hay, and his clerk of the court would have his inkstand set on a wash-tub turned upside down. The seigneurial gaols were still more rudimentary. At Nitry, in Burgundy, those convicted were put under a large wine barrel set over a hole dug in the ground.

This primitive and simple contrivance did not mean, moreover, that justice had been negligently rendered. We see in the pages of Retif de la Bretonne that these simple village tribunals were sometimes marked by the greatest conscientiousness. An atmosphere of great familiarity, in the best sense of the word, and a real concern to reach equitable conclusions, characterized them. A few good glasses of wine, especially in the vine-growing districts, were not neglected, and judge, litigants, advocates, witnesses, and the public clinked glasses together without any ceremony.

Retif speaks of his grandfather, Provost of Nitry :

" Audience was given at his own expense at his own house, and there was no other host but the judge." Each year, at Martinmas, after the harvest, the seigneur convoked in general assembly those subject to pay dues within the confines of his boundaries ; these were indeed rustic assemblies which in many provinces right down to 1789 recalled the memory of the feudal courts of old.   In Lorraine they were called *plaids annaux*, annual courts of pleas.

The inhabitants of the *seigneurie* would meet together in the great hall of the manor, or in the barn. The Bailli presided, assisted by the procurator-fiscal. The clerk to the court began the proceedings by reading out the list of the rights appertaining to the seigneur, and then asked if any present had any observation to make. Next in order came an enumeration of the fines and other penalties that had been pronounced by the seigneurial court during the current year. This was the moment for settling up any of the aforesaid fines which had so far been neglected. They were reminded of the rules laid down by the seigneur, and these were sometimes amended or completed ; they comprised the prohibition to frequent cabarets during the hours of divine service, or late at night, to disturb any wedding festivities by creating an excessive din, to bring to church very young children who might start to scream and disturb the service, to enter barns with a light, and cattle sheds with lanterns that were not closed, etc. Finally, if the occasion arose, they would proceed to appoint new seigneurial officials with the advice of those inhabitants present.

When it happened that the same seigneur had several villages under his jurisdiction, the baron, in his capacity as judge, together with his Bailli, might have been seen proceeding from one locality to another on their way to settle the differences which might have arisen among these worthy folk. The seigneur rode on horseback, and by his side ambled the Bailli on his more modest mule or donkey.

The village Bailli, a dispenser of justice marked with a sanctimonious air of solemnity, became the special favourite of comic authors in the eighteenth century ; he was represented as a worthy man, pompous and stupid ; he had a red nose, for he liked good wine ; those under his jurisdiction would find pleasure in making a mock of him, but without any malice, for below his flowing wig Messire Bailli bore a stout belly, and the pot-bellied are not vindictive.

Square posts, on the top of which were painted the arms borne by the seigneur, defined the limits of his jurisdiction, but, in spite of this precaution, there was still terrible confusion. The entanglement between seigneurial, abbatial, urban and royal jurisdictions, and between bailiwicks and *seneschalties* made up an inextricable confusion. Nothing was clearly defined. We should always bear in mind the origin of all the institutions which flourished under the Ancien Régime, those spontaneous products of thousands of family groups which had formed and spread all over the country, each one of them developing its active energies as far as possible. Thence came their wonderful vitality, originality and force, but also that confusion, which constituted the beauty, strength and weakness of the Ancien Régime.

We not only find the same village, but one and the same house saddled upon two different jurisdictions—the bedroom in one and the hall in another. The occupier would be informed that he was summoned to appear in a certain royal bailiwick, or in a certain seigneurial jurisdiction, and he took great care to receive the clerk of the court in the room of the house belonging to the other jurisdiction, where he was able to oppose a triumphant refusal.

To this confusion was added the multiplicity of officials employed by these tiny little jurisdictions, baillies, procurators, clerks of the court, *gruyers*, sergeants, mounted ushers, and ushers bearing wands, guardians of the peace and notaries in unimaginable numbers—"horrible animals who batten on law proceedings," as an Intendant under Louis XIV called them. One can well imagine the manifold items of costs involved in all this procedure. In the reports for Blainville, in Lorraine, we read : " The poor widowers, widows and orphans of the district, apart from the loss they may have sustained of a wife or other relations, often find themselves despoiled of the little that has been left by the deceased, after it has passed through the hands of the official procurators, clerks of the court and valuers for auction."

Since these officials of justice, including the Baillies, were badly paid—sometimes not at all—they had to make their money out of those subject to their jurisdiction. Some had bought their office and had to recover the price they had paid, both principal and interest ; moreover these official duties were often farmed out by the seigneur, and the contractor took care to get as much as he could out of them. In order to swell the number of plaints which would have to come before them for settlement, the seigneurial officials would create them. In a report presented by Saint-Sulpice-de-Roumagnac (Dordogne) we read : " Procurators crop up everywhere in great numbers in these country districts, without their being first called in, which fact is liable to foster suits, and they do not fail to seize the opportunity. They overawe the most peaceable peasant and compel him, in spite of himself, to bring an action, which assuredly he would not have thought of doing of himself . . ." " The flock," writes the Bailli de Mirabeau, " is devoured by lice."

As a set-off, and actuated by similar motives, the seigneurial officials of justice were singularly tolerant in dealing with criminals. Their watchword was to go to sleep. To summon offenders, lodge and board them, give a preliminary judgment and then send them on to competent jurisdictions entailed expenditure and no profit. Renauldon speaks of this in his *Traité des Droits Seigneuriaux* : " The seigneurs, their judges, from fear of incurring the expenses of a criminal trial, and from fear of instituting law proceedings for which they will not be paid, make no investigations into the most atrocious crimes."

On these grounds the attacks directed against the seigneurial jurisdictions from the beginning of the seventeenth century were justified. In his *Discours sur l'Abus des Justices de Village*, Loyseau terms them *mangeries* (process of eating up), where the people were devoured by the lowest grades of law practitioners : " In order to obtain a paltry fee," he says, " a man must fill up with drink the judge, the clerk to the court and the attorney in the case, in some fine tavern which is the spot where the documents are drawn up, and where very often cases are discharged in favour of the man who pays the reckoning."

The royal government, more particularly at the close of the reign of Louis XV, endeavoured to remedy these abuses. Abbé Terray kept a watchful eye that the Intendants should " put an end to this crying evil " (1772), which, like so many others, derived from the origins of French society and from its attachment to tradition.

In 1789 a number of reports drawn up by the people, some of which we have quoted, asked that the seigneurial courts might be retained. Means of communication were slow and difficult ; the court of justice of the Bailiwick was a long way off, and that of the Parliament still further ; in short, notwithstanding the disadvantages attaching to them as given above, the seigneurial courts entailed very little expense, sometimes none at all. Both the judge and his officials were acquainted with the people amenable to their judicial authority, and, as a rule, gave more equitable decisions than did the high-placed magistrates at a distance, who could only decide cases on forms of procedure that the most practised (not always the most honest) practitioners knew how to deal with. Peasants who refused to enter an appeal found they could receive a rapid decision from the seigneurial court, whereas the fantastically drawn-out length of Parliamentary procedure made their jurisdiction unapproachable by country folk. And we should be on our guard when we pass judgment on the past from the documents it has left to us, for only abuses and exceptional facts were drawn attention to, whereas anything that took place in conformity with custom called for no special notice. And then, as Guy Coquille wrote as long ago as 1612, we must remember that " the Parliamentary courts and the King's men had as their secret watchword to take note of and put in practice every method to lower the authority of the seigneurial courts . . . in order that they might draw more money from them when the exercise of that authority became extended."

XVII.—*The Arrogance of the Nobility*

The unceasing operations of the central power by depriving
the aristocracy of political action within their own domains, had
progressively obliterated the prestige which had adorned them.   In
proportion as the foundations upon which their eminence had been
built up became weakened, and its basis more fragile through the
enfeebling of their active part in the State, the nobility felt they
ought to cling more fiercely to their precedence and the honorific
distinctions which placed them in a favoured position.   It was by
this haughtiness of sentiment that the aristocracy paved the way
for its downfall far more than by those beneficial privileges which
it had preserved, or by the wealth—too often unjustifiable—which
its most important members had not failed to acquire.

At the Estates General of 1614, Councillor de Mesmes, speaking
in the name of the Third Estate, said that " France was the mother
of three Orders, the eldest of which was the Church, the second
the Nobility, and then came the Third Estate."   On hearing these
words Baron de Senecey fell into the greatest rage and hastened
to make complaint to the King :

"They compare your State to a family composed of three
brothers ! . . .   To what a miserable condition then are we fallen !
. . . and the nobility lowered to such an extent as to be put on
a level with the vulgar crowd in the closest form of society existing
among mankind, which is the relationship of brothers ! . . ."

We have shown the familiarity that existed between the seigneur
living in the country and his tenants.   At first sight he would
seem to be living among them as one of themselves, but, as Pierre
de Vaissière wrote, "these noblemen never forget that they are
gentlemen, and that noble birth assures them an undisputed
superiority over their *villeins*."   "There are some men," said the
old Marquis de Mirabeau, "made to obey, and others made to
command."

But in what respects was the superiority which should guarantee
this commanding position still in evidence ?   Parish affairs were
from now onwards conducted by people no longer dependent on
the authority of the seigneur ; the officials were controlled by the
Intendants and their sub-delegates.   The seigneur no longer
assembled the militia nor led them to join the army ; no longer
did he publish the King's commands ; he was now only the first
inhabitant of the place, with privileges which seemed to be no
longer justifiable.

Many noblemen recognized the position and accurately defined
it.   One of them wrote as follows : " We succour the peasant, we

protect him and rarely do him any harm ; but we look down on him. We make him subject to us if he be good and easy to deal with ; if he be difficult we aggravate and irritate him."

How different to the English gentry. Arthur Young relates that happening to be at the Duc de la Rochefoucauld's, at Lian-court, he expressed the wish to discuss agricultural matters with the principal cultivators in the district. The Duke thereupon ordered his steward to summon them to the château.

" The Duc de la Rochefoucauld had the kindness to order the steward to give me all the information I wanted relative to the agriculture of the country, and to speak to such persons as were necessary on points that he was in doubt about. At an English nobleman's there would have been three or four farmers asked to meet me, who would have dined with the family amongst ladies of the first rank. I do not exaggerate when I say that I have had this at least a hundred times in the first houses of our islands. It is, however, a thing that in the present state of manners in France would not be met with from Calais to Bayonne."

All the Revolution is contained therein.

Nevertheless, noblemen living in the country maintained a less haughty attitude towards their " subjects " than those in the town in regard to the bourgeois. Foreigners were struck by the difference.

" The seigneur living on his land," says De Tocqueville, " showed as a rule a certain good-natured familiarity towards the peasants, but his insolence to the neighbouring bourgeois was almost unlimited. This had always been increasing in proportion as his political power had dwindled, in fact just *because* it had dwindled ; for inasmuch as he had ceased to govern he had no longer any interest in keeping in with those who might have lent him their assistance in this task, and he liked to console himself for his loss of real power by making immoderate use of his apparent rights."

The great-grandson of a crusader might find himself in a pre-carious situation, but his insolent pride, far from diminishing on that account, only increased in proportion to his poverty. Chateau-briand had a cousin of the same name, a poor devil of an Abbé, tall, lean, and shabbily dressed, with a hat showing greasy finger marks and discoloured by age, his cassock frayed at the edges, and his black stockings in holes. The Prince de Condé offered him the post of tutor in the house of the Duc de Bourbon, carrying with it very handsome emoluments.

" Those belonging to my House may engage tutors," said the Abbé, bristling with pride beneath his poverty, " they are themselves never tutors to anyone." Only man's vanity could attain such heights.

Mme. du Châtelet was in the habit of calmly undressing before the members of her household. It had never been represented to her that there were men among them.

The famous quarrel between Voltaire and the Chevalier de Rohan-Chabot is one of the best known facts in our history. They took each other by the horns at the opera:

"What do you really call yourself?" said Rohan. "*Is it Monsieur Arouet,*[1] *or Monsieur de Voltaire?*"

"*Monsieur le Chevalier*, it is better to make a name for oneself than drag about the name one has received."

Rohan hired three bravos to give the writer a thrashing:

"I just set the men to work," he said pleasantly afterwards, and M. de Caumartin, a man of ready wit, made the following comment on the incident:

"We should be very unfortunate if poets had not shoulders!"

Twenty years later the illustrious author of *Candide* was raised to the nobility. The family of Arouet was of Poitou origin, and on that account the nobility of the district were open-mouthed with astonishment. The Chevalier d'Huilière wrote about it to his uncle, M. Ferrand-Meré:

"I have decided, after taking the advice of our noble relations, that there is good cause to close the doors against this Voltaire which the Court, to spite gentlemen of noble blood, has the assurance to elevate with a view to humble us."

Notwithstanding this attitude, my lords assumed a less arrogant demeanour when it was a question of obtaining a reduction in the matter of taxes. De Tocqueville notes that the Intendant, a mere plebeian and usually addressed disdainfully as " Monsieur," became under such circumstances " Monseigneur " (written in characters as thick as your arm).

In the following letter to the Intendant the point raised by a gentleman of noble birth is the *impot des vingtièmes*, to which the nobility were subject just as the Third Estate.

"Your sensitive heart will never consent to allow a father of my position to be taxed strictly at the twentieth part in the same way as any father belonging to the people."

The humiliations which the nobility did their utmost to impose upon members of the Third Estate began from their school-days, during which period sons of noblemen and of bourgeois sometimes rubbed elbows towards the end of the Ancien Régime.

In 1770, Antoine Barnave happened to be at the theatre at

---

[1] Arouet was Voltaire's family name. (H. W.)

Grenoble with his mother when up comes M. le Gouverneur of the Dauphiné, declaring that he required their box for his friends. Madame Barnave refused to leave it, whereat the Governor called in soldiers to drive her out. Barnave's father arrived on the scene just when the soldiers were entering the box, which he leaves, accompanied by his wife, after throwing out these words to the public:

"I am giving it up, with my wife and son, by order of the Governor."

We can imagine the rancour with which young Barnave preserved this incident in his mind after he had become one of the most brilliant orators of the Revolution.

Lacroix, the future member of the Convention, who voted for the death of Louis XVI, was leaving the theatre when he was jostled by a gentleman who was offering his arm to a lady; he gave expression to his annoyance:

"Who are you?" asked the gentleman.

Lacroix unaffectedly gave his name and particulars of himself.

"You have done very well to be all that; as for me, I am the Comte de Chabannes, and I am in a hurry." And taking his leave with a loud burst of laughter, my lord, the Count, got into his carriage with his pretty companion.

"Oh! what an appalling distance," said Lacroix, "do pride and prejudice interpose between men!"

Marie Jeanne Philipon, after she had become Madame Roland, also remembered the slight that had been put upon her when she and her mother had been made to dine in an aristocratic house in the servants' hall. She was spending eight days at the Château of Versailles with the ladies attached to the Dauphiness. "A few days more," she said to her mother, "and I shall detest these people here so strongly that I shall not know how to contain my hatred."

People cherished a feeling of rancour against them, wrote Taine, not only on account of the curt salutations they made to others, but also on account of the over-profound obeisance that was made to them. Chamfort relates with disgust that when d'Alembert at the height of his reputation was at Mme. du Deffand's house with President Hénault and M. de Pont de Veyle, there arrived a doctor of the name of Fournier, who, on entering, said to Mme. du Deffand: "Madame, I have the honour to present to you my very humble respects"; to President Hénault: "Monsieur, I have the great honour to salute you"; to M. de Pont de Veyle: "Monsieur, your very humble servant"; and to d'Alembert: only a mere "Monsieur, good day to you."

The Duc de Penthièvre, grandson of Louis XIV through his father, the Comte de Toulouse, was a man of good taste and easy of approach, but in his houses titled people sat at his own table while the bourgeois dined with his first gentleman-in-waiting ; after which humbler folk were admitted to the *salon* to take a cup of coffee. " There," Beugnot writes, " they would find the aristocratic tone and a crowded assembly of those who had been privileged to put their legs under the same table as His Royal Highness, and who did not fail to greet the new-comers with a complaisance that was full of patronage." Penthièvre, who at bottom was a good-natured man, pressed his attentions on each individual " even to excessive lengths," says Beugnot ; but Beugnot did not go there again.

At the close of the Ancien Régime the bourgeoisie and even the upper classes began to kick everywhere.

In 1725, Daucourt, the actor, was throwing out witty sallies at an assembly at which the Comte de Livry was amusing himself by telling jokes to his wife. Livry burst out, " I warn you, Daucourt, that if from now to the end of supper you show more wit than myself I will give you a hundred blows with my cane."

This closed the unfortunate actor's mouth, but after another half century had passed people were discussing politics and wrangling over them at the Opera. A mere dancer challenged the Chevalier de Keratry to a duel and killed him. At Rheims the ladies belonging to the nobility were in the habit of having square blocks of wood, trimmed with gold lace, and crimson velvet cushions carried to church to kneel upon ; in ridicule of which the market women would arrive with pillows and huge wallets. The nobility thought fit to distinguish themselves by wearing three-cornered hats and an affected attire ; the bourgeois youth countered this by a display modelled on it—round hats, hair cut short and curled, and Hessian boots with rosettes at the knee.

The Estates General assembled. The nobility, in spite of the rising flood of ill-will against them, and after the many concessions they had generously made, still obstinately wished to constitute a separate caste in the State. They consented to be no longer exempt from the *taille*, but on condition that what they paid should be qualified as " taille noble," and that the taxes they contributed should not be paid into the hands of the same receivers as those of the lower classes. They abandoned their useful privileges, but their honorific distinctions must be maintained in their integrity.

" Who could have believed it ? " exclaimed Rivarol. " It was not the taxes, nor *lettres de cachet*, nor all the other abuses of authority that irritated the nation the most ; it was the assumption of nobility that called forth their greatest hatred."

And De Tocqueville remarks :

" If one pays careful attention to the fact that the nobility, after losing their ancient political rights, had ceased to govern and lead the people . . . that while becoming an inferior class they had still continued as an aristocracy, and, in an increasing measure, a separate caste, one need not be astonished any longer that their privileges appeared so inexplicable and so detestable to Frenchmen."

BIBLIOGRAPHY

Arc (Le Chevalier d'), *La Noblesse Militaire*, 1756.—Avenel (Vicomte d'), *La Noblesse Française sous Richelieu*, 1901.—Brantôme, *Œuvres complètes*, ed. Lalanne, 1864–1882.—Calonne (A. de), *Vie Agricole sous l'Ancien Régime en Picardie et en Artois*, 1883.—Carré (Henri), *La Noblesse de France et l'Opinion publique au dix-huitième siècle*, 1920.—Chateaubriand, *Mémoires d'outre-tombe*. —Coquille (Guy), *Œuvres*, ed. 1646 and 1665.—Coyer (l'Abbé), *La Noblesse commerçante*, 1756.—Croÿ (Duc de), *Mémoires*, ed. Cottin and de Grouchy, 1906–1908.—Du Fail (Noel), *Propos rustiques*, 1547.—Du Fail (Noel), *Baliverneries*, 1548.—Du Fail (Noel), *Contes et Discours d'Eutrapel*, 1845.—Esmein, *Cours élementaire du Droit Français*, 1892.—Esmein, *Gouverneur Morris*, 1906. —Fagniez (Gustave), *l'Economie rurale de la France sous Henri IV*, 1897.— Flach (Jacques), *Les Origines de l'Ancienne France*, 1884–1904.—Fléchier, *Mémoires sur les Grands jours d'Auvergne*, ed. Chéruel, 1862.—Gouberville, *Journal*, ed. Robillard de Beaurepaire, 1892.—Guyot (Germ.-Ant.), *Traité . . . sur plusieurs matières féodales*, 1738–1751.—Guyot (Germ.-Ant.), *Observations sur les droits des patrons et seigneurs de province . . .*, 1751.—Guyot (Germ.-Ant.), *Traité des droits . . . à chaque dignité, office . . .*, 1786.— Loménie (Louis de), *Les Mirabeau*, 1889.—Luynes (attributed to the Duc de), *Des devoirs des seigneurs dans leurs terres . . .*, 1668.—Marivaux, *Le Spectateur Français*, 1758.—Mathieu (Le Cardinal), *l'Ancien Régime en Lorraine et Barrois*, 4th ed., 1907.—Mirabeau (Marquis de), *l'Ami des hommes*, 1756–1760.—Molière, *Théâtre*.—Montlosier, *Mémoires*, 1829—Oberkirch (Baronne d'), *Mémoires*, ed. L. de Montbrison, undated.—Palissy (Bernard), *Œuvres*, ed. Saint-Fond and Gobet, 1777.—Retif de la Bretonne, *La Prévention Nationale, Théâtre*, 1784–1793.—Richelieu, *Mémoires*, ed. de la Soc. de l'Hist. de France, 1908–1912.—Sully, *l'Economies royales*.—Taine, *Les Origines de la France contemporaine, l'Ancien Régime*, various eds. since 1875. —Tocqueville (Alexis de), *l'Ancien Régime et la Révolution*, 5th ed., 1866.— Turbilly (Marquis de), *Mémoires sur les défrichements*, 1760.—Vaissière (Pierre de), *Gentilshommes campagnards*, 1903.—Young (Arthur), *Travels in France*, 1794.

CHAPTER IV

THE KING

I.—*Family Origin of the Royal Power*

WE have described the reconstitution of France in the ninth
and tenth centuries around the family cell in the midst
of the anarchy produced by invasions. This is the essential fact
dominating our entire history down to the Revolution. As it
developed the family produced the mesnie, the mesnie, increasing
in extent, gave birth to the fief; the uniting together of several
small fiefs formed fiefs of intermediate size, and these, when
grouped together, the large fiefs. Hugh Capet in 987 was a feudal
lord who became King.

What was the argument on which Adalbéron, Archbishop of
Rheims, based the candidature of the new sovereign at the
assembly of the great men of the realm ?

" In him you will possess a father ; no one up till now has
invoked his patronage in vain."

" The patronal class," says Jacques Flach, " is a family which
has become extended, issuing from the family organization and
the system of patronage ; from this two-fold basis royalty also
took its constitution."

By the intermediary of the feudal baron, himself the head of
the family, the royal power thus sprang from the authority exercised by the father of the family. According to the observation
made by Hugue de Fleury (eleventh century), " The King represents
in the realm the image of the father."

And let us be careful not to see in this only some abstract connection, some remote origin taking shape in exterior forms, words
and formulæ ; we are face to face with a direct origin, established
by precise facts, and formed out of essential elements, the consequences of which we see being repeated century after century in
the clearest possible manner.

In his *Histoire des Institutions Françaises* Paul Viollet depicts the special character of this Monarchy:

" The King's authority was very nearly the same as that exercised by the head of a family, and thus patriarchal and royal power are very closely related in their origin." And Jacques Flach says: " The principle of the royal power is therefore a family one: the King is the head of the family."

Consequently the Queen must have her part in the administration, just as in any well-managed house. " She managed the royal household," says M. Flach in his *Origines de l'Ancienne France*. The State treasury was under her direct care and control. The chamberlain, who in our day would be called the Minister of Finance, was thus her subordinate. Robert II was pleased to praise the skill with which Queen Constance managed the public funds. As regards Bertrade, whom Philip I raised to sit on the throne, it would seem that she did rather too well: Yve de Chartres reproached her for trafficking in Episcopal sees and ecclesiastical dignities in order to bring in fodder to the State chests.

The executive power was quite naturally in the hands of the personnel ministering to the reigning family. They were grouped under six separate functions (*ministeria*), that is six separate offices. There were the pantry (*paneterie*, where the bread was stored, from *pain*); the *échansonnerie*, the cup-bearer's department; the kitchen; the fruit store; the stables and the bedchamber; all administered by high officials, namely the pantler, the bouteiller (cup-bearer), the seneschal, the *connétable* and the chamberlain, who were the personal servants of the monarch.

The Seneschal was the Master-carver and carved the meat placed on the King's table. After the meal he received from the Master-cook a piece of meat, to which the pantler and the butler added two loaves and two full pints of wine. When on a campaign the Seneschal superintended the arrangements of the King's tent; he always accompanied his master on his expeditions; in his absence it was he who took command of the armies. Louis VI diminished the importance of these functions; Philippe Auguste suppressed them. In the long run the office of Seneschal assumed such importance that it became a menace to the crown.

Together with the Seneschal there was the Connétable, *comes stabuli*, or Count of the stables. He superintended the King's stables, looked to the forage and purchased the horses. He saw that the grooms cleaned out the stalls. He had the right to feed four of his horses at his master's racks; in addition to this privilege the King's cook supplied him with raw or cooked meat, according to his choice. When Philippe Auguste suppressed the office of Seneschal, in 1191, the Connétable became the commander of the army ; but his functions assumed a too great importance, and Richelieu suppressed the office in 1627.

The Butler (*bouteiller*) was in command of the cup-bearers and administered the royal vineyards. He was entrusted with the duties of Keeper of the Royal Treasury, and presided over the *Chambre des Comptes* which regulated public expenditure.

The duties of the Chamberlain and High Pantler were of a similar character.

We come lastly to the Great Chancellor, whose office was slightly different in character inasmuch as, while domestic in its origin, it was at the same time religious. Among their relics the Merovingian Kings preserved the little cape (*capa*) that had been worn by St. Martin. This was the under-garment which the patron of the Gauls was wearing on the day he gave his tunic to a poor man. Hence is derived the word " chapel," the name given to the place where the relics of kings were kept, and that of " chaplain " to the clerics set apart for the duty of guarding them. These chaplains had to keep a register of the solemn oaths sworn on the *capa*. In this way there came under their charge the duty of drawing up deeds and diplomas attested by seals. Their head was the Chancellor, who always had to carry the seal suspended from his neck lest it should be stolen.

The above were the six great officers of the Crown who assisted the King in the exercise of his authority. Their essentially domestic character became weakened in course of time, but less quickly than one might be tempted to imagine. Even as late as the fifteenth century, on the very threshold of the Renaissance, Charles VII was waited on by the great officers on *fête* days, each one in accordance with the character and origin of his duties, and while the company were seated at table the Chamberlain read aloud to them.

The great ministers of State in the seventeenth century, men like Sully, Richelieu, the Colberts, and the Louvois, still continued to transact the family affairs of the Prince in conformity with the original character of their duties. They were still " domestic servants " at a time when, as remarked by Montlosier, these formed part of the family. On the rolls of the establishment they were listed in the same category as the comptroller of the King's kitchen and the men-servants ; they had a right to the usual allowance of two loaves and the fourth part of a measure of wine, and in addition, on non-abstinence days, a piece of game and a pound of bacon ; on days of abstinence they were allowed six carp and three pounds of butter.

Colbert and Louvois were on a confidential footing with Louis XIV. The Grand Monarch entrusted to them any special duties he had at heart, such as to provide for the lodging of Mlle. de La Vallière and Mme. de Montespan. Louise de La Vallière fled from the Court, and Colbert, in person—that grave, ever gloomy and silent man, his head overloaded with cares of State, whom even the most daintily shod ladies towering in their loftiest *coiffures* approached only with trembling—had to follow hot-foot on the track of the fugitive; he found her at the convent of Chaillot, made her listen to reason, if we may use this expression, and brought her back to the King. Mme. de Montespan gave birth to Mlle. de Blois; Louis XIV wrote to Colbert later : " My daughter de Blois has asked my permission to give up wearing her bib : I consent."

II.—*The King as Dispenser of Justice*

In his famous *Livres de la République* old Bodin wrote :
" The King receives his subjects and distributes justice to them, like a father does to his children." The first Kings, Hugh Capet and Robert the Pious, declared in precise terms that the King had no *raison d'être*, except to dispense justice. The King was the source of all justice in the realm, and all justice emanated from him. It could not have been otherwise. Among the thousands of local groups, families, *seigneuries* and towns into which the kingdom was divided, each one of which had an independent life and existence, the King was the sole link, and the sole superior authority capable of intervening in the differences arising between them. Inasmuch as each one of these groups lived and ordered itself independently, no other function was left to the King than to make them agree among themselves for the common good. Abbon, in the tenth century, gives expression to this concept in precise terms : " The moment that the King is consecrated he demands from all his subjects the oath of fidelity, lest discord arise in some portion of the kingdom." In the sixteenth century Bodin wrote : " The King must make his subjects live in agreement with each other, and all of them together in agreement with himself." Thus in two lines Bodin was defining the monarchical conception in a way that could not be bettered.

From the very fact that the King was the supreme judge he was also the pacificator, or " appeaser " as St. Louis said.

In the first ages this rôle of dispenser of justice was not, to tell the truth, exercised like a judge in session; we should rather say like a judge mounted on horseback. The robe bordered with squirrel's fur, was represented by the leather doublet or hauberk of steelmail. The supreme magistrate would be seen on the road, with his helmet laced over his head, wearing greaves, gorget and steel hauberk. This was not only the case with that fine king, Louis le Gros, but also with all the first monarchs of the line of Capet.

Picture to yourself Robert le Pieux, as the chroniclers have represented him, with his tall stature, "rather stooping, broad and long nose, gentle eyes and kind mouth ever ready to give the kiss of peace; always fighting, laying siege to castles, and ever striving, lance in hand, to promote the reign of peace and justice."

It was in this way that the kings by constant efforts succeeded in introducing relative order into the kingdom in the thirteenth century. St. Louis was then in a position to act the part of judge, no longer sword in hand on the high-roads, but seated at the foot of his bed in his chamber, or surrounded by his counsellors beneath the shade of the oaks at Vincennes.

A miniature of the fifteenth century, preserved at the Arsenal Library,[1] represents Charles V seated in the pillared hall of his palace facing the great open doors, just as the chroniclers of the thirteenth century represented St. Louis. He is surrounded by three or four counsellors, and before him two disputants are wrangling with such vehemence that the hat of one of them has fallen to the ground. While a procession of satisfied litigants are seen going out by the door, two by two, and along the road in the distance, the two litigants, now reconciled and arm in arm, are conversing in a friendly manner on the way in which the King had just settled their affair.

These traditions were maintained much longer and with much greater tenacity than one would be inclined to think at first. We treated above of the seigneurial dispensation of justice, proceeding from paternal authority just like that of the King himself. In the eighteenth century, and right down to the Revolution, the seigneurs or their representatives settled the differences of their subjects beneath the elms in the village square, or at the door of their manor, just as did St. Louis and Charles V in the thirteenth and fourteenth centuries.

The changes produced by time, the multiplication and greater facility of means of getting about, and the prodigious development of a town such as Paris in the neighbourhood of the royal residence, brought it about that a King like Louis XIV could not, like St. Louis, any longer give audience to his subjects who

[1] MS. 5187, f. 1.

might come to thrash out their disputes before him. However, Louis XIV did still receive every week the poorest and most ill-clad who presented themselves before him. On these occasions the Princes of the Blood residing at the Court were grouped round the King, and the worthy folk passed before him in single file, placing in his hands a *placet* (petition) in which the particulars of their case were given. These *placets* were laid by the King on a table near him, and were afterwards examined by him at a session of his Council, as is evidenced by the note, "read by the King," to be found on a number of them.

A popular engraving represents Louis XIV holding one of these public audiences. The setting is not very different from that of the miniature in which one sees Charles V sitting near the door of his palace. Underneath is the following inscription :

"Here is the great King, Louis XIV, giving audience to the poorest of his subjects in order to end their disputes promptly. Solomon sat on the throne to decide between those two poor women disputing as to whom the child belonged. Our Monarch imitates him perfectly, as did our great Kings and Emperors, Charlemagne and Louis Auguste (Saint Louis). Like him they gave public audiences to which they were bound by a special law which they caused to be published throughout the realm."

In this custom we have the origin and, as we shall see later, the reason for *lettres de cachet,* the form of which surprises us and arouses our indignation even to-day. They were however in harmony with the manners and strongest traditions of olden times.

But the growing number and the ever increasing complications of these matters compelled the King to delegate them to his counsellors. In this way the different Parliaments were created, to exercise justice by direct commission from the royal power in their capacity as representing the King.

III.—*The Religious Character of the Monarchy*

Such, therefore, in his essence was the King of France—a judge who not only dispensed justice but was the source of all justice in his realm, like a father in his family. And in his hands judicial functions carried all the more weight because they wore the appearance of being supernatural and almost divine.

"The Monarchy founded by Hugh Capet," writes Achille Luchaire, "is royalty of a sacerdotal character ; the King is a minister of God." Again he says, "The royal function is a divine mission." Suger represents Louis VI as "the Vicar of God Whose living image he bears in himself." As late as the fifteenth century the King was regarded as the foremost ecclesiastical personage in the realm. The people would rush forward when the King was passing so as to touch the hem of his robe, just as they would a relic. " It is nothing but the truth," said Saint Gelais when speaking of Louis XII, " that in every place where the King was going to pass, the people, both men and women, would assemble from all parts and run after him for three or four leagues, and when they were able to get near enough to touch his mule or his robe, or anything else belonging to him, they would kiss their hands and rub them on their faces with as much devotion as they would have done had they touched a relic."

Yve de Saint Denis, the monk who was present at the death of Philippe le Bel, has left an account of the last words spoken by the dying King to his eldest son whom he had called to his bedside : " Secretly, before his confessor alone, he instructed him how he should act when touching the sick, and gave him the holy words he was accustomed to pronounce when he touched them. Likewise he told him that with great reverence, purity and sanctity, cleansed in his conscience and in his hands, he must touch the infirm after that manner."

Louis XIV and Louis XV wrought cures on the scrofulous and those suffering from the King's Evil, in testimony of which we have many duly authenticated documents. " We see the King accomplishing this prodigy, not only in his own realm but in foreign States," we read in the account given by the Chigi Legation in Paris in 1604. " Thus when King John I was a prisoner in London after Crécy, and Francis I was detained in Madrid after Pavia, both English and Spaniards made haste to profit by the good fortune which had placed in their midst a personage whose hands put sickness to flight."

Locatelli of Bologna, as well as Doctor Nemeitz, a German, both gave a description of the ceremony in Paris at which they were present. It took place in the long vaulted corridors on the ground floor of the Louvre where the Museum of Antiquities is to-day. The sick suffering from scrofula, or the " King's Evil," were ranged in two files. Louis XIV would lay his hand on the head of each one and say :

" May God heal you." He would then bestow a kiss on them.

There would be assembled hundreds of sick people—on one day eight hundred were counted—affected by these skin diseases. Doubtless they had been washed beforehand, but in spite of this a strong stomach must have been required by the King to reach the end. It is very curious that this ceremony was not accom-

panied by any religious rite, but, on the contrary, was marked
with a military character. It proceeded to the sound of the loud
rolling of the drums of the Swiss Guard. What a din beneath
the bare and echoing vaulted roof of the long galleries !

After the ceremony in the Cathedral of Rheims, where he had
just been consecrated King of France (October, 1723), Louis XV,
aged thirteen, proceeded to the Abbatial church of St. Rémi to
hear Mass, in conformity with the traditional custom. The route
of the procession, hung with the Crown tapestries, was lined by
the Swiss and French guards. Mounted grenadiers, the black
and white musketeers, so called from the colour of the coverings
on their horses, opened the procession, followed by light cavalry ;
after them came the military establishment of the Household on
foot. The gentlemen of the Court in silk and lace, mounted on
their richly caparisoned horses, preceded the three chargers of
the King ; these were covered with a cloth of blue velvet embroidered in gold and silver, were led by the bridle, and carried
no rider ; then followed twelve mounted pages, and the trumpeters
of the Council Chamber, the hundred Swiss Guards in their deep
ruffs of many folds, shouldering their halberds. Immediately in
front of the King rode the Chief Equerry, Prince Charles of Lorraine ;
finally came the young King, Louis XV, dressed in ruby velvet
embroidered with gold. He looked charming with his large blue
eyes and handsome face encircled with fair curls. The reins of
his horse were held by two equerries ; six Scotch Guards walked
by his side. The procession was closed by the troops of the Guard.

There had been some hesitation in imposing upon the young
Prince the ceremony of touching for the King's evil, on account
of the extreme fatigue it would entail upon him ; but it was
recognized that it would be impossible to suppress it ; tradition
demanded it. Moreover the sick had been brought to Rheims
from all parts of France for the purpose.

On the 29th October, after hearing Mass in the Abbey of St.
Rémi, the young King proceeded to the large park adjoining it.
On either side of the long avenues, beneath the century-old elms,
the yellow leaves of which were already covering the ground
with a checkered carpet, the sick, scrofulous, and paralytics were
ranged in rows to the number of about two thousand. Louis XV
then came forward, wearing a mantle of cloth of gold on which
was displayed the light blue ribbon of the Order of the Holy
Spirit, with its emblem, a dove with outstretched wings, glittering
with diamonds. The two Ushers of the Chamber in white satin
doublets, mantles of white satin fastened with silver ribbons,
white satin caps surmounted by white plumes and gold lace

thick on their shoulders, walked in front of the King, who had just been hallowed by the sacred oils of his consecration. Before each of the sick he halted and gently touching the cheek with the back of his hand, uttered the words:

" The King touches you ; may God heal you."

The Lord High Almoner followed and placed a small silver coin in the hand of each one, while the drums of the Swiss Guard thundered out.

Not long afterwards the Intendants of the different provinces sent to the Court certificates attesting a certain number of cures.

IV.—*The Theory of Divine Right*

In this way we come to the theory of Divine Right. Taine was of opinion that it had been invented by the theologians who had endeavoured to make the King the " special delegate of God." On the contrary, it was the spontaneous creation of the people and had been opposed by the theologians ; it was the doctrine supported by the Gallicans and Parliamentarians, the declared enemies of the ultramontanists and the Jesuits. At the States General held in 1614—the last to be assembled before 1789—what section was it which proposed and with real passion insisted upon the insertion of an article proclaiming the Divine Right of Kings ? It was the Third Estate (the people), and with unanimity too, —that same Third Estate which later was to swear the oath of the *Jeu de Paume*.[1] And what section was it which combated this theory ? It was the clergy and the nobility. The clergy won the day, but, as stated by Richer, the historian of the States General, the maxim of divine right was to remain engraved on the mind of the people, and became, in the words of M. Hanotaux, " the touchstone of patriotism " for the country.

On the other hand, the partisans of Roman predominance—the Jesuits and Ultramontanists—alleged that Kings derived their authority from the choice of the people. This question, which was discussed for nearly two centuries, is a very interesting one for historians. The intermediate steps by which paternal authority had gradually mounted to the throne had long since disappeared, and in order to explain the origin of the royal power men's minds had to adopt one of the two hypotheses offered to them—divine delegation, and popular delegation. Only one notion has come

[1] *Serment du Jeu de Paume :* On the 20th June, 1789, the Deputies of the Third Estate took an oath not to separate until they had drawn up a Constitution for France. This assembly was held in the court of the Jeu de Paume at the Louvre, after Louis XVI had refused to place at their disposal the hall usually set apart for their deliberations. (H. W.)

down to us from the eighteenth century which is really correct ; it could only have proceeded from a historian who had studied the "monuments" of monarchy. Moreau, in his *Discours sur la Justice*, written for the Dauphin, states :

"The earliest societies were those composed of families, and the earliest authority was that of the father over his children. Kings exercised over nations the authority held by the father over the earliest families."

V.—*The Attitude of the Monarchy towards the People*

Bonald, the most brilliant theorist of the Ancien Régime in the nineteenth century, expresses himself as follows : "What a lofty conception of royalty must our fathers have had inasmuch as they reverenced their kings walking on foot, as it were, in their very midst, and lacking all the pomp which surrounds them to-day ! "

At the end of the eleventh century Guibert de Nogent contrasts the paternal friendliness of the Kings of France with the haughty attitude of foreign potentates. " A modesty quite natural to them shines forth from the Kings of France," he says, and quotes the words of Scripture which they recall, " Prince, lift not thyself up, but live amongst thy subjects as one of them."

The palaces of our Kings, which were open to every chance comer, possessed the simplicity of the humbler dwellings of the bourgeois. Walter Map, an Englishman, entered the Palace, like others, and approached the King, Louis VII. A conversation ensued.

Speaking of the Court in England, Louis VII said, " There is nothing wanting to your Prince—valuable steeds, gold and silver, silken stuffs and precious stones ; all these he has in abundance ; at the Court of France we have nought but bread, wine and gaiety."

The Englishman saw in these words high praise of the monarchs of his own country, and admired the courtesy the French King had shown.

In the thirteenth century the King used to walk on foot in the streets of Paris where anyone could approach him without any ceremony. History has preserved for us a dialogue which took place between a *jongleur* and Philippe Auguste. The play-actor asked for assistance from the King on the grounds, as he assured him, that he belonged to his family.

" In what way are you related to me ? " asked the King.

" I am your brother, my liege, through Adam, the first man ;

but what he left had been badly apportioned and I did not get my share."

"Come to-morrow, and I will give you your portion."

Next day Philippe Auguste perceived the play-actor among the crowd which had entered the Palace. He bade him come forward and gave him a *denier*.

"Here is the portion I owe you. When I shall have given as much to all our brothers descended from Adam there will barely remain to me a *denier* out of all my kingdom."

Even if this story should lack authenticity the fact of its having been noted down by a man living at the time is not the less significant.

Francesco da Barberino, the Florentine, went to France during the reign of the great and redoubtable Philippe le Bel. He was altogether surprised to see that greatly feared autocrat—whose power had made itself felt even to the most remote parts of Italy where it caused the pontifical throne to totter on its foundations, and drew cries of fury from the author of the *Divine Comedy*—walking in the streets of Paris, and returning with simplicity the salutes of passers by. Thus he saw Philippe le Bel stopped at the corner of a crossway by three low fellows of sour mien. The monarch remained standing there with his feet in the mud. He was wearing a white flat cap. He listened patiently to the complaints of the three companions and conversed for some time with them, and Barberino noted the contrast presented by the good-natured friendliness of these royal manners to the haughty pride of the Florentine nobles.

In their celebrated despatches the Venetian Ambassadors stated that no one was excluded from the presence of the French monarchs, and that people of the meanest condition penetrated at will the most private apartments, to such a point, said Michel Suriano in 1561, that when one wished to discuss any important matter with the Prince it was necessary to talk in a low voice so as not to be overheard. He added : "The French desire no other government than their King. From this fact arises the intimacy reigning between the monarch and his subjects. He treats them like comrades." Another Venetian Minister, Jerome Lipponano, mentioned in 1577 that "during the dinner of the King of France almost anyone might approach him and talk to him as one would to a private individual."

Louis XIV wrote : "If there is one particular characteristic of this Monarchy it is the free and ready access of subjects to their Prince." People went into the King's Palace as easily as into a mill, at which foreigners never ceased to express their surprise.

" I went to the Louvre," wrote Locatelli in 1665, " where I walked about at full liberty, and passing through the divers posts of the various guards I finally arrived at that door which is opened as soon as one touches it, more often than not by the King himself. It is enough merely to scratch on it, and one is forthwith introduced. It is the King's wish that all his subjects should freely enter."

The insignificant little priest from Bologna (Locatelli) was present at the Queen's *toilette* which was performed in public :

" While they were dressing her hair," he writes, " she was wearing a light corset of white linen well whaleboned and drawn close in at the waist, and a petticoat so tight that she appeared to be enveloped in a silken sack. When the Queen's hair had been dressed, pages brought in her outer garments made of pretty material of extreme richness, with blue and gold flowers alternating on a silver groundwork, and her ornaments were fastened to the waist by Court gentlemen. They even laced her up and finished dressing her, but her women arranged the jewels on her head and bust. When her toilette was complete she turned towards the foreigners present, made a fine curtsey and flew, so to speak, to the apartments of the Queen Mother (Anne of Austria)."

There were so many people in the room that Locatelli was only able to catch sight of the Queen at that moment, " and then only in the large mirror in front of her, wherein the whole room was reflected." The Italian notices the shortness of her stature which her " high-heeled slippers " had concealed up till then. The heels worn by the Queen were so high that they often caused her to fall, a detail which is confirmed by the correspondence of the Duchesse d'Orléans.

The same practice prevailed under Louis XVI. In 1770 the Dauphine, Marie Antoinette, took up her residence at the Château de la Muette. Her toilette was performed in public, and in order that as many as possible could be present benches were ranged in tiers like an amphitheatre. The Dauphine wrote about it to her mother : " I put on my rouge and wash my hands in front of everybody ; after that the men go out while the women remain and I dress in front of them."

Before the transfer of the royal residence to Versailles the public elbowed each other in the gardens of the Tuileries, and Locatelli was present at many little scenes of an interesting character between Louis XIV, Marie Thérèse and the Dauphin, which he relates with much charm. During the King's residence in Paris certain of the bourgeois found a distraction in going to the Louvre " for the sole pleasure of seeing the King, unable to tire of watching him when he was dining, or when he had gone down to the courtyard of the Louvre to match a team of coach horses."

The King's palace became a public resort where the first chance comer might comport himself with the utmost freedom, and everyone felt as if he were in his own home. One can imagine the difficulty there was in maintaining cleanliness and order. From morning to night there was a pushing and noisy crowd of people of every sort and condition. The spaces under the staircases and at the corners where they turned, the passages, balconies and the lobbies, were used to satisfy every kind of necessity. The palaces of the Louvre, Vincennes or Fontainebleau in places became mere latrines. The ladies would hold their skirts high when entering the Queen's apartments. As late as the third quarter of the seventeenth century the Louvre was noted for its ordures and stench.

In connection with this Nicolas de la Mare, house-steward to the Comte de Vermandois, writes :

" In many places in the courtyard, in the upper passages, behind the doors and almost everywhere, one can see a thousand heaps of ordure, one can smell a thousand unbearable stenches caused by the necessities of nature which everybody discharges there daily, those living in the Louvre equally with those who are in the habit of going there or passing through. In many places one can see the balconies and projections covered with these ordures and filth, the sweepings and contents of the chamber utensils which the valets and chamber-maids go and throw out every day ! " [1]

Certain parts of the palace of Versailles continued likewise to give forth all manner of odours as late as the close of the Ancien Régime. Viollet-le-Duc relates that while visiting the palace of Versailles at the time of the Restoration in company with an old lady who had frequented the Court in former times, they were passing through a corridor which smelt very strongly. The Marquise held her fingers to her nose with the following remark : " Ah ! that recalls a very happy time ! "

Louis XIV made an effort to remedy this state of affairs. Bussy-Rabutin admires him for having reached the decision of introducing a little order into his residence and of giving it " the cleanliness of a private house."

We can understand that these old traditions, which could not be changed, inspired the King with the desire to transfer the residence of the monarchy to Versailles. With the growth of the city and the increasing multiplication of contacts between the

---

[1] Bibl. Nat., MSS. N. de la Mare, ms. *franc.* 21688, f. 109.

King and his subjects in Paris, a stage had been reached when one could no longer breathe.

But as a matter of fact the same conditions prevailed at Versailles as in Paris. The royal residence remained open to all comers.

" We passed through a crowd of people, many of them not too well dressed," wrote Arthur Young ; " in viewing the king's apartment, which he had not left a quarter of an hour, with those slight traits of disorder that showed he lived in it, it was amusing to see the black-guard figures that were walking uncontrolled about the palace, and even in his bed-chamber ; men whose rags betrayed them to be in the last stage of poverty, and I was the only person that stared and wondered how the devil they got there. It is impossible not to like this careless indifference and freedom from suspicion. One loves the master of the house who would not be hurt or offended at seeing his apartment thus occupied if he returned suddenly ; for if there was danger of this, the intrusion would be prevented."

From time to time they did give the palace a sweeping out, but it gradually became invaded by beggars who waylaid every-body and held out their hands just as if they were in a street. We read in Dangeau's journal of the 2nd July, 1700, that " fifty Swiss guards were put on duty to drive out the beggars." Doctor Nemeitz, a German, gives us his impressions as follows : " It was easy to see His Majesty at supper. He would receive all his family at his table and unless there were already too many people present, which happened sometimes, anyone who arrived was admitted. Moreover one could always be admitted if one arrived in good time." Frequently a quite familiar conversation would take place between the King and people of the lower classes who were present. Traces of this are to be found in the letters of Mme. de Sévigné and in the *Mémoires* of Saint-Simon.

The public were more particularly admitted to the *grand couvert* (great banquet) which took place regularly every Sunday, and, we should note, on birthdays of members of the Royal Family. The entire family, including the Princes of the Blood, assembled on these occasions. Louis XIV compelled himself to dine in public until the last days of his life, down to the 24th August, 1715 ; he died on the 1st September. On that last occasion, owing to his condition of weakness, he was unable to appear except in his dressing-gown. " I noticed," remarks Saint-Simon, " that he was only able to swallow liquids and that it distressed him to be looked at."

Under Louis XV Parisians and provincials would come in to be present at the King's meals in order to admire his fine bearing and elegance, but still more, his skill in deftly striking off the top of a boiled egg with the back of his fork.

" Look ! the King is going to eat his egg ! "

At that moment the ladies sitting by the Sovereign would lean to one side so that the assembled crowd might have a better view. Louis XV knew the pleasure which this afforded to his subjects and so he compelled himself to eat eggs regularly at his *grand couvert*. Louis XV was the man who ate more boiled eggs than anyone else in the world. " The riff-raff who came on Sundays to Versailles," notes Mme. Campan, " returned home less enchanted by the fine figure of the King than by the skill with which he opened his eggs."

At dessert the King would offer fruit and ices to all the ladies present. In 1772 a young lady from Geneva, Rosalie de Constant, came in to be present at the *grand couvert*. " At dessert they offered ices to the ladies, who had come in to watch. I found them very good," she writes.

In order to take Parisians to Versailles who wished to go and see the King, a service of different kinds of omnibuses, some called " *carabas* " and other " *pots de chambre*," was organized. And here is a description of them :

" For ten sols (*sous*) each, twenty people packed themselves into the enormous cage with its grinding axles, and worn iron tyres bumping on the paved road, in the midst of a cloud of white dust. The rest sat by the side of the automédon,[1] perched themselves on the tilt, or squeezed themselves into the baskets hanging to the sides. Eight strong horses drew the vehicle, and when they began to sweat and pant and got tired at the ascent of the hill at Sèvres, all the company would get down to lighten the load a little, and climbed the hill chatting together."

Those who found a place in the front of the vehicle were called *les singes* (the monkeys) and those at the back *les lapins* (the rabbits). The expression " to travel *en singe* " still exists in Brittany to this day. People there can be heard saying, " I took my place *en singe*," meaning in the front, or *en lapin*, signifying the rear of the carriage.

" The *singe* and the *lapin* would get down at the gilded *grille* of the château," writes Mercier, " would wipe off the dust from their shoes, adjust their swords at their sides, and enter the gallery, and behold ! there they are contemplating at their ease the Royal Family and appraising the appearance and charm of the Princesses. After

---

[1] *Automédon :* the driver of the chariot of Achilles, used familiarly to denote the coachman. (H. W.)

that they play the courtier to their heart's content. They plant
themselves between two Dukes, jostle a Prince who is in too great a
hurry, whereupon he will restrain his movements if he has exceeded,
and there is nothing to prevent a *lapin* or a *singe* from figuring in the
apartment of the Court and at the *grand couvert*. And so," as Mercier
again observes, "in all parts of France people discuss the Court of
Versailles, and it is a rare thing not to find, even in the most remote
town, some one who can say *de visu*, from having gone there in a *carraba*
or a *pot de chambre*, ' what the King looked like, how very fond the
Queen was of oranges, whether the Dauphine was pretty, and if the
Princesses carried themselves well.' "

" Everybody, even those who had never seen him," writes Retif
de la Bretonne, " considers the King in the light of an intimate
acquaintance."

Events concerning the King and Queen were family events for
the whole of France. The King's House was literally the *Maison
de France*.

During the journey from Alsace to Paris made by Marie Leszczynska, betrothed to Louis XV, the people ran out to greet her.
Entire parishes assembled, carrying their banners, singing hymns
and kneeling before their future Queen. The roads were strewn
with herbs and flowers.

We find the same spirit animating the speeches made to her
by the market women on her arrival at Fontainebleau on the
14th November, 1725. Gellé, a market woman, addressed her in
the name of her comrades as follows :

" Madame, we present for Your Majesty's acceptance our finest
truffles. We hope we may have them in abundance. Eat a great
many, and make the King eat them, for they are very good for
getting children. We wish you good fortune and happiness, and
we hope you will make us all contented."

Everybody, I mean all the French people, were invited to the
ball given for the marriage of Marie-Josèphe of Saxony to the
Dauphin, the son of Louis XV ; it was a family affair. Some of
these cousins of the King were even rather badly behaved for
they stood on the silk covered benches in order to have a better
view of the ladies dancing, and answered the ushers, when they
tried to make them get down, with a remark as forceful as it was
laconic. The same spirit animated the marriage festivities of
Marie Antoinette and the Dauphin, afterwards Louis XVI. All
the world, with no distinction of class, entered the great glass
gallery where the Royal Family were assembled. Card tables
had been placed, and the ladies who did not play took their seats
on the raised benches ranged against the wall down the whole

length of the gallery. Facing them, on the side of the windows
looking on to the green lawn, a balustrade had been fixed which
went from one end of the gallery to the other, and behind this
the people passed by. Anybody was admitted with no formality,
provided that he was clean, and not in rags, and followed the
prescribed route. Mme. la Dauphine, the future Queen of France,
sat beside her father-in-law, the King, and with them the Royal
Family were disposed round a large table, where the King and
Queen, the Princes and Princesses chatted familiarly and played
cards in a simple and natural manner, while all the time the people
were defiling past, staring at the young bride, their future Queen,
and all the members of the House of France. On an occasion
such as that it was the King's duty to show himself with his
family to all his people.

"After the ball and royal banquet," writes the Duc de Croÿ, in
connection with the marriage of the Dauphin, the eldest son of Louis
XV, and Marie-Josèphe of Saxony, "we went to be present at the
toilette of the Dauphine which was performed in public up to the
moment when the Queen handed her nightdress to her; the King
then made all the men go and be present at the toilette of the Dauphin
to whom the King handed his night shirt, and both toilettes being
now completed everybody went into the Dauphine's bedchamber.
She looked rather well in her night cap, and rather embarrassed,
but less so than the Dauphin. When they had got into bed the curtains
were drawn back and everybody saw them for some time—a very
embarrassing ceremony which makes one see all the inconvenience
of this public presentation of Kings and great people."

Alluding to the putting to bed of the future Queen of France
on the night of her marriage the Maréchal de Saxe gives his views
as follows : "There are certainly moments when all the assurance
of a person, brought up to sustain this rôle with dignity, is required,
and one of them, among others, is that of the bed scene at the
moment of drawing back the curtains, after the husband and
wife have been put in the nuptial bed—which is a terrible moment,
for the whole Court is present in the bedchamber."

The Dauphine was going to present the Crown with an heir.
The *accouchement* had to take place in public before the whole
world, under the eyes of the people, to whom the child belonged.

"It is the high dignity belonging to yourself and to your child,"
said Henri IV to Marie de Médicis.

The midwife had recognized the signs of labour. Henri IV
immediately informed the Queen of the custom of the Court.
Marie replied that she had always determined to do all that he
thought right.

" I well know, my darling, that you are willing to do all I wish, but I understand your timid and bashful nature, and I fear, if you do not make a firm resolve on seeing them, that it may hinder your *accouchement*."

" The King went to open the door of the bedchamber," writes the midwife, " and caused all in the ante-chamber and the room beyond, to enter. I think there must have been two hundred persons, so that one could not move in order to carry the Queen to her bed. I was greatly upset on seeing this."

Mme. Boursier (the midwife) protested at the presence of so many people :

" The King overheard me and came and touched me on the shoulder, saying : 'Hold your tongue, midwife, hold your tongue ! Do not get annoyed ; this child belongs to everybody, and everybody must rejoice over it.' "

The child made its appearance ; it was a Dauphin.

" Throughout the town (Fontainebleau) and all through the night," continues Mme. Boursier, " one heard nothing but fireworks, beating of drums and blowing of trumpets ; great casks of wine were broached in order to drink the health of the King, the Queen, and His Honour, the Dauphin ; and people were mounting horses everywhere to ride off to the different districts, and carry the news through all the provinces and fine cities of France."

We now come to the *accouchement* of the last Queen before the Revolution. The Garde des Sceaux (Lord Privy Seal) and the Ministers and Secretaries of State were waiting in the large ante-room, together with the King's Household, the Queen's Household and the great ladies who had entry to the Court. The rest of the Court filled the card-room and the gallery. All of a sudden a voice rang out : " La Reine va accoucher ! "

The Court rushed forward helter-skelter with the crowd. Custom ordained that all should enter at that moment, and that none should be refused. The spectacle was a public one. They invaded the chamber in such a pushing throng that the screens placed round the Queen's bed were overturned. The room became transformed into a public place. Some Savoyards even mounted on to a piece of furniture to see better. A compact mass of people filled the bedchamber :

" Some air ! " cried the *accoucheur*, " some air ! "

The King threw himself on the windows, and opened them with the frenzy of a madman. The ushers and *valets-de-chambre* were compelled to push back the riff-raff who were struggling with each other. As the hot water, which the surgeons had demanded, did not arrive, the surgeon-in-chief lanced the Queen's foot without it, and the blood gushed forth. The two Savoyards who had climbed on to a *commode* began quarrelling and calling each other names. People near them intervened. There was a great uproar. At last Marie Antoinette opened her eyes ; she was saved.

In the same way as the King had come into the world so must he die—surrounded by his own people, that is, by everybody. Louis XIII was in the new palace at St. Germain, now almost entirely destroyed. Anne of Austria had her residence in the old palace which still stands to-day on the picturesque terrace overlooking the Seine. On those occasions when the King was well he was able to enjoy a little repose and rest there quietly in comparative seclusion ; but the moment his state of health became worse Court etiquette resumed its rights. We know what that meant. The host of courtiers living with the Queen in the old palace, augmented by a whole flood of Parisians who had hastened from the capital, invaded the chamber where the King lay dying and thronged around him, a moving, compact mass of people. "There was a trampling of feet, a dense throng, a din and a closeness of atmosphere terribly painful to the King who requested the favour that people would go further from his bed so as to leave him a little air " (Arvède Barine).

Napoleon, with his profound social intuitions, well understood the reasons of these hereditary customs so deeply rooted in the House of France. He had thought of re-establishing the *grand couvert*, that is, the practice of the reigning family dining in public ; then he gave it up ; it would have embarrassed him : neither Louis XIII, nor Louis XIV, nor Louis XV, nor Louis XVI had been embarrassed. And Napoleon added these words which mark well the character of those old customs :

"Perhaps one should have confined this ceremony to the Prince Imperial ; and only in his youth, for he was the child of the nation ; he must therefore belong to the sentiments of all, and to all eyes."

VI.—*The King as Head of all Families*

The Maréchal de Tavannes used to say : "Between ruling one's kingdom and ruling one's house there is no difference except their limits." Louis XIV ruled his kingdom as he ruled his House. In the latter no marriage could take place without his good pleasure. The Duc and Duchesse d'Orléans thought that they could marry their children according to their wishes, and a marriage was planned. The King summoned them to come to him, gave them a severe reprimand, and the project was broken off. The same thing happened in the case of the Prince and Princesse de Conti : Louis XIV decided the marriages of their children just as he had done for those of the Duc d'Orléans. The Prince and Princess ventured to offer resistance : Saint Simon writes that " the King employed all sorts of manœuvres, but finding that he made no progress he spoke to them as their King and Master and told Mme. la Princesse de Conti that he desired the double marriage of her children, that he had decided the matter, and that he would make them both marry as he wished, in spite of her." And this did not fail to take place.

No marriage amongst the nobility could be contracted without the King's consent. The King would often sign the marriage contract, and would sometimes elevate the rank of the husband on the occasion by raising the status of one of his estates to a Marquisate or a Duchy ; he sometimes even paid the expenses of the marriage ceremonies and gave a dowry to the bride. The same thing applied to magisterial families. Olivier d'Ormesson writes that he had to solicit the royal pleasure to unite his daughter with the future President de Harlay.

As a rule Louis XIV confined himself to giving advice. He said to the Duchesse de La Ferté :

" Madame, your daughter is very young."

" That is true, Sire, but there is need for haste because I want M. de Mirepoix, and in ten years' time when Your Majesty will recognize his merit and will have rewarded it, he will no longer want us."

To the Duc d'Elbeuf, on the other hand, who desired to re-marry at the age of sixty-four, the King objected that he was too old :

" Sire, I am in love."

That took Louis XIV on his weak side, for no one loved love and those in love more than he did. The Duc d'Elbeuf received permission to follow the dictates of his heart, and married Mlle. de Navailles the next day.

This paternal solicitude extended also to the provinces. The King was incessantly importuned by gentlemen of noble birth living in the country whom he did not know and whose name perhaps he had never heard of, to contribute towards the setting up of a daughter. The Comptroller General of Finance kept a fund set apart for this purpose. M. de Berlaymont, who lived in the neighbourhood of Lamballe, writes to the Comptroller : " Monseigneur, my family consists of five grown-up strapping daughters, very suitable for marriage, who bewail the fact of their being unable to fulfil their vocation because we cannot provide them with a dowry." " What grieves me most," explains

M. de Péguilhan-Laval, " is not being able to set up in life a well-developed daughter who has been excellently brought up in the house of the ladies of Mirepoix, and who is of an age to wish to marry."

We have alluded elsewhere to the large families of these country gentlemen. In these cases also, by virtue of the character of his functions, the King had to come to the rescue. How many examples could we not quote! Let us confine ourselves to the case of this Breton gentleman, bearing, by the way, the very bourgeois name of Monsieur Denis, who was familiarly described in the Comptroller General's office as " the gentleman who has three children at a time and awaits impatiently the King's bounty."

When once our people had secured the interest of the King in his capacity as *père de famille*, so as to concern himself in their marriage, he had to continue to take an interest in them. The Maréchale de la Meilleraye, who had secretly made a second marriage to Saint Ruth, went to Louis XIV to relate her woes to him : her husband was beating her. The King summoned Saint Ruth, and reprimanded him. He promised to behave more gently, but soon—it was more than he could help—he began beating his wife again. The latter complained to the King once more, and he again summoned Saint Ruth to his presence, who made fresh promises of amendment, which he again broke. Louis XIV decided to see to it. Now Saint Ruth was a good soldier. He was given a command in the army in Ireland, where the matter happily adjusted itself. Saint Ruth had his head shot off by a cannon ball, which made it impossible for him to go on beating his wife.

The young Duc de Richelieu was sent to the Bastille because he did not love his wife. This lively gentleman was kept under lock and key for several weeks in " dark solitude," as he expressed it, when suddenly the door opened and the Duchesse de Richelieu entered, charming and gracious, in her most dazzling attire. " Not even the beautiful angel," wrote the Duke, " who flew down from Heaven to deliver Peter looked so radiant." This was a good method for rekindling conjugal love when, by an ill wind, it had become extinguished, and it should make us forgive the Bastille one or two of its disadvantages.

The King's essential task was to open the doors of homes, as it were, to take part in their domestic honour, tranquillity and happiness, to see that the husband's affairs were prospering, that Madame's reputation remained intact, and that the children were well cared for and obedient.

Monsieur A. Joly, after studying in detail these facts as applying to the inhabitants of Caen, writes : " One can find cases there in which the King's majesty descended to offices unworthy of it, engaging itself in these domestic squabbles, saddling itself with the ridicule attaching to certain mishaps, and accepting all responsibility therefor." As a matter of fact the *dossiers* of provincial Intendants were crammed with reports of burlesque quarrels—sons-in-law with mothers-in-law, jealous wives, crabbed sisters-in-law and wrangling neighbours. We find mention of caps being torn, shoes being furtively put in the soup tureen, and slops showered down from a first floor on to a passer-by who opportunely received the charge full on his head ; and then too there were the boots of a musketeer very unexpectedly found in Madame's bedroom.

All these matters were scrupulously noted down, written out, examined, weighed, and considered again before being forwarded on to the Intendant who would transmit them to the Minister, and he in turn handed them to the King, who finally gave his paternal decision. We come across some amusing romances which engaged the Minister's watchful attention for two years ; and even then the matter had not been settled at the end of them, for on the last paper in the *dossier* is a note from the sub-delegate informing the royal government " that he will not fail to advise them of the course of events in this household."

Such were the functions of the King springing from the origins of the Monarchy. As for making administrative laws, regulating public education, civic affairs, the incidence of indirect taxation—in a word, occupying himself in what absorbs to a great extent the activities of a modern State—all that was like some foreign domain over which his authority did not extend.

The constitution of the monarchical power in France, such as we have described it, astonished foreign Ambassadors. Mercy-Argenteau, accredited by the Austrian crown to Louis XVI, writes to Prince Kaunitz on the 6th November, 1784 : " What seems an absurdity to say, but which nevertheless is only too true, is that the King has little influence in affairs of State." And Montlosier writes : " The King has no existence except inside his palace."

VII.—*The " Great Fear "*

France, living on her traditions, and governing herself with an independent mind by her customs and local authorities, saw these ancient traditions deteriorating in vigour during the course of the eighteenth century. The chief cause of this was the decay of those sentiments which had formed the old French family, the foundations on which the social edifice had been based. When the outbreak of the 14th July, 1789, burst forth, royalty still had at its disposal throughout the country nothing but a moral power formed on the patriarchal traditions which we have described. But all of a sudden these sentiments were brutally shattered by the unbelievable results which the taking of the Bastille produced in the provinces, and in one solid mass the entire edifice crumbled to the ground. But before it fell, offering no defence, for it was so constituted that it could not and ought not to make any defence, royalty was to add yet another page to its history, on which, strangely enough, was to be laid bare what it had been.

Towards the end of July, 1789, an unreflecting and frenzied panic suddenly spread East and West, North and South, over the different quarters of France. Dwellers in the country took refuge in the towns, and those in the towns rushed out to hide in the forests. On every side armed men assembled. The brigands are coming! they cried. They are approaching, people have seen them pillaging the farms, devastating the crops and violating the women; they are taking little children by the leg and crushing their heads against the walls! In some localities a messenger had been seen arriving from no one knew where, his eyes distraught, out of breath, and covered with dust, riding a horse white with foam! The brigands were over yonder, lying in ambush on the hill! Entire villages were abandoned; people were seen hiding themselves on the topmost branches of the trees in the forest, others buried themselves in large holes in the ground which they covered over with green foliage. In many provinces the towns were seized with a veritable access of frenzy, the inhabitants running this way and that in the greatest disorder, the prey of extravagant panic. The women fled through the gates of the ramparts dragging their children after them and carrying those who could not yet walk; and while the dwellers in the towns were escaping from their homes the people from the country were fleeing into the towns. After the taking of the Bastille there reigned throughout the whole of France what contemporary writers termed " La Grande Peur." On the coasts they talked of pirates, or a landing of the English; they were to make their appearance on the 22nd July, the feast of the Madeleine, and on that day anxiety redoubled on account of the fogs which had formed as though to facilitate the brigands in their work of pillage and bloodshed; from this arises the picturesque name, *les brouilles de la Madeleine* (*brume*, fog, and *brouilles*, disorders), by which those events were remembered.

The memory of this state of terror remained very vivid among those who were living at the time. It was this which, of all the events of the Revolution, penetrated most deeply into the minds of the people.

We have seen how the authority of the King had been built up and developed. Derived from the concept of *père de famille*, the King, instinctively and without their being aware of it, remained enshrined in the popular mind as the father from whom one seeks shelter and support. Towards him, throughout the centuries, all eyes were turned in times of necessity. And behold! by one shattering blow this patronal authority was overthrown, and there was uneasiness, and vague unreflecting fear, among all the people of France. What terrifying rumours went the round! " The brigands . . .! and the father is no longer there! " " The Great Fear " is the last page in the history of royalty in France. Perhaps none is more touching, none more glorious; certainly there is no page which reveals more clearly the character of those traditional relations between throne and country.

BIBLIOGRAPHY

Argenson (Marquis d'), *Considérations sur le gouvernement ancien et présent de la France*, 1767.—Bodin, *Les six livres de la République*, 1583.—Bourcier (Louise Bourgeois), *Récit véritable de la naissance de messeigneurs et dames les enfans de France*, 1625.—Bonald, *Œuvres*, 1859.—Campan (Mme.), *Mémoires*, 1822.—Croÿ (Duc de), *Mémoires*, ed. Paul Cottin and de Grouchy, 1906–1908.—Dangeau, *Journal de la Cour de Louis XIV*, 1770.—Flach (Jacques), *Les Origines de l'ancienne France*, 1884–1904.—Guibert de Nogent, *Histoire de sa vie*, ed. G. Bourgin, 1907.—Hanotaux (Gabriel), *Histoire du Cardinal de Richelieu*, 1893–1903.—Hanotaux (Gabriel), *Tableau de la France en 1614*, 1898.—Joinville (Jean, Sire de), *Histoire de Saint Louis*, ed. N. de Wailly, 1880.—Locatelli, *Voyage en France* (1664–1665), trans. Ad. Vautier, 1905.—Louis XIV, *Mémoires pour les années 1661 et 1665, suivis des réflexions sur le métier de Roi*, ed. Jean Longnon, 1923.—Montlosier, *De la monarchie Française*, 1814.—Nemeitz (Joachim-Christ), *Séjour à Paris*, 1727.—Retif de la Bretonne, *Monsieur Nicolas*, 1796–1797, new ed., 1883.—Saxe (Maréchal de), *Lettres et Mémoires*, 1794.—Saint-Gelais, *Œuvres*, 1719.—Saint-Simon, *Mémoires*, ed. Cheruel and ed. A. de Boilisle (Hachette).—Sévigné (Mme. de), *Lettres*, ed. de la Coll. des grands écrivains (Hachette).—Tocqueville, *l'Ancien Régime et la Révolution*, 5th ed., 1866.—Tocqueville, *Mélanges*, 1865.—Viollet (Paul), *Histoire des institutions politiques et administratives de la France*, 1890. —Visconti (Primi), *Mémoires sur la Cour de Louis XIV*, trans. J. Lémoine, 1908.—Young (Arthur), *Travels in France*, 1794.

CHAPTER V

THE COURT

I. The Splendour of the French Court.—II. The Courtiers.—III. Louis XIV.
—IV. The Boredom and Lack of Comfort at Court.—V. The Court of
Louis XV.—VI. Madame de Pompadour.—VII. The Court of Louis XVI
and Marie Antoinette.

I.—*The Splendour of the French Court*

UNDER the Ancien Régime the Royal Court had reached an
importance such as no Court of our times can ever realize
again. The motley and ill-regulated crowd of noblemen, gentlemen, intimates, favourites and courtiers within the circle, played
an active part in the direction of the State as successors of the
curia regis, which at the time of the early feudal Kings had consisted of the relations and closely united vassals of the Princes—
the *familia regis*—and had formed the Government. The Marquis
d'Argenson, Minister of Foreign Affairs, writes in this connection :
" The Court has become the Senate of the nation," and " the
chamber-women have a share in the government." This would
surprise us more, and seem wellnigh incomprehensible, did we not
constantly bear in mind the permanent facts of our history down
to the Revolution, and that the institutions, ways of thinking,
customs and usages of ancient France had their *raison d'être* and
explanation which may be summed up in these three words—
family, patronage, and tradition ; nay more, in one single word—
the family, for patronage proceeds from the family as it enlarges
its action, and tradition is the essential law of the family as continued from one generation to another.

It was not the action of the Kings themselves which in successive
ages welded together the elements constituting their greatness and
power, and created their renown. The dazzling monarchy of the
seventeenth century, at which posterity is still bewildered, and
which is sometimes held up to criticism by the foreigner through
envy, and because he has nothing like it to show, was built up

little by little, by unceasing alluvial deposits of the national stream.

Picture to yourself the Court of Honour at the Château of Versailles in the time of Louis XIV, a swarming mass of liveries, uniforms, costumes and retinues of a thousand brilliant and varied colours ; it might almost be likened to an immense cloak of Scotch tartan in perpetual motion, or a picturesque piece of Indian cashmere, the colours mingling in multiple designs.

And watch the Court issuing from the château in attendance on the King, and spreading down the avenues. " It is a fine sight," writes Primi Visconti, the Italian, "to see Louis XIV going forth escorted by his lifeguards, coaches, horses, courtiers, valets and a whole multitude of people all running about in a confused mass amid a noisy clatter. It reminds me of the queen bee flying over the fields accompanied by her swarm."

In the numberless and vast *salons* of Versailles on the days of the receptions—Mondays, Wednesdays and Thursdays of each week—the throng was so great that it was only possible to talk to the two or three people close to where one was standing. One was literally hemmed in, and only with great difficulty and patience managed to pass from one room to another. Persons of the highest rank, the King's own brother and sister-in-law, were pinned in a corner, and note their attire ! The Duchesse d'Orléans shall describe it :

" There was such a crowd that one had to wait a quarter of an hour at each door before being able to enter, and I was wearing a dress and underskirt so horribly heavy that I could hardly stand upright. My costume was of gold trimmed with black *chenille* flowers, and I had on my pearls and diamonds. Monsieur (the Duc d'Orléans) was wearing a black velvet coat embroidered with gold, and had on all his large diamonds. My son (the future Regent) had a coat embroidered with gold and different colours overlaid with gems. My daughter (Charlotte Elisabeth) wore a robe of green velvet embroidered with gold, the dress and underskirt, as well as the *corsage*, garnished all over with rubies and diamonds ; the embroidery was so well done that each rose looked as if it were worked into the material. Her *coiffure* consisted of several rows of brilliants and clusters of rubies, with golden ribbons sown with diamonds."

Madame Palatine (Princess Charlotte Elisabeth) also complained of the suffocating heat and the tumultuous hubbub which made people at the Court dizzy.

We owe to the most charming of writers the following description of an afternoon entertainment in the King's company at Versailles :

"At three o'clock," writes the Marquise de Sévigné to her daughter, the Marquise de Grignan (29th July, 1676), "the King, Queen, Monsieur, Madame, Mademoiselle, Mme. de Montespan, all the suite, courtiers and ladies—in a word, what is called the French Court— were assembled in the King's fine apartments which you know. All was divinely appointed and magnificent.

A game of *reversi* gave the note and fixed everyone's attention. A thousand *louis* were spread on the table ; there were no other counters. Mme. de Montespan held the cards.

I saluted the King in the manner you told me, which he returned as if I were still young and beautiful. The Queen talked to me about you. M. le Duc paid me a thousand of those kind attentions which mean nothing to him. The Maréchal de Lorges entered into conversation with me in the name of the Chevalier de Grignan, and so on, *tutti quanti*. You know what it is to hear something of everything that is going on. Mme. de Montespan talked to me about Bourbon and begged me to tell her about Vichy and how I felt there. I thought her back was very flat, as the Maréchale de la Meilleraye said, but seriously, her beauty is something surprising. She was dressed entirely in French point lace, her hair done in a thousand curls, with the two on the temples falling very low over the cheeks ; and black ribbons on her head—in a word, a triumphant beauty, enough to arouse the admiration of all the Ambassadors. She knew that people complained that she was preventing all France from seeing the King ; she has given it up, and you cannot believe what a joy this is to everybody, nor what a brilliancy it gives to the Court. This agreeable confusion without confusion, of all that is most choice, lasts from three o'clock until six. If any couriers arrived, the King would retire to read his letters and then come back again. Some good music was going on all the time, to which he listened, and he talked to the ladies accustomed to have that honour. And then the cards were given up at the hour I said.

At six o'clock we got into open *calèches* and then we went on the lake in gondolas. There was music, and at ten o'clock we returned and then there was the play ; at midnight supper—and that is how Saturday passed."

The setting of all this is well known—the *salons* of Versailles in all their robust magnificence, of a kind never before produced in such completeness by royal artistry. But these *salons*, although still of incomparable splendour, are to-day robbed of some of their finest adornments : pictures by Rubens, Van Dyck, Titian, Fra Angelico, Veronese and Guido, and their marvellous furniture with its wonderful richness and glitter, which varied according to the time of the year ; in the cold season green and flame coloured velvet predominated, but in the summer the light would play on brocades in gold and silver flowers, or woven in silken threads.

The lustres and their fittings were of crystal and wrought bronze, and on the golden console tables were baskets fashioned of glistening silver.

Let us place ourselves in the Galerie des Glaces, of which the *Mercure Galant* of December, 1682, gives a description :

"Eight portable silver stands bearing branching candlesticks are placed between four silver boxes of orange trees resting on feet of the same metal, and adorn the spaces between the windows, and eight silver vases match the stands on each side of the doors. Four gilded torch holders carry great silver chandeliers in the angles of the gallery. Eight silver branching candlesticks rest on round gilt tables placed in front of the windows. At each end of the gallery hang two silver lustres with eight branches. The footstools are of green velvet bordered with a band of gold brocade, with a fringe of the same."

And think of the fairy-like effect of the bright coloured costumes, and the glistening of precious stones and diamonds, for no black coat cast its funereal shadow there. Everything was elegant, brilliant, bright and luminous.

The society was exquisite.

Taine writes :

"All the men and women were chosen one by one ; they were all accomplished people of the world, gifted with every grace that birth, education, wealth and custom could bring ; they were perfect of their kind. There was not a toilette, not a turn of the head, not a voice, nor turn of phrase which was not a masterpiece of worldly culture, the distilled quintessence of everything exquisite which social art could elaborate. However polished society in Paris might have been, it did not come near to it ; compared to the Court it wore a provincial air."

The Comte de Tilly shows us a lady of quality saluting ten persons at one and the same time in one single inclination, "returning with her head and look the bow each of them gave." This was done in so delicate and subtle a manner as to be almost imperceptible, but so well carried out as to be noticed by all onlookers.

"A hundred thousand roses were required to make one ounce of that exquisite essence used by the Kings of Persia," continues Taine. "Of such a kind was this *salon*—a flask of gold and crystal containing the substance of a human vegetation. To fill it, it was necessary that a great aristocracy, transplated into a warm climate, and henceforth barren of fruit, should bear only flowers, and then that all its sap, purified in the royal still, should be concentrated into a few aromatic drops. The cost was excessive, but only at such cost can the most delicate perfumes be manufactured."

With the exception of our worthy country gentlemen, all the
nobility at Versailles were in quest of fortune, pleasure, and the
sun to shine on their vanity. In the words of Saint Simon :
" All France filled the great reception room."

Rank, dignities, renown of birth or public service—all were
blended together there. " I was stupefied with amazement,"
writes Visconti, " to see Cardinal de Bouillon, Cardinals de Retz,
Bonzi and other ecclesiastical dignitaries, who hold such lofty
rank in Rome, jostled about in the crowd here. It was explained
to me that there were too many persons of distinction at the
Court to stand on ceremony." There was a block in the stream
of the time-honoured crowd which from every point in a great
country had ceaselessly pushed forward in the same direction.
For the great personages in the kingdom, whether of the nobility
or clergy, the ever present concern came to be to live under the
eyes of the King.

How to make oneself conspicuous in the crowd ? Molière shall
tell us. We are in the ante-chamber of the *Œil-de-Bœuf* [1] :

Vous savez ce qu'il faut pour paraître, marquis ;
   N'oubliez rien de l'air ni des habits :
Arborez un chapeau chargé de trente plumes
   Sur une perruque de prix :
Que le rabat soit des plus grands volumes,
   Et le pourpoint des plus petits.
Mais surtout je vous recommande
Le manteau, d'un ruban sur le dos retroussé ;
   La galanterie en est grande
Et parmi les marquis de la plus haute bande
   C'est pour être placé.
   Avec vos brillantes hardes
   Et votre ajustement,
Faites tout le trajet de la salle des Gardes ;
   Et, vous peignant galamment,
Portez de tous côtés vos regards brusquement ;
   Et, ceux que vous pourrez connaître,
   Ne manquez pas, d'un haut ton,
   De les saluer par leur nom,
   De quelque rang qu'ils puissent être.
Cette familiarité
Donne à quiconque en use un air de qualité
Grattez du peigne à la porte

---

[1] *Œil-de-Bœuf :* The ante-chamber to the King's bedroom at Versailles
was so called from being lighted by a single window like a bull's eye, and
was where the courtiers assembled, waiting for the King to come out. (H. W.)

De la chambre du roi ;
  Ou si, comme je prévoi,
La presse s'y trouve forte,
Montrez de loin votre chapeau
  Ou montez sur quelque chose
  Pour faire voir votre museau ;
  Et criez, sans aucune pause,
  D'un ton rien moins que naturel,
" Monsieur l'huissier ; pour le marquis *un tel*."
Jetez-vous dans la foule, et tranchez du notable ;
Coudoyez un chacun, point du tout de quartier,
  Pressez, poussez, faites le diable
  Pour vous mettre le premier.

(Remercîment au Roi.)

II.—*The Courtiers*

" Whoso will consider the fact that the King's countenance constitutes the entire happiness of the courtier," says La Bruyère, " and that he occupies and fills his whole life in regarding him, will understand in some measure how God constitutes all the glory and felicity of the saints."

" The passion evinced by men at Court to be noticed by the King," writes Primi Visconti, " is incredible ; when he deigns to cast a glance at certain of them, the one who receives it thinks that his fortune is made, and boasts of it to the others, saying :

" ' The King looked at me ! '

" You may take it that the King is fairly acute," adds the Italian, " how many people does he not thus repay with a look ! "

This life in common, which was lived in such close promiscuity, had consequences which Taine has clearly pointed out :

" The Court of Louis XIV was the place in the world where men best learned the art of living together.   They reduced it to maxims, and drew up its guiding principles.   They made it the subject of reflections, matter for discussion, the end and purpose of education, the outward sign of merit, and the employment of life."

On the other hand, this constant close contact of so many people, often divided by conflicting interests, ambition, or vanity, gave to people of that time a singular skill in studying character : whence sprang that admirable literature which portrayed the human soul and its passions like none other in the world : Mme. de la Fayette, La Rochefoucauld, La Bruyère, Molière, Racine and Bourdaloue. It still has its influence even in our times.

It was a bustling, moving, buzzing crowd, agitating round the monarch from morning to night, " an appalling crowd," writes the Duchesse d'Osnabrück, " that makes a most fatiguing racket."

Visconti calls it " a fair of nobility," and adds, " I wish you could see the Court; it is a real bear-garden of men and women." Voltaire emphasizes it as " the crowded life of a great town house, a kind of huge caravanserai which concealed underneath it many miseries and had not even the advantage of being comfortable."

The highest nobility were attached to Versailles like an oyster to its bed.

The Maréchal de Noailles had gone to bed and was going to sleep. Drawing the curtains round him, his valet asked:

" At what o'clock does Monseigneur wish me to call him ? "

" At ten, if no one dies during the night."

The oldest courtiers who had reached the most advanced age— and these the best of them—had passed the greater part of their existence in the royal ante-chamber, like herons standing motionless in the muddy marsh. One of them remarked to a young débutant in this noble career:

" You have only to do three things: say nice things to everybody; solicit every post that is likely to become vacant, and sit down when you can."

" What is a nobleman ? " asks de Mesmes; to which he replies, " a pillar of the ante-chamber."

This appalling rôle—and one may as well say here, this basest of rôles—imposed thus miserably upon so many men adorned by the greatest names in France, proud of their lineage, and of the glory shed forth by the standard they bore, resulted in deforming the character of even the best of them. Read the Memoirs of the Duc de Croÿ, a fine and upright man.

Who to-day would not prefer to sweep the gutters in the town rather than drag along the existence of an everlasting beggar, more often rebuffed than favourably received, not only at the hands of the Prince whom no one could dare to approach freely, but at the hands of his mistresses and favourites, of Ministers and their clerks ? The Duc de Croÿ took his son to Versailles: " I showed him the doors where I had so constantly waited."

In his book on Le Gouvernement et les Mœurs Senac de Meilhan quotes these lines of Montesquieu:

" Ambition in idleness, meanness accompanied by pride, the desire to grow rich without working, an aversion for truth, contempt for the duties of a citizen, apprehension from the virtue of the Prince, and hope from his weaknesses—such was the character of the greater proportion of the courtiers."

But let us not judge with too great severity those unfortunate beings in Court dress—a poverty-stricken nobility pushed on into an *impasse*. It was a class of society which had fulfilled its task, and, taken all in all, had fulfilled it magnificently; there was no further reason for them to remain at home on their lands, on which, moreover, it was becoming difficult for them to live. As a social class at least, it should have disappeared, but to renounce its rank, privileges and precedence, and become a commercial, trading, financial and industrial class, this it could not do. Humanity does not free itself by a mere turn of the wrist of the stamp with which it is imprinted in its inmost recesses.

Do not compare our aristocracy under the Ancien Régime with the English nobility, as is too often done. The latter was by heredity and tradition the product of quite a different formation, just as the English monarchy in its origin and development was fundamentally other than the French monarchy. Let us mention only one fact, a very important one it is true, among many others that might be cited : by its rôle in Parliament the English nobility and gentry continued to be the directing power in the country ; the French nobility no longer directed anything. Listen to the furious cries of Saint Simon, who, moreover, would have been more incapable than anyone else of directing anything.

" All those people were lodged in Versailles," writes Gustave Geffroy in his fine book on the Palace of the Great King, " Versailles was pulsating with the animation and ambitions of ten thousand persons. One or two narrow rooms, partitioned off from the large apartments, which temporary makeshift lasted for years, formed the only lodgings of these privileged ones."

We see the Duc de Saint Simon giving up the regiment of which he was Colonel to shut himself up at Versailles in " a hole in the entresol " without any air or light, so as to be near to the rays of the sun. In the end the Duchesse de Saint Simon was appointed to be a lady-in-waiting to the Duchesse de Berry, and the noble Duke was then able to lodge in the château in an apartment containing five rooms.

" Huddled one against the other in this way," proceeds Geffroy, " outwardly satisfied, and feverish when behind their closed doors, inwardly filled with the tumult of their conflicting interests and passions, and maintaining with difficulty on their pinched countenances the marks of an amiable impenetrability, the seigneurs came and went, descending from their miserable garrets in the roof, the honour of occupying which they had persistently solicited, and assisted at the daily ceremonies attaching to Court life, le grand lever, and le petit lever, the royal repasts, and the morning Mass. More than one would groan over the new conditions attaching to life, more than one would curse that immense palace which absorbed the activities of the kingdom, wherein were accumulated the Ministries, the public

services, the services of the Court, those of the chapel, of the King's
bedchamber, of his private office, of the King's table, of the most
trifling amusements, of the King's stables and military household."

A few rare individuals had the strength to resist this fatal
attraction, like the Marquis de Mirabeau, so closely resembling
Saint Simon in the piquancy and colour of his style, and so far
above him in intelligence and character : " Inasmuch as the nobles
at Court make a profession of dabbling in the mire of intrigue,
I have never wanted to go to Versailles, I, a wild bird nesting
between his four towers . . . "

Consuming anxieties and feverish preoccupations pursued their
course in undertones beneath the brilliant play of colour of those
most wonderfully arranged *fêtes*. " The beauty of things and the
virtue of art are powerless to discipline the ebb and flow of the
passions " (Geffroy).

Under Louis XIII the amusements of the Court assumed a popular
guise ; there was dancing to airs of the Auvergne,[1] going so far
as clog dances and beating together of heels as at village weddings.
The ladies and gentlemen danced in circles, holding each other
by the hand ; distant reserve was effaced, the ladies engaging the
gentlemen by offering them bouquets ; the King himself would
take part in them just like any private individual, and the first-
comer could invite him to dance.

This was no longer the fashion at the Court balls under Louis
XIV and Louis XV. The *pavane* was replaced by *la courante*,
and that in its turn gave way to the *passe-pied*,[2] which enjoyed a
long run of favour ; it was a nimble, light-footed dance, the special
feature of which was the movement of the left foot advancing along
the floor like the paw of a kitten. The ladies did not dance after
reaching the age of twenty-five.

The balls given on State occasions were called *bals parés*, and
etiquette ensured that they should be magnificent rather than
agreeable. The ladies could only appear *en grande toilette* with
enormous *paniers* ; the weight of the heavy material on their
shoulders was so great that they could hardly lift their arms ;
they wore narrow pointed shoes with high heels ; their dresses
were immensely long, made of a thick rich material embroidered
with gold, or of a brocaded silk ; the hair was arranged in a very
high *coiffure* loaded with precious stones. Heavy clusters of
diamonds, hanging from their ears, completed their costume, in

[1] Auvergne : *chansons des bourrées et des branles :* a kind of lively village
round dance swaying round the fire of faggots. (H. W.)
[2] *Passe-pied :* a lively Breton dance. (H. W.)

which it was very difficult for them to dance with any lightness. The men wore richly ornamented coats, embroidered down all the seams, and a sash ; in the time of Louis XIV they also wore an ample wig, but later on they had their hair pressed down and plaited.

At ordinary Court balls—called *bals de la reine*—the ladies were in *dominos* with long folds falling behind, from the neck to the heels. These *dominos*, which were made entirely of white taffeta, were worn with small *paniers*, floating sleeves and short trains. The ladies were therefore all in white, while the gentlemen were decorated with multi-coloured and brilliant embroideries.

As regards paint, if fashion no longer required the men to cover their faces with it, as in the time of the Médicis Queens, it was nevertheless *de rigueur* for the ladies. It was not a question of painting themselves so as to resemble nature, or of giving to their lips and cheeks the radiance of springtime beauty. " This rouge which seemingly wished to be natural is truly ridiculous," the Comtesse says in Mme. de Staal's *La Mode*. A rouge was required " which told you something," and of these there were different kinds according to the rank and position of the lady using it. In this way the kind of rouge used would announce the person appearing in it, as was remarked by the Goncourts : " The rouge worn by the lady of quality was not the same as that of the lady at Court ; the rouge of the woman of the *bourgeois* was merely a suspicion of rouge—a mere hint of it."

The Princesses, on the contrary, wore it very much accentuated and of a very pronounced colour, and they wished the ladies of the Court to be no less pronounced.

" Nevertheless, the startling rouge used in the time of the Regency, colouring Nattier's portraits with purple—and due no doubt to the use of Portuguese rouge, thickly applied—gradually lost favour under Louis XV, and was only seen on the cheeks of actresses, on which it marked that vivid patch which the artists of the time made a point of showing in their paintings of opera costumes."

And beneath all this outward splendour and superficial varnish, under all this beauty of form which has never since been attained, what an oppressive gloom and boredom brooded ! The Duchess of Osnabruck emphasizes the trouble they gave themselves at the French Court to be amused. " I see many *fêtes* at the French Court," Madame Palatine writes, " but no gaiety of heart." Even Mme. de Sévigné's letters, despite her efforts to write in a light, lively, and smart strain, draw some depressing pictures when speaking of the Court. It clung to frivolities and vanities which even a market woman would despise, so as to work them up into occasions for joy and pleasure. Boredom at the Court affected even those seemingly the most favoured, even Mme. de Maintenon, who, from a most humble condition, had reached the pinnacle of fortune. This she confided to her friend, Mme. de Maisonfort : " How impossible it is for me to tell you what I go through, or to make you realize the boredom which consumes the great, or the difficulty they have in filling the day ! Do you not see that I am dying with depression in circumstances it would be difficult to imagine ? " To her brother d'Aubigné she said : " I can stand it no longer ; I wish I were dead ! " To which he replied jokingly : " *Vous avez donc parole, ma sœur, d'épouser Dieu le père !* "

Poor uprooted nobility ! " We get our meals in all kinds of different places," writes Visconti, " and we are always on the move, like Bohemians. . . . In Paris there are twenty thousand gentlemen who exist haphazard."

The Duchess of Osnabruck writes to her brother : " The position of the French nobility created by the royal predominance has deprived them of their dignity. The life the courtiers lead would not suit me ; necessity reduces them to slaves."

" One day I heard someone say about Louis XIV," writes Visconti, " that with one glance he sees everybody, whether he be in his study, in the chapel or in the country, and facts show him to have been right. On one occasion when he was on horseback at Versailles he was the only one to notice a thief putting his hand into the pocket of young Villars Orondate."

Thus vanished the fine independence of the country nobility of earlier days, when Montaigne still spoke of them with enthusiasm.

Louis XIV made it an essential point that all his nobles should be seen around him. Saint Simon tells us : " It was accounted to be failing in all that was most distinguished for a man not to make his usual sojourn at Court, for others to come there only rarely, and certain disgrace never, or almost never, to go there." And the *Grand Roi*, with his eye ever on the watch, made a daily inspection of the crowd surrounding him.

" In short," concludes Visconti, " the great men of the land live under the King to-day like so many novices under a father director."

And in what a wonderful degree did this aristocracy—which the Monarchy by removing its foundations had committed to unavoidable destruction—dazzled by the Fate that was sweeping it away, remain faithful to the Prince who was ruining it, burning to serve him with most generous devotion in the army, and ready to sacrifice both life and fortune for his sake. We find touching evidence of this, such as the following letter written in 1707 to Louis XIV by the Marquis de Naucaze :

This old nobleman, at the age of 107, was telling the King that he was writing *without glasses* " to assure him of his hope not to die until God should vouchsafe to him the favour of seeing His Majesty crowning his glory by giving peace to Europe, and compelling his enemies to accept it."

On the other hand, note the amount of esteem on the part of the Prince which all this unwearying devotion and submission secured for the nobility ! The scene takes place in the Low Countries :

" Louis XIV had just sat down to table with his leading courtiers who were in the habit, when on a campaign, of sharing his meals ; he declared in rather harsh tones (he had just come from a long conference with Louvois, his War Minister) that he had decided upon the siege of Maestricht, that he had no use for chattering courtiers and that he did not care a rap what became of them. He repeated this, saying that he had nothing but contempt for them. All remained silent, and trembling, when the Comte de Grammont, rising from the table, and with a lowly sweep of his hat, answered, ' Sire, courtiers are poor men ; they are the foremost of your subjects ; it is on them that all misfortune falls. They sleep on the ground, expose their persons and belongings in the service of Your Majesty, and say nothing to Your prejudice ; they are not like those (the Ministers) who have just held conference with Your Majesty ; *they* sleep in good beds and run no risks, and much more than that, are all arrayed in gold and silver.' The King did not breathe a word in reply, and all the courtiers present ran and embraced the Comte." (Primi Visconti.)

III.—*Louis XIV*

Such were the innumerable satellites which gravitated round the centre planet, so aptly named the *Roi-Soleil*. The following is one of Saint Simon's wonderful portraits :

" There was nothing to equal him (Louis XIV) at reviews, *fêtes*, and wherever an air of gallantry might find occasion owing to the presence of ladies—gallantry that was always majestic though sometimes accompanied with an air of gaiety, and never in any degree either out of place when in company, or too bold ; but down to the smallest gesture, his walk, his carriage, his whole make up, was measured and restrained ; all was becoming, great, majestic and yet very natural, to which habit and the unmatched advantages of his whole appearance, gave a great ease. And so, when it came to serious things, such as giving audience to Ambassadors, and at ceremonies, no man was ever more imposing; and it was necessary to begin by making a practice of looking at him if one did not wish to run the risk of coming to a full stop when addressing him. His replies on these occasions were always short, just, full, and, when the matter under discussion deserved it, very rarely without some little courteous, and sometimes flattering turn of phrase. The respect too produced by his presence, in whatever place he might be, imposed silence amounting to a kind of fear.

He was very fond of the open air and exercises. . . .   He excelled at dancing, croquet (*mail*), and tennis (*paume*). He was an admirable rider, even to a great age. . . . He greatly loved shooting, and there was no better shot than he, nor one possessed of such grace. . . . In all things he loved splendour, magnificence, and profusion. He made this taste a maxim, and inspired all his Court with it. It pleased him that people should throw themselves into entertaining, fine clothes, retinue, building houses and gambling. . . . He found satisfaction for his pride in a Court that was superb in every detail."

Through his energy, and his remarkable gift of organization, Louis XIV succeeded in imposing order and punctuality in the life of the feverish Court. Even in the midst of the confusion and crush we have described above, the King maintained a deportment in which majesty, inborn as it were in him, seemed to be reflected—an order and deportment which aroused the admiration of Elzéar Spanheim, Minister of the Elector Palatine:

" It was irksome to the Dauphine (Princess of Bavaria) to rise at a fixed hour, to have to get ready to go to Mass, and dine at the King's table, to take her place in the circle and to go to a full dress dinner in the evening—all done by set rule as in a convent, a rule which the King meant to be punctually observed. This ordered existence seemed to her like the wearisome existence of a nun."

Louis XIV rose daily at eight o'clock. At ten he went to his Privy Council at which he remained until half-past twelve, when he went to hear Mass with his family, accompanied by the Queen. At one o'clock he paid a visit to the ladies, with whom he remained until two, at which hour he dined with the Queen in public. Then followed an airing out of doors, or a hunt, and after that an hour or two of work with his Ministers in Council. From night-fall until ten o'clock there was the reception (*appartement*), that is chatting in the *salon*, card playing, a play, or a ball. At eleven o'clock, after supper, he would again spend a few moments with the ladies. At midnight he went to bed, as also did the Queen. This constituted what Saint Simon called " the machinery of the Court."

IV.—*The Boredom and Lack of Comfort at Court*

It should be added that in the midst of so great luxury, the courtiers and even the King himself were singularly lacking in comfort. Who has not been surprised, when reading the correspondence of Madame Palatine, the sister-in-law of Louis XIV, to hear her complaints in this respect ? Most of the nobles were lodged at the Château of Versailles in the servants' quarters. In winter the wine and water on the royal table would freeze in the glasses, in spite of which the ladies chatted laughingly with bare shoulders. It was so cold in the King's bedroom that he was obliged to go into his private study to get warm before he could enter it.

" When I rise before they have come in," writes Louis XIV, " I light my fire myself. I do not wish to summon them. One must let these poor people sleep. I have prevented them often enough from doing so."

We have sketched the severe trials and lack of comfort which the nobility suffered at Versailles, and now we come to the boredom they endured. To drive away the latter they took to gambling.

" Here, in France," says Madame Palatine, " as soon as they get together, people do nothing but play *lansquenet*. They gamble for frightful sums, and the players are like madmen ; one will roar at the top of his voice, another will strike the table so hard with his fist that the whole room re-echoes with the sound, a third will blaspheme. . . . All appear to be beside themselves and present a terrifying aspect."

In the beautiful chapel at Versailles, in the presence of the courtiers and the King himself, Bourdaloue with his rugged eloquence would brand the gambling that went on in lively terms :

" Gambling with no restraint or rule, which is no longer an amusement, but an occupation, a profession, a traffic, a bondage, a passion, a frenzy, and as a consequence, a forgetfulness of duties, a disordered household, a dissipation of revenues, unworthy cheating and knavery leading to avidity of gain, outbursts of passion, cursings and despair."

Such was the ransom paid for so much glory, beauty and splendour, in which a social life of unparalleled magnificence mingled with the brilliancy of art and traditions still young and vital in spite of the centuries that had passed over them.

V.—*The Court of Louis XV*

On the morning of the 1st September, 1715, Louis XIV died in his Palace of Versailles, three days before reaching the age of seventy-seven, and in the seventy-second year of his reign.

The clock on the new chapel was striking a quarter past eight when there appeared on the gilded balcony overlooking the marble court, an officer wearing a hat with black feathers. The court-yard was full of people—gentlemen in lace and ribbons, officers, artisans and a few women of the people with their starched linen collars turned down over their shoulders. The officer on the balcony removed his black plumed hat and cried out in a loud voice :

" The King is dead ! "

The people in the courtyard below stood open-mouthed. The officer disappeared. A few moments later he came back ; white plumes had taken the place of the black ones on his hat and waving it aloft he cried aloud three times :

" Long live King Louis XV ! "

The Swiss Guards were drawn up along the long gallery, the mirrors of which reflected the fresh morning light.

In the park the trees, still green, were casting their chequered light and shadow on the water of the lake, on which were mirrored at intervals the marble nymphs in their pure whiteness, and the busts of the gods on their square pedestals.

Down the length of the gallery officers and men of the Swiss Guard, of lofty stature, were stationed. They wore black velvet caps with white, red, and blue plumes, and red and blue tunics of frieze ornamented with silver tufts. The soldiers stood with their picturesque halberds at attention. The Princes, led by Philippe, Duc d'Orléans, the nephew of Louis XIV, the Princesses, the lords and ladies of the Court, Archbishops, Bishops and Abbés, all went to pay their homage to the young King.

There was no gloom.

" Some, in hopes of cutting a figure, of taking a part and obtaining a footing therein, were overjoyed," says Saint Simon, " on seeing the end of a reign under which there was nothing more for them to expect ; others, weary of a heavy, ever crushing yoke, and of the Ministers in a far greater degree than of the King, were charmed at finding themselves in a freer atmosphere ; all, in general, were delivered from a feeling of perpetual constraint, and were athirst for something new."

The Princess Dowager, Charlotte Elisabeth of Bavaria, sister-in-law of Louis XIV and daughter of the Elector Palatine, generally called Madame Palatine, arrived escorted by two noblemen wearing the blue Ribbon of the Order of the Holy Ghost. Her grief was sincere, for she had had a great affection for Louis XIV, whom she called " the good King." The Duchesse d'Orléans and Princesse de Conti were likewise escorted by noblemen wearing the blue Ribbon.

The Court made its entry before Louis XV whom his governess, the Duchesse de Ventadour, was holding by a silken cord. He was then five years old and was wearing a close-fitting violet tunic, the mourning for Kings. His face and delicate features were rather pale, and he was wearing on his pretty little curly head a round, broad-brimmed hat with large white feathers ; round his waist was a white silk sash falling down at the side to his white satin shoes which were fastened on with white silk ribbons. The child was holding in his hand a little malacca cane topped with an ivory ball.

The Duc d'Orléans was the first to speak :

"As the first of your subjects, Sire, I am come to offer my humble homage to Your Majesty."

The little fellow was charming with his graceful manner and air of majesty, and, as worthy Buvat states, "with his collected bearing as though he were of a much more advanced age."

A reaction began to set in against the elaborate and ceremonious tone which Louis XIV had imposed on his surroundings, and the younger courtiers nicknamed the representatives of the former Court "antiques."

When the little King had attained the age of reason, that is seven years old, he was summoned to preside at the Council of the Regency at which he took his seat on a big arm-chair which up till then had been left vacant. The boy naturally understood nothing of what was going on. He played with a kitten which he took care to bring with him, a fine kitten with black and white marks on it, and Saint Simon, who was a member of the Council, made a point of including it in the number of his colleagues. One day, when the little Monarch had to carry out some formality connected with his succession, he got tired, and the Duchesse de Ventadour, his governess, wrote to Mme. de Maintenon : "He made his own soup afterwards and found solace in no longer having to play the part of King." The child was quite happy a little later on in the park at La Muette when he was able to play at being a dairyman with a very small cow and all the appurtenances of a little dairy which Mlle. de la Chaussenaie had given him, or digging for truffles with a hoe and tiny dogs trained for the purpose, a present from his grandfather, the King of Sardinia.

Philippe, Duc d'Orléans, the Regent, was as unlike as possible to the dead King whose place he was called upon to assume for a time. Affable and witty, the Regent lived at the Palais Royal as a private individual. "M. le Duc d'Orléans," writes Saint

Simon, "was not made for stiff rules nor severe decorum, but allowed everyone to make free of each other's precedence, taking no notice of their customary rights and careless of all accepted procedure." He laughed at all ceremonial.

Court life became bourgeois, a kind of family life embellished with sociable friends who amused themselves and each other. Even Madame Palatine, in spite of her great affection for her son (the Regent), found herself unable to take part in it : "There is no longer a Court in France," she writes on the 23rd May, 1720 ; and again, on the 22nd November, 1721 : "Would to God the late King were still alive ! I then had more pleasure and satisfaction in one day than I have had during the six years of my son's Regency. There was really a Court then, and none of this bourgeois existence to which I, brought up at Court where I have spent my whole life, cannot accustom myself."

The young King gave evidence of the same tastes as the Regent, even more closely resembling those to be found in family life ; in after years, amid all the splendour of the throne, one of his favourite distractions was to make the coffee in the company of his daughters sitting round and doing their tapestry work.

We shall see the King, in order to escape for a moment from pomp and ceremony, betaking himself to the little private rooms in the palace, those celebrated little rooms which provided material for so many stories all the more intriguing because hardly anyone knew what took place there. The publication of the Memoirs of the Duc de Croÿ eventually lifted the veil of mystery. These private rooms, or little suites of rooms, had been arranged for Louis XV by Gabriel, the architect, and were decorated with de Troys paintings, the *Déjeuner d'huîtres*, the *Rendez-vous de chasse*, and the *Cerf aux abois* (1734), and with Lancret's *Déjeuner de jambon* (1735). These two *déjeuners* are now at Chantilly.

Access to them was by a private staircase. An usher standing by the door of the staircase would read out the names of the gentlemen to be admitted to an evening in the privacy of the royal *entourage*. "One entered discreetly," says the Duc de Croÿ, "and went up to the little private suite."

"The dining room was charming, and the supper delightful, without any stiffness. Only two or three valets of the wardrobe served the meal, and they retired after setting what was necessary before each guest. Freedom combined with correct manners seemed to be the rule ; the King was lively and at his ease, but always maintained a grandeur which one could not help noticing."

"Generally speaking, everything in this private suite was on a

very grand scale and very well ordered in accordance with the
rules of the great world of fashion."

In another place the Duc de Croÿ describes in greater detail
these famous suppers in the little private suite :

" The King was already seated at table when I arrived. I modestly
took my seat at the little table in the corner by the window, alone with
M. de Lameth. The King sent dishes over and looked after me. He
even gave me a friendly wave of his hand which showed a greater
degree of familiarity.

He made us pass the time in unpacking his fine white and blue and
gold service from Vincennes which had just been sent from Paris
where it had been on exhibition for the eyes of connoisseurs. It was
one of the masterpieces of this new manufacture of porcelain which
claimed to excel and put in the shade that of Saxony ware. The
Marquise, to whom the King had given the village of Sèvres, was
putting in hand large works there in order to establish it next to the
glass manufactory."

These were intimate gatherings of sociable people. " The King
made himself charming in this little suite, combining ease of manner
with infinite politeness." He would have a wood fire lighted and
made his guests sit round, " and we chatted with the greatest
familiarity, but all the time it was impossible to forget that we
were with our master."

There you would find the Maréchal de Saxe, of whom the King
was very fond. He only thought of his dinner, " and seized upon
choice morsels only, for he was a great *gourmand*."

Mme. de Pompadour, very lively and sprightly, would also be
there. After supper she would take part in the gambling although
she did not care for it. " She gambled for the purpose of playing
the wanton and getting firmly established rather than from love
of it " (Croÿ). The King, on the contrary, liked heavy stakes and
played very skilfully and quickly. " All this was very different,"
Croÿ notes, " from the time of Louis XIV, who only very rarely
had supper parties with a few members of his Court." De Croÿ
also mentions that at the beginning of the reign of Louis XV the
number of gentlemen admitted to the privacy of the little suite
was small, but it continued to grow larger—" people of all ages,
degree and kind—all, nevertheless, members of the nobility." A
few ladies, two or three of an evening, were admitted from time
to time.

As narrated by the noble Duke courtiers—all men of the highest
rank—might be seen waiting every evening at the little door of
the private staircase for it to open, when the usher would call
out the names of those privileged to be admitted that evening

to the presence of their master. The rest would return crest-
fallen to their rooms. " It was very mortifying to be refused,"
says the Duc de Croÿ. A nobleman, even of his rank, was exposed
to this humiliation any day after a long wait by the closed door.
What a life !

And all the time the etiquette of the public life of the Court
was being subjected in an ever increasing degree to a minute and
rigorous observance. It became crystallized, narrowed down, and
hardened.

Those courtiers who were housed at the palace were now better
lodged and furnished than in the time of the Grand Monarch—
there were hangings of white damask on gilded poles, mirrors
everywhere to increase the light, and choice furniture, and with
it all there was always the same luxuriousness of apparel—coats
of cloth of gold and silver worn with Spanish point lace, or made
of those marvellous silks of Lyons which Marie Leszczynska, the
Queen, had brought into fashion. Diamonds and precious stones
were all the rage ; the *corsage* and *coiffure* of a lady in Court dress
streamed with them ; they would lend their jewels to each other ;
even the Royal Princesses did so to the ladies of their suite.

The passion for gambling went on increasing. People, quite
strangers to Court circles, and mere commoners with no kind of
title, obtained admission by reason of the money they were able
to put on the tables. In 1741 a Royal Decree had forbidden the
crudest forms of games of chance, such as *Bassette, faro, Biribi*
and *Petits-paquets*, but this was naturally a dead letter for those
staying in the King's palaces. Several of the leading members
of the Court, such as the Duc de Richelieu, the Prince de Montbarey, and the Marquis de Chalabre, were frenzied gamblers.
M. de Chalabre, a brigadier in the King's army, was kept by a
professional woman gambler ; M. de Rostaing allowed himself
to be maintained by his mistress whom he ruined ; M. de Muret,
after losing his fortune in gambling at the Court, left to become
a cab driver at Lyons ; he was the most honourable of the lot.

Do not, however, let us imagine a Court that had lost its greatness and its imposing beauty. The noble figure of Queen Marie
Leszczynska made its impression on everyone, and even Louis XV,
whatever we may think, showed more outward decorum and
dignity in his life as a sovereign than his great-grandfather had
revealed. Louis XV had his mistresses, but he did not allow
them to ride in the same coach with the Queen, nor did he
legitimize his natural children ; he never dreamt of reserving to
them any right to the Throne of France, as Louis XIV had done.

A contemporary writer, Dubourg, the famous prisoner of Mont

Saint Michel, where he remained for so many years shut up in a wooden cage and died, has left in his *Espion Chinois* (1745) a remarkable description of the character of Louis XV which deserves to be reproduced here, all the more so from its being little known.

" His character is uniformly consistent; it is difficult to acquire his favour, but it is only necessary for a man to be sure of himself to be sure of him. The one thing he never pardons is an abuse of his confidence ; when that has been lost it is never regained. He follows the same method even in his love affairs, and never makes it up with his mistresses ; what is surprising is that he sacrifices them on occasion in the interests of his people. In making a choice his heart counts for nothing ; his mind always derives more pleasure from them than his eyes, because he has more regard for intelligence than for beauty. . . . He is very phlegmatic and possesses a marvellous *sang-froid* in regard to everything. He often esteems but never admires. He punishes vice, and rewards virtue, with an equally indifferent hand. . . . He is a bottomless well in which even love has never been able to lay bare anything. Reason and decorum ceaselessly guard the entrance to his heart. Such a Prince is made for the diadem he bears. In France the love felt for him by his subjects leaves almost nothing for the sovereign's ability to do, but on a throne shaken by a storm he could not maintain himself for long."

For some years historians in general have been reconsidering the severe judgment brought to bear by their predecessors on Louis XV. Without going so far as to think, with the Duc de Croÿ, that the official laudations lavished on him were justified in a greater degree than those poured forth on his predecessor, one should recognize that, taking him all in all, he carried out very worthily his rôle as King.

The results of the War of the Austrian Succession have afforded matter for blaming him to people overlooking the perfidy of Frederick II, who cynically left his ally in the lurch as soon as he had obtained Silesia, the object of his covetousness ; people have reproached him still more sternly for the Seven Years War, alleging that he brought it about, and concluded it with a Treaty which was so unfortunate for France ; they forget the acts of brigandage carried out by England, who, with the design of seizing our colonies, attacked our ships on the sea before she had even made a declaration of war, and robbed us of our colonial possessions by a piratical warfare while we were powerless to defend them owing to the complications the war on the continent laid upon us ; above all, they forget the treachery of Russia after the death of the Tzarina Elisabeth (3rd January, 1768), and the singular *volte-face* of her successor, Tsar Peter, who not only threw

up his alliance with us at the very moment when the affairs of
Frederick II were desperate, but turned his troops against us.
When an honest man plays fairly with knaves he has every chance
of being duped. Is it for the historians to reproach him with
this ?

His was a remarkable figure and one which remains enigmatic
on many sides. Three points at any rate seem to be well established. Louis XV had been very badly brought up; he was
extremely intelligent; and he was very handsome, the finest
looking man in his kingdom in the eyes of many of his contemporaries, as had been Louis XIV, and like him of a physical beauty
suited to the taste of his times. The sculptor, Pigalle, who had
visited the principal Courts in Europe, said that the heads of the
two sovereigns which had struck him as the most remarkable
were those of Louis XV and Frederick II, the former from its
plastic beauty, and the latter from its extraordinary appearance
of intellectual refinement.

At the end of his reign Mme. de Genlis makes a further comment
in speaking of Louis XV: "Although no longer young he was
very good looking; his Sèvres-blue eyes—royal blue as the Prince
de Conti said—and his glance were the most impressive things
one could imagine. When speaking he adopted a curt and pecu-
liarly laconic tone, which had however nothing ungracious about
it; and his whole personality gave forth something royal and
majestic which distinguished him from everyone." He has been
called hard, unfeeling and heartless: contemporaries represented
him as being deeply penetrated with the most acute sorrow on
account of the death of his son. He loved his daughters like a
good father, taking pleasure in their company; he called them
familiarly "Coche," "Loque," "Graille" and "Chiffe." There
are still people who make a grievance of this. Certainly some
writers are easily aggrieved.

The games in which Louis XV indulged with his grandchildren,
when he had become a grandfather, have provided compilers of
memoirs with material for charming pictures. The King had his
mistresses; what a disgraceful thing! It would have been
amusing to have seen these rigorists, on emerging from childhood,
married to a woman eight years older than themselves! Louis
XV certainly showed much more regard for his wife than Louis XIV
had shown to his. True, his mistresses, a superior woman like
Mme. de Pompadour, and a delightful creature such as Mme. du
Barry, had not been chosen from among the nobility of the
highest distinction—the former a Poisson, the latter a Bécu—what
an abomination! Ah! if the favourite in the eighteenth century

had been a Rochechouart, a Mortemart or an Athenais de Monte-span,[1] from whose virtuous modesty our modern Catos borrow their most pointed shafts, they would have placed crowns of laurel leaves on her brow.

It is quite true that the King was bored; he was bored with the pompous life for which he was not made. Let us call to mind what we have said on a former page—the King enjoyed little influence in the State, and took little part in its administration. We should remember also what Saint Simon said of Louis XIV : " he thought he was governing, and no Prince ever governed less." And Louis XV was under no misconceptions on this point. Hence this weariness of the rôle of being a King, and possibly even weariness of life itself. Acute depression held him in its grasp, and never left him. More intelligent than those surrounding him, and, with a few exceptions, more intelligent than his ministers, he soon formed his own judgment of them, just as he did of his Court and of all the reformers by whom he was constantly approached. He saw through men's ambitions, and laid bare the hidden end of so many eloquent professions and protestations of devotion. Bernis [2] submitted to him a scheme of reforms, saying " It needs for the right conduct of affairs a central point to which everything tends." The King smiled, looking up to the ceiling with his beautiful Sèvres-blue eyes : " *Central point,* which means that he wants to be Prime Minister. Is he not on his way to being a Cardinal ? See his astute cleverness ; he well knows that by reason of his dignified position he will force the Ministers to meet at his house, and Monsieur l'Abbé will be that central point."

Louis XV summed up his courtiers at their true value. Comte d'Argenson, Minister for War, together with the administration of the Department of Paris, fell from power, and, in accordance with the custom was punished with a *lettre de cachet* exiling him to his own property. One of the gentlemen of the Court came up rubbing his hands with a joyful air, and announced the news, emphasizing it with " I have just seen his baggage going off ! " Now this man had been one of the most obsequious and assiduous

[1] Mme. de Montespan : Françoise Athenais de Rochechouart, Marquise de Montespan, of the family of Mortemart, the favourite of Louis XIV (1641–1707). (H. W.)

[2] François Joachim de Bernis, a Prelate and French poet, whose verses procured for him the name of Babet la Bouquetière, and the favour of Mme. de Pompadour. Under Louis XV he became Ambassador and Minister for Foreign Affairs at the beginning of the Seven Years War, Archbishop of Albi and a Cardinal, and ended by being French Ambassador in Venice and Rome (1715–1794). (H. W.)

flatterers of the statesman now in disgrace. Louis XV heard him, looked him up and down, and then went up to Mme. de Montespan and murmured, with a shrug of his shoulders :

" And the cock crowed ! "

And thus Louis XV resigned himself to the sway of long years of discouragement. One day a new Minister arrived with some fine plans for reform, and set before the Council grand projects for the future. The King, with his greater intelligence and experience, thought to himself, " He has displayed his wares like anyone else and promises the finest things in the world, none of which will come to pass ; he does not know this country of ours ; he will see."

Everyone knows the celebrated and often repeated remark : " If I were Chief of the Police, I would forbid hackney carriages." The reader is asked to be good enough to recall what I have said in the preceding chapter : the King had no power to forbid hackney carriages. He could, strictly speaking, dismiss the Chief of Police and give the post to another after receiving from the latter an assurance that he would forbid hackney carriages ; but he would have found himself at loggerheads with the new official on other and doubtless more important points than that concerning the use of light vehicles, and would have again been powerless to exert his will. From *Le Secret du Roi*, the celebrated work by the Duc de Broglie, we learn that Louis XV was obliged to have recourse to secret diplomacy, conducted by himself apart from his Ministers, in order to be able to give effect to his will. This contradiction sometimes crops up in writers treating of the Ancien Régime : they thunder with eloquence and sincerity against the royal despotism, and then, on finding themselves faced with the barriers placed in former times against absolute power, they wax indignant, with no less eloquence and sincerity, that the King did not cast them down.

VI.—*Madame de Pompadour*

In the *entourage* of Louis XV Mme. de Pompadour was the most conspicuous personality at the French Court for nearly twenty years, from 1745–1764. She was the daughter of Antoine Poisson, a bank clerk, and had married Lenormand d'Etiolles, the son of a paymaster. She was tall, a little thick-set, and of a majestic bearing ; she had fair hair and a transparent and clear complexion. There was nothing seductive about her features, but her whole personality shed forth an indefinable charm.

We have her portrait by La Tour, the *chef-d'œuvre* of that marvellous artist. He even painted her twice, the first time when

she was still Mme. Lenormand d'Etiolles. After the decree of
separation of the young wife from her husband had been pronounced
by the Court of le Châtelet, the latter kept the portrait. Seized
with the desire to possess it, for she was very attached to it, the
fair Marquise charged the Abbé Beyle to go and reclaim it :

" It is all that remains to me of my wife," the husband replied.
" Well, tell her to come and take it back."

Mme. de Pompadour did not dare to do so.

It was necessary to beg La Tour to paint the portrait of the
favourite a second time. The illustrious artist agreed to do so,
on condition that no one should enter the room where he was
working—something like the story of Michael Angelo and Pope
Julius II. La Tour arrived with his easel, palette, and box of
colours ; he got into position, laid aside his collar and garters,
unloosed the buckles of his shoes, and took off his wig, replacing
it with the skull-cap he usually wore. He had started to work
when the King silently entered. La Tour perceived him and
flew into a great rage. He seized his collar, buckles, garters,
wig, palette and box of colours and fled in spite of the King's
protests and his efforts to detain him. A fresh embassy on the
part of Abbé Beyle became necessary ; the artist allowed himself
to waver. At the last sitting La Tour permitted the King to
come and pay his court to his mistress. Louis XV arrived,
accompanied by her brother, the Marquis de Marigny, Superintendent of the Department of Fine Arts, and the Duc de Choiseul.
Then a famous dialogue took place. The King, Choiseul and
Marigny were discussing marine subjects :

" Why talk of marine subjects," interrupted the boorish painter,
" we have not got any ! " To which the King answered in his
usual serene manner :

" Hey ! Monsieur La Tour, and what about the marine subjects
of Joseph Vernet ? . . . "

The portrait was placed in the King's private room. The
Marquise de Pompadour died on the 15th April, 1764, and Mme.
du Barry succeeded to the royal favour. The picture was removed
and placed, face to the wall, behind an old clock. In the year
1780 Louis XVI happened to have his clock-maker, the celebrated
Janvier who afterwards became a member of the Institute, called
in to repair the regulator. Janvier discovered the portrait :

" Sire, what a wonderful painting ! "

" What ! that . . . still here ! Take it away from me ! "

He had to remove the picture, which is now at the Louvre.

Great exception has been taken to Mme. de Pompadour for
having followed the march of the French armies during the Seven

Years War by sticking flies on the map of the countries where their operations were taking place. During the last world-wide war we stuck little flags on our maps, and one cannot see that the difference between these markers offers very solid grounds for cries of indignation; but perhaps we may be allowed to give expression to a little gratitude to the memory of the fair Marquise when we remember that she was the foundress of the Ecole de Guerre which she created with the help of the celebrated financiers, the brothers Paris. Léon Mention relates in his history of *l'Armée de l'Ancien Régime* that:

" Comte d'Argenson was Secretary of State for War at the time of the foundation of the Ecole Militaire. We may say, however, that the institution came about apart from him and from above him. All he had to do with it was to put his signature at the foot of a project all the details of which had long before been drawn up between Paris-Duverney and Mme. de Pompadour."

The foundations of this great scheme were really laid when Mme. de Pompadour visited the Academy of Saint Cyr. She writes about it on the 18th September, 1750, to Paris-Duverney as follows (we retain her orthography which is charming, especially by reason of her delightful use of the letter *s* in marking the plural of verbs):

" We were at Saint Cyr yesterday. I cannot tell you how greatly I was moved by this establishment. . . . They all came and told me that another one like it should be built for men. That made me want to laugh for they will think (*croironts*) when our scheme becomes known (*cera scue*), that it was they who conceived the idea. I embrace you with all my heart, my dear booby." In this way we may see how the greatest and most glorious institutions may come about at the light touch of a pretty woman gifted with intelligence and patriotism—even though she may have followed the march of French armies with the aid of flies stuck upon maps. We should also remember that we owe to Mme. de Pompadour the manufacture of Sèvres porcelain and the Petit Trianon with its plantations of exotic trees, the horticultural experiments directed by Claude Richard, the celebrated gardener, and the famous Bernard de Jussieu, which gave to France the large garden strawberry. The experiments carried out at the Trianon rendered services of the most varied kinds. Observation was kept on the ravages caused by blight, as a result of which instructions were issued to the Intendants, and henceforth the careful grower did not sow his seeds before washing them with a mixture the ingredients of which were indicated—

water mixed with verdigris or alum, sea water with a mixture of quick lime, or liquid manure.

On the heights of Bellevue arose a delightful country house in which the Marquise de Pompadour, with her rare taste, assembled the most characteristic examples of that marvellous style to which her name has been given—in architecture, paintings, sculpture, furniture, decorated wainscottings and carvings, hangings of Lyons silk, bronzes and porcelain, all in a wonderful and exquisite harmony. But inasmuch as the Château of Bellevue had been the work of the favourite, who had given it to the King, the men of the Revolution considered that their "immortal principles" bade them demolish it.

If reproach is to be laid at the door of the Marquise it should be for not having received insults and calumny with indifference, and for not having allowed them to pass into oblivion in a spirit of unbounded good nature, as did the Comtesse du Barry, or to lose themselves in tears and weeping, as was the case with Marie Antoinette. Madame de Pompadour caused the Comte de Maurepas, who, it is true, had outrageously affronted her, to be expelled from the Ministry, and the doors of the royal prisons were bolted on more than one writer who had insulted her in pamphlets.

VII.—*The Court of Louis XVI and Marie Antoinette*

On the 10th May, 1774, at four o'clock in the afternoon, a lighted candle placed on the window-sill of a room in the palace of Versailles brought the news to France that Louis XV had just expired. A witness relates that " at that moment a terrible din, just like thunder, was heard rising from the principal chamber of the suite ; it proceeded from the crowd of courtiers deserting the ante-chamber of the dead King in a rush to greet the new power."

The most arresting personality in the French Court under Louis XVI was the Queen, of whom the Goncourts have penned a wonderful description :

" A bounding heart, giving freely and prodigally of itself, a young girl rushing open-armed to welcome life, eager to love and to be loved. . . . She loved all things which lulled into reverie, all the joys appealing to young wives and offering distraction to youthful sovereigns ; the seclusion of the family circle in which kindliness may expand, intimate conversations wherein the spirit is free, that kind friend nature, the woods to which one may confide one's secrets, country scenes and the far horizon in which eye and thought may lose themselves, and the ever renewed gladsome feast of the flowers. In singular contrast to all this an outward gaiety concealed a touching and almost melancholy disposition in the young Queen. A frenzied, heedless

and petulant spirit of gaiety filled the whole of Versailles with movement and life. A spirit of restlessness, *naiveté*, thoughtlessness, and
mischievous fun was communicated to all by the Queen and exhaled
around her by the turmoil excited by her thousand charms. Youth
and beauty—everything combined in her to attract, everything
within her was up in arms against etiquette, everything about the
Princess was charming ; she was the most adorable, the most womanly,
if one may say so, of all the women at the Court. Ever in movement,
tip-toed and fluttering, flitting by like a song, like a flash of lightning,
heedless of her train, or of her ladies-in-waiting."

"One could have eyes only for the Queen," wrote Walpole who
saw her in August, 1775, at the festivities on the occasion of the
marriage of Madame Clotilde. "The Hebes, the Floras, the Helens
and the Graces are mere street women compared with her. When
standing or sitting down she is grace personified. She wore a robe of
silver worked over with scattered leaves of oleander, and only a few
diamonds and feathers. They say that she does not keep time in
dancing, but in that case it must be the time that is at fault. . . ."

More than any other human being Marie Antoinette was doomed
to suffer from the strict rules of etiquette with which her lively
and spontaneous nature was in conflict at every step.

"One winter's day," writes Mme. Campan, "it happened that
the Queen, already in complete *déshabille*, had reached the stage of
putting on her chemise ; I was holding it ready unfolded ; the *dame
d'honneur* enters, removes her gloves in haste, and takes the chemise
from me. There is a tap at the door ; it is opened for Mme. la Duchesse
d'Orléans ; her gloves are taken off too, and she comes forward to
take the chemise ; but the *dame d'honneur* must not hand it to her ;
she returns it to me, and I hand it to the Princess ; there is another
tap at the door ; it is Mme. la Comtesse de Provence ; the Duchesse
d'Orléans presents the chemise to her. The Queen was holding her
arms crossed over her breast and appeared to be cold. Madame (de
Provence) sees her pitiable attitude, contents herself with throwing
aside her handkerchief, and keeping her gloves on while putting on
the chemise ruffles the hair of the Queen who bursts into a laugh to
conceal her impatience, but not till after saying several times between
her teeth : ' It is odious ! what a tiresome fuss ! ' "

Mme. de Genlis too relates a conversation she had with Madame
Louise, the younger daughter of Louis XV, who had taken the
veil as a Carmelite nun :

"It requires a miracle to bring up a Prince or Princess at the Court.
The wet-nurse has no other function than to give suck to the child
when it is brought to her ; she may not touch it. There are *remueuses* [1]

---

[1] *Remueuses :* nurses whose sole duty it was to put the child to bed and
change its linen. (H. W.)

to do that, but they may take no orders from the wet-nurse.   There
are certain hours for changing the child, three or four times a day.
If the child be asleep, they wake it up to change it.   If, after its linen
has been changed, it wets its swaddling clothes, it remains like that
for three or four hours.   If a pin should prick it, the wet-nurse may
not remove it ; another woman has to be fetched and waited for,
and the child begins to cry. . . . All these ceremonies are a real
misery."

When Marie Antoinette, Queen and mother, wished to lay her
child in its cradle, the Comtesse de Noailles, her *dame d'atours*
(tire-woman), opposed it : it was not in accordance with etiquette.
The Comtesse de Noailles, whom the young Queen jokingly called
"Madame Etiquette," was a woman conspicuous for the irreproachable dignity of her life and manners, but also for her harsh
attitude and her narrow and heavy disposition.

One day it happened that Marie Antoinette was riding a donkey
when the animal, kicking up its hind legs, threw her on to the
sward.   The Queen landed in the tall grass and there she sat
with rumpled skirts clapping her hands and crying out :

"Quick! go and find Mme. de Noailles that she may tell us
what is the etiquette to be observed when a Queen of France has
fallen off the back of a donkey ! "

Just as Louis XV took refuge in his private suite from all this
formality, so Marie Antoinette found a shelter from it in that
enchanting retreat, the Petit Trianon, which Louis XVI made
over to her as her private property in May, 1774.

The Petit Trianon had been the creation of Louis XV.   The
Duc de Luynes writes about it in a letter dated the 14th January,
1753 : "The King makes great use of this country house to which
he has added several apartments, and on the side towards Versailles a new kitchen garden with hot-houses for all kinds of
fruit, vegetables, and shrubs, of this country as well as from foreign
lands."

Marie Antoinette's work consisted of the *hameau*, or imitation
country homestead.   "She created Trianon in order to escape
from Versailles and Marly," writes M. de la Rocheterie ; "she
wishes to be alone there with a few guests of her own choice.
There she is no longer the Sovereign of a vast empire, but the
owner of a small estate ; there the charm of private life reigns
after the worries of life lived in public."

So too Pierre de Nolhac writes :

"This country life gave a greater freedom and ease.   The Queen
of France kept up less state there than Mme. de Montesson or the

Maréchale de Luxembourg in their circle in Paris. She was like the mistress of an unpretentious house, willingly allowing her guests to group themselves round any particular woman friend—Mme. de Polignac, for instance—while she reserved for herself the special duties of hospitality. Her one pleasure was to please her guests who were also her friends, chosen by the dictates of her heart, friends by whom she felt she was loved."

When she came into the room the ladies did not leave the spinet, or discard their tapestry work, nor the men their game of billiards or *tric-trac*.

Of a sentimental turn of mind Marie Antoinette conceived of life just as a young girl imagines it in the springtime of youth—to go out early in the morning and watch the dawn growing bright from the top of a hill, to run along in the tall grass among the flowers in the meadows, and to wander in the woods after dark under the light of the moon. And so she made this favourite abode, the *hameau* of Trianon, as like the real country as she possibly could, somewhat naively no doubt, for the Queen and Hubert Robert [1] thought of every detail, even to painting cracks in the masonry, breaches in the plaster, protruding beams and bricks in the walls.

But beneath all this artificial setting, a little too much like that of a theatre, Trianon was no village of comic-opera as the brothers Goncourt pictured it, but a real little village :

There was a real farm, with thatched roofs, live animals, Swiss cows that gave milk, sheep covered with wool, rabbits with long ears, pigeons that cooed, a turkey that gobbled and hens that clucked. There was a farmer of the name of Vély, a watchman called Bercy, a small field of pasture for the cows, and a milk-maid to carry the milk. The dairy possessed a rural appearance as mirrored in the fine lake ; its slabs were of white marble, and the milk was kept in porcelain bowls.

The Queen meant to be a real farmer, and used to milk her cows " Brunette " and " Blanchette " herself ; she combed the hair of the big goat, although he had a strong smell, and the pretty she-goats that came from Freibourg ; she would scatter grains of wheat and oats for the hens to peck ; and, watering can or shears in hand, tended the flower beds and borders.

" One could go from the dairy to the barn, from the barn to the mill ; one could eat fresh eggs at the farm, drink the milk warm in the cow-shed, fish in the stream, cross the lake in a gondola, and, when tired with all this exercise, one could return and sit down in the

[1] Hubert Robert : a French painter, who made some fine reproductions of ancient monuments and buildings (1733–1808). (H. W.)

shade, drinking in the scent of the flowers and working ; for no one
was idle at Trianon ; the women would embroider, make tapestry,
or wind their thread ; the men would make nets, read or walk about
chatting together " (Maxime de la Rocheterie).

" The Court of Louis XVI," writes Sénac de Meilhan, " during
six days of the week presented the appearance of a family, or
private country house party drawn together by affection ; on one
or two days it would assume a more imposing character, but it
was easy to see that official ceremonies were a painful task, and
every effort was made to curtail them."

But the consequences of this abandonment of the forms established by tradition at the French Court were not long in making
their appearance.

At the Salon of 1783, Mme. Vigée Lebrun exhibited a portrait
of the Queen in a simple white dress, without any ornaments :
" She dresses like a *femme de chambre*," murmured the Parisians.

Marie Antoinette was the first Queen of France to admit men
to her table, and, notwithstanding that the manners of the Court
became more correct under her influence, this gave occasion to
the most ribald comments.

When Marie Antoinette was still the Dauphine, Louis XV had
foreseen the dangers to which her contempt for etiquette would
eventually expose her, and, later on, the unfortunate Louis XVI
had to confess the same in those cruel hours.

" The Queen," he said, " adopted a manner of living removed
from all forms of etiquette. This custom she has continued on
the throne, and these ways, which were a novelty at the Court,
were too much in accordance with my own natural tastes for me
to oppose them."

The time came when the unfortunate King had to learn to his
discomfiture how greatly the public, who had applauded the
abandonment of ancient usages, now resented this in their
sovereigns.

One morning, taking a charming fancy into her head, the Queen
went out to watch the sun-rise on the heights of Marly, with a
few intimate friends. This gave rise to a horrible pamphlet, *le
Lever de l'Aurore*, which the courtiers were the first to pass round
under their cloaks.

During the warm evenings in the summer the Queen liked to
walk about freely on the terrace of the palace among the public,
for whom she had caused the gates of the park to be opened. The
music of a band could be heard, and nothing seemed more charming.
But the English newspapers distorted these royal evenings into

unclean orgies, and, under the title of *les Nocturnales de Versailles*, the proceedings were reproduced in France in a still more outrageous manner.

These horrible pamphlets even came to the Queen's knowledge at the Court where there were enemy hands to place them on the little round tables in her bedroom.

One morning at the Trianon, the 13th September, 1786, Mme. Campan, her first woman-of-the-bedchamber, on entering the bedroom of her royal mistress found her still in bed crunching between her fingers some letters that had been thrown on the bed, her face bathed in tears and her voice choked with sobs : "Ah! the wicked wretches, the monsters!" cried the unfortunate Princess. "What have I done to them? . . . I wish I were dead!" and when Mme. de Campan wanted to offer her some orange water and ether she went on bitterly : "No, no! leave me if you love me! It would be better that I should die!" She was holding her head between her two hands and the tears were trickling through her fingers.

Napoleon too, when meditating at St. Helena, was to discern the havoc wrought on public opinion by weakening the maintenance of forms consecrated by long use :

"Had she been guided, watched over, and held prisoner by etiquette, the Queen of France would have had no suspicion cast upon her, no scandal would have arisen, and no calumny would have been spread abroad."

It was just a village life that was led at the *hameau*, "a pastoral life," said the Chevalier de Boufflers, "in which only the wolf was wanting." The wolf was to come.

The buildings of the *hameau* at the Trianon were very simple, but the newsmongers conjured up foolish things about them. Mazières painted on canvas a piece of decorative work in a setting of Venetian glass beads. People talked of walls set with diamonds. These latter were soon to glitter so brilliantly in the popular imagination that when the Deputies of the States General visited Trianon in 1789, they stubbornly demanded to see the chamber of diamonds, and, since it was impossible to show them any such place, they left with the firm conviction that this evidence of the King's squandering of the public money had been concealed from them.

As the Goncourts have written in an eloquent passage :

"Private life, its charm and attachments were forbidden to Sovereigns. Kept as State prisoners within their palaces they could not leave them without weakening the religious faith of the people and the respect of public opinion. Their pleasures must be grand and regal; their friendships must be lofty and without intimacy; their smiles must be for the public and shed over all. Even their own heart must not belong to them, nor can it be lawful to them to follow its dictates and abandon themselves to its impulses. Queens, just as Kings, came under this condemnation, this penalty of royalty. When they descended to their private tastes, their sex, age, the simplicity of their minds, the artlessness of their inclinations and the purity and devotion of their affections, won for them neither the indulgence of courtiers, the silence of the malicious, nor the charity of history ! "

We find details of the Court of Louis XVI in the memoirs of the Comte de Ségur, which show its falling off from what it had been in the course of the century which had just come to a close. Young members of the nobility " considered those who held positions round the throne as so much old rubbish of an antiquated régime." Going to Court had come to be regarded as a *corvée*; it was no longer the centre of wit, elegance and luxury.

Men went to Versailles in black coats in order to save the expense of the embroidered costumes which hitherto had been worn there.

" Whom have you lost ? " people would enquire.

" No one; I am going to Court."

In February, 1778, Voltaire was in Paris. Ségur makes a comparison between the Court of Louis XVI at Versailles " where the good King lived in simplicity without any show like a sensible man in peaceful retirement," and the Court of King Voltaire on the Quai des Théâtins, resounding from night to morning with the shouts and acclamations of a worshipping crowd.

" The outer display of former times no longer existed," writes Sénac de Meilhan. " The most wealthy people wore simple and inexpensive costumes; the majority of those whose birth called them to Court confined themselves to putting in an appearance there for a few hours once a week, and then hastened to return to town to solicit an entry into social circles which gave some distinction."

The exterior formalities of the days of Louis XIV were preserved, but they no longer held any majesty, brilliancy, or gaiety. Nevertheless, as Mme. de Genlis states, mind and character were on a higher level, " Meanness and vile actions were more severely judged at the Court than anywhere else."

Like the nobility for which it had been the point of concentration, the French Court had reached the last page of its rôle, and the black gulf of night, the great void, is often preceded by blood-red twilight.

BIBLIOGRAPHY

Argenson (Marquis d'), *Considérations sur le Gouvernement . . . de la France*, 1767.—Bourdaloue, *Œuvres*, 1900.—Carré (H.), *La France sous Louis XV*, 1891.—Croÿ (Duc de), *Mémoires*, ed. F. Cottin and de Grouchy, 1906–1908.—Druon (H.), *Histoire de l'éducation des Princes . . .*, 1897.— Dubourg, *l'Espion Chinois*, 1745.—Dumoulin (Meurice), *Le Caractère de Louis XV; Revue des Etudes Historiques*, 1898.—Geffroy (Gustave), *Les Chefs-d'œuvre de Versailles*, 1907.—Genlis (Mme. de), *Mémoires*, 1825.—Goncourt (Edmond and Jules de), *La Femme au dix-huitième siècle*, 1862.—Goncourt (Edmond and Jules de), *Histoire de Marie-Antoinette*, 1884.—La Bruyère, *Caractères.*—La Rocheterie (Maxime de), *Histoire de Marie-Antoinette*, 1892. —Luynes (Duc de), *Mémoires sur la Cour de Louis XV*, 1860.—Marion (Marcel), *Dictionnaire des Institutions de la France aux dix-septième et dix-huitième siècles*, 1923.—*Mercure Galant*, Dec., 1682.—Mention, *l'Armée sous l'Ancien Régime*, 1900.—Montbarey (Prince de), *Mémoires*, 1826.—Nolhac (Pierre de), *Le Château de Versailles*, 1898.—Nolhac (Pierre de), *Etudes sur la Cour de France : Marie-Antoinette Dauphine*, 1898.—Nolhac (Pierre de), *Etudes sur la Cour de France : la Reine Marie-Antoinette*, 1899.—Nolhac (Pierre de), *Etudes sur la Cour de France : Louis XV et Marie Leczinska*, 1900.—Nolhac (Pierre de), *Etudes sur la Cour de France : Louis XV et Mme. de Pompadour*, 1903.— Oberkirch (Baronne d'), *Mémoires*, 1853.—Orléans (Duchesse d'), called "Madame Palatine," *Correspondance*, trans. Brunet, 1857–1859;—*Lettres nouvelles*, ed Roland, 1883;—*Correspondance . . .*, ed. Jaeglé, 1880.—Sabran et du Chevalier de Boufflers (*Correspondance inédite de Mme. de*), ed. Magnien and H. Prat, 1875.—Saint-Simon, *Mémoires*, ed. Cheruel and Regnier Fils, 1873– 1881 ; ed. A. Boislisle, 1879.—Ségur (Comte de), *Mémoires*, ed. du Marquis de Ségur, undated.—Ségur, *Au couchant de la Monarchie*, undated.—Sénac de Meilhan, *Du gouvernement, des mœurs et des conditions . . .*, 1795.— Sévigné (Marquise de), *Correspondance*, ed. Monmerqué, 1873–1881.—Spanheim (Ezéchiel), *Relation de la Cour de France en 1690*, ed. Em. Bourgeois, 1900.—Taine (H.), *Les Origines de la France contemporaine, l'Ancien Régime*, ed. 1875.—Tilly (Alexandre de), *Mémoires*, 1828.—Vigée-Lebrun (Mme.), *Mémoires*, ed. P. de Nolhac, undated.—Voltaire, *Le Siècle de Louis XIV*.

CHAPTER VI

LETTRES DE CACHET

I.—*The Importance of this Institution*

THE history of *lettres de cachet* is closely linked to that of the constitution of the family and of the royal power which we have endeavoured to sketch in the preceding chapters. They represent that institution belonging to the Ancien Régime which at the present time is perhaps least understood by us, because our minds do not envisage it amid the social conditions, traditions and manners of olden times. One fact is predominantly evident ; and that is that during the space of several centuries not only did our ancestors not think of protesting against this institution, a faithful sketch of which we are about to give, but the idea never entered their minds ; and if in the concluding years of the Ancien Régime the use of *lettres de cachet* aroused numerous and often vehement protests, that was because the manners and traditions of which they were the expression had themselves changed.

In his studies on *Les Lois Fondamentales de la Monarchie Française* M. André Lemaire arrives at the conclusion that " Public law itself considered the State as one large family of which the King was the father."

We have described the manifold bonds by which the royal authority was shackled. *Lettres de cachet* were the sole means possessed by the monarch for putting his will into effect in the kingdom, and even they had each to be countersigned by a responsible Minister. Moreover, they did not apply solely to orders of incarceration or exile, but to all matters wherein the King desired to intervene directly, and always under the *ægis* of a Secretary of State, for the King could do nothing of himself. In

201

the following pages we shall only consider orders by the King relating to the incarceration or exile of private individuals, or what general opinion understands by " *lettres de cachet.*"

Lettres de cachet were made use of not only in public life, but also in the privacy of the family life of old French society, and in such a profound and extensive degree that on the eve of the Revolution there were few families of any consideration who had not at some time or other experienced their effects. Malesherbes had been Minister of the King's Household, together with the Department of Paris, and in this twofold capacity had been concerned in the issue of a considerable number of *lettres de cachet*; with an interest almost amounting to a passion he had unceasingly occupied himself with these *ordres arbitraires*, to borrow the expression commonly used at the end of the eighteenth century, and had taken pains to make himself acquainted with their incidence from every side, and as completely as possible. In 1789, when the different jurisdictions were already assembled for the election of Deputies to the States-General, he drew up a valuable memorandum on *lettres de cachet*, still unpublished, which he addressed to Louis XVI : " I am only giving a vague idea ; it is impossible to give any other, and I doubt whether anyone in France could present an exact table of the different orders (*lettres de cachet*) which take effect in the provinces " ; further on he returns to the same idea : " I will relate what I know about France, for I do not know everything that takes place in France." A study of the documents in the archives provides us with a fuller knowledge.

II.—" *Lettres de Cachet* " *for Affairs of State; as a Police Measure; in Family Matters*

A common error is to think that *lettres de cachet* were confined to affairs of State. A pamphleteer published lampoons against those in authority, against religion, or against the authority of the King ; he was seized and put in the Bastille—such is the general opinion of the meaning of a *lettre de cachet*. Cases like the above, and others of a similar kind, are to be found, no doubt ; but they were so rare that we may safely affirm that out of a thousand *lettres de cachet* issued by the administration, we can barely find two or three, or four at the utmost, connected with a matter of this kind, and a historian desirous of forming a judgment, or bird's-eye view of this institution as a whole, may practically neglect them. With what kind of matters then were the remaining 996 *lettres de cachet* concerned ? Usually with matters connected with the police or with family affairs.

As regards the police, *lettres de cachet* were not without their use, when we take into consideration the astonishing system of jurisdiction, the procedure of which went back to remote times and was sedulously preserved under the Ancien Régime. In his Memorandum Malesherbes writes :

" Except in cases of *flagrante delicto* a judge cannot arrest without a writ, and this cannot be issued without an information duly laid ; witnesses are not heard until they have been officially summoned ; the Minister does not cause them to be summoned until after he has obtained permission to lay an information, and he cannot receive permission to do this except by entering a plea. Meanwhile the guilty person takes to flight. In such cases the Procurator General, or his substitutes, request a *lettre de cachet.*"

The accused would be in prison when a writ for his arrest (*prise de corps*), issued by a regular tribunal such as the Court of le Châtelet, or Parliament, arrived ; forthwith the *ordre du Roi*, as the executive called a *lettre de cachet*, was cancelled, and the prisoner passed into the hands of the ordinary judicial authorities. Under these circumstances the *ordre du Roi* might be compared to the warrant issued by our police magistrates.

Another category of *lettres de cachet* used by the police was peculiar to Paris. "In many towns," writes Malesherbes, "the police officials punish those who are a nuisance to society with summary imprisonment, without any judicial procedure or right of appeal ; in Paris the public authorities and the acting head of the Police, that is, the Lieut.-General of Police, obtain *ordres du Roi* instead of giving instructions in their own names." To this practice must be attributed the fact that *lettres de cachet* in connection with police matters were more numerous in Paris than those issued in relation to family affairs, whereas in the provinces the opposite was the case. Our readers will agree with us that the *ordres du Roi* relating to family matters will present great interest. In a way we might perhaps not have expected we shall see them characterizing a state of society from which our own has emerged, although it differs very considerably from it. We will therefore pause and consider more particularly the *lettres de cachet de famille.*

III.—*Procedure of a " Lettre de Cachet "*

A second mistake is to think that the issue of a *lettre de cachet* was bereft of all forms of procedure and formality.

The following is an account of an *ordre du Roi* taken haphazard from one of the numerous *dossiers* preserved in the archives of the Bastille. We will relate it in detail for it possesses the advantage of demonstrating in a rather striking manner, not only the procedure followed by the administration, but also the spirit inspiring it, the end in view, and the results sometimes obtained.

Towards the end of the year 1750, the Lieut.-General of Police, Berryer by name, received a complaint from Marie Adrienne Petit, the wife of François Ollivier, a vendor of gloves and perfumes established in Paris in the Rue Comtesse d'Artois. From the time that her husband had made the acquaintance of a young dressmaker, called Marie Bourgeois, living in Rue Saint-Denis-aux-Rats, all had become upside down in the home. The poor wife described herself as being despised and even called names by her husband, and customers had given up coming to a shop where the master was now only to be seen on rare occasions; moreover the savings they had been able to put by were being squandered on finery for the smart young girl to whom master Ollivier could no longer refuse anything. The Lieut.-General of Police sent one of his subordinates, a man called Grimperel, to Marie Bourgeois with instructions to make her listen to reason. Grimperel gave her a severe dressing down in the name of the *Magistrat* (the title given in the documents to the Lieut.-General of Police), as representing the royal authority, and forbade her for the future to frequent the company of the said Ollivier. It was good advice, but it happened to be given to a light-headed young woman:

"Meanwhile she continues to receive him in her own lodgings," writes Mme. Ollivier in a second petition, "which causes much trouble in our own home and in our business, and it is easy to foresee that if this continues it will be impossible for us to meet our liabilities. In view of this, Monseigneur, I appeal to you, imploring you to have Marie Bourgeois shut up." This petition to the Lieut.-General of Police was signed by Mme. Ollivier, and (this is an important detail) was countersigned by "the tenant of the house where the pretty dressmaker was living, a man called Charpentier." The Lieut.-General of Police put the matter in the hands of Chaban, his secretary, who was more particularly charged with investigating all questions relating to the issue of *ordres du Roi*. Inspector Dumont was delegated "to verify the facts entered in the petition and to report on them," in conjunction with Grimperel. The two officers sent in similar reports: "The said Bourgeois has not given up seeing the *sieur Ollivier* in spite of having been forbidden to do so."

Berryer, however, hesitated to have recourse to the severe remedy of a *lettre de cachet*, and wanted to make further endeavours by gentler means to bring the guilty pair back to better ways. He therefore wrote about them to the Curé of the parish in which the two lovers were living, begging him to summon them before him and try to lead them back to the right road by persuasive methods. How did she find out that there was a question of bringing her before the Curé ? In order to provide against this eventuality Marie Bourgeois changed her lodgings, and set up in another parish where she gaily resumed her relations with the perfumer of the Rue Comtesse d'Artois, in spite of further admonitions on the part of Grimperel. Of a surety Berryer had doubts as to the effect these reprimands were producing when he instructed his secretary to " keep the papers until fresh complaints come." Fresh complaints did come in the following May. Mme. Ollivier writes that her husband has fallen into the worst excesses, and that she is certain that he means to leave Paris with his mistress : " Have pity, Monseigneur, and order Marie Bourgeois to be locked up ! " In spite of this appeal Berryer did not come to a decision until he had made a second investigation by other police officers, and had received a fresh petition from the wife : " My husband is making preparations to leave Paris any day, and his mistress has already given up her room."

Marie Bourgeois was arrested on the 15th July, 1751, at nine o'clock in the evening, in virtue of a *lettre de cachet* signed by the Comte d'Argenson, then Minister for War and also for the Department of Paris. She was taken to For-l'Evêque,[1] and soon afterwards was transferred to the Salpêtrière. Under lock and key at the latter reformatory the young woman had time to consider the consequences which the attentions of a perfumer might bring in their train, while her family were interceding with the " Magistrat." Her sister Madeleine, and Mme. Herbon, one of her aunts, the head of a dressmaking establishment, assured him that Marie was a respectable girl, and backed up their statements with the testimony of several lodgers in a house where she had lived. On the other side Mme. Ollivier was imploring the Lieutenant of Police to keep her under lock and key.

Berryer chose the latter alternative. However, another petition for mercy met with a better reception. On the 20th February, 1752, the Lieutenant of Police wrote to the Secretary of State for the Department of Paris : " The aunt and sister of Marie Bourgeois have signed an undertaking to watch over her conduct, and François Ollivier another to break off all relations with her." The

---

[1] For l'Evêque : a prison formerly situated in the Rue St. Germain-l'Auxerrois in Paris, and used for debtors and delinquent comedians. It was demolished in 1780. (H. W.)

prison gates were opened, and the Lieutenant of Police heard no more about Mlle. Bourgeois or of Master Ollivier.

The archives of the Bastille provide a large number of similar documents relating to *ordres du Roi*, but the one we have just given should suffice to show that the issue of a *lettre de cachet* was surrounded in Paris by a fairly complicated procedure, which was not, strictly speaking, necessary, but was imposed by custom. However, we will add a few other examples.

A woman of the name of Catherine Randon had been locked up in the reformatory, and M. Menjol, an auditor at the Public Accounts Office, sent to the Lieutenant of Police a protest which may be summed up as follows : (1) In the report concerning the manner of living and morals which had been drawn up about the prisoner, M. Lemoine, tenant of the house in Rue Bourtibourg where she had been living for eighteen months, had not been heard, nor had any of the neighbours in the same street ; (2) Before being punished with a *lettre de cachet* the prisoner had not been summoned before the Curé of St. Paul, the parish in which she was living ; (3) The *ordre du Roi*, which should have been executed by Inspector Bourgoin, had been carried out by one of his subordinates without calling in the proper police official, and without fulfilling the formalities requisite in such cases. Catherine Randon was set at liberty.

On the 22nd June, 1721, a young girl called Leclerc was locked up in the Salpêtrière ; she had been in prison a fortnight when the Lieutenant of Police received a petition beginning with the following words : " Sir, since it is not at all usual, and is contrary to the procedure and rules, and even the laws, to lock up a woman on the deposition of one person alone, and since the order (*lettre de cachet*) creates a scandal and gives cause for complaint to her neighbours and even to the Curé, we have thought it our duty to represent to you that the Abbé de Maignas has outwitted you in the matter of the said woman Leclerc." She too was set at liberty.

But if it be true that the issue of a *lettre de cachet* necessitated a procedure and formalities which had become regular and fixed by tradition, it is likewise true that all this procedure remained secret. That is the most serious reproach which should be levelled by history against this institution. Now, it is a curious thing that this secret character of the procedure and formalities surrounding the issue of an *ordre du Roi* constituted, in the eyes of the people of those days, not only an excuse for *lettres de cachet*, but their *raison d'être*. The administration was not satisfied with covering up under the most complete silence everything connected with the issue of an *ordre du Roi* ; when the person was once in prison the Secretary of State caused all the papers relating to the affair to be destroyed so as to prevent their ever falling under the eyes of indiscreet individuals in the offices of the Ministry.

When the matter related to people of not much importance, and the investigation had not gone outside the office of the Lieutenant of Police, they did not trouble to burn the papers, but consigned them to the most secret place in the kingdom, the bottom of one of the towers of the Bastille, and it is from that hidden spot that they have come down to us. Once in the Bastille the papers never left it ; whatever reasons might exist for demanding their return—an action brought before Parliament, or a question relating to the succession to a property—the Lieutenant of Police always gave an inflexible refusal to communicate any document whatsoever forming part of the *dossier* of a prisoner sentenced by a *lettre de cachet*. The same principle was followed by the Ministry, where it was forbidden not only to communicate the *dossiers*, however grave the motive for the request, but even to give a copy of the very brief notes concerning the case which had been entered in the registers of the office as a matter of form.

This secrecy was part of the family organization of which we have spoken. When we read the circulars issued by Ministers, the instructions of Police officers, the correspondence of Intendants and their subordinates, the replies given by Louis XVI to the remonstrances of Parliament, and also the requests and petitions sent in by private individuals, the same notion never fails to crop up again and again in every kind of form, viz. " the *raison d'être* of *lettres de cachet* is the preservation of family honour." An *ordre du Roi* entailed no shame on the person dealt with in this way, and that was its essential characteristic ; and this is why it seemed necessary, in cases where the reasons for issuing it touched the personal honour of the prisoner, that these reasons should remain secret. " By this means I have been successful in doing a service to respectable people so that the misbehaviour of their relations has not been reflected upon them," writes Berryer. A *lettre de cachet* entailed none of the ignominious circumstances attaching to a criminal trial. The King's procurators in the courts of justice stated in their reports : " No evidence against this individual has been found on which to pronounce sentence of punishment against him, but it would meet the situation to cause him to be imprisoned by an *ordre du Roi*." This did not therefore involve a sentence after judgment had been pronounced ; it was rather a precaution, a personal act of the Sovereign as a fatherly form of correction. This expression is repeated by

Monsieur A. Joly in the course of a study on the incidence of *lettres de cachet* in the district of Caen.

In 1773 the Chevalier de Baillivy, in a lampoon upon *lettres de cachet*, or rather in a campaign against them, wrote as follows : " When considered in the light of the principles animating them, *lettres de cachet* are merely private favours which the King kindly extends to families in order to screen them from the dishonour to which, according to precedent, they fear to be exposed." Vergennes said in 1781 : " There are a whole crowd of cases that the King, in the exercise of his paternal kindness, endeavours to correct so as to prevent punishment by regular justice." Saint-Florentin too was able to write : " An *ordre du Roi* is rather a favour than a punishment," and Malesherbes in his Memorandum to the King in 1789 : " It is to the interest of the family to remove a relative from the possibility of an ignominious sentence ; when the King, as an act of kindness, is good enough to have him locked up, it is a favour."

IV.—" *Lettres de Cachet* " set in Motion for Family Reasons

An *ordre du Roi* issued by the Minister on the report of the Lieutenant of Police used to be requested by the parents or relations of the delinquent. It was for the father, in his capacity as judge over his children, to claim the assistance of the royal power. Malesherbes writes : " Only the father has the right to demand a *lettre de cachet*." When the honour of their family was at stake the people of the lower classes were no less severe than those of higher position. A glazier named Allan, living in the Rue Neuve-Guillemain, who perambulated the streets of Paris looking out for broken windows, informed the commissioner of police that he had solicited a *lettre de cachet* against his son because " he was giving him just reasons to fear ignominious consequences for his family on account of his thieving propensities." The worthy man further declared that he was so poor that it would be impossible for him to offer any contribution towards his son's keep in prison. Henry Clavel, an " actor comedian," requested that his son might be locked up at the Bicêtre,[1] where he would pay an allowance of 150 *livres* for his keep, " because there is cause to fear that this son of mine, who is unable to work for his living, may bring dishonour on his family by a miserable end." Louis Armand, a fan-maker, had his daughter Euphrosine shut up in the Salpêtrière because " he feels himself on the point of being dishonoured by the bad conduct of this unfortunate daughter." We could multiply similar instances indefinitely.

[1] *Bicêtre :* a place of detention for old people and lunatics. (H. W.)

We should, moreover, follow up the principle in all its consequences. For a father to be able to shut up one of his children it was not necessary for the latter to have committed a crime, or even a misdemeanour; that would have been a blot against which the family not only had the right, but the duty of preserving itself. Hence no accomplished acts were required; all that was necessary was a well-founded fear of their happening. The family of Charles de l'Espinay had recourse to the King's authority " in order to be protected from the bad actions which this young man *may* commit and which *might* bring dishonour on them." Danchin, a commissioner of the Royal Buildings, asked that his son might be locked up at Bicêtre because " there is reason to think that he will dishonour his family."

A request from a father was rarely rejected. " Paternal authority by itself should be all that is required in such circumstances," observes a sub-delegate, " because it is not to be presumed that the right instincts and affection of a father could be affected by any prejudice." The Vicomte du Chayla approached Comte d'Argenson in favour of a friend who was being threatened by his father's anger; but the Minister replied, " It is customary to arrest the children of whom their fathers complain." When a *lettre de cachet* had been already issued, the father had power to suspend its execution. Jacques Avisse, a carpenter living in the Rue Saint Roch, wrote to Berryer as follows : " A few months ago I obtained a *lettre de cachet* in the case of my daughter, but from fatherly affection I prevented the order from being carried out." We have mentioned the case of Euphrosine Armand, the fanmaker's daughter; her father had asked for a *lettre de cachet*, and his request had been handed to Inspector Bazin. Shortly afterwards the father wrote : " I think that the presence on the spot of the said Bazin has sufficiently intimidated her, and that fear will bring her back to better ways, and this prompts me to suspend the execution of the *ordre du Roi*." After a little time Armand again requested the incarceration of his daughter, " convinced," he wrote, " that she is worse than ever." The order was carried out.

The father even chose the prison himself. When asking for a *lettre de cachet* against one of his sons, Guillard de Fresnay wrote to Berryer : " We will discuss together in the family to what spot he shall be taken by your authority." When the son was once in prison the father still possessed full power over him. He would draw up the régime to which he was to be submitted, he might mitigate the treatment he had demanded for him, could have him transferred from one place to another, or have him released any day. D'Argenson writes to Vicomte Du Chayla : " The father is so incensed with him that in all likelihood he will keep him a long time in prison." In a letter sent by Lejeune, the son of a paper-maker at Marais, to his mother, we read : " The Father Prior (of Charenton, a lunatic asylum) tells me that I shall never leave here until my father is dead ; although he is severely punishing me, I still love him and hope he will live longer than myself."

Chabrier de Laroche, a captain on half-pay belonging to the Lusignan cavalry regiment, and the son of a President in the Public Accounts Office, was taken to the prison of For-l'Evêque on the 24th October, 1751, on the petition of his father. On the ensuing 12th November his father requested that his son might be set at liberty, but with an *ordre du Roi* returning him to his regiment. This was done, and on the very same day that the young man left the prison, namely on the 14th December, his father obtained a second *lettre de cachet* giving him the power, should he leave his regiment, to have his son arrested on any future occasion wherever he might be, and to keep him in prison for twenty years.

If, for some cause or other, the Minister should hesitate to place this royal thunderbolt in the hands of an irritated father, he was exposing himself to the hard words which one such father gave Malesherbes :

" When the tutelary and sovereign authority refuses to give its support to domestic authority, it knows, doubtless, where to find suitable means for watching over the head of each individual in particular. I therefore resign myself thereto ; but one day it (the royal authority) will not be able to refuse a hearing to my old age when it comes to demand restitution for the prostitution of a name which had been handed down without blemish, and which I had tried to preserve as such ; nor its aid in keeping that name from the slur cast on it by the law."

In the absence of the father, the mother drew up the request, and in the absence of both father and mother, the chief members of the family—brothers, uncles, cousins and even friends of the house—joined their signatures to obtain a *lettre de cachet* against the libertine who by his bad conduct was threatening to tarnish their fair name. The authority of the mother had very great weight with the administration, especially in the case of a daughter. Catherine Flaubert, aged seventy, the widow of Pierre Fontaine, a working plumber, " Having a daughter who had disobeyed her in wishing to marry a youth in spite of her mother, *found herself obliged* to have her sent to the reformatory of Salpêtrière by an *ordre du Roi.*" As the mother was seventy years old, we may well ask what could have been the age of her daughter!

Marie Brache, the widow of a master iron-worker in Paris, had her daughter locked up on account of her misconduct; she supported her request in these words: "Her position as a mother (these petitions were always drawn up in the third person) is less respected than if she were her servant."

In 1751 Thomas Bouillette, a journeyman carpenter, was imprisoned at Bicêtre in virtue of a *lettre de cachet* which had been solicited by his mother, the widow Bouillette, a tripe-seller. She states that "the family profess to be respectable people and are apprehensive of the grievous consequences of his frequenting the company of loose fellows." The young man had been in the Bicêtre for several weeks when his mother addressed a fresh appeal to the Lieutenant of Police. "Her son," she said, "was desirous of enrolling himself in the East India Company, but his afflicted family feared that he was only seeking an opportunity to escape," and asked "that he might be sent in chains to the West Indies with the deserters." The widow Bouillette added that she was willing to pay the entire cost of the voyage, "preferring to make this sacrifice to the grief of being dishonoured by a libertine." Her request was granted. The reader should not imagine that these examples have been chosen for mention here as being exceptional, but as being types, each of which is representative of a large number of similar cases.

We need hardly say that questions of morality form the greater proportion of the motives on which the petitioners based their appeals. Georgette Leloir, the wife of a working man in the Faubourg St. Antoine, had a daughter who had consoled herself for the death of her husband, Jante, without the formalities prescribed by the rules of the Church and the laws of the State. She was living with a night-watchman and "the poor afflicted mother had endeavoured in vain to persuade them to get married"; she therefore demanded "that her daughter should be locked up in the prison where abandoned women were enclosed." Louise Jante was incarcerated in the Salpêtrière on the 18th January, 1752. The night-watchman forthwith declared he was ready to marry his mistress, and her mother consented to her daughter being set at liberty on condition that the marriage should take place in the prison chapel before she came out. Everything seemed on the point of being happily settled, but they had not taken the future father-in-law into account. In a letter signed "Clément" he refused to suffer the insult of seeing one of his sons married in a prison, and made it a condition of his consent that the marriage should be celebrated in the neighbouring church of St. Paul. The mother proved accommodating, and the authorities went so far as to provide the necessary witnesses. In the registry of marriages in the church of St. Paul, dated 15th February, 1752, we read :

" In consideration of the licence granted by the Vicars-General of Paris : betrothed and married on the same day : the husband aged twenty-nine years : the witnesses for the husband were Féral, and. Perrault, *Lieutenant de la Prévôté des Monnaies et Maréchaussée de France ;* [1] the wife's brother, a casual labourer, and Jean Toussaint, licensed hackney carriage driver, attended the wife : the last two stated they were unable to write their names."

As we have just said, the pleas drawn up by parents with a view to having their children incarcerated were nearly always connected with questions of morality ; other cases had reference to frenzied extravagance—the ever recurring story of the young heir allowing his inheritance to get into the claws of the money-lender for the sake of the *beaux yeux* of a girl. The reasons advanced for requesting a *lettre de cachet* were not always very serious. Brunek de Fraudenck had one of his sons locked up in For-l'Evêque when he went to Paris to complete his studies with the intention of entering the corps of engineers, in order. to secure for him the most favourable conditions for preparing for his examinations. His father drew up for the young man a frugal régime, and set him up in a well-lighted room in which there was a large table on which to draw his plans, and every day the prisoner received visits from his instructors, the Sieurs Beauchamp, Thuillier, and Gravelot, the celebrated designer, who gave him lessons in drawing and geometry.

Lettres de cachet were of assistance to a certain father-in-law who was alarmed at the prodigal expenditure of his son-in-law. The Marquis de Brisay was an ancestor of Gaston de Presle, the son-in-law of M. Poirier. As a young man he was fond of luxurious living and, being very extravagant, he soon came to the end of his resources. He then found a very rich and vainglorious family of good bourgeois stock, who were dazzled by his title of " Marquis " and gave him their pretty daughter in marriage, together with a still finer dowry. He then resumed his extravagant living in fine style, and the father-in-law, M. Pinon by name, charmed as

---

[1] This resounding office appears to correspond with the origins of the Marshalsea prison, immortalized by Dickens. The *Maréchaussée* was formerly a corps whose duty was to watch over the safety of the roads in France, and was superseded by the *gendarmes* in 1791. (H. W.)

he was to hear his daughter called " Mme. la Marquise," nevertheless frowned on seeing her dowry so rapidly squandered by her husband. He therefore took their children to live with him, and drew tight his purse-strings ; the Marquis got into debt, M. Pinon became angry and petitioned for a *lettre de cachet*. We have it on the table beside us as we write ; it is dated the 24th January, 1751, signed " Louis " and countersigned " d'Argenson," and it committed the Marquis de Brisay to the fortress of Lille. The latter betook himself unconcernedly to the prison, where he arrived on the 3rd February attended by a servant. All went well for the first month, and the Marquis paid the tradesmen who supplied him, but before the end of the two following months Brisay owed considerable sums to the prison caterer, the tradesmen and the officers of the garrison. The governor of the citadel of Lille, M. de la Basèque, thereupon wrote to the Lieutenant of Police and demanded that the family, that is the father-in-law of the Marquis de Brisay, should add two thousand *livres* a year to the two thousand allowed him by his creditors. When M. Pinon was informed of this he protested loudly " this is too much ! " and sent word to the Minister that the Marquis had children whom he, Pinon, was obliged to bring up, that he had kept Brisay for twelve years, and that the utmost he was disposed to do was to increase his allowance by 500 *livres*. In a second letter, written shortly afterwards to the Secretary of State, M. Pinon made representations that his son-in-law's sojourn in the citadel of Lille, " where the *cabaret* was always full of officers and chorus girls," was of a nature to lead the prisoner to spend money. He therefore requested that the Marquis might be transferred to Fort Escarpe-lez-Douai, or to Fort Saint Français, near Aire.

V.—*To Save the Family Honour*

The circumstances giving the most satisfactory explanation for *lettres de cachet*, and the only ones which the spirit of modern times can admit, were those having in view the rescue of a delinquent from the terrible judicial system of the time as applied by the tribunals of Châtelet or Parliament, and the saving of a whole family from the disgrace of a public sentence which was always pronounced with pompous notoriety. The action of *lettres de cachet*, grafted, as it were, on to the action of the law-courts, is particularly interesting when studied in connection with the lower classes of the people.

In the course of a report to the Lieutenant of Police giving particulars of a patrol through the quarter of Saint-André-des-Arts, made on the 31st January, 1751, Inspector Poussot states that a man called François Bunel, a soldier in the French guard, when taking part in a sanguinary brawl at the back of a cabaret had been arrested ; he then discovered that this individual had been charged with many robberies and that he was living with a woman of the worst kind. He was, therefore, on the King's order committed to the jurisdiction of the Châtelet ; but his mother, the widow of a soldier who had been in the French guard, succeeded in coming to an arrangement with the civil court in order to save her son and all his family from the shame of a sentence by the tribunal, and managed to get President de Boulainvilliers himself, at whose house her son had committed one of his robberies, to write to the King's Procurator requesting, in her name, and in that of the family, that Bunel might be allowed to enlist for the West Indies, or be imprisoned by *lettre de cachet* at Bicêtre, which would remove him from the jurisdiction of le Châtelet.

This was done, and the sergeants recruiting for de Briqueville's regiment found him at Bicêtre. He was a well set up man, and the Lieutenant of Police authorized him to enlist in that regiment. A *lettre de cachet*, dated 22nd March, opened the prison doors, and a second exiled him to be placed on the strength of the infantry regiment of de Briqueville. We are without any further news of him for a year and a half, but on the 4th November, 1752, the Marquis de Briqueville wrote to Berryer asking him to cancel the order of exile which hung over Bunel's head. He said that Bunel had been behaving in an exemplary manner throughout, had never incurred the least censure, and that his superiors were anxious to give him promotion, which could not be done so long as he was under the sentence of a *lettre de cachet*. Another note, signed by the Captain of Bunel's company, was attached to the Marquis de Briqueville's request, and ran as follows :

" Monsieur, you did me the honour to promise that when you received a letter from M. de Briqueville, you would cancel the two letters exiling Antoine Lachambre and Bunel. Allow me to have the honour of begging you to grant me the cancellation of that attaching to Bunel. I make bold to assure you that he is a very good fellow who has been behaving wonderfully well for the two years he has been in the regiment, that all his superior officers are very well satisfied with his behaviour, and wish to promote him to sergeant as soon as the *lettre de cachet* is cancelled, and that I for my part will take upon myself to watch over his conduct and give you an exact report should he fail, contrary to my expectations, in the obligations he will owe to you. And this favour, Monsieur, I am making a special point of requesting of you."

The last paper in the *dossier* is a report of the Lieutenant of Police to the Comte d'Argenson, the Minister in Paris :

" Toussaint François Bunel was placed on the strength of de Brique-ville's regiment by an *ordre du Roi* of the 21st March, 1751, because he was a dissolute fellow living with a woman who passed as his wife, had stolen linen within the jurisdiction of Brittany, and had committed another robbery from M. d'Houvant, custodian of the Kitchens to M. le President de Boulainvilliers ; as he has been of very good behaviour since being in the regiment, and as M. de Briqueville requests the recall of the order with the intention of promoting him to sergeant, M. le Comte d'Argenson is begged to have the necessary instruction sent to this effect."

This report bears a marginal note in the hand of the Minister : " Cancellation authorized, 3rd December, 1752."

For the proper comprehension of the bearing of this brief record a knowledge is required of the severe sentences given by the tribunals of that period, to which philosophic writers continually drew attention, and of which Voltaire speaks in the following terms : " They (the tribunals) were the upholders of ancient barbarous customs against which nature aghast called out loudly. They consulted only their worm-eaten registers and if they found in them any senseless and horrible usage they regarded it as a sacred law. For this reason no proportion was observed between the penalty and the offence. They punished some thoughtless act of a young man as they would have punished a case of poisoning, or one of parricide." The *lettre de cachet* obtained by the mother of François Bunel not only saved the young French guardsman from the gallows, but proved his moral salvation, rehabilitated and transformed into an honest man of service to his country a miserable being lost to all moral principles and sinking into ever greater degradation in the most ill-famed slums of Paris. Many *dossiers* similar to that of François Bunel have come under our eyes. We should add, however, that not all parents anxious to preserve the honour of their families acted under so legitimate an emotion. A lady of the name of Leblanc stubbornly persisted in living with her husband, although he had no more money left, " with an obstinate infatuation (in the words of the record) which even her confessor was unable to overcome." The mother of the young wife had her shut up in a convent of the Mathurines. " It is not without sorrow," she wrote to the Mother Superior, " that I have seen my daughter reduced to the lot she is experiencing, and it is a fearful thing, doubtless, to be deprived of one's liberty when one has nothing for which to reproach oneself beyond a too great attachment to one's husband."

VI.—*In the Interests of Morality*

The Lieutenant of Police often considered parents to be too severe, and instead of giving the *lettre de cachet* asked for, he would summon to his private office the father and mother, together with the young person who merely wanted to follow her bent. The young girl would listen to the reprimands of the Lieutenant of Police and next day, in spite of the threat of a *lettre de cachet* to punish her disobedience should she disobey, would become all the more infatuated with her lover. Such episodes of a paternal and gracious character give us a life-like picture of the period.

When the parents neglected to intervene in putting a stop to the irregularities of their children it sometimes happened that other lodgers in the house, neighbours, and people living in the same quarter, would send an expression of their indignation to the Lieutenant of Police. Details such as these are valuable evidence for the history of the Paris population in those times.

The *dossier* of another young French guardsman has come into our hands. He had fallen in with a young dressmaker named Marie who had just reached the age of seventeen. The two children went to lodge in the attic of a large house in the Rue des Bourguignons belonging to the Chevalier d'Hautefort. Their little garret looked over the surrounding roofs. In the boxes of earth, placed on the window ledges, they had planted convolvulus, and the flowers standing out in their bright colours from the green leaves, between which little glimpses of the sky could be seen, had climbed along the wire netting. The young couple felt themselves left alone to the enjoyment of their happiness when a letter arrived at the office of the Lieutenant of Police signed "Thierry Petit, tenant of the buildings and out-buildings inherited by M. le Chevalier d'Hautefort." He represented that "the said Jean Foulard, a soldier of the French guard on half pay, was living a scandalous life with the said Marie Boutillier," that all the neighbourhood was indignant, and that even the Curé of Saint Médard, "with true pastoral zeal," had expressed his determination that "the King's authority should remove these erring sheep from his flock." The Curé of Saint Médard, Abbé Hardy, supported this request : "I have the honour to certify that Foulard and Marie Boutillier, both minors, are living in a manner that scandalizes and gives rise to indignation in the entire district, and refuse to listen to anyone, or to separate."

Berryer, the Lieutenant of Police at the time, exercised his formidable authority with a kindness of heart and an indulgence which was recognized by the testimony of his contemporaries. He preferred to keep his eyes closed until fresh complaints were brought to him, and he had not long to wait. Another petition arrived from the inexorable M. Petit, countersigned by the young woman's family : " Monseigneur, the entire family of the said Boutillier join with the Sieur Petit and implore Votre Grandeur to grant them an order to have her shut up in the reformatory. This favour the family awaits from your goodness—you who are justly considered as the upholder of family honour." The petition had been dictated to a public scrivener, as is evidenced by the handwriting, but the signatures bear witness to the humble position of these worthy folk : François Billard " ocquele " (*oncle*), Nicolas Frangel " cusen " (*cousin*), François Royé " cousien " (*cousin*).

Nevertheless Berryer still hesitated, and in consequence received a further complaint on the 12th February : " M. le Curé de Saint-Médard has made every effort to persuade the young people to get married, or to separate and change their manner of life ; but far from taking into consideration his prudent remonstrances they go on living together in sin." Pierre Bercion, a disabled soldier, and his wife, Jean Cochet, a gauze weaver, Catherine Lallemand, called La Joye, a silk winder, Marguerite Regnaud, wife of a practising lawyer, Louise Paillard, gauze worker, Louise Macomble, widow of a journeyman brewer, and Antoine Macomble, gauze worker, all neighbours or lodgers in the building where Jean Foulard and his little friend were living, added their complaints to those of M. and Mme. Petit, and all signed the petition with the exception of two or three of them who could not write. *Lettres de cachet* ordering the imprisonment of the young man in the Bicêtre, and that of the young woman in the Salpêtrière, were issued by Comte d'Argenson on the 22nd March, and carried out on the 1st August, 1751.

After a few months' detention in the reformatory the young girl wrote to the *magistrat* (Berryer) a very touching entreaty, imploring his pardon and her liberty. Her family got wind of this and protested : " The whole family have the honour to humbly implore Votre Grandeur to grant them the favour of keeping the said Marie Boutillier in the reformatory as a bad lot having every appearance of wishing to begin her dissolute life again." A further petition is dated 18th December, 1751 : " In their fear that she will sink back into her life of debauchery and thus dishonour them, they very respectfully beg Votre Grandeur not to grant her her liberty." A third petition is dated 23rd March, 1752 : " No sooner will she have come out than she will resume her licentious life to the great scandal of the family." Berryer wrote on the back : " Her family is opposed to her being granted her liberty. To be attached to the *dossier* and produced at the inspection."

Meanwhile "J. B. Foulard, twenty-two, cobbler's apprentice," had enlisted in the army with the approval of the Lieutenant of Police ; he left the prison, and shortly afterwards Berryer received a letter from him imploring him to set his little friend at liberty. Foulard stated that if he had sheltered Marie Boutillier, an orphan, with no father or mother, it was with a view to marrying her, and added "that as a result of their true affection for each other the young girl had given birth to a boy," who had been baptized under his father's name in the church of Saint Médard, and that, having had the grief of losing the child, they had had him buried in the same parish. He ended up by saying that " as the petitioner and the young girl had been living together all the time, M. le Curé of the parish had brought about their separation by causing the petitioner to be imprisoned in the Bicêtre, from which he had now come out, and the girl at the Salpêtrière where she still remained. The said Foulard, in a full spirit of probity and religion, requests permission to marry her in order to repair her honour, and the said girl, who has no other wish than to live with him, urgently implores Votre Grandeur to be so good as to give command for them to be married at the reformatory." The marriage took place on the 29th July, and the Inspector, in his report of the ceremony, states that "the orders of the *magistrat* were carried out there with all possible exactness." Our two young friends, thus set at liberty, were now able to follow their love in a regular manner, and with no further scandal to the neighbourhood they could retake possession of their little garret in the Rue des Bourguignons.

We have seen that the priests of the different parishes in Paris played an important part in the history of *lettres de cachet*, especially in cases like the preceding one. Their zeal in endeavouring to bring back members of their flock who had strayed away sometimes led them to adopt excessive rigour. In 1751 Jeanne Velvrique was twenty-one years old, and, to quote the expression of Abbé Feu, Curé of Saint Gervais, "gentle and shy, pretty and graceful." A woman of the world got hold of her and procured for her the protection of an American. The Curé intervened : "The American talked reasonably to the two persons I sent to see him," he wrote to the Lieutenant of Police. All seemed going to be satisfactorily settled when it came out that this "reasonable man" was not the only one to contribute to the welfare of the young lady, and that a man called Lheureux, postman to the Salpêtrière, "a pernicious man," as the old priest wrote, enjoyed a no less happy position in her heart and favours, and was far less disposed to relinquish her. "I claim my sheep," wrote the

Curé of Saint Gervais to the Lieutenant of Police, " and hope that you will be so good as to have her arrested and placed in Saint Martin's, where she should amend her ways, and then I will put her in a convent." It should be noted that Saint Martin's was the roughest prison for women in Paris.

Berryer charged Commissioner Rochebrune to inquire into the following facts : " What is the behaviour of the young girl like ? Is she a cause of scandal ? Has she any parents, and does she live with them ? Are they able to pay anything for her keep in case it may be necessary to punish her ? " On these different points Rochebrune made the following reply : " Her parents are poor and the girl has left them since the first week of Lent." He added that having learnt of the move that had been made by the Abbé Feu she had made application to join the Opera, " with a view to being protected from her Curé by the privileges attaching to the Royal Academy of Music." Any little dancer or chorus girl at the Opera, engaged on that footing in the service of the King, could no longer be punished by a *lettre de cachet*. But Jeanne Velvrique had not time to carry out her plan and was arrested on the 22nd February, 1752. When in prison she lost no time in writing to her protectors, of whom she had many. To the Duc de Duras, Marshal and Peer of France, she wrote : " *Mon cher papa*, I beg of you the favour to use your influence with M. Berryer in procuring my release from prison. If for some time past you have felt indifference towards me, do this out of charity. You are the only one to whom I look for my future destiny." The Duc de Duras made a fervent appeal to the Lieutenant of Police, the girl's mother added her entreaties to the noble Duke's urgent demands, and the Curé of Saint Gervais consented to Jeanne's leaving Saint Martin's on condition that before being restored to complete liberty she should spend some months in the Community of the Good Shepherd : " I count on the good influence of the Mother Superior," wrote the old priest, "to save this strayed sheep."

VII.—*Disagreements between Husband and Wife*

As we should expect, cases of husbands desirous of having their wives shut up are very numerous, and still more numerous are those of wives anxious to have their husbands put under lock and key. So, too, it was always on the plea of the honour of the family being imperilled. The hubbub created over an affair of morals pleaded before Parliament was perhaps greater at that time than it would be to-day. An action for a separation filled all the gutter press. D'Argenson writes : " The public is delighted with the scene presented to it, and no one is charitable enough to draw down the curtain in order to hide such an absurd spectacle." The lawyers had taken to having the memoranda, cross examination and pleading all printed and distributed on sale in Paris in large quantities. These were passed from hand to hand; in the corner of a *boudoir* they were read by Clitander who would season them with his comments to bursts of laughter on the part of Célimène and the Marquis. The verdict of the judge was also printed, together with the considerations that had led him to it, and one could hear the news-hawkers—already they were swarming in Paris—shouting them out in the streets even in front of the houses of the persons concerned.

One remark must be made in reference to *lettres de cachet* solicited by one of the married pair against the other : the King's order was far more easily obtained by the husband against the wife, than *vice versa*, which fact, however, did not prevent *lettres de cachet* against the husband from being the more numerous, for the reason, as stated by Malesherbes, that " they were importuned with far greater insistence than all the others." In the course of his memorandum to Louis XVI Malesherbes makes another interesting observation on this subject : " I ought to reveal one of the secrets of the Administration," he writes, " and that is that there are more of these—that is, *lettres de cachet*—against husbands, than of those granted against the wives. But there is a difference ; the wife does not make her petition in her own name. Those who are interested in her lot relate her misfortunes to the officials entrusted with issuing the *ordres du Roi*. Investigations are thereupon made into the husband's behaviour, and when they find pretexts for having him shut up, they seize upon them." Thus the wife was not in a position to demand a *lettre de cachet* in her own person ; when an order against her husband was granted, Royal authority was supposed to have acted spontaneously.

This observation of Malesherbes must, however, be qualified with one reservation. These subtleties were rarely applied except among the nobility and the upper classes ; the people acted with more simplicity, and we have had the opportunity of perusing an infinite number of appeals drawn up by the wives themselves and in their own names.

The King's authority intervened in married life even when there had been no scandal, as is testified by the reports of d'Argenson's Lieutenant of Police, which are full of keen observation and humour.

" A young woman, named Beaudoin," he writes, " openly makes it known that she will never have any love for her husband, and that she considers everyone is free to dispose of their affections and of their person as they wish. She places no limit to the impertinences she utters against her husband who is so unhappy as to be at the point of despair. I have twice spoken to her, and although for many years I have become accustomed to impudent and ridiculous assertions, I am unable to restrain my surprise at the line of reasoning advanced by this woman in support of her systematic attitude. She means to live and die with these views; she says a woman must have lost all sense to follow any other, and rather than continue to live with her husband she will turn Huguenot or enter a convent. On receiving the report of all these impertinences I was led to think she must be mad; but unfortunately she is not sufficiently so to be shut up by the public authorities; she has only too much intelligence, and I was hoping that after spending two or three months in the Asylum she might come to see that that abode was even more melancholy than the presence of a husband she did not love. Moreover the latter is of such an accommodating temper that he will put up with not being loved if only his wife will be willing to return to him and will stop saying at every moment that she hates him more than the Devil.

But the wife replied that she could not tell a lie, that a wife's honour consists in speaking the truth, that everything else is but an idle fancy, and that she should kill herself on the spot if she foresaw that she should ever have the least affection for her husband."

Such causes for obtaining imprisonment are repeated with constant uniformity—attractions apart from the home, dissipation of their common resources, ill-treatment, and frequent instances of misdemeanour punishable by the courts, from the jurisdiction of which it was hoped to save the delinquents. A husband had his wife shut up for having been smitten by excessive love for the god of wine. When the bad conduct of the wife was witnessed by the children, especially by girls of a certain age, the appeal was never refused.

In 1722 Nicolas Cornille, a bourgeois of Paris, returned to his home after a long voyage overseas. He arrived with joyful countenance and presented himself to his wife; but she received him with a distant manner and told him it was a poor practical joke to try and make himself out her husband. In short, in spite of the insistence of the worthy man, she not only refused to allow him to resume the enjoyment of his conjugal rights, but, what Cornille considered still more serious, the enjoyment of his fortune as well. A *lettre de cachet* consigned the recalcitrant wife to the Salpêtrière.

After one of a married couple had been put in prison the other retained the right to prescribe the régime to be observed, and to have the prisoner transferred elsewhere if the latter place appeared to be safer. The husband remained the judge of the proper moment for setting his wife at liberty and *vice versa.* " I have spoken to the wife of the man called Lécuyer," wrote a Police commissioner, "who is desirous of having her husband released from the Bicêtre ; she tells me that she finds him in very good dispositions." The Lieutenant of Police wished to take the opinion of the overseer of the prison, in addition, and received the following reply : " His wife came to see him a short time ago, and he seemed to be willing to accommodate himself to her views." And so Philippe Lécuyer was set at liberty.

A few hyper-sceptical persons will feel no astonishment at the fact that some husbands who had been shut up at the instance of their wives asked permission to remain in prison when the latter came to reclaim them. Taschereau de Baudry, Lieutenant of Police, writes on the 6th September, 1722, to the Minister in Paris : " Michel Arny asks permission to remain in prison for the rest of his days, assuring me he will be happier there than living with his wife." This spirited individual was a cobbler by trade, and as the Overseer of the Bicêtre stated that employment could be found for him in the prison he was authorized to remain there and was promoted to the grade of " well-behaved paupers."

VIII.—*Family Affairs become Affairs of State*

After expressing surprise at seeing the Government under the Ancien Régime busying itself over the most insignificant disputes among the humblest families of the kingdom, the few writers who have had occasion to touch on the history of *lettres de cachet* are still more astonished to find Ministers, when asked to issue a *lettre de cachet,* giving so much attention, taking such pains and assuming the burden of infinite worry with a view to coming to a decision after acquainting themselves with the facts. Monsieur A. Joly speaks of it in the following terms :

" In all of this the Ministry showed a wonderful forbearance. There was no matter too trivial, no detail too paltry, to engage their attention. One can scarcely imagine to what puerile details the curiosity of the minister descended, or what ridiculous tittle-tattle the Intendants reported—complaints of angry parents, remarks made by neighbours, incidents happening in small towns, etc. And it was not at all necessary that a family should occupy a great position. Domestic disputes of the humblest bourgeois were safe to come to the ears of the Minister and to find him good-naturedly open to receive them.

One of these *dossiers* contains quite a voluminous account which is interesting to read on this point, dealing with the quarrels of a bourgeois with his wife's family. All the incidents of this burlesque affair and the wrangling of a giddy-pated son-in-law with a cross-grained mother-in-law supported by her daughters, are detailed therein at great length. The *dossier* is crammed full of accounts of caps torn, chests of drawers emptied, soup thrown about, and unseemly chastisement of his wife by her husband in the open street. And let no one think that all this information failed to reach the right quarter. For the space of two years the Minister's attention was kept on the alert."

Correspondence of the above kind is not found in the *dossiers* dealing with *lettres de cachet* in Paris, because no distance intervened between Paris and the Minister, and also because the organization at the disposal of the Lieutenant of Police enabled him by means of his commissaires and inspectors, speedily to provide the Minister with the information desired. None the less the Secretary of State for the Department of Paris bestowed no small attention on the family matters to which his notice was drawn.

Who does not recall one of those strange scenes depicted by Marivaux in his delightful *Vie de Marianne*, at the family meeting in the private office of the Secretary of State ? They were discussing a *lettre de cachet* for which a petition had been made against Marianne, a girl whom a young man of good family was anxious to marry, although she had neither birth nor possessions. The discussion went on for a long time ; the Minister summoned Marianne to his presence and listened with interest to what every-one had to say. From Marivaux's description one might be tempted to believe that the Minister only took all this trouble in the case of aristocratic families, but if we go through the *dossiers* we find humble bourgeois, and people of the lowest classes obtaining similar access to his private office.

Claude Huisse, a drunkard and a brute, was a tavern keeper in the Pré-Saint-Gervais, and was in the habit of beating his wife " to the extent of smashing her with his blows," as we read in the documents. He had also another failing, being " such a mad fool that in spite of the fact that he was hugely in debt he dressed like a musketeer, with embroidered hat and green cockade trimmed with gold, and ordered a suit from his tailor costing 600 livres." He was sent to the Bicêtre. After two months his wife, who had petitioned for him to be imprisoned, requested that he might be set at liberty. Saint Florentin, Duc de la Vrillière, and Minister of the King's Household, wrote to the Lieutenant of Police ordering an inquiry to be made by the Provost of the Pré-Saint-Gervais with a view to enabling him to decide as to the desirability of such a measure. The Provost drew up a detailed report in which he represented the prisoner as a man of extremely violent tempera-

ment, and of a weak and vicious disposition, especially when he
had been drinking; he added that he had summoned Huisse's
wife before him. "She appeared to me extremely embarrassed,
and I think, judging by her request to you, that she must have
been born feeble-minded and unlucky considering that she has
everything to fear at the hands of this man who sooner or later
will do her a bad turn." The poor woman persisted in requesting
the release of her husband, whereat the Minister, Saint Florentin,
summoned to his office the nearest relations of the prisoner, and
after a discussion with them over Huisse's character he made
them promise to keep a watch over his conduct, to be responsible
for him, and to come again if required.

Louis de Loménie very justly observes, "Possibly people will
pity the Ministers of the Ancien Régime and will allow them some
indulgence when they see to what extent these inextricable private
matters took up their time and attention at the expense of public
affairs."

IX.—*Their Abuse*

The institution of *lettres de cachet* engendered on the other hand
great abuses by reason of the preponderating weight given to
the personal opinion of the men entrusted with carrying them out,
and the absolutely secret methods surrounding their procedure.

In 1713 a member of the King's bodyguard, Du Rosel de Glatigny,
"gentilhomme de l'Isle de France," wrote to the Minister requesting
an order to have his daughter, Marie du Rosel, aged nineteen,
imprisoned in a reformatory in Paris. He set out in his petition
that she wanted to marry "a trumpeter" to the prejudice of
an officer of the guard who had asked her hand in marriage. As
a measure of prudence, and to spare his daughter the attentions
of her lover, he said he had already placed her in a convent at
Meaux, but he had every reason to apprehend that the young
man would carry her off as he had learnt that he had already
found means of seeing and speaking to her. "It would bring
dishonour on a family owning amongst their numbers Lieutenant-
Generals and Knights of Malta," he said in conclusion. Cardinal
de Noailles, Archbishop of Paris, was asked his opinion, and replied
that religious communities were often unsuitable places for keeping girls of that sort, that they got no better there and often corrupted the nuns, that the only safe thing to do was to put her
in a reformatory where she could be hidden away, and that the
institution of Sainte-Pélagie, otherwise called the Refuge, seemed
to be the most suitable place for the present.

Marie du Rosel was transferred accordingly from the convent,

where she then was, to the prison in Paris. Shortly afterwards
the Minister received a very sharp letter from Mme. de Richelieu,
the Mother Superior of the convent at Meaux ; she gave the highest
testimony in favour of the young girl whom, she stated, she knew
to be pious and good, and that far from allowing herself to be
courted by soldiers the girl was disposed to become a nun ; but
that her father, being anxious to have the use of the fortune which
Marie du Rosel held from her mother, had had her transferred to
Saint Pélagie in the hope that they would keep her there for the
rest of her days. D'Argenson, whose business it was to verify
the facts, summoned Du Rosel to his presence and plied him with
questions to such good purpose that he was compelled to admit
that he had no proof of his allegations. This made a great stir
and people demanded the severe punishment of the gentleman
" for having obtained the order on a false declaration, and for
having desired to bring dishonour on his daughter." Marie du
Rosel returned to the convent at Meaux, whence she sent a petition
for the pardon of her father.

At about the same period Mme. Chantray d'Ormoy had likewise
been taken to the Refuge. In league with a lady, one of his neighbours, her husband had previously sought various means to get
rid of her. He had first of all, in 1682, charged her with adultery
before Parliament, but had been nonsuited. On two subsequent
occasions he returned to the same charge, but with no further
success, and he then fell in with a man who stated that he was
possessed of special facilities for obtaining the grant of *lettres de
cachet*. The two plotters drew up the following agreement :

" We, the undersigned, have come to the following understanding,
to wit, that I, Seigneur des Aulnez, with Seigneur d'Ormoy, have
agreed that I, the said Des Aulnez, promise to the said Seigneur d'Ormoy
to obtain for him a *lettre de cachet du Roi* bearing an order to have
the wife of the said Seigneur d'Ormoy shut up in a convent, and within
a fortnight's time, and I, the said Seigneur d'Ormoy, promise the
said Seigneur Des Aulnez to pay him, one month after he shall have
handed to me the said order, the sum of four hundred *livres* for his
pains, attentions, and negotiations ; in faith of which we have this
day signed these presents. Written in Paris, this 12th April, 1692.
Signed : d'Ormoy, des Aulnez."

Had it not been for the vigilance of the civilian official the prisoner
would have remained under lock and key for a long time.

A similar affair concerned an innkeeper, named Curieux, whom
his wife had had arrested and imprisoned by her lover, a police
constable. This bold accomplice took possession of her husband,
locked him up in the Bicêtre on the alleged plea of a *lettre de cachet*

and did not leave him until he had seen him safely behind solidly
locked doors. When later on he was asked on what authority he
had acted, he boldly replied that he had received a verbal order
from his Chief.

Another case of this kind is the account of a gilder, named Gillet,
who was locked up in the Bicêtre, the most horrible of all prisons,
where he remained for six months, because his wife was in love
with a police constable. We can read of still more startling incidents. The following is the account of a poor blind woman,
who, after the death of her husband, was shut up in a convent.
The relatives of the husband had obtained an *ordre du Roi* on the
pretext that she was seeking to enrich herself with the effects left
by her husband, but in reality it was they who were trying to get
possession of them for themselves. The Mother Superior of the
convent of Charonne, in which Mme. de Morsant had been placed,
had just received fresh instructions forbidding her, on the part of
the Minister, to allow the prisoner ever to come out again on any
pretext whatsoever. To this she replied :

"Monseigneur, the unfortunate plight in which Mme. de Morsant
finds herself compels me to trouble you by very humbly begging you
to take compassion on her misery, and to allow her to leave our house
in which she has been since her husband's death, in order that she
may attend to her affairs and be in a position to draw something of
what may lawfully be hers for her own and her son's subsistence. I
am able to tell you, Monseigneur, that she is reduced to such extremities that she has nothing wherewith to pay for her board. It is a
very great misfortune to her that people believe that she has made
herself rich over her late husband's death, but I can assure Votre
Grandeur that she has been so simple-minded as not to have derived
any advantage on that head, and that far from having profited by it
she has left behind what is her own—a thing quite easy to believe
by those who know her, not only as a good woman but quite blind,
and not in a position to be able to look after herself."

The above examples of the abuses engendered by *lettres de cachet*
are not the only ones we have come across. On the other hand,
we must bear in mind the fact that Malesherbes—who, as philosopher
and official, had not ceased throughout his whole life to combat
the practice of *lettres de cachet*, and had only consented to enter
the Ministry on the promise that he should be allowed to work
for their suppression—in the course of his famous investigation
in 1775 into cases of people imprisoned on *lettres de cachet*, only
discovered two cases in the whole of Paris in which he considered
the prisoners were deserving of being set at liberty. And in his
memorandum to Louis XVI the official condemnation of *lettres*

de cachet, drawn up in 1789, after the reports from the Bailiwicks had already made public their unanimous feeling against this doomed institution, he had frankly stated : " The complaints raised in these last few years have been greatly exaggerated."

From the preceding pages the reader, like ourselves, will have drawn a two-fold conclusion : firstly, that the institution of *lettres de cachet* possessed living roots in the social instincts of the time, from which it drew the sap that had nourished its formidable development. It had grown spontaneously within a society which had issued from the Renaissance, made our seventeenth century, and deteriorated in the course of the eighteenth century ; and grown in such a way that the abuses of *lettres de cachet,* instead of diminishing were continually on the increase—not because the Administration was becoming more powerful and tyrannical, but just the contrary as can be shown ; the real reason was that *lettres de cachet* were meeting with greater opposition year by year and becoming more grievous and more painful to tolerate in the state of society in which they were continuing to function.

On the 16th March, 1790, on the King's initiative, the Constituent Assembly obliterated from our laws this institution characteristic of a former age, thereby accomplishing a sound and just work which was applauded by France and all Europe.

It is, nevertheless, a curious fact that although the whole of France came to set its face against the régime of *lettres de cachet,* the Revolution found its strength and its very reason in what had constituted the strength and first cause of that institution. Have we not been struck by the character of the people of Paris which the history of *lettres de cachet* discloses in so remarkable a light ? When pointing out the keenness with which these orders were demanded, and the motives dictating them, Malesherbes, who had had to make a particular study of them in his capacity of Minister of the King's Household, wrote these memorable words :—

" The members of a patrician family are indignant at a young man acting in a manner unworthy of his birth. Plebeians have other prejudices which possibly are based on a very sound moral code, but they cling to them with too great a rigour. There are faults which every one blames, but which people of condition, and those we call men of the world, regard as pardonable ; these, however, in the opinion of a bourgeois family, are offences which may not be excused. It is to the obscure classes of society that simplicity and purity of morals have been relegated. It could be wished that these simple modes of thought were those of the entire nation, but they are not, and we ought not to go so far as to deprive of their liberty those who have allowed themselves to share in the vices common to their century."

At that time the Maréchale de Luxembourg used to say : " There are now only three virtues left in France, namely vertuchon ! vertubleu ! and vertugadin ! " [1]   She was judging French morals from the point of view of a frivolous nobility. Since then these same morals have been judged on what the clever writers of the time calumniously said of them. A priori, one ought to think that they had remained sound and strong among the bourgeoisie and the popular classes who gave vent to their prodigious energy during the Revolution and the wars of the Empire.

The apparent cause and pretext for the Revolution was the arbitrary methods of the Ancien Régime as characterized by lettres de cachet ; the real cause, the social cause, was the persistence in the mass of the people of those sound and vigorous traits, strong in moral feeling and a rigid sentiment of honour, which have been revealed to us in our study of lettres de cachet. The people were led to revolt against a Government and directing class who, owing to their having lost the tradition of these moral principles, showed by their actions that they had become incapable of sustaining the rôle which was incumbent on them.

X.—" Lettres de Cachet " in the Provinces

It remains to add that the picture presented by the history of lettres de cachet in the provinces, as studied by Monsieur A. Joly in so far as concerned Caen, by M. Ant. Dupuy in Brittany, M. Emile Duvernoy in Lorraine, M. Vander Haeghen in Languedoc, M. Ch. Latune in Provence, and ourselves in Flanders and Artois, offers the same aspect as lettres de cachet in Paris, with this added grievance, that in a very large number of towns—often the most insignificant—the municipalities themselves issued valid lettres de cachet, identical in their procedure and effect with the ordres du Roi of which we have been speaking. When Breteuil's circular of 1784, and the royal orders of the 31st October, 1785, and 1787, well before the first revolutionary movements, decreed the suppression of the system from henceforth called " ordres arbitraires," our municipalities protested with the greatest energy, indignant that the King should wish to demolish the prisons in which the mayors and local magistrates were accustomed to lock up those against whom there were complaints in the town.

[1] Vertuchon : a play on the word vertu which is difficult to paraphrase in English. Vertuchon and vertubleu were formerly used as expletives, and vertugadin was a cushion or bustle worn by the ladies of the time. The bon mot is an allusion to a story going round Court circles of a lady having unfortunately dropped her bustle in a public place. (H. W.)

M. Joly has related the edifying history of the Châtimoine Tower in Caen. The municipal council highly praised it : " it was a roomy fort, and of such solidity as to discount any fear of escapes," said the local magistrates.

An Inspector of Prisons gives the following account of it in 1784 :

" This tower, forming part of the ramparts of the town, has been from time immemorial under municipal administration." It was a real Bastille, and had subterranean dungeons.

" This place is so deep and wet," said the Inspector, " that several times in the year it is flooded to such a depth that the water has to be pumped out. In the thickness of the walls of this underground vault four or five cavities have been hollowed out in which they place prisoners, who are in very truth sealed up, as it were, in the wall, for once immured in these cavities the door by which they enter is not opened again, being secured to the wall by iron bars which are soldered into it. In the middle of this door is an opening of about a foot square by means of which the prisoner obtains air to breathe, receives his food, and throws out his excrements—an unheard-of kind of dungeon of the most barbarous sort it is possible to conceive. On the other floors the prisoners are each placed in a kind of cage which cannot be better compared than to the cabins on wheels used by shepherds for guarding their sheep at night in the open country, having but one opening like those in the underground dungeons for maintaining life."

In comparison with the municipal Bastille at Caen that of the King, in the Faubourg Saint Antoine, offered an agreeable sojourn !

Now it happened that about this year 1785, of which we are speaking, when the régime of *lettres de cachet* was virtually suppressed in France, the year in which the Ministers of Louis XVI closed the Donjon of Vincennes, an auxiliary branch of the Bastille, and decided, as is now proved, upon the demolition of the Bastille itself, the Government were likewise desirous of closing and demolishing the horrible Châtimoine Tower at Caen.

From what quarter did the liveliest opposition arise ? From the Town Council of Caen itself : " What they regret," wrote the Intendant to the Minister, " is what they call their jurisdiction over the tower ; they do not like to think they will no longer be able to imprison on their own authority those bourgeois in the town who are a cause of complaint to their families. I do not hesitate," he added, " to assure you on this point, that the municipal officers would not have troubled you if I had been willing to promise that the establishment I am going to build would provide them with the same satisfaction as they derive from the Châtimoine Tower, which they must lose."

Let us conclude by saying that the philosophers, those eloquent apostles of individual liberty and violent adversaries of despotism, were not backward in soliciting *lettres de cachet* against those displeasing to them. We may state that the most inveterate petitioner of *lettres de cachet* in all the Ancien Régime was Voltaire ; he wearied Ministers and Lieutenants of Police with his insistence, and waxed indignant, with that petulance we know he possessed, when he was unable to obtain an order for imprisonment against some person of whom he said he had to complain. We may see his signature among those of people of the lowest classes, requesting the imprisonment of some neighbouring lady he did not like.

XI.—*" Lettres de Cachet" in Blank*

One last point to touch upon concerns the alleged issue of *lettres de cachet* in blank. It is now established, and no one thinks of contradicting it, that contrary to what so many renowned historians have written, *lettres de cachet* could not be obtained bearing the signature of the Minister with the name of the victim left blank. The famous allegation, repeated hundreds of times, is well-known : " The Ministers of Louis XV sent as presents to their mistresses *lettres de cachet* leaving the name of the victim blank." It is astonishing that such absurdities could have been believed for one moment. Will French people one day become convinced that their great-grandparents were not savages !

Never, under any circumstances, or by authority of any Minister, was the practice of *lettres de cachet* abused to the extent of blindly placing the liberty of citizens at the mercy of private revenge or criminal machinations. True, in very rare circumstances, *lettres de cachet* with the name left blank could be placed by the Government in the hands of the representatives of authority, as has been shown by M. Marcel Marion in an irrefutable manner ; but such a proceeding took place under regular circumstances and under the responsibility of the high administrative authority making use of it, and this had to be confirmed by the King. We know what were the judicial powers of the representatives of royal authority in the provinces ; let us not play with words ; in the above very rare circumstances these terrible *ordres du Roi* were nothing else but summonses to appear before the court as issued by our judges of the present day.

BIBLIOGRAPHY

Argenson (René d'), Lieutenant Général de Police, *Notes de* . . ., ed. Lor Larchey et Mabille, 1866.—Argenson (René d'), *Rapports inédits* . . . (1697–1715), ed. Cottin, 1891.—Carré (H.), *Histoire d'une lettre de cachet*, 1895.—Dupuy (Ant.), *La Bretagne au dix-huitième siècle* . . . *Ordres du Roi, lettres de cachet*, *Bullet. de la Soc. Acad. de Brest.*—Duvernoy (Emile), *Les Lettres de cachet en Lorraine*, *Rev. des Etudes Historiques*, Nov.–Dec. 1907.—Flammermont, *Remontrances des Parlements de Paris au dix-huitième siècle*, 1888–1898.—Fr. F. B., *La Constitution de la famille et les lettres de cachet*, *Réforme sociale*, 16 Feb., 1893.—*Les Lettres de cachet en Province*, *Revue bleue*, 29 July, 1899.—*Les Lettres de cachet en blanc*, *Compte rendu des séances de l'Académie des Sciences morales et politiques*, 1895.—*Les Lettres de cachet à Paris*, 1903. —Joly (A.), *Les Lettres de cachet dans la généralité de Caen*, 1864.—Latune (Charles), *Les Lettres de cachet en Provence*, 1905.—Lemaire (André), *Les Lois fondamentales de la monarchie française*, 1907.—Loménie (Louis de), *Les Mirabeau*, 1879.—Marion (Marcel), *Les Lettres de cachet en blanc*, *Compte rendu des séances de l'Académie des Sciences morales et politiques*, 1898.— Marion (Marcel), *Dictionnaire des institutions de la France aux dix-septième et dix-huitième siècles*, 1923.—Marivaux, *Vie de Marianne*, 1731.—Mathieu (Cardinal), *l'Ancien Régime en Lorraine et Barrois*, 4th ed., 1907.—Prévost d'Exiles, *Histoire du Chevalier Desgrieux et de Manon Lescaut*, various eds. since 1753.—Van Schoor, *Les Lettres de cachet*, Brussels, 1895.

CHAPTER VII

THE MAGISTRATES

I. Attributes and Functions of the Parliaments.—II. Origin of Parliament.
—III. The Registration of Acts and the drawing up of Protests to the
King.—IV. The *Lits de Justice.*—V. Chancellor Maupeou.—VI. The
Magisterial Aristocracy.

I.—*Attributes and Functions of the Parliaments*

O NE can imagine the aversion felt by the Parliaments for the
ordres du Roi, which they regarded as a detestable infringe-
ment of their rights. The majority of *lettres de cachet*, as we have
seen, were concerned with family matters. When a husband or
wife had obtained one against the other party and their differences
came before a Court of Justice, the Magistrates did not fail to
consider the *ordre du Roi* as a grave insult to themselves, which
ran the risk of causing the petitioner to lose his case.

It is a common error to think that the Parliaments were entrusted
exclusively with the administration of justice. They carried out
the most various functions, the first of which undoubtedly was
the administration of justice, since that was the essential function
of the King whom they represented. But their additional attributes
possessed great importance.

Since the King was endowed with an ecclesiastical character
the Parliaments had to concern themselves with religious matters,
about which they busied themselves with the liveliest enthusiasm.
They set themselves up as the defenders of orthodoxy, they discussed theology, gave discourses on consubstantiation, on efficacious
and efficient grace, branded incorrect propositions, condemned
books classed as heretical to be burnt, and did not hesitate to tear
up a Pontifical Bull when they considered it to be prejudicial to
the Church. Did they not possess an infallibility which the Bishop
of Rome does not yet enjoy ? They said so at all events : " The
Magistrates only utter the oracles of infallible truth " (*Remontrances*
drawn up in 1753). One might almost call them a council of Mitred
Prelates, in which capacity they did not exceed their attributes—
the Kings they represented were ecclesiastical persons.

Our Magistrates defended Catholicism against the Reformation with a fury in comparison with which Louis XIV and his Bishops appear like shrinking *bravos*. At the beginning of the reign of Charles IX, Parliament refused to enrol the Edict of pacification granted by the King to the Protestants ; in 1598 it opposed the Edict of Nantes whereby Henri IV shed forth some gleams of toleration, and in 1685 it applauded its revocation. Again, as late as the eighteenth century, the Parliament of Toulouse beheaded people who took part in preaching the Gospel after the methods of Luther or Calvin. Ah ! if the Protestants had had to deal with our Magistrates instead of the *Roi-Soleil* and his Bishops, they would have witnessed some singular scenes of which the fate of the aristocrats in 1793 might give some idea ! Right down to the end of the eighteenth century, when Louis XVI appointed Wurmser, a Lutheran, to be Commander-in-Chief in Alsace (1778), and published edicts granting civil rights to members of the " reformed " sects (1787), the Parliaments offered to royal liberalism a tenacious opposition.

Louis XIV had no love for the Quietism of that soft-hearted Mme. Guyon whom Fénélon took under his protecting wing, but it would not have entered his head to condemn Quietist Curés to the stake as the Parliament of Burgundy did. In 1663, Simon Morin, an *illuminatus*, gave out that he was incorporated in Jesus Christ. Had the matter been left to the King it would have resolved itself into a *lettre de cachet* consigning him to the Bastille or to Vincennes : the Paris Parliament condemned him to be burnt alive.

Parliament was Gallican. Bossuet's Four Articles constituted its formula of truth. It consecrated them by its decrees, and by decree it likewise gave the force of law to the doctrine proclaiming the supremacy of Councils over the Pope. In a far greater degree than Louis XIV Parliament was an advocate of religious unity, and wanted a State Religion far more than he did.

Unfailingly the Parliaments defended ideas springing from French origins ; it was a magistracy composed of families of the old stock, rooted in the soil. Protestantism drew its inspiration from Germany and England ; the Jesuits, who were " ultramontane," received their orders from Rome, and the Parliamentarians strove equally to bar the way to them. With D'Aguesseau at their head they condemned the celebrated Bull *Unigenitus* (8th September, 1713) directed against Port Royal and its adherents, and when the French Prelates, who appealed to the Council against the Pontifical Decree, were excommunicated by the Pope, Parliament opposed the admission into France of the Pontifical document and forbade its publication. They proceeded to still greater lengths. When Christophe de Beaumont introduced "Roman" ideas into the Archiepiscopal See of Paris (where Cardinal de Noailles had shown himself inclined towards Jansenism), and forbade priests in his diocese to give Holy Communion, and even Extreme Unction to those who had not adhered to the Pontifical doctrine, Parliament took steps to compel priests to do so, banishing from their jurisdiction those who did not obey their injunctions, and ordering to be burnt the instructions of the Bishops depriving of the Sacraments those of the faithful suspected of Jansenism.

Parliament made war on the Jesuits as it did on the Protestants, condemning books written in their favour to be burnt, and going so far as to exile their most distinguished defenders. We do not intend to go into the question as to whether the maxims Parliament defended were good or bad ; all we wish to say is, that in setting up as theologians its members were not exceeding their attributes.

In its capacity as the King's Court of Justice, Parliament personally represented the King. It is well known that in order to emphasize this the Kings arrayed Councillors in the garb proper to themselves, even to the mortar cap of the Presidents which with its gold circlet represented the royal diadem. And in order that no one should be ignorant of this fact our Magistrates preserved, hung on the wall of their Council Chamber, a portrait of Charles VI dressed as a President and wearing the mortar.

Another point clearly emphasizing the identity existing between the Royal and Parliamentary functions is that the King, when he visited the assembly of Magistrates, did not preside over them ; he effaced them. When the King was present, Parliament no longer existed. In the words of La Roche-Flavin, "*Adveniente principe cessat magistratus.*" Parliament, in the strictest sense of the word, was the King's Lieutenant, that is, it stood in place of the King. When the Captain speaks and acts, the Lieutenant has but to do his bidding. Our old legal historians, Bodin, Lhommeau and Roche-Flavin, are all agreed on this point. "And just as rivers leave behind them their names and their force when they enter the sea," writes Bodin, "and just as the lights of the heavens fade in the presence of the sun," so do we see the Courts of Justice shorn of their authority the moment there appears amongst them he who has endowed them with it.

The magistrates exercised censorship over books. They had their own ideas on Aristotle's Categories, and the doctrines of Confucius. Rousseau struck them as horrible, and the economists as " perturbers of the public peace." After being examined by the Advocate General, books considered to be bad were burnt at the foot of the steps of Saint Barthélemy as being " heretical, schismatic, erroneous, violent, blasphemous, impious, attacking authority," and many other things of the same kind ; but they were only burnt in effigy, or rather not at all. The executioner would merely throw into the flames a few bundles of papers, for the book-loving magistrates took care to keep for their libraries the books that had been seized and had now become famous from the very fact of their having been condemned.

The origin of this exercise of authority was entirely a family one also. In the beginning their Councillors and Prime Ministers were chosen by the Kings from among their own household, their *familia*. They meted out justice in the King's circle, and the Queen took her place among them. We need not therefore be astonished that they came to mix themselves up in family matters, just as the King did. Thus we find the Paris Parliament forbidding Cinq-Mars to marry Marion de Lorme. It considered the morals of this charming woman to be somewhat too frivolous to figure on the untarnished coat-of-arms of a French gentleman. Our magistrates, " on account of the bad example," likewise forbade Mme. de Limoges to make a marriage for her daughter, doubt-less an honourable one, but a love-match—in conformity with the views of the Grande Mademoiselle (Montpensier). For the same reason they opposed the marriage of Mlle. de Piennes to M. de Villequier ; but if Parliament declared war against the lovers Louis XIV extended his protection to them. On the interven-tion of the Bishop of Chartres, he smiled on the wishes of the young people and set them up in life. In the case of Mme. de Pibrac, Parliament forbade her to marry again " on account of the absurdity of the thing " ; true, it was for the seventh time.

In this way Parliament, like the King, came to busy itself directly in all that concerned French life. The Court of Dijon forbade— a very bold measure—Burgundians to enter a cabaret. Our magistrates interested themselves in the various arts, manufactures and inventions. They issued their decrees as to the manner in which silk was to be woven, how flax was to be corded, glass to be blown, and bolts to be riveted. They had no use for vaccine, and after a vigorous inquisition by the Advocate-General against the " hydra of inoculation," Jenner's therapeutic discovery was duly condemned. Parliament secured for poor people the right of gleaning after the harvest, and forbade landowners and farmers to turn cattle into the fields to pasture until three days had elapsed, so as not to diminish what was left to the gleaners ; it was for-bidden to scythe the wheat ; it had to be cut with a reaping hook so as to leave the stubble for the poor ; it was forbidden to keep goats, for they browsed on the young blades and caused great waste ; any goats seized were killed.

The Courts of Justice were authorized to make administrative regulations, and to draw up rules for the police ; they would summon the Government agents to appear before them, and would keep a watch over the municipalities whose regulations they claimed the right to register officially. They were responsible for the high police officials. The rôle of Parliament, when the throne was vacant, or during the minority of the King is well-known. In 1593 it preserved the crown for the House of Bourbon by suppressing the plot to bestow it on an Infanta of Spain. By a decree of the 28th June, Parliament upheld the Salic Law, and on the 25th July, Henri IV heard at Saint Denis that Mass for the sake of which he had no mind to renounce Paris. We know the part played by Parliament during the minorities of Louis XIV and Louis XV when, in the latter case, it over-rode the testamentary instructions of the late King. Some historians have thought that in this it had out-stepped its prerogatives, but in the absence of the King, when the King was a minor, Parliament represented Sovereign Authority.

II.—*Origin of Parliament*

Just as people in the seventeenth and eighteenth centuries disputed over the origins of the royal power on account of the consequences springing from it, so did they dispute over those of Parliament, and for the same reasons. The seventeenth century writers, mentioned above, define them in more exact terms : Parliament was the *lieu-tenant* of the King. But this tradition became lost in subsequent generations. In Diderot's *Encyclopédie*, Boucher d'Argis only regards it as a Sovereign Court set up to administer justice in the last resort. For their part the Councillors of Parliament claimed that they went back to the time of those Councils on the battlefield which the Carlovingian Kings used to assemble. Others asked themselves whether Parliament was not an emanation of the States General. Its frequent opposition to the royal power gave it a popular origin in other quarters. All these ill-defined hypotheses created a false idea of its assumed rôle and activities, which were qualified by its opponents as an intolerable usurpation.

The power of Parliaments, like that of the Kings, was theoretically unlimited. They claimed to be superior to even the States General, whose decisions had to be submitted to them, " le siège du trône royal et le lit de la justice souveraine " resting with them. They pronounced judgment in the last resort, and received appeals against all royal, municipal, seigneurial and ecclesiastical jurisdictions. They had acquired the right to examine, amend, and protest against all public Acts, which had to be registered by them. Treaties made with foreign powers were submitted to them, and even the appointment of officials. Finally, by means of the successive decrees they pronounced, and which became law, they modified the oldest established customs and laws.

There were thirteen Parliaments in the Kingdom : these were, in the order of their creation, those of Paris, Toulouse, Grenoble, Bordeaux, Dijon, Rouen, Aix, Rennes, Pau, Metz, Besançon, Douai, Nancy. In Artois, Roussillon, Alsace and Corsica there were no Parliaments, but Superior Councils which performed similar functions. The jurisdiction of the Paris Parliament extended over the entire ancient domain of the Kings, including, besides l'Ile de France, Picardy, Brie, Perche, Beaux, Maine, Touraine, Sologne, Berry, the Nivernais, Anjou, Poitiers, Aunis, Rochelais, Angoumois, la Marche, the Bourbonnais, Macon, Auvergne, the Forez, the Beaujolais and Lyons—ten million inhabitants.

III.—*The Registration of Acts and the Drawing up of Protests to the King*

The Parliaments preserved the custom of registering edicts, orders, regulations and other public Acts emanating from the King's Government and the properly constituted authorities ; they copied them into their registers with their own decrees, so that their subsequent decisions should be in conformity with them. An Act which had not been registered by them had no existence in their eyes, and could not be applied within the extent of their jurisdiction. "The law of the realm is such," wrote La Roche-Flavin, Président des Requêtes of the Parliament of Toulouse, " that no edicts, no ordinances have any effect, we do not obey them, or rather, they are not held to be edicts and ordinances, if they have not been verified by the Sovereign Courts after deliberation thereon."

This registration might be compared to publication in the *Gazette* at the present day. The custom went back to the beginning of the fourteenth century, that is, to shortly after the time when Parliament definitely received a regular organization. It sometimes happened that our magistrates, if they did not consider the proposed edict, ordinance or measure to be in conformity with French customs, or in the interests of the district, suspended its registration and forwarded protests (*remontrances*). If no notice was taken of their observations, and the assembly still persisted in its opinion, registration was refused, and the magistrates continued to pass judgments and to act as though the incriminated measure had no existence.

Occasions arose when the Parliaments punished village officials for obeying the King's orders transmitted by the Intendants, when these tended to the carrying out of some ordinance which they had refused to register.

On the other hand, historians have viewed this over-riding of the royal commands as an arbitrary encroachment and usurpation. It could be vexatious in many circumstances, and in others might serve a useful purpose ; in our opinion it was justifiable, if not in law,—theory played so small a part with men in olden days —at any rate in fact. La Roche-Flavin pictures to us King Louis XII riding on a little mule through the gardens of the precincts next to the Palais de Justice. The good King suffered from gout. In the alleys of the garden he would give directions on public affairs, and when some difficult question or other required consideration he would go up to discuss it with Parliament : " For this purpose a sloping ascent had been erected from the bottom step to the top, made of thin planks covered with matting, by which his mule was able to ascend and take him to the doors of the Grand Chambre."

When a sovereign requests from an assembly its counsel and approval he must also allow its criticisms, and when a Prince, as was the case with Henri IV, owes his crown to the decision of a body of councillors, neither he nor his successors should be surprised if those same councillors consider they have a right to intervene in the affairs of the Government. When a Government, as happened during the Regency, asks a judicial assembly to annul an Act so serious and authoritative as a royal Will and Testament, it must not be surprised if these same men, or their successors, should not feel themselves under the obligation to bow to all its decisions.

There is a celebrated story of the sitting of Parliament on the 13th of April, 1655, when Louis XIV, aged seventeen, is said to have appeared booted, his hat on his head and a whip in his hand, and put an end to the deliberations of Parliament in these words : " L'État c'est moi." The tale is legendary, even if it is true that the King, wearing his ordinary dress, forbade their further deliberations " in a strange manner, very far removed from that of his predecessors."

Twelve years after (April, 1667), Louis XIV published his Ordinance touching the reform of justice. He wished to regulate the right of Parliament to examine and register the Public Acts : " Our Courts of Parliament shall be held to proceed forthwith

with the publication of ordinances, edicts, declarations, and other documents as soon as they have been registered, without causing any delay thereto, and in precedence of all other matters." Any observations might be made during the space of a week, " after which time Our Ordinances shall be taken as having been published."

On the 24th February, 1673, other prescriptions followed : " It is Our will that Our Courts register purely and simply Our Letters Patent without any modification, restriction or clauses added thereto . . ."

If Louis XIV did not actually declare to Parliament in April, 1655, that " *L'Etat c'est moi*," his great-grandson and successor, Louis XV, affirmed the same sentiment in March, 1766, to the same assembly, and in a form which though less concise, possessed at any rate a lofty clearness in its cadenced rhythm :

" In my person alone resides Sovereign Authority. . . . To me alone belongs legislative power, independent and undivided. Public order in all its entirety emanates from me ; I am its supreme guardian. My people form one with me, and the rights and interests of the nation, which men dare to separate from those of the Monarch, are necessarily united to my own, and rest in my hands alone."

These injunctions and expressions of opinion did not prevent Parliament from continuing its activity in the most efficacious manner. No tax or public loan could be realized apart from its authorization. During the whole of the eighteenth century M. Marion considers that it ruled French policy. " So great was its authority," states Sénac de Meilhan, " that after a long war the King had to undergo the embarrassment of proposing the continuation of a grant in aid, necessary for the purpose of paying off the debts contracted during it."

IV.—*The Lits de Justice*

In order to bend the resistance of Parliament recourse was had to the famous *lits de justice*. In the presence of the King the power of the Councillors was suspended, and the registration of Acts took place as of due right.

The *lits de justice* were held in Paris in the Grand' Chambre. Louis d'Orléans has given us a description of one of them at the end of the fifteenth century :

" The bed was set up under a canopy, vault, or structure resting on pillars, covered with cloth of gold or velvet ; it was provided with cushions, and was adorned with another great covering of azure-blue velvet decorated with golden fleurs-de-lys which made a background to the royal throne and went under the cushions whereon the King was seated, descended over the steps and spread well on to the floor of the room, giving a magnificent appearance to the King's seat, which in other respects resembled an ordinary bed with canopies, backs and pillows."

In the succeeding century the azure-blue material was changed to violet.

The *lit de justice* was also called the "*trône du tribunal royal.*"

The King's "bed" was placed in the corner of the Grand' Chambre, also called the "*chambre du plaidoyer*" because it was the only place where petitions were heard; another name given it was "*la grand' voûte,*" and the public spoke of it as "*la chambre dorée*" on account of the gilded pendants with which Louis XII had decorated the ceiling. A triptych hung on the wall with portraits of Charlemagne, and Saint Louis, a French painting of the fifteenth century, now in the Louvre; it used to be attributed to Albert Dürer. Underneath hung a portrait of Charles VI, "dressed like the Presidents of the present day in their round cap of office," in the words of the *Encyclopédie Méthodique.* The loss of this last portrait cannot be too much regretted. The remaining decoration of the Chamber dated from 1721.

The King was in the Sainte Chapelle when four *Présidents à mortier* and eight Councillors came to fetch and conduct him to the Grand' Chambre to the sound of a fanfare of trumpets and drums. At the feet of the King, who had now taken up his position in the angle of the room on his bed of purple velvet sown with golden fleurs-de-lys, sat the chief Equerry. To the right was the Great Chamberlain who bore the King's sword hanging from his neck. Kneeling on the floor in front of the King were two mace-bearers, holding their silver-gilt maces, and six heralds.

The King was seated with covered head and the assembly took up their positions; the King removed his hat in salute and replaced it again; he then gave the Chancellor permission to speak, who proceeded to explain the object of the meeting.

Nearly all the *lits de justice* were held at the Palais de Justice, and only exceptionally in the royal palaces. In his *Journal* the advocate Barbier has given us a description of the one commanded at Versailles on the 3rd September, 1732 :

"Parliament in red robes repaired to Versailles at 10 o'clock in the morning; they were received by the Master of Ceremonies and conducted to the Salle des Gardes, which had been arranged on the model of the Grand' Chambre. At the same hour the King returned from Marly. . . . The *lit de justice* began at about 11 o'clock. The King took up his position in the corner of the chamber on an elevated seat under a pillared canopy like the one at the Palais de Justice, and sitting at his feet were M. le Prince Charles de Lorraine, Chief Equerry, who on the occasion of great ceremonies wore a large belt to which was attached a huge sword, and the Great Chamberlain, M. le Duc de Bouillon.''

Barbier notes that it was a magnificent assembly by reason of the distinction of the people present and the variety of the costumes.

'' The King said : 'I have summoned you here to convey to you my intentions which my Chancellor will explain to you.'
The Chancellor made a speech in which, after speaking of the dis-obedience of Parliament to the King's orders, and of His Majesty's clemency, he told them that the King intended to have his declaration registered. . . . The President, M. Le Pelletier, in conformity with the decision of the Court, gave us the reasons which decided the assembly to refuse the registration of the declaration. Then M. Gilbert de Voisins, Chief Advocate-General, demanded the registration in satisfaction of the King's commands, at the same time betraying the grief he felt in exercising his functions on such an occasion.
The Chancellor caused the registration to be inscribed on the coun-terfoil, after which the King said to him :
'I command you out of my own mouth to carry out all you have heard, and especially to continue to execute your functions.' ''

The assembly then separated.
The King enjoined upon Parliament to continue in the exercise of its functions, but these gentlemen had contrived an ingenious method of suspending the exercise of justice when they had been compelled to register an ordinance or declaration which did not please them, and that was to call together '' all the different cham-bers in consultation '' in order to discuss political or administrative questions, and even religious matters, with the result that as all the Councillors were engaged on these important deliberations the exercise of justice throughout the land was in fact suspended for the time being.
Cardinal Mathieu describes the procedure of a *lit de justice* in a provincial Parliament. It relates to that of Lorraine whose councillors rejected the Edict of December, 1781, augmenting the price of salt by 3 *sous* a pound.
M. de Choiseul, the Governor of the Province, and representing the King, advised the Chief Councillor that he had received *lettres de jussion*.[1] The Court, after deliberating in black robe and square cap, repaired to the Audience Chamber. Choiseul received them

[1] *Lettres de jussion :* letters sent to an acting provincial court by the King requiring them to register an Edict. (H. W.)

surrounded by great military pomp, and handed them the royal
letter :

" I bring you the King's commands. . . .   With a view to carrying
on a costly, indispensable, and just war (it concerned, O Americans !
the war in which we were engaged for your independence), His
Majesty is in need of aid proportionate to the expenses it entails. . . .
I know the hearts of my fellow-countrymen, and am well assured,
Gentlemen, that I have only to record your submission. . . ."

After this the fiscal Procurator-General was introduced, and
demanded the registration of the edict in the following terms :

" This imposing presentation of sovereign authority offers to the
province a spectacle as new as it is painful. . . .   You have laid your
representations at the foot of the throne.   The result has not corresponded with your hopes.   This sorrow can only give place to that
of having caused displeasure to a beloved Monarch.   We must believe,
Gentlemen, that only impossible difficulties have restrained the inexhaustible benevolence of a King who is the father of his people.   Of
this he has given fresh proof by entrusting the carrying out of his
wishes to a Commander whose name, dear and precious to this province, has never been known but as an instrument of good. . . .
It only remains to us to give the example of our submission."

The Clerk to the Court then registered the Edict at the Governor's
order, and the Chief President closed the *lit de justice* in the words
following, which should be remembered.   The wonderful social
courtesy of the Ancien Régime, its appreciation of *nuances*, the
strength underlying the most moderate expression of its views,
and the firmness of its resistance beneath a varnish of deference
and submission, are seen therein in a light which has now passed
away.   The Chief President addressed the Governor in the following terms :

" The love for the King with which we are penetrated and the inviolable fidelity of which this assembly has given unceasing proofs to
His Majesty have done violence to our desire to obey his commands.
. . .   You will be able to report to the King that this Edict has been
registered at his express command and that you have found no obstacles
in carrying out the commands of which you are the bearer."

The doors were then opened to the public and the *lettres de
jussion*, together with the Edict to be registered, were read to
them.   " M. le Duc de Choiseul standing with his head uncovered
then saluted all these gentlemen, who returned his salute, and
then he stepped down from his place ; on leaving the chamber
he turned round and again repeated his salute which was returned,
and he was escorted out as he had been received."

But it must not be thought that the matter was at an end. It was sometimes closed in this manner when Parliament approved of the measure ; but in the event of their disapproval the matter was only settled in appearance. At the conclusion of the ceremony Parliament would protest against the violence which had been done to it, and in all its subsequent pronouncements—the regulations it would decree, and the police measures it would prescribe —it acted as though the Edict it had registered did not exist. It would call meetings of the different Chambers, which of set purpose would make it impossible for them to carry out their judicial functions as regards private cases, and if the King refused to acknowledge his defeat, the only resource left to him was to banish all the members of Parliament, who were possessed of posts from which they could not be removed, to a distance from their seat of jurisdiction.

But meanwhile the public would be in need of having their cases adjudicated upon, and so the King would endeavour to replace his exiled Parliament by judges drawn from other tribunals— and how great was his difficulty in collecting them, for these makeshift judges lacked prestige ! Advocates and attorneys would refuse to take cases, for our Councillors always had a large crowd of the legal profession on their side on whom they could rely, and these would follow them in their exile or refuse their services to the judges replacing them : " A plaintiff," says Besenval, " in the certainty that any verdict he might obtain would only be temporary, would fear to transfer his case to a new tribunal, knowing well that if it had not been concluded when Parliament returned the prejudice attaching to his having had recourse to other judges would be a sufficient reason for his losing his case."

In the end it would be necessary to recall the exiles who meanwhile had been posing as martyrs ; they had sacrificed themselves in the popular cause ; for the masses—when, for instance, the Parliament of Lorraine opposed the levies made for carrying on the American war—were not in a position to understand the great issues at stake nor that the country really required them to make this sacrifice ; all they understood was this : *Messieurs les Conseillers* did not wish the taxes to be increased.

Thirty members of the Besançon Parliament were exiled in 1762, but were recalled. There was an explosion of enthusiasm throughout the province, and the local town councils were also greatly elated. A hundred young girls on horseback and a like number in carriages met the exiles with flowers in their hands, and another delegation of sixty girls to the accompaniment of a great hubbub of kettle-drums and trumpets proceeded to offer laurel wreaths to the illustrious victims of despotism.   Antoine Cleradius, Cardinal de Choiseul-Beaupré and Archbishop of Besançon, gave a dinner in their honour ; it was a triumphal banquet at which, as a kind of " entremet," appeared twelve graceful shepherdesses, decked with flowers and ribbons, as in Boucher's pictures, escorted by fifty youths, each bearing a drawn sword in his hand.   They had come to sing the praises of the heroic conquerors.

When the thirty members of Parliament were exiled, the Inten-dant, the acting representative of the royal power, had declared : " They will not return until we see Jacquemart at the theatre joining in the fun."   This referred to the great figure of Jacque-mart made of lead and wood which struck the hours on the brazen bells on the top of the church of Sainte Madeleine.

This figure was taken down from its perch and brought into the hall of the theatre where the piece then being played was cheered at every turn.   Thanksgiving services were held in all the churches, tables were spread in the streets where the citizens, mingling to-gether in rejoicings shared by all, did not fail to embellish their happy transports with Bacchic libations.   The guilds of workmen, mercers, drapers, silversmiths, carvers of statues, carpenters, poultry sellers, domestic servants, masters and mistresses in the schools, and street cleaners organized noisy processions carrying flowers.   Songs in great numbers were composed for the occasion, and everyone vied in learning them, while street singers standing on trestle tables made the streets and squares resound with them to the accompaniment of hand organs, with the people standing round following them in chorus.   The same thing happened in other provinces.   " Compulsory registration, determined protests, the exile and ever triumphant return of the Councillors, were the usual vicissitudes of these wars of jurisdiction "—such was the conclusion of Cardinal Mathieu who was making a study of the Ancien Régime in Lorraine.   The incidents in the above picture of the scenes that took place in Franche Comté are taken from Albert Babeau.

V.—*Chancellor Maupeou*

The preceding observations explain only too well the re-forms attempted by Louis XV and René Nicolas de Maupeou, the last Chancellor of the Old Monarchy.   The Parliament of Brittany was among the most determined of them and included among its members an unusual number of gentlemen of the old nobility.   Notwithstanding the prohibitions of the Chancellor it continued its law-suit, which had been begun in 1769, against the Governor of the province, the Duc d'Aiguillon.   The action was

referred to the Paris Parliament, and as the Paris Councillors felt
bound to take sides with their Breton *confrères*, a *lit de justice* was
held on the 27th June, 1770, at which Louis XV annulled all the
proceedings that had taken place up to that day. But on the
2nd July, in defiance of sovereign authority, Aiguillon was condemned. This was the origin of a conflict between the high officials
and the Crown in which all the Parliaments of France united
solidly together, the vicissitudes of which have been often described.

Louis XV possessed more character, energy and power of decision
than he has been credited with. He detested the Parliamentarians
—those " republicans " as he called them. Maupeou was a determined man. On the 13th April, 1771, Louis XV held at Versailles
the celebrated *lit de justice* at which he compelled the registration
of three edicts, one of which suppressed the *Cour des Aides*,[1] the
second replaced Parliamentary posts, which for the most part were
hereditary, by posts appointed by the King, without the right of
passing them on in the family, and the third created in place of
the Courts of Justice, which he abolished, a fresh Parliament—
the famous Maupeou Parliament—in which were to sit the members
forming the Chief Council, or as we should say the Council of State.

Louis XV expressed himself on this occasion as follows :

" It is not without the most painful regret that We have witnessed
officials of Our Parliament giving way to a disobedience condemned
alike by the laws, by their oath, and by public interest, in making the
arbitrary suspension of their functions a matter of principle, and
openly proclaiming their right to prevent the carrying out of Our
wishes. . . . For a long time We have suspended the exercise of
Our Authority in the hope that reflection would bring them back to
their duty ; but Our very benevolence has only served to encourage
their resistance. . . ."

" We have recognized," the King continued, " that the purchase of
offices, a custom introduced in unfortunate times, has been an obstacle
in selecting Our officials, and has often kept out from these offices
those most worthy to fill them . . . that we owe to Our subjects
prompt, clean, and free justice, and that the least mingling of personal
interest could only offend the delicacy of judges charged with uphold-
ing the inviolable rights of honour and property."

The King alluded to the unimaginable slowness of the procedure
and the deplorable custom of *épices* (giving presents to the judges).
He then spoke of the excessive extent of the jurisdiction of the
Paris Parliament " as being hurtful to litigants obliged to leave
their families in order to solicit slow and costly justice. Exhausted

[1] *Cour des Aides :* the Chamber which regulated public expenditure.
(H. W.)

by the expenses of the journey and finding accommodation, this long drawn out and complicated procedure ended in their ruin."

The Parliaments were replaced by superior tribunals whose officials, appointed gratuitously and without having to buy their posts, were to have no other emoluments than the salaries attached to their offices. This suppressed the system of *épices*.

Besides the superior tribunal set up in Paris, Councils were established at Arras, Blois, Châlons, Clermont, Lyons and Poitiers, forming the curtailed jurisdiction of the Paris Parliament. The other Parliaments were likewise replaced by Councils.

At that time, the 15th December, 1770, the Duc de Croÿ had a conversation with Bertin, the Comptroller General, which he relates in his *Mémoires*, explaining the deciding motives of the Court and the opposition to its policy which was aroused.

"A revolt on one side or the other was inevitable," said the Minister, "one secret and the other of a resounding character. For ten years past Parliament has been making one secretly."

It seems to be certain that under the ferment of men's minds, then beginning to make itself felt, under the movement for a political and social transformation then being manifested, the Parliaments thought that by uniting together they might be able to acquire the direction of the State, thereby reducing the King's prerogatives to a kind of constitutional monarchy. Anglomania, which at that time was all the rage, strengthened them in their convictions.

"I own," writes the Duc de Croÿ, "that the Parliaments had gone too far and that their sole thought was to increase their authority."

"It was more than that," interrupted the Minister, "it was a plot and a general partnership having in view the destruction of the monarchical system and transferring it to the hands of an aristocracy which should be under their sole control. Thus it was a complete and secret revolution, with its plans well advanced."

Croÿ considered that the King had done very well in again becoming monarch, but that Maupeou had made him into such an absolute monarch that he could not be warned too strongly of the danger he was incurring.

The opposition of the Provincial Parliaments to Maupeou's reforms was not so general as has often been said. M. Carré recalls the fact that in several towns, such as Rennes, Aix and Lyons, the new officials met with a good reception. At Besançon the upper classes made common cause with the Parliamentarians who had been dismissed, but the people execrated them. In many towns, notably Toulouse, a number of judges belonging to the

Court of Justice which had been dissolved consented to take office in the new tribunal, and at Aix and Dijon the *Maîtres des Requêtes* took their seats in those that had become vacant.

But in Paris the opposition was unanimous. It aroused de Tocqueville's admiration, and the great historian writes :

" When, in 1770, the Parliament of Paris was annulled, the Councillors belonging to it sustained the loss of their position and power without one of them yielding to the royal will. Further, Courts of a different kind, like the *Cour des Aides*, which were in no way affected or threatened, voluntarily exposed themselves to the same rigours at a time when these rigours were certain to be put into force ; still better, the leading advocates who pleaded before Parliament associated themselves voluntarily with its fortunes, thereby renouncing what had brought them fame and wealth, and condemning themselves to silence rather than plead before judges they considered a disgrace. I know of nothing greater in the history of free peoples than what happened on that occasion. . . ."

Even the Royal Princes, and the Peers of France, ranged themselves on the side of the suppressed Parliaments, and their womenkind showed themselves extremely tender to the victims of royal authority. Besenval writes " that they were not behindhand at such a fine opportunity of supporting what they called the fundamental institutions of the State. In conversation and at suppers nothing else was talked of, and these gatherings of society and pleasure became, as it were, States General in miniature." Ladies of the highest rank were among the most enthusiastic, and at Grenoble Mme. de Pina boxed the ears of a secretary of M. de Bérulle whom she suspected of not entertaining a sufficiently vigorous hatred for Maupeou.

We may however be certain that the Maupeou reform inspired by Louis XV was a just one. It cannot be denied that the principles on which it rested—the suppression of the sale of offices and of the system of *épices*, that is to say, presents made to the judges by litigants, the simplification of the forms of procedure, the multiplicity of Courts of Appeal in the immense jurisdiction of the Paris Parliament at a time when moving about was a slow process and proportionately more costly than it is to-day—were reforms of such a useful character that the matter cannot be disputed. Voltaire enthusiastically praised the reform when it had been carried through.

Why was it not better received ? There were many reasons for this. The Parliament of Paris, against which the reform was especially aimed, had latterly made itself conspicuous for its hostility to the Jesuits. Maupeou, whether rightly or wrongly,

was regarded as being favourable to them. The policy of Louis
XV in regard to the Parliaments was therefore looked upon as
a " clerical " move, if we may apply this ugly word to it, and
at a time when a liberalism much resembling the state of mind
characterized by the same term at the present day, was emerging
from the dying embers of Jansenism.

The reform of Louis XV, who henceforward would have to
pay the salaries of the judges, reduced their numbers in all the
Courts, and the members of Parliament felt that they were being
threatened.

However able and energetic Maupeou might have been, his
personal reputation was only of a second-rate order. And then the
case of Goezmann blazed into notoriety. Louis Valentin Goezmann
was a member of Maupeou's Parliament and a native of Alsace where
he was a member of the King's Council. He was accused of corruption by Beaumarchais, and Mme. Goezmann too was implicated
in the affair. Beaumarchais' *Mémoires*, written with sparkling
animation and circulated in thousands, created a great stir. Mme.
Goezmann was condemned, Goezmann was obliged to resign, and
the unsavoury notoriety of the affair was reflected upon Maupeou's
Parliament itself.

We can hardly imagine the frenzy of passion and invective let
loose in pamphlets and satires by these events. Collections were
made of them—lampoons, songs, rhymes, skits and epigrams—
under the name of *Maupeouana*. A list of them under the heading
" Maupeou " gives some idea of what it was possible to print under
the Ancien Régime in defamation of the first personage in the
kingdom, after the King, without being brought to book. The
mere enumeration of the charges brought against him occupies
four-and-a-half columns.

Louis XV died, and Louis XVI was young and inexperienced.
A strong reaction, as usual, set in against the previous reign. The
members of Parliament who had been deprived of their offices
were recalled. The Edict of Fontainebleau (November, 1774), re-
establishing the Parliaments in their former powers, has been often
made a reproach to Louis XVI. M. Carré observes " that Louis
XVI, while forming a Ministry of reform dominated by Turgot,
at the same time re-established the Parliaments, the enemies of
reform." For our part we are convinced that had Louis XV lived
for a few more years, and if his reforms had had time to take root,
or if Louis XVI had had the force of character and prescience
requisite for carrying on the policy of his grandfather, the Revolution, at least with its accompaniments of violence, could have
been avoided.

Maupeou's reforms realized an important part of those principles which the men of 1789 and 1792 were to put into practice. When the Ministers of Louis XVI, men like Turgot, Malesherbes, Vergennes, even Loménie de Brienne, and Breteuil, with a decision and willingness which we will discuss later on, projected and sought to realize numerous reforms conceived in the most modern spirit, and in harmony with the aspirations which were to bring about the Revolution, from what quarter came incessant obstacles, repeated and multiplied in every form ? With a strength and audacity augmented by their triumphant return, the Parliaments stubbornly strove to bar the way to any measure which might do away with the routine and customs which had been condemned. Their minds were essentially conservative in the strictest meaning of the word, " ever on this side of the ideas prevailing in their century," as Sébastien Mercier writes, and far less tolerant towards new philosophies and ideas than were the heads of the Church.

Voltaire was beside himself with rage : " Scurvy pedants, fanatics, religious contortionists, monkeys changed into tigers, assassins of the Chevalier de La Barre that you are, learn that philosophy counts for something ! " The economists, who were seeking after a better basis of taxation and more favourable conditions for national productivity, were dubbed by the Parliamentarians " disturbers of the public peace." With aggressive obstinacy the Parliaments systematically opposed the most incontrovertible reforms of the royal government, such as the abolition of torture, the suppression of the *corvée* and the prerogatives of masters over their apprentices ; they interfered with the working of provincial assemblies, blindly refused to pass the taxes necessitated by the American war, and, in the last half of the eighteenth century, went so far as to resort to the most audacious proceedings in order to hamper the action of the Government.

The King held a *lit de justice*, and commanded the registering of an edict ; next day Parliament declared the registration to be null, and the edict non-existent. Parliament was exiled and Justice consequently suspended. The position of the King's Government became untenable owing to the systematic opposition of the Courts of Justice.

Let us suppose a similar state of affairs in our day : The Court of Appeal, the Accountant General's Office and the Provincial Courts opposing the execution of the laws and decrees officially published, opposing the taxes and loans necessitated by the war in Morocco or by our external debts, and having the power to make null and void the decisions of the Government.

We may feel certain that the Parliaments, taking up the notion

conceived by Louis XV and Maupeou, were seeking to seize upon
the direction of the State for themselves. When the Constituent
Assembly prolonged the vacation of the acting Courts on the 3rd
November, 1789, thereby preventing them from continuing the
exercise of their functions, the Parliament in Paris refused to
register the Act. But the time for sulking was over, and on the
6/7 of September, 1790, the Constituent Assembly definitely
suppressed the Parliaments.

The Convention completed the work—in its own fashion—by
guillotining a certain number of the Parliamentarians, and a long
and brilliant history was definitely closed.

VI.—*The Magisterial Aristocracy*

The history of this order had been great and glorious, especially
on account of the powerful constitution of the Parliamentary
families whom centuries of tradition had made into a class eminent
by the position it occupied in the State, its influence, its wealth,
and often, by its virtues.

" Once they had entered into the patrimony of certain families,"
writes the Vicomte d'Avenel, " offices in the judicature never left
them. . . . The son succeeded his father, the nephew his uncle,
the son-in-law his father-in-law. Parliament became one vast
family."

An appointment in a Parliament was an item of the patrimony
which was handed on by will; it figured in the stipulations of
a contract of marriage. At the end of the fifteenth century (1499),
Louis XII tried to put a stop to it—the officials were to be freely
elected, two members of the same family were not to be allowed
to sit in the same Court. . . . His efforts were in vain; the feeling of heredity throughout France was too strong. At about this
same time Imbart de la Tour notes the formation of the great
Parliamentary families. Foreigners spoke of the magistracy in
France as " some new order."

For fiscal reasons Francis I maintained the family system in
the handing on of offices in the judicature. The selling of appointments was introduced ; each was purchased, money down, by the
holder. The system was regularized. A Councillor of Parliament
was given the right to resign his office to anyone he liked on condition that the transference took place forty days before the death
of the then holder. Henri IV made this transference a simple
hereditary right in return for an annual fee fixed at a sixtieth part
of the value of each office. This right, a celebrated one in the
history of the French magistracy, was called *La Paulette* from the
name of the tax gatherer, Paulet, who farmed it at the time of its

origin (December, 1604). *La Paulette* made the transference of a
judicial post to the heir safe at all points. It was also called *l'Edit
des femmes*, for it was especially favourable to them ; on the death
of the husband the value of the appointment remained in the wife's
hands. *La Paulette* lasted right down to the end of the Ancien
Régime, with brief interruptions and a few modifications, and a
notable increase in the amount of the annual fee to be paid.

The eagerness of Parliamentary families to pay the tax of *La
Paulette* was extreme right from its commencement. Loyseau
gives us a graphic picture of this, dated 1608 :

" At the beginning of January, being in Paris, I thought I would
go one evening to the house of the agent for the annual fee (Charles
Paulet) and have a talk with him. I found him very much taken
up ; I had chosen my time badly. There was a great assembly of
officers (Parliamentary) there, jostling each other and pushing forward
to be the first to pay down their money ; some were still in their
riding boots covered with mud, not having had time to change them.
I noticed that as soon as they had been dealt with they went out
straightway to a notary, near by, to have authenticated their right
to resign (the appointment which they held). . . . Afterwards,
when night had fallen, and the agent had closed his register, I heard
great murmuring among those who still remained, insisting that he
should take their money, not knowing, as they said, whether they
might not die that very night."

The nobility showed themselves determined opponents of this
measure, which threatened to create an aristocracy rivalling themselves.

The selling and purchase of appointments has been often attacked.
The practice also found defenders among the highest ranks, notably
Richelieu. It has been remarked that it ought not properly to be
spoken of as venality, since there was no raising of the price to
the highest bidder, and the rich man had no advantage over one
who had less ; so too it has been said that the price was a guarantee
that the judge's means placed him above the temptations of corruption. Lastly, people saw in it the great advantage of placing
at the disposal of the State a body of officials forming a source
of revenue through the value of the fees to which *La Paulette* was
eventually raised. New functions and offices in the judicature
grew in numbers ; the importance of the Parliamentary class increased, and their families became united with each other by
marriage. From the middle of the eighteenth century especially,
the essential condition for entering the magistracy was to belong
to it already in virtue of birth. In this way arose the great Parliamentary families in Paris, those of de Mesmes, de Thou, Séguier,

Môlé, Pasquier, Feydeau, d'Aguesseau, d'Ormesson, Maupeou, Lamoignon and Phélypeaux. In the Parliament of Provence we find that seven members of the family of Rabasse de Vergons were Procurators-General, seven of the family of Coriolis and four Grimaldis were supreme Presidents, six Thomassins were also Presidents, without counting six of this same family who were Councillors, and one an Advocate General. In the Parliament of Rouen we find a President administering justice surrounded by his four sons, all of whom were likewise Councillors.

This aristocracy of Parliamentary executive officials was recruited from the upper classes of the people, from families conspicuous for their wealth or distinguished by Academic honours. The hereditary nobility disdained to enter their ranks, except in Brittany where a tradition dating back to the earliest Dukes placed the offices of the magistracy in the hands of the aristocracy. The Breton officials, therefore, by reason of their large landed properties, their illustrious descent, and the importance of the functions they exercised, came to form a body of exceptional weight and activity in the province, which fact accounts for their energetic resistance to the representatives of the King's authority.

Independent of the Crown owing to their constitution and the nature of their offices to which they succeeded by hereditary descent, the magistracy were no less so by reason of their traditional customs. It was forbidden to an office-holder to exercise any functions at the Court, or to receive any honour therefrom. When Louis XIV decided to raise the property of Villemort into a Duchy in favour of President Séguier, Parliament returned to him the letters patent—Government favour was not fitting for a magistrate.

The sole members of Parliament who might be nominated by the King were : the Chief President of the Grand' Chambre and the " gens du Roi " in the law courts, the Procurator and Advocates General. Further, as Beugnot indicates, the independent organization of the magistracy was so strong that these very nominations in point of fact depended on the chief Parliamentary families who imposed their selection on the Government.

It was an independence based as a rule on a position postulating considerable wealth. Offices in the magistracy were paid for at a very high price. The following figures must be multiplied by ten to arrive at their present-day value. For a simple position as Councillor in the Parliament of Paris 80,000 to 150,000 *livres* were paid to the holder willing to resign his post, averaging 1,000,000 francs at the present time ; that of an Advocate General 150,000 to 300,000 *livres* ; that of *Président à Mortier* 500,000 *livres* ; that of Procureur General 700,000 *livres*—seven million francs at the present day. In the Parliaments of Toulouse and Rouen the same offices fetched from 20,000 to 200,000 *livres*, in that of Dijon 130,000 *livres*.

The possession of wealth seemed necessary for the proper exercise of the magistracy, so much so that the Parliaments used to inquire into the private means of candidates, and if these did not appear to be sufficiently assured the competitor was rejected. " One must be able to live independent of accessory emoluments, and of other work, which should not interfere in any way in a position to which honour calls one," were the words of the Procureur General of the Normandy Parliament.

This wealth often consisted of large landed properties ; the members of the Parliament of Bordeaux owned several of the finest vintages—Château-Laffitte, Château-Latour, Saint-Estèphe, Château-Margaux and Haut-Brion.

Then there were the wealthy marriages. Our nobility of the magistracy followed in the steps of the nobility by birth. Présidents Môlé and Lamoignon married respectively the daughter and grand-daughter of Samuel Bernard, with dowries of eight and twelve million francs at the present value.

> O temps ! O mœurs ! O siècle déréglé !
> Où l'on voit déroger les plus nobles familles,
> Lamoignon, Mirepoix, Môlé,
> De Bernard épousent la fille :
> Ils sont les recéleurs du bien qu'il a volé.

We must add too the rise in the social scale entailed by the exercise of high judicial functions—a *quasi*-nobility of the highest degree, and hereditary ; so much so that members of the Courts of Justice became insensibly separated from the Third Estate, from which their families had sprung, and sought alliances among the nobility by birth ; they would no longer admit into their ranks anyone who was not of their caste, or one not sprung from a Parliamentary family ; they too came to form a class apart, a special caste enjoying great privileges. Especially in towns in which commerce and industry had but slight importance the Parliamentary families acquired such a preponderating influence that nowhere else, with the exception perhaps of the Court, could the real nobility, properly so called, lay claim to any similar position. Certain towns, such as Rennes and Dijon, lived upon their courts of justice.

The people acknowledged this fact. At Aix the members of Parliament were considered " as kings." They proceeded to the seat of justice followed by a crowd of their faithful adherents like the "clients" of Roman times. At Dijon they were qualified with the term "*hauts et puissants seigneurs.*" When they entered any place within their jurisdiction the officials of the town would offer them a *vin d'honneur.* The Chief President would be received with all the pomp and circumstance of royalty, with the thunder of cannon, beating of drums and flags flying.

The offices in the *Cour des Comptes* and the *Cour des Aides* were transmitted hereditarily, like those of Parliament. We mentioned[1] the famous example of the Nicolai family who occupied in hereditary succession the post of Chief President at the *Cour des Comptes,* from the time that Louis XII appointed Jean de Nicolai in 1506 down to the reign of Louis XVI. The humblest office, such as that of a mere clerk, followed the same rule.

From among these great Parliamentary families eminent personalities stand out, such as Chancellor Séguier whom Louis XIV had wished to make a Duke. He refused the letters patent granting him an annuity of 200,000 *livres* which Anne of Austria wanted to bestow on him. He got together an admirable library where men of learning and letters used to meet.

Another famous man was Chancellor d'Aguesseau, the son of the Intendant, Henri d'Aguesseau. "My father," he relates, "nearly always took us with him on his frequent journeys ; his coach became a kind of class-room in which we had the good fortune to work under the eyes of so great a master." The Chancellor was a terribly hard worker and extremely conscientious about his heavy responsibilities ; to those who remonstrated that he would wear himself out he replied : "How can I rest when there are people suffering ?"

He also cultivated the art of poetry, and used to dig in his garden at Fresnes. He afterwards made his father's home his own, and has given us a description of it :

"His house was open to all, but more especially for transacting business than for pleasure, and presented to those who came there a picture of most worthy magistracy. No luxury or display offended the humblest eyes ; fitting without being magnificent, it was large for his occupation. On arriving one felt one was entering the home of wisdom, and its very simplicity formed its chief dignity. His table, well served and amply provided, without being sumptuous, expressed like everything else in the house, that character of moderation which was natural to him ; a decent freedom and a countenance always serene and gracious gave to it its most pleasing adornment."

The habits of the magistracy appear also to have been more serious and better regulated than those of the greater part of the

[1] Page 65.

nobility, at least of the nobility at Court. Their wives as a rule
had the appearance of bourgeois women of the upper class, and
wore a grave demeanour in which was reflected in a somewhat
strained manner the dignity of the husband. They did not go to
Court where they could not enjoy the privileges of the nobility
having the *entrée*, and would console themselves by seeing ladies
of the highest birth coming to wait in the antechamber of the
President à Mortier, or of a mere Councillor.

But our judges liked to unite together as good comrades in
good cheer, drinking jovially and eating heartily. The banquets
of President Hénault, celebrated by Voltaire, acquired a real
renown, but President d'Aligre's table formed an exception.
Lauraguais said of it, " If one did not devour one's neighbour's
reputation while eating his bread, one would have died of hunger."

How many charming figures they present, from whom the
wrinkles of time have not obliterated their smile ! President de
Brosses, a hard worker, a great judge, antiquarian and historian,
whose letters are among the pearls of our literature ; President
de Bachaumont, a very indolent man, but an energetic protector
of our old monuments, the counsellor of some of our best artists
—Boucher and Bouchardon—of subtle wit and charming humour ;
President Bouhier too, a man of profound learning, but one who
gave expression to it with a light touch. One day Piron[1] found
out he was in danger of being prosecuted for his *Ode à Priape ;*
he was a young man and the matter might have entailed unfortunate consequences for him. " You are an imprudent fellow,"
the judge told him, " but if they press you too far to find out the
author of this offence, you may tell them it was I." A delightful
episode, and one could add a hundred others. He stands out a
live and charming figure, the serious and at the same time the
jovial judge of the Ancien Régime ; but the strong, fine family
organization of the Parliamentary families of old had also its
reverse side.

Young candidates for the magistracy were obliged to hold a
diploma of licentiate in law, to spend a certain number of terms
with an advocate, and to have some knowledge of law and Latin ;
an examination was held by a jury of Councillors which generally
lasted three hours, but if the examination took place during Lent
the candidate was questioned for four hours, for what reasons
we do not know. The examination began with a discourse which
the candidate had to deliver in Latin, taking Cicero for his model,

[1] Alexis Piron : a witty, satirical and licentious poet, born at Dijon (1689–
1773). (H. W.)

but it would seem that all this was only an elegant pretence. "Judges are too easily passed for the tribunals," said the clergy of Saintes in 1789; "a young man purchases an office, and shortly afterwards, without any preliminary studies, or knowledge, and often possessing no talent, he decides cases involving the honour and fortunes of citizens, and later on, their lives." Roederer, a Councillor in the Parliament of Metz, deplored the too often insufficient qualifications of the Councillors : "They learn the little law they know from the advocates they hear pleading." "But in truth, when one penetrates into their private chambers," notes Servan, Advocate General of the Parliament of Grenoble, "one may see imposing bookshelves of large volumes bound in brown leather and gold, making a fine display." Seats in Parliament were often occupied by fledglings, "still barely weaned from their foster-mother's milk," in the words of Norvins. We come across Councillors of nineteen, eighteen and even seventeen years old, and *Presidents à Mortier* who had scarcely reached the age of twenty-five.

Then there was the appalling practice of *épices*, the name given to the presents made by litigants to the judges. These originally took the form of comfits, boxes of preserves, game, fruit and especially oriental sweetmeats (*épices*) which litigants who had won their cases presented to the judge as a thankoffering ; but these *épices*, while still keeping their original name, soon changed into presents of money and became almost obligatory. The edict of 1673 endeavoured to regulate this practice and to tax it ; it forbade the refusal on the part of the judge to pronounce judgment, under the pretext that the *épices* had not yet been paid. The edict was observed with more, or less, scrupulosity, but the abuses became more and more aggravated. President Rolland de Challerenge writes in 1765 : "The unbridled licence of this practice dishonours the judges, and it would be very desirable to find means to put an end to this shameful and base side of their functions." The *épices* were in proportion to the intricacy and duration of the procedure involved—domiciliary visits, inquiries, reports and judgments. According to Fléchier, Guillaume de Lamoignon did his best to put a stop to the results too easily obtained by some *épiciers*. "How often did he not endeavour to banish from the Palais de Justice those artificial delays, those well-nigh interminable side issues invented by avariciousness to lengthen out cases by means of those very laws which were made to terminate them, and to obtain profit from the spoils of both the loser and the winner of the case."

Even the tradition which concentrated judicial functions in the hands of certain families came to engender abuses. Here is a petition addressed to the King in 1777 by the municipal officers of Brest with a view to preventing the appointment of a certain Sieur Bergevin to the office of Seneschal. These gentlemen explain that all the judicial functions in the town, to whatsoever jurisdiction they belonged, were fulfilled by members of the same family, "and therefore, supposing M. Bergevin were put in possession of the office of Seneschal, the only office left which is not held by his family, we should have but one sole judge."

The magistracy occupied a judicial position such that no one could dream of prosecuting them. They openly engaged in contraband on the frontiers of Dauphiné and Provence. They stored merchandise in their country houses. In 1726, at Grenoble, a band of smugglers, when prosecuted by the excisemen, found sure protection even at the Palais de Justice. The farmers of taxes, though so powerful, did not dare to complain against them.

As Besenval says, the magistracy was above the laws. "How many unfortunate holders of property are dispossessed of their inheritance for the sole reason that it suited some member of Parliament to look on while a judgment, as iniquitous as the bad faith which brought the action, has been given!"

Arthur Young is no less severe :

"The conduct of the parliaments was profligate and atrocious. Upon almost every cause that came before them interest was openly made with the judges : and woe betided the man who, with a cause to support, had no means of conciliating favour, either by the beauty of a handsome wife or by other methods."

The reports drawn up in 1789 tell the same tale. It was like the statuette, spoken of by Voltaire, made of clay and gold ; must it be broken up because it contained clay ?

After pointing out the greatness of the magistracy of old resplendent in its independence of the Government, and after showing also the abuses resulting from its unceasing interference in matters outside its judicial functions, Tocqueville concludes as follows :

"We have, it is true, banished the administration of justice from the sphere of the executive government into which the Ancien Régime had allowed it to intrude unduly ; but at the same time the Government itself unceasingly intruded on the natural sphere of the administration of justice, and there we have left it, just as if the confusion of authority was not as dangerous to one side as to the other, and even more so ; for the interference of the dispensers of justice in the Government is merely prejudicial to public affairs, while the interference of the Government in the sphere of justice depraves mankind and tends to render them both revolutionary and servile."

BIBLIOGRAPHY

Aguesseau (H.-Fr. d'), *Œuvres complètes*, ed. Pardessus, 1819, 16 vol.—
Avenel (Vicomte G. d'), *La Noblesse Française sous Richelieu*, 1901.—Babeau
(Alb.), *La Ville sous l'Ancien Régime*, 1880.—Beaumarchais, *Mémoires dans
l'affaire Goezmann*, 1878 ed.—Besenval (Baron de), *Mémoires*, an VIII–1805,
3 vol.—Beugot (Comte), *Mémoires*, 1866, 2 vol.—Bodin (Jean), *Les Six Livres
de la République*, 1583.—Boscheron des Portes, *Histoire du Parlement de Bordeaux*, 1877.—Busquet (Raoul), *Histoire des Institutions de la Provence*, 1920.
—Cabasse, *Le Parlement de Provence*, 1826.—Carré (H.), *La Noblesse de France
et l'Opinion publique au dix-huitième siècle*, 1920.—Carré (H.), *Essai sur le
fonctionnement du Parlement de Bretagne après la Ligue*, 1888.—Carré (H.), *La
Fin des Parlements*, 1912.—Castéras (Paul de), *La Société toulousaine à la fin
du dix-huitième siècle*, 1891.—Croÿ (Duc de), *Mémoires*, ed. P. Cottin and de
Grouchy, 4 vol., 1906–1908.—Dubédat, *Histoire du Parlement de Toulouse*,
1885.—*Encyclopédie méthodique* (Diderot's), section *Jurisprudence*, 1786,
articles by Boucher d'Argis.—Flammermont (Jules), *Le Chancelier Maupeou
et les Parlements*, 1883.—Flammermont (Jules), *Remontrances du Parlement
de Paris au dix-huitième siècle*, 1888–1898, 3 vol.—Floquet, *Histoire du Parlement de Normandie*, 7 vol., 1840–1849.—*Journal historique de la révolution
opérée dans la constitution de la monarchie Française*, by M. de Maupeou,
7 vol., 1775–1776.—La Cuisine, *Le Parlement de Bourgogne*, 1864.—La Roche-
Flavin, *Arrêts notables du Parlement de Toulouse*, ed. Graverol, 1682.—Le Moy,
Le Parlement de Bretagne et le pouvoir royal, 1909.—Loyseau, *Œuvres*, 1701.—
Marion (Marcel), *La Chalotais et le Duc d'Aiguillon*, 1898.—Marion (Marcel),
Dictionnaire des institutions de la France aux dix-septième et dix-huitième siècles,
1923.—Mathieu (Cardinal), *L'Ancien Régime en Lorraine et en Barrois*, 1879.
—*Maupeouana (les), recueil des écrits patriotiques publiés pendant le règne du
Chancelier Maupeou . . .*, 1775.—Saulnier (Fréd.), *Le Parlement de Bretagne*,
2 vol., 1910.—Sémichon (Ernest), *Les Réformes sous Louis XVI*, 1878.—
Sénac de Meilhan, *Le Gouvernement, les mœurs et les conditions . . .*, ed.
Lescure, 1862.—Tocqueville (Alexis de), *L'Ancien Régime et la Révolution*,
5th ed., 1866.

CHAPTER VIII

THE VILLAGE

I. The Peasant.—II. Village Assemblies.—III. Rustic Interiors.—IV. Wealth and Poverty of the Rural Classes.—V. Their Dwellings.—VI. Their Garments.—VII. Their Food.—VIII. Their Education.—IX. Charitable Customs.—X. The Division of Property.—XI. Progress realized in the Eighteenth Century.—XII. The Village.

I.—*The Peasant*

IN France of old the country districts were of far more importance than the towns, especially towards the middle of the eighteenth century, at which period we see industry attaining a brilliant scope ; here too we may say that under the Ancien Régime the family, of which we have already treated, and the village, which we are about to deal with, formed the foundations of the whole of society.

The celebrated picture of the tiller of the soil sketched by La Bruyère is well known :

" We see certain wild animals, male and female, spread over the country, dark, livid and tanned by the sun, clinging to the soil which they dig and turn up with invincible perseverance ; they have some sort of articulate speech, and when they rise to their feet they display human faces, and are, in fact, men. They retire by night into their dens where they live on black bread, water and roots ; they spare others the trouble of sowing, ploughing and gathering their daily bread, and in this way do not deserve to be lacking in what they have sown."

Perhaps nothing in our literature is more celebrated than this steel etching *à la Callot*, the quintessence of the history taught in French schools. Elsewhere La Bruyère says, " In towns one is brought up in utter indifference to things rural and of the fields." Doubtless he wished to give us a personal example.

The above lines of La Bruyère are only literature, written by a good writer for the sake of effect, which he attains. We might make of them one panel of a diptych, the second of which might be the following picture given by Sébastien Mercier :

259

" A rustic wedding at which the couple are seen proceeding to the church with their fingers lovingly intertwined and glancing at each other with looks expressing their simple feelings ; the parents are following behind to that same altar where they themselves were married ; the groomsmen in their Sunday clothes, with ribbons in their hats and flowers in their button-holes ; the girls in white bodices looking with more assurance at their sweethearts on that special day ; and the violin, somewhat squeaky it is true, gaily closing up the procession. . . ."

Then comes the wedding feast :

" The village banquet, with its unaffected laughter, the table on the grass, the joy of the relatives, the wine pitcher ever replenished, the calf cut up and roasted whole." Next, " the sprightly dances and lively frolics ; the old white-haired folk wiping from their eyes their affectionate tears, the bridegroom, petulant and watching impatiently for the evening star to gleam forth, and on the morrow the bride somewhat pale, confused and happy, wondering and triumphant. . . ."

Greuze, where are thy brushes ?

But let us leave La Bruyère and Sébastien Mercier to reconcile their differences, and let us talk seriously.

Among the writers on the Ancien Régime there is one possessing a unique value in connection with country life. Retif de la Bretonne, the Burgundian peasant, who followed the plough up to the age of twenty, and lived in close relations with the people in his village, has described with robust pen the life led by his own people. In a large number of his books, particularly *La Vie de mon Père*—a masterpiece; in *Monsieur Nicolas*, an autobiography ; *l'Ecole des pères*, and the *Paysan perverti*, we find descriptions of exceptional value, owing to their reality, relish and sincerity, of the village people and peasants of Burgundy in the first half of the eighteenth century.

Speaking of the two villages of Sacy (Dept. of the Yonne, *canton* of Vermenton) and Nitry (*canton* of Noyers), Retif writes :

" The inhabitants owned their land almost entirely ; each one cultivated his share, and possessed cattle proportioned in number to the quantity of forage raised and the amount of manure he required."

II.—*Village Assemblies*

In addition to privately owned property each village (they called them communities) possessed *communes* (common lands) belonging to all. But let us leave the description to our peasant :

" As the small parish of Sacy," says Retif, " possessed *communes*, it was governed like one family." The following words are of special interest and should be remembered. " Everything in it was decided by a plurality of votes at meetings which were held in the public square on Sundays and *fête* days, to which they were summoned by the ringing of the great bell. At these meetings were appointed the syndics, collectors of the *taille*, the watchmen to guard sown land and the vines, and the public herdsmen." On 'a former page we discussed these village assemblies in connection with the jurisdiction of the seigneur. The syndics were the officials of the rural communities and had nothing to do with the municipal administration.

" The seigneur's representative presided at these meetings ; the taxing officer (*Procureur Fiscal*) laid the matters to be discussed before the meeting, but each individual had the right to denounce any abuses he knew of, or to propose any measures that he considered to be useful. These matters were discussed then and there, and if they were of any consequence they would send the syndics to the Intendant's subdelegates to have them authorized. Further, at these meetings they would designate each year the section of the common woods to be cut by each member ; this was drawn by lot, with the exception of the Curé, the chief (seigneur), when he was living there, and the two syndics to whom were assigned by name the best sections."

As we can see, this was rural self-government in all its integrity. We should particularly note that this picture of a village meeting given by Retif agrees in all its details with that presented at a later date by Cardinal Mathieu in the case of Lorraine, as the result of his study of the local archives.

Albert Babeau writes : " Forty thousand natural associations deliberated about their own interests and chose their own agents."

But let us look at the picture drawn by Cardinal Mathieu of the village assemblies in Lorraine :

" The syndic was elected every year. The inhabitants assembled on a Sunday after Vespers either in front of the church, under the shade of the huge tree which had sheltered their rustic deliberations, sometimes for centuries past, or on the market-place ; or may be in the seigneur's audience chamber, when there was one. There they would discuss among themselves almost the same matters as our own municipal councils do, and a few other questions besides. They would appoint the assessors and collectors, would agree upon the tithes which had been presented by the tithe collector for payment, fix the date for beginning the harvest, the wages of the herdsman and the schoolmaster ; would decide upon what repairs were needed for the belfry tower, the Curé's house, the bridge over the stream, and the road leading to the next village. They would settle the sharing, sale or letting of the common lands, the manner of fulfilling the obligation of the *corvée* ; would delegate the mayor (representing the seigneur) or the syndic (acting for the community) to go to the office of the Intendant, to the magistrate's court, or the person in authority, to ask permission, may be, to remove a cow or horse impounded by the watchman of a neighbouring village ; lastly, they would listen to the statement of dues to be paid. Often the meetings became heated. . . . It sometimes happened that they would decide to bring an action against the seigneur, the Curé, or against a neighbouring community. . . ."

It was not in reality a deliberative assembly, but a sort of public meeting of which the village notary kept the minutes.

Similar meetings of mothers were held on a Sunday after Vespers, to choose the official village midwife, and the Curé would preside. Possibly he may not have had sufficient acquaintance with the subject, and so there were sometimes complaints of the routine methods of the midwives chosen, some of whom were imbued with the quaintest superstitions.

It is clear that such a communal administration, comprising all the inhabitants of a village, would no longer be possible to-day, not only on account of the extent of many of our villages, but principally because of the multiplicity and complicated nature of the questions with which such assemblies would have to concern themselves. The autonomy of the different families forming the communities of earlier days, each one of which administered its own affairs like a small State, rendered the questions to be discussed very simple and few. There were some villages in which the only expenditure in common was for the upkeep of the clock in the belfry of the church. It was the schoolmaster's duty, as a rule, to wind up the weights.

As regards the election of the dignitaries and officials of the communities, this took place under the most ordinary circumstances in the world—amid the canvassing and intrigue which generally flourish in this kind of operation ; they would elect the syndic, the schoolmaster, the tithe collector, the collector of the *taille*, the herdsman or common shepherd, the *va-de-pied*, that is, the rural postman, and the carrier whose duty it was to place the locality in communication with the neighbourhood.

We can readily imagine the confusion and disorder which could find their way into these meetings, especially in the eighteenth century with its changing customs and the lessening of the traditional respect for the head of the family, whose authority up till then had been the preponderating influence at the assemblies. Turgot complains of the uproar and commotion into which these meetings under the old elm had degenerated. Compelled to extend the field of their deliberations, the peasants no longer possessed the requisite knowledge, and groped about in the dark. Busybodies gave ready tongue to their grievances and the community lost its way in a host of law-suits, for in the course of the eighteenth century our peasants became madly litigious. It sometimes happened that Parliament quashed their decisions, but the Intendants constituted themselves their defenders.

The seigneur's voice was listened to no longer, nor that of his agent. In many localities the sale of the domain had brought a new family to the manor house; it was no longer the same family with which for centuries the parish had held close relations. How many parishes which willingly had followed the counsels of their old seigneurial family came into conflict at the very outset with the one which had taken its place! The seigneur now lived at Court, and his domain was administered by a steward, and his land by a farmer. Seigneur and vassal no longer took any interest in each other. Towards the close of the Ancien Régime many parishes had reached the point of delegating their powers to various forms of municipal councils, as we do at the present day. The collector of the *taille* and the syndic had slipped more and more under the authority of the Intendant, or his subdelegate; in many villages the syndic had even become the King's agent in proportion as the seigneur, whether from absence or indifference, had become more or less a stranger to his " subjects," for it should be noted that the importance and independence of these village assemblies went on diminishing during the course of the eighteenth century, in proportion as the importance of the part played by the seigneur among his tenants grew feebler.

III.—*Rustic Interiors*

The Seigneur of Nitry was a Knight of Malta. On the death of Maître Boujat, the judge of the seigneurial domain, who for the space of forty years had carried out his functions to the satisfaction of those in his jurisdiction, Retif's father was called upon to succeed him at the request of a deputation to the seigneur from the village. Retif speaks in terms of the greatest praise of the Curés of the two parishes of Nitry and Sacy. Messire Antoine Foudriat, the Curé of Nitry, " assisted the poor to pay the *taille*." Marriages were celebrated at four o'clock in the morning, a custom which was widespread.

Retif introduces us inside the homes of these worthy folk;

we can see the heavy curtains with their woven patterns surrounding the beds, and the earthenware plates leaning against
the dresser.

Several families would unite " to make up a three-horsed plough."
Nicholas Retif had gone to a distance from Nitry with a comrade,
and when passing through the village of Puits-de-Bon (Dept. of
Yonne, *commune* of Noyers-en-Serein), he and his young friend
knocked at a door. There they found some worthy peasants
supping on a dish of salt pork, after which appeared black
puddings. A great jug of wine was warming in front of the fire—
they drank it hot. " The party was made up of three families
regaling themselves together after sowing their crops. They were
' *suitiers*,' that is, associated together to make up a three-horsed
plough."

Let us now enter Retif de la Bretonne's own home :

" In the evening at supper, the only meal at which all the family
could assemble together, Edmond Retif (the father) looked like a
patriarch at the head of a numerous household, for, as a rule, there
were twenty-two at table, including the ploughman, and the vine
dressers (who in winter became threshers), the cowman, the shepherd,
and two female servants, one of whom worked with the threshers,
and the other looked after the cows and the dairy. All the company
were seated at one table, the head of the family at one end, near the
fire, with his wife by his side within reach of the dishes to be served
—for she alone had the care of the kitchen. The female servants,
who had been working all day, were sitting eating peacefully ; then
came the children of the family, seated in order of age, which was all
that settled their places ; next, the ploughman of longest service
and his mates ; then the vine dressers, after them the cowman, and
the shepherd ; the two women servants closed up the ranks. . . ."

It was supper time, and as we said above, it was the only meal
uniting the whole family together, and in the " family," following
a good old custom, were comprised the women servants and
labourers ; during the daytime, their different occupations did not,
in fact, allow of everybody meeting together at the same hour.

After supper the head of the family would read a few pages of
Holy Scripture, accompanied with explanations and kindly remarks.
This was followed by a short prayer, said in common, and then
the last part of the catechism was recited by the little children.
" After that all went to bed silently, for after evening prayers,"
said Retif, " laughter and loud conversation were forbidden."

In winter, when the evenings were longer, after the recitation
of the catechism the head of the family would tell stories and
old legends of the countryside, and give them the latest news,

and then everyone was free to speak, and there would be laughter and joking. During Advent, Christmas carols were sung. We are far from La Bruyère's "wild animals," as one can see.

A mother sends his scanty wardrobe to her son who had left the village to go to the town :

"Edmond, I am sending you thick floss stockings and breeches of *fort-en-diable*,[1] two vests and your homespun coat for you to make a brave show on Sundays and *fête* days."

And how easy it is to understand this old peasant making his son, who wanted to become a bourgeois in the town, return to his native village :

"They would like to settle you in the town, would they ! Tell me, my future posterity, what would become of you in a few years when lost among the population of the towns ? Let us remain here, where everything is full of us, where everything reminds us of our honourable position ! . . ."

We have another picture of village conditions and habits sketched by Marmontel. He too, like Retif, was a son of peasants, worthy people among whom he passed his early days. Marmontel is more literary than Retif, and his style is polished. His aim is to present us, not only with accurate pictures, but rounded and well-balanced sentences. Marmontel's pages do not possess the same zest, intense life, and high relief of the Burgundian's portraits, but the similarity between the two is none the less useful. They wrote at the same period, and while Retif introduces us to Burgundy, Marmontel takes us to the Limousin district.

Marmontel first saw the light of day and passed his early boyhood at Bort (Dept. of Corrèze), a little rustic village. In addition to the father and mother there lived under the same roof the two grandmothers, three aunts, and a "swarm of children." "Bort on the Dordogne was a place where any inequality in condition or fortune was scarcely felt. A little property, or some small form of industry and commerce made up the condition of nearly all the inhabitants. . . . Everyone was free, and usefully occupied."

He makes the following interesting remark : "The marriages they made were no anxiety to the family ; there was so little inequality in their condition or fortune that the fathers and mothers were in agreement almost as soon as their children, and rarely did marriage end in a lessening of mutual love. . . ."

Marmontel had a little friend whose fair hair was always carefully combed, his clothes were clean and simple, and his linen

[1] *Fort-en-diable :* a familiar term, denoting a special material of very strong texture. (H. W.)

always white. His name was Durand, and his father was a labourer in a neighbouring village. Marmontel was always delighted to go there. " How the good old man welcomed us ! What fine cream, rich milk and good brown bread ! "

The little fellow was spoilt by his grandmother. " She used to show me, like so many treasures, the provision she had made for the winter, her bacon, hams, sausages, pots of honey and jars of oil, her store of buckwheat, rye, peas and beans, her pile of radishes and chestnuts, her straw beds covered with fruit."

Marmontel continues :

" The sheep-folds of Saint-Thomas clothed the women and children with their wool ; my aunts spun the wool, as well as the hemp which provided us with linen ; and in the evenings, by the light of a lamp burning oil made from our own walnuts, the young people near by would come and help us beat this good hemp, making an enchanting picture.

The harvest of the little farm provided our subsistence ; the wax and honey from the bees, which one of my aunts cultivated with care, gave a return with little expense ; the oil pressed out from our walnuts when still fresh, had a savour and odour which we preferred to the taste and smell of olive oil. The flat buckwheat cakes, buttered when hot with that excellent butter of Mont d'Or, were a great treat for us. I do not know anything we enjoyed more than our radishes and chestnuts, and on winter evenings when these fine radishes were roasting round the fire, or when we heard the water boiling in the saucepan wherein were cooking those savoury tender chestnuts, our hearts would palpitate with joy. . . .

Consequently in a household where everything was made use of, these little things combined made up the comforts of life in a small way, and not much expense was entailed in providing for all our necessities. There was dead wood in abundance in the forests near by which was of little value, and my father was allowed to take what he wanted. The excellent mountain butter and most delicious cheeses were local and cost little ; wine was not dear, and my father drank it sparingly. . . ."

Christmas ! And the Christmas feast ! " How the same delight came round every year ! " writes Marmontel. " We looked forward to it, but took care to conceal our expectations. While we were at Mass the soup of green cabbage, the black puddings, the sausages, the dish of rosy salt pork, the cakes, apple-fritters fried in lard, were all mysteriously made ready by her (the grandmother) and one of her sisters. . . . After Mass all these wonderful things were found on the table, and we would shout with cries of delight. . . ."

Here again it is a far cry to La Bruyère's " wild animals."

Retif has drawn in many places portraits of these heads of peasant families, called in Lorraine " *chefs de feux* " ; in the Midi " *caps d'hostal* (chefs d'hôtel, chefs de maison)," and in other localities " *ménagers*." Ch. de Ribbe states that " the *ménager* has been for centuries one of the corner stones of the edifice of local liberties." Henri de Sourdis, when sent by Richelieu on one of his centralizing missions, came up against the independent spirit and resolute will of these robust peasants. " What is to be done with them ? " he exclaimed in despair when met by the claims of " an impossible assembly of ' consuls ' who return to their plough after casting aside their ' *chaperons* ' (the ' consul's ' insignia) ? "

The period during which they exercised rule over their families is called in Provençal documents a " reign " . . . " en Olliol [1] (Ollioules) *renhava ung mien reyregrand que si appelava Guilhem Deydier-Baralha*." The Latin texts of the district of Briançon call these ruling peasants " *rois et chevaliers* " ; *reges et milites*. We might think we were reading the Iliad or the Odyssey. " Heads of families were content to wear on *fête* days a good smock of the closely-woven homespun then in vogue, and another for working days of good linen with an old jacket underneath ; maintaining their families in freedom and tranquillity, taking little interest in outside affairs beyond knowing how much wheat fetched in the market of the next village. . . . " In the evenings they might be seen " chatting freely together on some trifle or other, laughing heartily, telling stories of olden days *et neiges de l'année passée* [2] ; and on returning home from the fields everyone would have his broad jest with which to chaff his fellows, and incidents of the day to relate, each content with his lot and the calling which gave him an honest living. . . . " The above sketch is by good Noel du Fail, describing the types to be found in the sixteenth century. We have already given instances of these rural patriarchs cited by Retif; they did not disappear with the Revolution, and Mistral was able to give us a similar portrait of his father at the beginning of the nineteenth century :

" Quite a crowd of retainers, some hired by the month and others as day labourers, would go to and fro over the land belonging to the *mas* (Provençal farm) with harrow and rake, or with a fork over their shoulder. . . . My father dominated them by his height, by his good sense, and also by his noble birth. He was a fine and imposing type of an old man, dignified in his language, firm in his commands,

[1] " In Ollioules reigned one of my ancestors who was known as Guilhem Deydier-Batalha."

[2] Cf. page 71.

benevolent to the poor and severe on himself alone. During the Revolution he engaged as a volunteer in defence of France, and in the evenings he would take pleasure in recounting his old battles. . . . My father had deep religious faith. At night time, summer or winter, he would pray aloud for us all, and when the evenings were long, he would read the Gospels to the children and servants."

As we see, it is just the same scene that took place under Edmond Retif's roof at Nitry in Burgundy. Mistral goes on :

" My father used to celebrate Christmas with much ceremony, and after he had reverently blessed the logs on the hearth, he would speak to us of our ancestors, praising their lives, and praying for them. Whatever the weather he was always content, and if he sometimes heard people complaining about it on account of the high winds or torrential rain, he would say to them, ' Good people, He who is up above knows quite well what He is doing, and what is good for us.'

All his life he had worked and saved ; but his table, like his purse, was open to every comer, and when any one was mentioned in his presence, he always asked whether he was a hard worker ; and if they replied ' Yes,' he would say, ' Then he is an upright man, and I am his friend.'

He died like a patriarch. After he had received the last Sacraments all the household were weeping around his bed.

' Come, children ! ' he said, ' I am going away, and I give thanks to God for all I owe to Him, for my long life and my labour which He has blessed.' "

Almost in every feature the above is also the faithful portrait of Retif de la Bretonne's father, as traced by his son.

We have already spoken of village weddings. It was a custom doubtless common in most of the French provinces—M. Dagnan-Bouveret has given us a delightful picture of it as still practised in the nineteenth century—for the bridegroom and bride-elect to kneel at the feet of the head of the family before proceeding to the church. All present knelt likewise. A prayer was recited aloud, and the father gave them his blessing, after which they left to the sound of violins to be married in the church.

" In addition to the fine clothes of the bride," writes the Abbé de Marolles in the eighteenth century, " and a head-dress of embroidery jingling with tinsel and glass beads, the relatives wore their well-pleated blue dresses which they would take out from their chests perfumed with lavender, dried roses and rosemary—I speak of the men as well as the women. . . . The wedding favours were not forgotten, each one wearing them at the waist or at the top of the sleeve. There would be the strains of pipes, flutes and hautbois, and afterwards a sumptuous banquet and rustic dances which lasted till the evening."

A red dress seems in most provinces to have been the bride's special "livery" just as white is to-day. The seigneur of the village, often a man of the highest rank, would take part in these rustic weddings. This was a tradition of which we have accurate record. The Duc de Croÿ writes, "we went to the house of the bride, where we saw preparations for a fine wedding feast laid for forty people consisting of only the brothers and sisters of the two families; great store of turkeys and meat pies. We took one away with us and we danced with the bride. The Prince and Princess (de Condé) acted with quite good grace and in a popular spirit as was expected of them." This scene took place at Vanves.

IV.—*Wealth and Poverty of the Rural Classes*

We must not however draw a too favourable conclusion of prosperity from what has gone before. There is much authentic testimony showing the poverty which overtook the rural classes in one or other province after a bad harvest. The Ancien Régime could not bring great steamships from the New World, the East, or North Africa, laden with sufficient supplies to make up for the deficit due to the failure of the crops. The provincial customs houses, in maintaining which the people displayed the blindest obstinacy, were a further obstacle to the relief of the stricken districts; and so too was the violent hostility to the prudent provision that might have been made by the authorities beforehand to meet the exigencies of a possible food crisis. The economic notions of the period were still of a rudimentary kind, and the people were very severe towards speculators, or monopolists, to apply the term with which they were branded. With unreflecting prejudice the whole of France opposed "these monopolists who desolate the kingdom," against whom the Third Estate of Rheims was later on, in 1789, to demand the severest laws. Arthur Young, however, an experienced agriculturist, observes more justly, "It is necessary in order to secure a regular provision to give great encouragement to the monopolists."

Under conditions like these, poverty could not have failed to ensue after terrible winters such as those of 1709, 1740, 1767, 1771, 1775, 1784 and 1789, or in different parts of the country after a long drought. But the pictures drawn by Vauban, Massillon, the Marquis d'Argenson, and Arthur Young, of the distress of the agricultural classes in France before the Revolution, are much too darkly coloured. For instance, Vauban writes in his *Dîme Royale* (1707): "The evil has certainly gone too far, and if it be not remedied the people will fall into such extremities that they will never be able to recover." And yet the same writer declares

in the same work that on Sundays and *fête* days the village taverns
were never empty. He should be more consistent. The Marquis
d'Argenson had been embittered by his disgrace and exile. We
have, on the other hand, an equal number of rose-coloured descriptions to contrast with these darker views—Voltaire's for instance :

"I know not how it happens that in our villages, with an
ungrateful soil, heavy taxes, and an intolerable prohibition against
selling outside the district the wheat they have sown, there is
hardly a single cultivator who does not possess a good cloth suit
or is not well shod and well fed."

We have, too, the testimony of foreigners who judged our social
conditions with no *arrière pensée*; for example, in 1739, Lady
Montagu remarks upon "the air of abundance and contentment
everywhere in the country districts of France," and Horace
Walpole, as he passed through Artois in 1765, states, "I find this
district thriving prodigiously . . . the smallest villages possess an
air of prosperity." An Intendant of Roussillon takes note of the
numerous meals eaten by the country folk, "four, five, even six
daily, with meat and wine at every meal. . . ."

This varying testimony, however, cannot be taken as representative, either on one side or the other.

V.—*Their Dwellings*

One would like to give a general description of the houses of
the peasants, but their diversity from North to South, sometimes
even in the same district and the same village, would be too great.

In the North the most important buildings were made of brick,
but such houses were seldom to be found in the villages, where
they used a composition of clay and straw cased in by wooden
beams. The foundation was formed of pebbles or rubble. They
presented the appearance of those old village dwellings which we
still often see at the present day—in comic opera. Arthur Young
declares that in the Cotentin district he came across the best built
houses and barns he had ever seen : "They build in this country
the best mud houses and barns I ever saw, excellent habitations
even of three stories, and all of mud, with considerable barns and
other offices." In the Cahourcin district the English traveller
passed some houses "extremely well built of stone, and roofed
with slate or tiles ; but they had no windows." Similarly in the
Montauban country "there were well-built cottages, without
windows, and some having no other light except what came through
the door." In Limousin windowless cottages were common.

In the time of Louis XVI, Cottereau, an engineer of Lyons,
invented a method of construction in *pisé*, which was very econ-

omical and was much advertised by engineers. From the district
of Lyons the process spread to Laon and through Picardy. The
monotony of the peasants' dwellings was sometimes broken by a
gabled window at the height of two or three storeys—the village
inn. The seigneur's house was often only distinguished by its more
important dimensions : a large farm at the end of the courtyard,
which was surrounded by farm buildings ; but on the top of the
roof creaked a square-shaped weathercock. As for the presbytery,
it generally bore the appearance of the humblest of dwellings, a
straw-thatched hovel, with no gable, cellar, or wood shed, and
possessing only one serviceable room.

The roofs were almost all thatched, and on them grew various
parasitic wild plants, such as mullein and house leek. Roofs with
wooden tiles (*aissangles*) were very common in wooded districts ;
they were made of oak, shaped like narrow slates, and these turned
brown in the course of years. People were apprehensive of them
on account of fire, and for this reason it was generally the wind-
mills, which had no fire-place, that were roofed with them. Fear
of fire brought it about that thatched roofs came to be more and
more prohibited. The Paris Parliament, by decree dated 1786,
ordered that new houses should be roofed with tiles. And the
Intendants only assisted those who had been visited with fire on
condition that they should roof their new dwellings with " something hard." Arthur Young states that he found in the district
of Saint-Gobain the most beautiful slate roofs he had ever
seen.

The dwellings of the poorest peasants, agricultural and day
labourers, were narrow and low ; the cattle shed was often ill
kept, and the dung was only cleared away at long intervals.

It was the French custom, continued down to our times in so
many villages, to have the manure heap in front of the house.
It very often happened that the soil at that spot became gradually
raised in the course of time by deposits of all sorts, so that the
door of the house was below the level of the manure heap, from
which the liquid manure would trickle in. Raymond de Saint-
Sauveur, the Intendant of Roussillon, gives us the following
description :

" It was in the course of a tour of inspection that I came to know
of the lack of cleanliness in the villages, especially the mountain villages, where the inhabitants are accustomed to pile their manure
heaps by the door, and keep their pigs under their own roof, a practice
which taints the badly paved streets, infects the air, and is the cause
of frequent illnesses, and occasionally of epidemics in such a warm
district as this. . . ."

The lack of public fountains in so many places aggravated the evil. Saint-Sauveur took pains to have as many constructed as he could.

The poorest peasant dwellings consisted of only one very low room, giving access in many cases to a few little out-houses. The floor was of trodden-down earth, the ceiling of beams blackened by the smoke of time. Light entered through an opening over the door, or one or two windows which in the South of France were unglazed; in other districts they were glazed with coarse glass having great bubbles like the bottoms of bottles. The walls were whitewashed, but at some time long forgotten in the past, and the years had covered them with a brownish mould. The farmers had two or three rooms, sometimes more, and in important houses these were of very large dimensions. We should recall the description given on an earlier page of the *chauffoir* in the *maisons de village*.

There was little difference in the furniture of the simplest and most wealthy houses—great beds with flowered curtains, or of grey or green serge, that is, when they did not use the huge cupboards for sleeping in; by the hearth the ancestral arm-chair of the head of the family, the salt tub, the chests, often carved with branches and flowers, wherein were kept the Sunday clothes, and serving also the purpose of seats; the side-board or dresser with its pewter and earthenware plates; *objets de piété* in wood, bronze, or pottery representing Christ, the Virgin or the patron saint of the village; drinking pots of stone or pewter and the flask of cordial. Lastly there was the great press of oak, walnut, or white wood. The panels were often carved in the style of the period, assuming a fine dark polished gloss. In it were kept the family treasures, often of greater value than one would imagine. Pieces of plate were not rare in these humble dwellings, especially drinking goblets.

We should note too the old arquebus, gun, or musket hanging over the chimney; the churn, and sometimes a clock and spinning wheel. In the Northern provinces especially, there was scarcely a house where Marguerite's spinning-wheel was not humming. A little girl would learn how to spin from her mother and grandmother; on becoming a mother and grandmother herself she would still continue to spin, while humming to herself old songs with an unintelligible refrain which had come down and had been passed on from ear to ear, growing less uncouth and more musical in the course of time, just as pebbles are polished by the streams.

Life in the home centred round the hearth whereon brushwood, faggots and logs, vine branches or lumps of peat (according to the district) blazed and crackled—in front of which the head of the family sat in his rudely constructed oak arm-chair.

VI.—*Their Garments*

The peasant's dress varied little from the Renaissance to the Revolution, but it differed in one province from another. Thirty years ago one could still see the same dress that had been worn in the seventeenth and eighteenth centuries.

There was a great difference between the peasant's everyday working garb and what he wore on Sundays, his *habits à la viande* as they were called in Berry, for they were only worn when there was meat on the table. English travellers visiting France were struck with the poverty-stricken appearance of the dress of our peasants, often composed of pieces of material of different colours like that of a Harlequin. Many wore sabots, clogs, or they merely bound their feet round with cord or straps. Arthur Young uttered cries of pity at the sight of our country districts, particularly those of the South where the people went bare-footed. This English gentleman compared them with those of his native land, and concluded that our country folk were all poverty-stricken, which was a rash deduction. Contemporary writers remarked that the French peasant was often bare-footed, but never bare-headed. As I write these lines two yokels from my own village are talking under my window. One of them has just headed the list at the municipal council, and has bought a fine piece of land facing my own little property, for which he paid thirty francs the square metre ; he is very comfortably off. His friend talking to him is still better placed, a great and successful grower, the pride of the district. What an imposing appearance he presents on Sundays in his blue cloth blouse and round black felt hat ! Now at the present moment these two are wearing the humblest garments ; the vest of one of them is patched and the other is in sabots. If Arthur Young had happened to pass by and had learnt that before him were two of the richest cultivators in the district, he might have drawn forcible conclusions about the poverty of French agriculturists.

Towards the middle of the eighteenth century the garments of our peasants were certainly made almost entirely of coarse linen :

Le pauvre laboureur
Il est vétu de toil' comme un moulin à vent . . .

as the admirable old song says ; but the blue blouse had not then come in, and the word " blouse " was for the most part unknown. The peasant wore the old *sayon* of his Gallic ancestors of coarse grey linen.

About the middle of the eighteenth century clothes made of woollen material, cloth or velveteen of a grey, blue, or olive shade, came in, and grew more and more in general use. It is a remarkable fact that with the use of all this linen, and possibly on account of it, under-clothing was almost unknown. It was one of the reforms introduced in the middle of the eighteenth century ; after that time the use of under-linen became general, and itch and scurf and other skin diseases due to the want of cleanliness, and resulting from not wearing underclothes, became less common, if they did not entirely disappear.

The hat was generally round, with a large brim, as still worn in our day by so many peasants in Brittany and Velay ; they were black, white or grey, and decorated with silver thread.

The peasant women wore different kinds of dresses, according to the province—bright-coloured skirts, the front of the bodice of flowered damask, and a delightful variety of lace and fine linen coifs, varying in different villages. In Alsace the usual broad black or red ribbons, or red embroidered with flowers, were then of narrow dimensions. The skirts were red or green according to the district. With the advent of Louis XVI peasant women in striped cotton skirts made their appearance. This fashion was rendered illustrious by the volunteers of 1792, a large number of whom in the fore-front of battles were to cover with glory and blood the under-drawers—it was no question now of breeches— which a mother, sister, or sweetheart had made for them out of the cotton material of her village skirts, with pink and white stripes, blue and white, light green and white, mauve-crimson and white, or yellow and white.

VII.—*Their Food*

The diversity in food was the same as in clothing, and it would be difficult to trace any general lines, not only on account of the varying conditions in different provinces and their varying products—for instance, clearly more wine was drunk in Languedoc than in Artois, and more cider in Normandy than in Burgundy— but also by reason of those years of want which, as we said on a former page, were far more severely felt in some places than in others.

Moheau—believed to be the famous Montyon—a writer of sober mind, who made no attempt to stir his readers with any vivid descriptions, writes as follows in his treatise on the French people : " I saw the last period of distress ; I saw hunger trans-

formed into frenzy, I saw an inhabitant of one district where the
harvest had failed, crazed by grief and despoiled of everything,
envying the lot of domestic animals, and wandering over the
fields eating grass and sharing the food of wild animals. . . . ''
On the other hand, at the beginning of the reign of Louis XVI
we find the inhabitants of Nouans, a poor little village in the
district of Mans (canton Marolles-les-Braults, Sarthe), living as
follows :

" The food of the inhabitants, even those less well-off, was sub-
stantial and abundant. The bread, consisting of only a third of
barley to two-thirds of wheat, was very good, and no one lacked cider
more or less diluted with water. At dinner and supper the soup
was followed by a dish of meat, eggs, or vegetables ; for lunch and
' collations ' there were always two dishes, cheese and butter, and
often a third of raw or stewed or dried fruit, apples, nuts, etc. . . .''
(Bernard, *Souvenirs d'un Nonagénaire.*)

These quotations refer, as regards the former, to a temporary
calamity limited, as the author states, to certain cantons ; the
latter to more permanent, though also exceptional, conditions.

Legrand d'Aussy says of the Auvergne peasants on their mountain pasture land : on Sundays and *fête* days the soup would be
enriched with a piece of bacon ; on other days it was seasoned
with butter, or merely salt. Peasants in comfortable circumstances
had milk and cheese on the table ; they all ate rye bread. As
regards their drink, apart from pure water, they drank only
skimmed milk.

The average would doubtless be found in the following lines
by the Marquis de Turbilly in his celebrated *Mémoire sur les
défrichements* (1760) :

" No farmer or peasant either eats meat or drinks wine in his
own home at ordinary times ; their food consists of soup seasoned
with butter, vegetables, fruit, milk products and bread, which is
often very bad during the lean years, when they put buckwheat
in it, though sometimes this is better than the other meal they
mix with it."

Arthur Young, proud gentleman-farmer but a good fellow all
the same, on seeing the French peasant generally rather meanly
housed in his tumble-down thatched dwelling of mud and clay,
poorly clad in his coarse linen garments, wearing sabots unless he
went bare-footed, and hardly ever eating meat except on Sundays
and holidays, stiffens up and tells us with British pride, though
very friendly all the same : " In England I could show you a race
of peasants well clothed, well fed, and enough over for good drink,

well housed and comfortably off ; but not one in a thousand could be found owning land and cattle." Arthur Young had just stated that an infinite number of French peasants, though poor to all outward appearances, owned the land they cultivated and the cattle they drove to pasture—one advantage possessed by the French peasant. And here is another, contained in the charming remark, which we have already quoted, made by Louis VII to Walter Map, the Englishman : " There is nothing wanting to your Prince—valuable steeds, gold and silver, silken stuffs and precious stones ; all these he has in abundance ; at the Court of France we have nought but bread, wine, and gaiety."

A large number of French peasants owned their land—every one was his own master at home ; and—as was not always the case with their comrades on the other side of the Channel—they had their dancing, songs, and their gaiety.

" In England," observes Abbé Leblanc (1728), " the villages have a more cheerful aspect and are better built than those in France, the peasants are better off, the women more elegant, but the former are not so light-hearted ; with us every one sings." And these songs, drawn from an inexhaustible stream of folk-lore, are delightful, among them being the purest and most exquisite that a refined mind could gather. They sang and danced every-where, except in church, but especially in the space before the church, under the great trees, in the shadow of the clock tower. They danced on the green grass to the music of the pipe, flute, sackbut or trombone, the Breton bag-pipes, hautbois, hurdy-gurdy, and tambourine. Girls taking the veil were led to the church, where they were to make their vows, to the sound of the violin. People danced to the tune of pastoral ballads and songs —the *bourrée* of Berry and Auvergne, the *sauteuse* (two-step) of Nivernais, the gavotte of Dauphiné, the round dance of Burgundy, the *farandole* of Provence, the *gaillarde*, the *laitière*, the *sabotière*, the rigadoon. " There is no street or public square which we do not see full of people dancing," writes Fléchier in his over-jovial *Journal des Grands Jours d'Auvergne*. The inhabitants of Agde used to dance on the sea-shore in the evenings. " There were over a hundred sets of people dancing in the space of half a league round," noted a contemporary.

But let us get back to our village from which our interlude on dancing has not, however, taken us very far.

VIII.—*Their Education*

Primary instruction in the country districts was developed in a far greater degree than is generally thought. The consequences entailed by the Revocation of the Edict of Nantes—which, be it remarked, the modern mind cannot too strongly condemn— favoured in a quite unexpected manner the development of village schools. In a large number of districts the funds of the suppressed Protestant institutions, and a portion of the property of the fugitives from France, were set aside for the creation of fresh schools. The Government saw that teaching by Catholic masters would be a means whereby to combat Protestantism. " We enjoin upon all fathers, mothers, guardians, and other persons entrusted with the education of children," Louis XIV made declaration on the 13th December, 1698, " and particularly upon those who have made profession of the so-called Reformed Religion, to send them to school up to the age of fourteen years." The King fixed the minimum annual salary to which teachers would have a right at 150 *livres* for masters, and 100 *livres* for mistresses. Later on, under Louis XVI, the great majority of parishes were provided with primary schools. Statistics drawn up by Albert Babeau for the Department of Aube, state that out of 446 *communes* there were only 23 without public education. Schools were widely spread, particularly in the North and East, in Lorraine, Champagne and Franche-Comté.

We have seen that the schoolmaster was elected at the village assembly by the votes of all. The votes were given orally, for many of these good folk did not know how to write, having neglected to go to school. The voting was preceded by an examination of the candidates by the Curé, assisted by the leading *chefs de famille* of the village. This examination was on lines we can guess : the candidate would have to present a specimen of his handwriting, and in addition to this two branches of knowledge were required which would not be expected of our modern teachers —the liturgical chant, and palæography. The ability to decipher old texts and mediæval charters was of great importance on account of the disputes that might arise, not only as regards the possession of certain parcels of land, but the amount and nature of the tithes and the various feudal dues. A curious instance occurs in one of Retif's works, of property having been restored to a village community by the discovery of some dusty parchments at the top of an old cupboard where they had lain for a long time. A knowledge of the liturgical chant was of no inconsiderable value either, for the schoolmaster was called upon to support the Curé as he intoned the service, and in the registration of births, marriages and deaths. When the examiners, consisting of the Curé and the village notables, hesitated between two or more candidates, the deciding test took place at the reading desk in the church : in front of the entire parish assembled there, the candidates would chant an *Agnus Dei*, a *Kyrie Eleison*, or a *Tantum Ergo*, and the one whose voice had filled the nave with the greatest credit was assured of his election.

The schoolmaster was usually elected for one year, at the end of which his mandate to teach the village children had to be renewed. It sometimes happened that a teacher who had failed to give satisfaction to the parents was judged to be incompetent to continue. As in the case of our elections to the Legislature, the local cabaret was called upon to play its part ; little glasses of old liqueur and ratafia, handed round by the threatened schoolmaster, did not fail to reassure unsteady voters—so far as their votes went at any rate.

The master was generally paid by the parents for each pupil individually ; two or three *sous* a month to teach him to read, three or four a month to teach him to add, and four or five to teach him to write. When these fees did not amount to the yearly sum of 150 *livres* fixed by Louis XIV, the village had to make it up. The pupils hardly ever went to school regularly, except during the winter months ; on fine days they were engaged in helping their parents in the fields.

In a large number of villages it was the custom for the master to have his daily dinner in turn with the parents of his pupils. In some places the education was free on account of foundations left for the purpose. A schoolmaster would often add to his emoluments by carrying on some other occupation at the same time, for instance, that of mason, cobbler, or tailor, and in some cases his workshop would also serve as a class-room. He was, however, forbidden to sell wine. Many of these teachers were scriveners, as they are at the present day, or clerks to the community as they were called.

We know that the peasant school children, following a surprising tradition, learned to read from Latin books up to the time when the intelligent zeal of Jean Baptiste de la Salle and his lay brothers substituted reading from French books. La Salle prosecuted his fine campaign with such energy that he wished that the masters in his schools should not know Latin, whence arose the name *frères ignorantins* [1] given to them in derision by those who did not know its glorious origin. The teaching was still individual : instead of taking the whole class together the master would take each pupil, one after the other, and give him a lesson. Schools

[1] *Ignorantins :* the name originally taken for reasons of humility by the Brothers of St. John of God who tended the poor. St. Jean Baptiste de la Salle founded the Christian Brothers, a teaching congregation. (H. W.)

for girls were rare and those that existed were generally kept by
nuns, whereas the schoolmasters in village schools were nearly
always laymen. A great number of schools were mixed. A very
curious picture, drawn by Binet for Retif's *Vie de mon Père* under
the author's direction, represents the schoolmaster of Nitry seated
at the end of the class-room under a crucifix ; on benches ranged
along the wall are seated the girls on one side, and the boys on
the other, opposite to each other, while the centre of the room
is empty.

As regards the results obtained by this form of teaching, in which
the moral side occupied a large place, they appear to have been
satisfactory, especially as far as writing was concerned. Village
handwriting was famous for its excellence.

One can easily imagine that under the conditions described
above, the value of schoolmasters differed very considerably.
The master at Nitry, of whom Retif de la Bretonne gives an admirable portrait, was a man of very rare qualifications. Later on
the Subdelegate of Lunéville said, " there is no kind of merchandise
that can be described as more mixed than the schoolmasters."

At the close of the Ancien Régime it may be stated generally
that two-thirds of the men, and one-third of the women, knew
how to read.

We will conclude this rapid sketch of rural schools under the
Ancien Régime with this observation : men in olden times did
not attach the same importance to the education of the people
as we do in our day. The reports drawn up in 1789 display surprising indifference in regard to primary education. The clergy
(those famous partisans of obscurantism !) were almost alone in
demanding the diffusion of education among the people ; the
few reports of the Third Estate which alluded to the matter,
regarded the question as of secondary importance. Voltaire, a
seigneur de village, and very sincerely solicitous for the well-being
of his tenants, gave it as his opinion that " one pen is enough for
a hundred inhabitants."

Together with the schools we must mention, alas ! the *cabarets*.
For long these had been the most formidable plague of our country.
The reports of 1576 laid vehement stress on this problem. " On
Sundays men spend in taverns what they have earned during the
week, and wife and children perish of hunger." A report from
Ferté-Loupière (Yonne) demanded the penalty of death against
tavern keepers and their customers. The authorities would have
liked to confine the use of inns to passing travellers. The Dijon
Parliament enacted a fine of 50 *livres* to any man of the parish
found drinking at an *estaminet*. A royal decree prescribed the

closing of taverns during the hours of Divine Service and after eight o'clock on winter evenings, and 10 o'clock in summer, and the proprietors, as well as those found drunk on the premises, were punished.

IX.—*Charitable Customs*

Nearer neighbour to church and school than to the cabaret comes charity. This sentiment was widely held in the France of old, to the extent of engendering occasional abuses, especially in the neighbourhood of religious houses, on to which a whole crowd of people foisted themselves whose real calling developed in time into one of professional begging—"weevils collected round an Abbey to consume it," as an old writer notes. One of the best customs due to the spirit of charity was the right of gleaning in the fields after the harvest. The owner was forbidden to glean on his own land. For three days after the harvest was carried "the old and young, the crippled and those unable to work" took possession of the land. The Parliaments forbade the able-bodied to glean or to send out their children for the purpose; owners of land might not permit the families of their harvesters to glean, nor might they put out cattle to pasture on the land until these three days had elapsed. But nevertheless abuses resulted from this fine custom of which the reports of 1789 made complaint.

The same thing arose over the *éteules*, that is, the relinquishing to the poor the stubble left on the spot after the harvest. Custom required that the standing crop should be reaped with the sickle, which allowed a considerable height of stubble to be left uncut; but the Flemings used to employ the scythe, a practice which tended to spread into France about the middle of the eighteenth century, and the Parliaments endeavoured to put a check to it with a view to preserving for the poor their right to the stubble. The proprietors, however, made great efforts to enforce their demands. By compelling them to cut their crop with the sickle, they alleged that they were obliged to spend a longer time over their harvesting, "to do in a week what they could have finished in three days," adding that "stubble used for any other purpose than to enrich the soil was robbing the ground, and a great robbery too, since in certain spots half the straw was left."

To this the poor replied that "by substituting the scythe for the sickle the French tyrant, out for new methods, will add to our poverty by depriving us of the stubble which covers the roof of our hovels, and helps to warm our families half dead with the cold." A battle ensued between the two interests. The poor were defended by the Parliaments; the farmers, disregarding the decrees issued, scythed their wheat in contravention of prohibitions, and allowed themselves to be prosecuted, joining together to defray the cost of lawsuits in Paris, where they engaged the most famous advocates to plead their cause. These things occurred in 1756 and the following years. Finally the rich carried the day and the Government allowed them to use scythe or sickle as each thought fit; but this was towards the close of the Ancien Régime, and for centuries the poor had enjoyed the precious right to the stubble.

The same thing occurred in reference to the *glandée*, that is, the right to send pigs to feed in the forest, and the right to gather the dead wood; but the above usages were not general. We should mention, further, the right of *vaine pâture* permitting poor people to drive their cattle to pasture on the land of the proprietor after the hay-cutting and aftermath.

To conclude, there was also the custom among well-to-do country proprietors and farmers of offering food and lodging to passing beggars and tramps. This was a tradition observed everywhere and so strongly established that in this case, too, abuses resulted therefrom. Beggars and vagabonds claimed an absolute right to it, and did not fail to come and sit down at the table without being invited. We read in a report sent in to the Government:

"Beggars make a practice of coming to farm-houses in the evening and demanding lodging; they take the best seat at table and hearth, get drunk and then sleep it off in the out-houses at the risk of setting fire to them. Lorrainers—as the enemies of the Government were called—and deserters from the Militia associate themselves with these brigands, whose audacity knows no bounds in fleecing the farmer whom they order about. Sometimes they demand money, sometimes food; they steal the vegetables under the proprietor's own eyes, and he dare not say anything for fear of having his place set on fire."

The terrible "brigands"[1] found in these charitable customs the most dangerous auxiliaries for their misdeeds. A compassionate farmer would naturally welcome an out-at-elbows beggar when he knocked at his door in the evening; but in the middle of the night he would be awakened by an evil-looking band of men with their faces blackened with soot. The tramp had opened the door to his accomplices, and the farmer, with his feet held roasting over the fire on the hearth, would be compelled to hand over his money and anything valuable he possessed.

[1] *Brigands :* the French word is "*chauffeurs*," so called from their practice of holding their victim's feet over the fire, as described above. (H. W.)

The charitable customs of ancient France did her honour. In times of scarcity the rich, the seigneurs, and the religious houses, were called upon to come to the aid of the unfortunate, and Intendants and Parliaments compelled them to do so at need. In addition there were the charitable confraternities, relief offices, the gift of free medical treatment in a great number of places, and also the free distribution of boxes of remedies by the official authorities. In a word, dominating all this great social organization of compassion towards the poor and needy was that same family spirit, that solidarity bringing together the members composing it, accompanied by inconveniences repugnant to the modern spirit, but also by advantages, and among the latter was the imperative duty of coming to the aid of the less fortunate.

On the other hand, the rights of gleaning and of free pasture formed obstacles to the progress of agriculture. Arthur Young considered that French agriculture in 1789 was still in the condition that obtained in the tenth century. That was an exaggeration, but there was some truth in it. The French peasant, so tightly bound by tradition, followed a little too faithfully the counsel given by the illustrious Olivier de Serres :

"Never change your ploughshare and hold everything new as suspect."

The " carillon du fléau "—the rhythm of the beating flail—still resounded in Autumn in the barns at a time when England was already putting into use her mechanical threshing machines.

X.—The Division of Property

The chief cause of the little progress realized in French agriculture from the sixteenth century, according to Arthur Young, who laid great stress on it, lay in the minute division of property : due partly to the equal distribution of an estate among the heirs, which was the general law for the greater portion of the rural classes ; and partly to the fact that from the beginning of the second quarter of the eighteenth century the peasants were buying their land from the proprietors piece by piece, and in large numbers. The oft-repeated dividing up of the land among the cultivators was certainly a great benefit, but formed an obstacle to technical progress. On this point Arthur Young's showing is illuminating. According to him only a large landed proprietor has the means at his disposal to introduce new methods by reason of the cost entailed thereby, such as powerful machines doing the work of several men and giving a greater return. On small holdings where is there room for large pasture lands sufficient for a numerous head of cattle, which improve the strain and which provide a fertile source of manure ? Only large proprietors have the means to break up the soil properly, to drain it, to bring waste ground into cultivation and to import artificial manures, often from a great distance. A large landed proprietor in Lancashire or Devonshire will import from Italy, Holland, and even from Normandy and Brittany, fresh stock of cattle, sheep, and pigs to improve his strain, whereas a small proprietor cannot even dream of doing so.

" Everywhere the peasants possess small properties," writes Young, " to an extent we have no idea of in England ; this is the case in all parts of the kingdom. . . . I have more than once seen this dividing up carried to such an excess that a single fruit tree on about 10 perches of land constituted a farm and the local situation of a family.

" The small farmer is powerless," concludes Young, " and he is poor. He is in no condition to put forth the efforts required by good cultivation. . . . In a small farm division of labour is impossible ; the same man does all the work of the farm in turns. On the larger farms there are labourers, threshers, hedgers, shepherds, cowmen, bullock drivers, pig men, lime burners, men to drain the land and others to water it ; in this way the work must be done better on a large farm than on a small. One of the most useful things is a sheep-fold ; this can only be found on a large farm, otherwise the labour it entails absorbs all the profit."

This is just what was said in the 1789 reports of the Tiers Etat. That from Cernon (Marne, canton of Écury-sur-Coole) states : " Although we are all owners, many of us are without the neces-sities, and hardly anyone possesses the means required for good farming."

Many holdings, according to Arthur Young, were so small that the owner had not enough to do to employ his time. Some did not consist of sufficient land for the employment and feed of a plough horse, and so the proprietor might be seen digging his field from one end to the other, after the advice of La Fontaine's worthy labourer to his children. Young noticed peasants at the foot of the mountains in Languedoc carrying earth in baskets on their backs, to form soil on the higher levels. " At Landivisiau," writes the Englishman, " I saw a man who had tramped two-and-a-half leagues in order to take two chickens to market which, in my opinion, were not worth twenty-four *sous* for the pair. I came across people at Avranches, each with a horse, carrying about four bushels of sea-weed." Others ended by doing nothing at all ; in order to occupy the time they would remove stakes from one place to another, and change the position of a bed of cabbages or turnips.

Another cause of the backward state of cultivation in France is shown in the agricultural associations at the end of the eighteenth century. We are referring to those vast stretches of land held in common, the exploitation of which was split up among the inhabitants of the village, and to those woods and fields the pasture of which was free ; in other places there was marshy land where they would cut the reeds. A third obstacle to progress, according to academic opinion, lay in those admirable *maisons de village*, those associations of the different members of one large family of cultivators for the exploitation in common of their ancestral domain. Too rigorously attached to their traditional practices and customs, they hesitated to adopt new methods within their wide boundaries.

Yet another reason, according to Young and certain modern historians, would lie in the development and multiplication, from the year 1750, of rural manufactures, under the encouragement of the parish priests themselves.

Yet in spite of everything, the division of property, land held in common, *maisons de village*, and crafts giving work in the home, were, in a social sense, the greatest benefits that could be desired.

XI.—*Progress Realized in the Eighteenth Century*

Whatever value may be attached to Arthur Young's judgment on French agriculture at the close of the Ancien Régime, it cannot be denied that, from the middle of the eighteenth century, it profited by the great movement drawing the whole of France towards a new future opening out for her by reason of the progress she had realized in every domain of national activity. The peasants were buying their land all over the country in a real passion for possession. The prices paid exceeded the value of the land ; the rents of farms doubled ; in the Marne Department they increased by two-thirds. Any land offered to rent at once found a tenant, and farmers soon found there was no more to be had. An increase in the value of leases followed : " From the middle of the eighteenth century till 1790 the rise became more accentuated," writes the Marquis d'Avenel, " and in the second half of the eighteenth century perhaps the most rapid upward movement ever remembered in our economic annals took place."

Under the influence of agricultural societies, and even of members of the aristocracy who took an interest in the cultivation of the land, many of the methods were improved, and agricultural machines were brought over from England ; barns which cost so much to build were superseded by hay-stacks in the fields, and the growing of foodstuffs for the cattle increased to a very great extent. Arthur Young states that the cultivation of lucerne in France was on such a remarkable scale that his country-men came over to our country to learn our methods. The introduction of maize, the rearing of silk-worms, the cultivation of the potato under the impulse given to it by Parmentier, and the Spanish breed of merino sheep acclimatized in our country by the labours of Daubenton, mark in France at the close of the Ancien Régime the achievement of victories of such importance that the nineteenth century can show nothing comparable to them.

XII.—*The Village*

Let us now endeavour to present a bird's-eye view of what a French village was like under the authority of its seigneur.

Vauban has made an attempt to represent it in a statistical form. At the head comes the lord-of-the-manor, married, with children, six men servants, two women servants ; the parish priest, one man servant, one woman servant ; his curate, one man servant. Next in importance come the local judge, an advocate, married, with children ; the Procurator Fiscal representing the Government, living in the same house as the notary ; the schoolmaster, married, with two children. The above formed the directing officials, and all of them were closely united by beliefs into which no doubts had yet found any entrance, and by common traditions, and under the direction of their chief were bound by an almost religious attachment to the person of the King who personified for them their country. This group of authorities sprang from the organization of the family which had enlarged its borders and had grown stronger with every century. Even in the eighteenth century we can quote from many documents in support of this. On the 17th February, 1774, the Parliament of Provence writes to the King :

" Each community among us is a family governing itself and imposing its own laws. . . . " This system of self-government we have already described when dealing with the village assemblies.

Living under the group of village authorities, as given by Vauban, were the inhabitants consisting of the tillers of the soil with their farm servants, both men and women, the vine growers, the wood-cutters, the wheel-wright, the carpenter, the farrier, the tool maker, the baker, the miller, two masons and two women spinners.

We have already seen their domestic organization in the quotations from Retif de la Bretonne and Mistral; everything was based on tradition and a close solidarity between each family and neighbouring families. " The rural community," writes Cardinal Mathieu, " therefore seems to us like a little kingdom independent of its neighbour, and governed by its lord who administers justice and decides upon everything connected with his subjects, after deliberation with them."

Under Louis XIV we see the able-bodied men of the village organizing themselves into companies under the leadership of their lord and the parish priest, and harrying the armies of Prince Eugène.

Right in the midst of the Revolution, in Vendée, in the Bocage of Poitiers and in the Marais, lord and peasant still preserved this close union : " They would meet in the fields, in church, at market," writes Pierre de la Gorce ; " on holidays the manor house would lend its lawns for dancing." The seigneur and his *métayers* would hunt together. As we said on a former page, the seigneur, when among his own people, only seemed like one of them, but always the foremost. In Bourbonnais, at the height of the Revolution, peasants might have been seen tearing down the Jacobin mayor's pew in the church which had usurped the place of that of their lord. " They have burnt the pew of our good lord," pleaded these worthy folk in excuse.

We should add to this the depth and intensity of their religious beliefs. The practice of their faith entered into every detail of their lives, always presenting the same warm and kindly family character. The peasant lived under the shadow of the church, and this was surrounded by the cemetery, where his father and grandfather rested in hallowed soil.

Can we not see at a glance the beauty, social force, power of cohesion and life-giving energy of that social cell, the village community, itself sprung from the primitive cell of the family, and while increasing in size and development, still preserving its same character ?

The community, the village, was a family. Such was certainly the view held by everybody in those times, as Ch. de Ribbe writes in his study of society in ancient France. Their usages responded to this spirit by creating an identity of customs from which arose an identity of traditions and features special to each one of these groups.

These thousands and thousands of groups—forty thousand in the whole of France—were all united to each other, not as neighbours, but from beneath to above, by an ascending scale of *seigneuries*, as has been shown, right up to the keystone of the arch itself—the King. Society was not built up horizontally, if we may say so, but vertically.

And now we can understand how in each of the groups forming society, the community of beliefs and traditions was necessary. Religion was not then, as it is now, a matter of personal opinions ; it permeated the traditions of the family through and through, and made up the most solid portion of the cement holding together its moral structure. Imagine to yourselves a new religion springing from a conception different from what had made up their common life, imported moreover from abroad as in the case of Protestantism in the sixteenth century—imagine it falling like a thunderbolt into the midst of one of those country parishes of which France was formed, and which we have been describing. It meant the disorganization and destruction of a marvellous, living, palpitating social cell. We can imagine and understand the formidable opposition to this foreign element, instinctive in its intense and fierce repugnance, for of a surety it was not the importance of the doctrine of the Virgin, nor the worship of images, nor even the supremacy of Rome, so lightly held by the great Gallicans of the seventeenth century—that was at stake ; no, it was a question of the strongest ties linking together their everyday life.

Cardinal Mathieu saw rightly that each of these family communities had lived for centuries isolated from its neighbour, like a small State governing itself, and that in the course of time they were brought into closer contact with each other through the development of means of communication, the progress of industry and commerce, by the requirements even of agriculture, finally by the sentiment of nationality then coming into being. Henri IV proclaimed his edict of toleration, and Louis XIV thought fit to revoke it. For my own part I am convinced that had Henri IV been in the place of Louis XIV he would himself have revoked his own edict just as his grandson did. It was necessary because a closer relationship and a fusion between the social cells had taken place. Religion formed an integrating element in family life, and from that very fact, in public life also at the time of which we are speaking. Under Henri IV these cells were still living in isolation, and each could have its own religion ; but from the day they tended to unite to form a national life they had to tend likewise to unity of belief. A study of the *dossiers* of prisoners incarcerated under *lettres de cachet*, among whom religious sectaries occupy such a large place, has convinced us that in 1685 it was again the King and the Bishops who showed the most moderate spirit in the kingdom. Supposing that in 1685 France had had an elected assembly, a National Convention, to govern her, as was the case in 1790 ; the Protestants, being a minority in the country, as were the Federalists in 1793, would have been treated as these latter were, and far more harshly.

The Jacobins cut off heads by the thousand, shot people down in heaps, and drowned whole masses in hulks with the hatches battened down, just because they did not hold the same ideas as themselves about administrative centralization ; what would the French of the seventeenth century, in their still uncultured state, have done to men who came among them to tear apart the innermost fibres of their family and national life ?

Thus a study of the modest village community leads to far wider questions, inasmuch as, being based on the organization and traditions of the home, it was the foundation on which the State rested. In harmony with the *seigneurie* and the monarchical principle, it formed the strongest, finest and most fruitful social organization that the world has ever seen, and by means of the family instinct was the real founder of French greatness. But what happened to it ? The French village community, like the old French family, like the *seigneurie*, and like the monarchy, was bound to disappear or be transformed after it had accomplished its work.

In some of the most admirable pages of his fine work, de Tocqueville has shown how the fact that a large number of peasants had become the owners of land, and that on the other hand the seigneurs had lost all acting authority in their domain, was bound to lead the peasants to revolt. Feudal rights burdened the land, hunting rights damaged the harvests, tolls interfered with the sale and exchange of produce on seigneurial lands. The peasant did not trouble his head very much as long as the land, the harvest and produce of the domain were no longer his. " What does the tithe matter to a man who is not a farmer ? " writes de Tocqueville. " It is levied on the produce of farming. How does a ground rent affect the man who is not the landowner ? What does all the trouble entailed in improving land matter to a man who is working for another's profit ? " As regards the personal dues paid to the seigneur in *banalités*, fees on succeeding to property, and honorific privileges, the peasant, acknowledging established rights as legitimate, willingly paid them so long as his lord was the protector of his tenants, saved them from military service by going to the wars himself, and preserved order and safety for them on his domain. De Tocqueville notes that the same obligations existed in England ; whereas in Germany the burdens were far heavier ; but neither in England nor in Germany did the tenants think of revolting, nor even of murmuring against them, because their suzerain still carried out the duties incumbent on him.

In the third quarter of the eighteenth century we find a distinct change taking place in the sentiments and attitude of very many peasants throughout France. This transformation became accentuated in the reign of Louis XVI. Mme. de Genlis relates :

"It happened in the country ; an officer of high rank ordered a farmer to carry out some work which he had no right to demand ; the farmer refused, and the officer said to him :
'You have got to do what I wish, or I will give you twenty strokes with my cane.'
'Monsieur,' replied the farmer in a calm voice, 'I advise you not to, for you would not have the time to count them !'"

Mme. Vigée-Lebrun went to Romainville on a visit to the Maréchal de Ségur, of whose family she painted so many charming portraits : "Not only did they (the peasants) not doff their hats to us, but they looked at us insolently ; some even threatened us with their heavy cudgels. . . ."

And not long afterwards in many villages the old bell in the church tower sounded the sack of the seigneurial château.

BIBLIOGRAPHY

Ardascheff (Paul), trans. L. Jousserandot, *Les Intendants de province* . . ., 1909.—Argenson (Marquis d'), *Mémoires*, ed. Jannet, 1857–1858, 5 vol.—Babeau (Albert), *Le Village sous l'Ancien Régime*, 4th ed., 1891.—Broc (Vicomte de), *La France sous l'Ancien Régime*, 1877.—Calonne (A. de), *Vie agricole sous l'Ancien Régime en Picardie et en Artois*, 1883.—Clément (Fr. P.), *La Corvée des chemins en France et spécialement en Poitou*, 1899.—Croÿ (Duc de), *Mémoires*, ed. P. Cottin and de Grouchy, 1906–1908, 4 vol.—Du Fail (Noel), *Propos rustiques*, 1547.—Guillory, *Le Marquis de Turbilly*, 1862.—Kovalewsky, *La France économique et sociale à la veille de la Révolution, les Campagnes*, 1909.—La Borderie (Pierre), *Le Procès des serfs du Mont-Jura (1767–1777), Feuilles d'histoire*, 1st Aug., 1919.—La Bruyère, *Caractères*, various eds.—La Gorce (Pierre de), *Histoire religieuse de la Révolution française*, 1909.—Leblanc (Abbé), *Lettres*, 1758.—Legrand d'Aussy, *Voyage d'Auvergne*, 1788.—Levasseur, *Des progrès de l'agriculture dans la seconde moitié du dix-huitième siècle, Acad. des Sciences morales . . . Seances et travaux*, 1898.—Marion (Marcel), *Etat des classes rurales au dix-huitième siècle dans la généralité de Bordeaux, Revue des Etudes historiques*, 1902.—Marmontel, *Mémoires*, ed. M. Tourneux, 1891, 3 vol.—Mathieu (Cardinal), *L'Ancien Régime en Lorraine et Barrois*, 4th ed., 1907.—Mazon (A.), *Une paroisse de montagne et son Curé au dix-septième siècle*, dans le Vivarais et Velay, 1891.—Messance (La Michodière), *Recherches sur la population* . . ., 1766.—Messance, *Nouvelles recherches* . . ., 1788.—Mistral (Frédéric), *Les Iles d'or*, 1876.—

Moheau (Montyon), *Recherches sur la population de la France*, 1778.—Retif de la Bretonne, *La Vie de mon père*, publ. under the title of *Le Village*, undated libr. Fayard, *Coll. de Mémoires illustrés*.—Retif de la Bretonne, *Monsieur Nicolas*, 1796–1797, 16 vol.—Ch. de Ribbe, *La Famille et la Société en France avant la Révolution*, 4th ed., 1879, 2 vol.—Tocqueville (Alexis de), *L'Ancien Régime et la Révolution*, 5th ed., 1866.—Turbilly (Marquis de), *Mémoires sur les défrichements*, 1760.—Vauban, *Projet d'une dixme royale*, 1707.—Wolters (Fritz), *Agrarzustande u. Agrarprobleme in Frankreich von 1700 bis 1790*, 1905.

CHAPTER IX

THE TOWN

I. The Family Origin of Town Communities.—II. The Ruling Authority.—III. Appearance of the Towns.—IV. Feudal Traditions.—V. The Town Militia.—VI. The *Mairie.*—VII. The General Assemblies.—VIII. Internal Dissensions and Financial Disorder.—IX. Civic Development and Industrial Progress.

I.—*The Family Origin of Town Communities*

BODIN heads the thirteenth chapter of the third book of his *Six Livres de la République* as follows :

" Showing how corporations and communities have issued from the family."

And nothing is truer. Paris did not develop, as one might be tempted to think, by the progressive action of a central nucleus growing and gradually extending in size ; on the contrary, it was the result of a certain number of generative nuclei developing independently, and these came nearer together as they grew and in course of time coalesced. Contrary to widespread opinion, the city did not spread like a large patch of oil until it gradually reached to either bank of the Seine, and then extended over the district until it filled the present extent of the fortifications. It was formed out of an indefinite number of small cities, this one under episcopal, that one under royal authority, some under the jurisdiction of Abbeys—Saint-Germain-des-Près, Saint-Martin-des-Champs, the Dames de Montmartre, the Abbey of Saint-Antoine, etc., and others under the rules of a Military Order, such as the district of le Temple. But the great majority were under the suzerainty of a seigneur, such as the fief of Châtelet, and these were built up and developed, each by itself, into living cells, growing in size and importance by the force of their internal vitality until the time came when, owing to their expansion, they pulled down the walls inside the common enclosure.

Thus the city of Paris was built up by the juxtaposition of a certain number of fortified residences, each one of which was the seat of a seigneur, and the latter, as we have endeavoured to show, issued from the family through the intermediary of the mesnie. Each of these strongholds had its own defensive works, and was surrounded by gardens, thickets, fields and open spaces, the whole closed in by a fortified wall, often supported by a moat filled with water. Each formed the abode of a seigneur who grouped his mesnie around him, like a Roman patrician and his clients, a *pater-familias* living surrounded by his *familia*, or an ecclesiastical lord—who likewise filled the rôle of a father among his people.

In this respect Paris presented during the Middle Ages the appearance of Moscow in the eighteenth century as related by the Comte de Ségur—a vast grouping together of castles, each surrounded by its own village, defended by its own donjon, and walled in with its own fortifications.

Inside these walled enclosures many houses of merchants and artisans could be seen, but these were the *ministeriales domus* employed in serving the *seigneurial familia*, or *fèvres-mesniers*, workmen of the mesnie, as they were then called. They supplied the requirements of their lord and his kinsmen, and worked and trafficked under his patronage. As the prosperity of the community grew, the population within the surrounding walls of these different feudal *seigneuries* grew and multiplied, and we find the seigneurs beginning to build within their enclosure, withdrawing themselves to the centre of their property and cutting up those portions of their land bordering on the public roads so as to make dwellings for their people. Each little family town enjoyed its own autonomy, with its private enclosure within the common one. In the hey-day of the seventeenth century under Louis XIV more than half of Paris was still split up in the hands of thirty-four seigneurial owners. The same was the case in all old French towns. In his admirable study of the town under the Ancien Régime, Albert Babeau testifies to the existence of these inner divisions, and concludes : " By the natural sequence of events the towns were split up into judicial, religious, military and municipal administrations." This fact is true, but the process had been the opposite to what that eminent historian thought. Those divisions were in the nature of the very origin of the town, the conditions that had contributed to form it ; and far from having been split up in the course of time, on the contrary, the towns had gone on breaking down their former divisions into boroughs each separate from the other, in order to blend them into one city.

In the sixteenth century Tours was still divided into thirty-one different fiefs, and thirty-one ruling seigneurs still shared amongst themselves all authority in the town, which fact shows that the city of Tours owed its original existence to the grouping together of thirty-one feudal chiefs, or we might say, to thirty-one heads of families, each one possessing its feudal domain, its walls, its tenants, and seat of justice. As time went on the industry of the inhabitants gradually filled up with buildings the enclosure surrounding each of these fiefs; houses began to take the place of the open spaces round the Abbeys and donjons, and the inner walls were thrown down so as to leave only one outside wall round the whole for external defence. In this way was the city of Tours formed.

This process of aggregation of social centres, originally independent of each other, can be seen also in every detail in the towns of Amboise and Arles. In Burgundy we find quite unimportant towns divided among five, six or even seven different seigneurs, showing that these towns had been originally formed by uniting five, six or seven different *seigneuries* within one surrounding wall.

It was the same with Angers, Moulins, Rouen, Bourges and Troyes; we think we are justified in stating that it was the same with all towns dating back to the Middle Ages, with the exception of those *bastides*, or towns built *en bloc* by feudal lords, which likewise, it should be noted, bore a family imprint.

From the point of view with which we have been dealing the most remarkable of all was the town of Metz, the six different quarters of which were noted for their independence and the wonderful vitality each retained right down to the opening of modern times; five of these *pariages* (wards) as they were called—a word which signifies " family "—bore the proper names of families, thus testifying to their origin, and the sixth was called *le commun* because it had been formed at a later date by the union of those citizens who had settled in the town and did not belong to one of the five great seigneurial families, or were not acknowledged by them. Strasbourg was divided into clanships, which term sufficiently denotes their family origin.

II.—*The Ruling Authority*

The constitution of French towns should be explained here because it is the only way to enable us to understand their outward physiognomy, and the special and sometimes curious features which characterized them at the period of which we are writing.

Municipal administration was never concentrated in the hands of one individual, as it is in our day. This feature was common to all towns, and, bearing this in mind, the different kinds of municipal authority, taking them as a whole, may be defined as coming under three types.

1. The Syndicate. Best fitted for the needs of insignificant

communities; it was their usual form of municipal government, haphazard, and possessing no statutes. We have described the village assemblies; these were to be found in the smallest towns, electing one or several syndics according to its importance, and administering it as a family concern. By the end of the seventeenth century the syndicate only existed in rural communities.

2. The Consulate in the south, or *Echevinat* [1] in the north. This form of municipal administration was centred in the hands of two or several officials acting as one body, with no precedence of one over the other. These Consuls or *Echevins* might be presided over by an officer of justice, a royal official affiliated to them. This system was chiefly in force in the south.

3. The *Mairie*. This system of administration was practised in the northern and central provinces, and was in force in every town of any importance. But even in these *Mairies* the executive authority was not concentrated in the hands of one individual, as it is at the present day. The Mayor formed one of the Town Council whose members were called *échevins*, governors, councillors, *pairs*, consuls, *jurats* or *capitouls* according to the locality. The Mayor could not act without his *échevins*, a body consisting of several persons, to which the northern provinces applied a characteristic term—the Magistracy; elsewhere it was called the *corps de ville*, or Town Council. It constituted the executive authority of the town. "The Mayor was President of the *corps de ville*, not the administrator of the city" (de Tocqueville). Thus it formed a collective administration.

Now, note this: among the attributes attaching to the *corps de ville* was one which demands our special attention. The Mayor and the *échevins* held audiences at which they issued decrees similar to those of the royal tribunals; they condemned people to prison, to fines and banishment. The Magistracy was a real judicial tribunal of executive Magistrates.

These officials wore very fine robes, like those of the royal judges, "the robe being distinctive of the Magistracy" (Loyseau); they were red in colour, even in the most insignificant towns. Racine writes in 1661: "It is a fine thing to see gossip Cardeur and carpenter Gaillard in their red robes, like a President, issuing their decrees (at Uzès)." Often the robe was of two colours, one of which was always scarlet or purple, "a mark common to the magistracy," as Loyseau observes in his treatise on justice; the other was the colour special to the town. Thus the robes of the

---

[1] *Echevinat*: the *échevins* corresponded to our sheriffs and aldermen. (H. W.)

town council of Bourges were red and green, those of Bordeaux
and Saint-Emilion, red and white, of Gaillac, red and black, and
Troyes, blue and purple. Sometimes their attire was enhanced
by more brilliant decoration, such as that bought by the people
of Bayonne in 1766 for the "*robe de justice*" of their Mayor, consisting of facings of gold lace and black beaded braid. In their
municipal accounts for 1786 we read : " 36 *livres* for the dressing
of the Town Council's wigs." The Mayors and *échevins* or consuls
all wore wigs.

It is very interesting to note that this municipal jurisdiction
The justice administered was of a patriarchal kind. The *Magistrat* (the Magistracy)—that is, the municipal authority—issued
lettres de cachet, for we must not think that these were the attribute
of the King alone, and both Mayor and *échevins* exercised the
same care in this respect as their eminent *confrère*, the King :
care for the honour and integrity of the family. Our *corps de
ville* possessed their own prisons which, as we have seen, were of
a far more rigorous character than those belonging to the King.
The banishments pronounced by them were accompanied by
solemn rites. The exiled citizen would leave the town to the
sound of the ringing of the bells in the belfry tower, which were
kept ringing until he had passed out through the gates of the city
wall. Cases may be found of private individuals being banished
from the town, like some latter-day Aristides, because they did
not please their fellow citizens. The origin of this municipal
justice was again the same as that exercised by the King ; the
feudal chiefs and heads of families, whose union had made the
town, these exercised in their own quarter, or by delegation to
those they had elected, that same family justice which each of
them wielded over his own people.

It is very interesting to note that this municipal jurisdiction
was recognized by the central power, for we find officials, appointed
by the Government under the title of *Procureur de Roi*, or *Avocat
du Roi*, or *Substitut*, sitting in these tribunals.

The Magistracy—Mayor or Town Council—issued decrees dealing
with most private matters. For instance, it would prescribe the
dress to be worn in the town by the bridegroom and bride on their
wedding day, the number of dishes to be served at the wedding
banquet, and the kind of presents which should be made. The
Magistracy would previously have forbidden the swain to frequent
the house of his bride elect except during the hours of daylight
"so as to enable him to return home without a lantern." The
same thing occurred in connection with baptisms, the details of
which became a municipal affair, and similarly with the banquet
and presents accompanying the churching. The number and

minutiæ of the sumptuary regulations enacted by the municipalities may again find their explanation in family origins.

All these, and other precious directions, were announced to those concerned by the town trumpeters or drummers, heralds arrayed in fine costumes marking the importance of their functions. At Dijon these officials wore a broad-sleeved scarlet surcoat lined with silk and decorated with silver braid ; at Troyes, a blue and violet robe trimmed with gold lace ; the arms of the city were embroidered on their sleeves, and on the banner attached to their trumpets. The trumpeter of Albi wore a purple mantle embroidered with the armorial bearings of the town. The municipal trumpeters and drummers were generally accompanied by a sergeant who read out the proclamations of the town authorities. Proclamations were very seldom posted up, for part of the population were unable to read, but with the advance of education in the eighteenth century this practice became more general, and the heralds lost their importance.

In their official capacity these worthy towns willingly undertook the office of god-parents to the children of people with whom they were friendly. Thus even d'Artagnan had the honour of seeing the city of Bayonne holding one of his sons at the font, and the child received the names of Louis-Bayonne. And Bayonne—we do not mean the infant d'Artagnan, but the town—followed with interest the careers of its godsons and god-daughters ; to one of the latter, Mme. de Piis, the city gave a ball, and presented her with a bracelet on the occasion of her marriage. To the Mayor's son a present of game was given on his wedding day, and to his daughter, boxes of sweetmeats. In the case of a large city, such as Lyons, they would go so far as to present a set of diamonds. On New Year's day the Mayor would receive from his fellow citizens gifts of oranges, lemons, and bouquets of flowers, and the Mayoress a fine hat in the fashion of the day.

III.—*Appearance of the Towns*

These traditional customs flourished in towns which had preserved their old-time appearance down to the seventeenth century. The streets were narrow and winding, and the gutter was in the centre of the road which rose up on either side—hence the expression " *tenir le haut de pavé*," keep on the pavement, as applied to people who on the road of life keep to the high level, away from the muddy stream trickling in the gutter. The houses had projecting gables, the upper floors being well over the street, and picturesque signs creaked on their iron poles over the heads of the passers by. There were shops the arched fronts of which were closed up with large shutters and when these were taken down by day they formed boards whereon to display their goods on the public thoroughfare. The streets were usually encumbered with different objects, cases, barrels and handcarts ; people would settle themselves down in them, tables and chairs would be brought out, and worthy old women would turn their spinning wheels ; the old gossips, men and women, would chatter and tell each other the news, sitting over the trap-doors of the cellars ; animals of all kinds, poultry, and pigs especially, could be seen wandering about in search of what they could pick up. Albert Babeau made a very true and important observation when he wrote that the streets of ancient France were not made for passing through, but for living in. In our own day, the prey as we are to a frenzied scurrying to and fro, we can scarcely understand the serene immobility of the people of former times. Everything held together in the France of old, forming a tranquil stability of family and tradition : dress, usages, beliefs, tools and local ideas are hard to change.

Down to the middle of the seventeenth century the country also retained its aspect of olden times, and fortresses of stone might be seen everywhere. There was no accessible height but had its corbelled and machicolated towers. A traveller made the remark that almost every town was perched on a height from which its ramparts dominated the plain ; these were exigencies of defence in those rude times the people had passed through. Arthur Young too remarked that there was no town in France that had not been built round a castle. To this castle it had owed its birth and first development down to the time when it had won the position of being treated as a fortified place on its own account. In the twelfth and thirteenth centuries the term " town " and " castle " were synonymous.

The towns came to act the part of the castles when, as in former days, the country population fled to take refuge within their walls as soon as the alarm was sounded. The Curé of Provins gives us a description of the appearance of his native place in 1576, filled with peasants from the neighbouring countryside, who had taken refuge there with their families, cattle and booty : " It was very pitiful to hear the cries, uproar, and the lowing of so many beasts."

The same transformation that had taken place in the country occurred also in the towns, and far more rapidly. The seigneur, the protector of his bourgeois folk and working people, who without him could not have traded and worked, had become of no further use. And so the townspeople would have now liked to be free of him. This was the " revolt of the commons," and when they gained the day they planted the belfry tower of their municipal authority in front of the crenelated fortress of their lord. A decree of 1626 ordered the destruction of the castles and fortresses within the kingdom. This Act was hailed with joy by the bourgeois who found in those formidable structures of olden times a stone quarry ready to hand for their bridges, churches, hospitals and ramparts. Thus baronial influence had disappeared almost entirely from the towns by the eighteenth century, save in those few provinces which formed the appanage of a Prince of the Blood. In the city of Orleans, the Duc d'Orléans still nominated the Mayor from a list of names submitted to him. In a certain number of small towns the seigneur, as in the villages, still preserved a few of his rights, such as those pertaining to administering justice, to intervening in the election of the town authorities, and honorific privileges.

The *beffroi*, the town hall with its turrets, became the boast and pride of the townspeople. The town clock would ring out the hours, often with chimes, and the keeper of the *beffroi*, or governor—these two terms used to be synonymous—was often a clockmaker, or locksmith. Beneath the clock were painted the armorial bearings and battle-cry of the town, and these served a decorative and sometimes an entertaining purpose. At Beaune, a globe representing the phases of the moon revolved on the town clock with the passing of the hours ; at Aix seven statues, representing the seven days of the week, appeared by turn ; quaint figures striking the hours on resounding bells were as frequent as they were varied ; and from the top of the belfry tower, especially in the northern towns, the mechanism would chime forth over the roofs, from a multitude of crystal clear bells, those old airs so dear to the memory of all good folk.

IV.—*Feudal Traditions*

From feudal days, of which the *beffroi* was proud testimony, more than one town had still preserved its traditions ; for we must not lose sight of the fact that in the twelfth and thirteenth centuries the towns which had been raised into communities were under feudal authorities, like the barons. In the eighteenth century a number of communities still existed which were really *seigneuries*, and their Mayors took from them the title of Count, Viscount, or Baron, according to their rank. Their feudal rights had for the most part disappeared. Those that still remained were carefully preserved by the municipalities who kept a record of them, maintaining for the purpose a paid expert on feudal dues—rent quittances, *lods et ventes* (fees on transmission of property)—and these

the towns farmed out in the same way as the seigneurs did. Some
towns levied tolls on bridges or roads outside their walls. At
Badonviller, in accordance with a feudal right, the town authorities
exacted the tongue of every beast killed. Several cities exercised
a real suzerainty over neighbouring towns, including them in their
seigneurial territory. Within the limits of his Intendancy in the
Limousin district, Turgot was careful to see that the towns did
not abuse their supremacy over the country districts and villages
round about. In return the towns gave up all the seigneurial
obligations, such as, in the case of Bordeaux, the gift of two gold
spurs which the city had to present annually to the King from
whom it held *in fief* the right to possess its own ramparts, which
right continued to be claimed as late as 1785.

The cities used to attach as much importance to their ramparts
as to their *beffroi*. Moated ramparts, even in the Middle Ages,
had been the distinctive feature which marked a " *bonne ville* "
or rightful city. They all still preserved their stone walls at the
beginning of the seventeenth century ; a picturesque setting with
its draw-bridges and portcullises, its corner turrets and pepper-box
watch towers. Armed peasants kept watch on the boulevards.
In the evening the gates were shut, the draw-bridges raised and
the keys of the city were given into the hands of the Mayor.

Then came the decree of 1626 which declared that this large
number of fortified places " was a permanent incitement to civil
war," and in the course of the seventeenth century the ramparts
of cities in the interior parts of France were for the most part
demolished. Richelieu showed himself a great enemy to ramparts
and donjons. The townsfolk required more space, and thus we
see a factor in that movement towards the unification of the country
which was proceeding under every shape and form. The ramparts of some towns were allowed to remain when they happened
to be on the frontier, and to this we owe the preservation of those
marvels—Aigues-Mortes, Carcassonne and Saint Malo. Avignon
was situated in pontifical territory ; but the keys of the towns
remained after the locks had disappeared. In the eighteenth
century the Duc d'Orléans, having made a visitation of the principal
towns in his Duchy, wrote about it to his sister :

" They presented me with the keys of many a town, but I could
not discover their gates."

Despoiled as they had been of their ramparts, the cities could
only attach a greater value to their artillery, consisting of cannons,
mortars, carronades, falconets, culverins, fire-throwers, escalators,
scaling towers, instruments for discharging a hail of iron from
the barbettes, arquebuses mounted on a crook, and other quaint

pieces decorated with the municipal arms, recalling memories
sometimes triumphant and often heroic. Most of these weapons
were more for the sake of appearance than for any utility. At
the time of the rising in the Fronde, the city of Aix closed its gates
to the King's troops, and decided to offer a defence ; but the
wooden cannon which they hoisted to the top of the ramparts
burst at the first shot !

A few large cities like Paris succeeded in retaining their artillery.
In towns where it had been decided to deprive them of it, the
citizens would hide their old guns, burying them in the glacis of
the ramparts. " The inhabitants of Epernay," Albert Babeau
recalls, " desired to preserve their cannon which they had named
the ' chien d'Orléans,' from its having fired on the army of Henri
IV. They wanted to lower it from the tower from which it had
been pointed with a view to hiding it, but it slipped from their
hands and was broken into several fragments."

V.—*The Town Militia*

The Town Militia used to mount guard on the ramparts under
command of the Mayor or a captain elected by the town council
or the assembly.

Louis XI once reviewed the Paris Militia on the plain of Saint
Antoine so as to make a display of them before the eyes of the
foreign Ambassadors ; but this parade made so great an impression upon him that he took care not to have one again for fear
of giving the people of Paris too clear an idea of their strength.
The Town Militia as late as the end of the sixteenth century formed
a force which had to be reckoned with.

Their dress was most magnificent in all respects—red uniforms,
of the brightest shade as at Bayonne, under the command of
officers in gold seamed coat and scarlet mantle embroidered with
the city arms. The drummers wore large-sleeved coats of red
and white silk taffeta. The arts and crafts of Lyons formed bat-
talions resplendent in gold and tinsel. " Every soldier in the same
company is dressed alike," according to a document of 1622. In
this way the idea of a uniform began to be realized.

Louis XIII declared his wondering astonishment at his first
glance at the Marseilles Militia when drawn up on the whole length
of the Cannebière, in " their splendid and gorgeous accoutrements."
But what must have afforded the King the greatest satisfaction
was their dress. The people of Marseilles had still further accentuated the terrifying appearance of those formidable warriors, for
some were dressed as savages, others as Red Indians, Turks with
enormous turbans, and Moors.

From the beginning of the reign of Louis XV the uniforms, as a rule, recalled the three colours dear to France—red coat, blue facings and white waistcoat and breeches; for the non-commissioned officers epaulettes of gold and silver. The reforms made in 1786 were intended to allow only officers of the royal army to wear epaulettes—the protests raised can be well imagined!

The standards were of the municipal colours in parallel strips, squares or stripes; the Colonel displayed a white flag with the fleurs-de-lys in gold.

Even members of the Religious Orders were under obligation to guard the ramparts, at least down to the reign of Louis XIV; some municipalities placed them under the command of a priest.

The Burgundians felt they should exempt a newly married man from guard duties and reviews during his honeymoon.

During the good old times of the independence of the towns, and as late as the seventeenth century, the citizens took pride in serving. The clergy were the first to get their places taken by others, sometimes by needy ne'er-do-weels lacking any smartness; the wealthy bourgeois followed their example, and so decadence set in.

It would happen that the night patrols of our worthy militia would turn into rollicking outings, with " continuous discharge of musketry," which robbed the citizens of their sleep. Among our fine Turks, Hurons and Iroquois Indians at Marseilles, every one wanted to be an officer.

The Militia had no love for the excise men, preferring the contrabandists. On one occasion the Châtellerault Militia had received orders to guard the salt warehouse, and this duty they carried out by setting free all the salt smugglers who had been imprisoned. A decree of 1781 found it necessary to forbid " militia men to leave the posts assigned to them by their officers, or to make any discharge of musketry without orders."

In considering their decline we should not, however, refuse to the town Militia the justice due to them. In many circumstances they rendered valuable services in guarding prisoners of war and in defending the frontier strongholds, as was the case with the Militia of Saint-Jean-de-Losne, who, shut up with forty soldiers belonging to the Enghien regiment, defended their ramparts against forty thousand assailants, and forced the enemy to raise the siege.

The importance of the Militia was otherwise increased by the fact that in many towns the King of France had not the right to maintain a garrison, one of the many facts characteristic of the Ancien Régime which has been too little emphasized. When

Mehemet Effendi, the Turkish Ambassador, crossed France in 1720, he was quite surprised at this.

" Toulouse," he wrote, " possesses the privilege of not allowing the King's garrison within its walls. For this reason the fifty soldiers, with the Captain and Ensigns, who had accompanied me from Toulon, took leave of me before the gates of the city, and returned. Two other companies of the city (militia) passed in review before me and conducted me to my lodging." The same ceremony occurred at Bordeaux. " Since this is a free city," continues Mehemet Effendi, " the soldiers remained outside. Several companies of the Town Militia, with their Captains, passed in review before me, and conducted me in state to my lodging." Marseilles, Saint Malo, and twenty other cities had like privileges.

Even in towns where the King maintained a garrison the Mayor exercised authority over them. He commanded them in the absence of the Military Governor ; in other places, as at Toulon, the Mayor presided over the councils of war of the royal army.

VI.—*The Mairie*

The functions entrusted to the Mayors varied greatly in different places, together with the utmost variety in the customs. We have already said that in certain localities there was no Mayor at all, at least as late as 1692, in which year Louis XIV sought to establish one everywhere. The Mayor was sometimes called " *Mayeur*," in other places " *Syndic*." In Paris and at Lyons he went by the name of " *Prévôt des Marchands*." The manner of electing the chief magistrate of the town showed likewise the greatest variety.

The reforms attempted by Louis XV in 1764 and 1765 endeavoured to bring more uniformity into municipal administration, but without meeting with equal success in all places. Thus the city of Langres bought back in 1773 its municipal functions in order to have power to administer the city according to its liking. The reform instituted by Louis XV, which would seem so natural at the present day, aroused the most violent protests from all parts.

The Edict of 1692, establishing the office of Mayor in all communities with a population of more than 4,500 inhabitants, had a fiscal end in view. When making the office of Mayor one to be held in perpetuity, Louis XIV thereby created something that could be bought and sold. Thenceforth the office of Mayor could be bought in the same way as a Councillorship in Parliament, and advertisements like the following could be read in the public notices :

" For Sale : Excellent Burgundy at thirty *sous* the bottle, including
the bottle. For Sale : Office of the *Maire Royal* at Sarreguemines."
(From the Lorraine Public Notices, 1787.)

This introduction of the Treasury into the sphere of urban
Mayors did not in reality produce the effect one might imagine,
for a large number of towns bought back the office of Mayor. In
Burgundy the *mairies* were acquired by the States General of the
province who thereby obtained the right in future to appoint the
first Magistrate in the different towns, " with the exception of
Dijon, where," they said, " divisions and cabals were less to be
feared than in the small towns."

In other cases, the office of Mayor had been acquired by the
seigneur of the place, or by some corporation, as at Chartres,
where the corporation of merchants became the possessors of it,
in 1692, for the sum of 35,000 *livres*, after outbidding the town
itself which only offered 20,000 *livres*.

We give the following account of the manner of electing the
Prévôt des Marchands (Mayor) in Paris after the Edict of 1692.
The *Prévôt* was elected for two years, and the date of the election
was fixed for August 16th. The sixteen candidates for the administration of the capital arrived at the Town Hall in coaches, together
with the thirty-two notables of the city, who, by a somewhat
complicated procedure, had been nominated to take part in the
election. They listened to the reading of a Royal *lettre de cachet*,
in which the name of the new *Prévôt des Marchands* to be elected
was coolly stated. After this they wrote down this name on little
slips of paper and after swearing to conduct themselves as faithful
and loyal electors they placed their vote in a crimson velvet bag.
Barbier, the advocate, was one of the electors in the year 1750,
and was of opinion that this was the best of all possible methods
of election, for, as he said, if the notables had been allowed to
record their votes as they thought fit, they would have been able
to sell them.

When the proceeding was ended, writes Barbier, the elected
and the electors " strolled about in the Town Hall, had a drink
if they so listed while the table for the great banquet was being
laid . . . for ninety-six guests. All down the middle of the table
were twenty-two trays, each containing four baskets of dried
sweetmeats worth at least ten francs apiece, which each guest
took away with him at the end of the banquet. . . ." A band of
trumpeters and drummers was massed in the courtyard, and saluted
in deafening strains the various courses as they were brought in.
Each guest had a lackey in attendance behind his chair. As

was the case when the King dined, the public were admitted as spectators, and this afforded, as one of those present said, "a magnificent and august scene."

Barbier gives us the details of the menu : soup, two *entrées*, two dishes of roast meat consisting of white meat and game (*viande noire*), salad, melon ; then came the *entremets*. For dessert there were pastries, stewed fruit and baskets of peaches. Wine and water were handed round in iced pitchers ; for wine there was Meursault, champagne, and Cyprian wine. "One drank in a very decorous manner there," states our advocate. At dessert the *Prévôt des Marchands*, in his robe of crimson satin, proposed the health of the Governor of Paris, the King's daughters, the Dauphiness, the Dauphin, the Queen, and lastly the King. For the royal toast every one stood. Each toast was accompanied by the resounding din given forth by the trumpeters and drummers in the courtyard.

The nomination of the Mayor by a *lettre de cachet* was exceptional and only large cities were thus privileged.

The functions of the first municipal Magistrate were unpaid, but they brought with them fairly valuable advantages. The position was a caste of nobility, and in important towns it became hereditary, and the nobility by birth and the *noblesse de robe* (the official caste) eagerly sought after these positions. We may fairly say that at the close of the Ancien Régime the most important municipal functions had become the hereditary patrimony of the aristocracy. In addition there was the exemption from taxation.

The Worshipful Mayor had the right to station guards and to have a barrier before the gate of his house. In some large towns *mais*[1] was planted in front of his door. The Mayor identified himself with the town, and did not wear mourning for anybody, like the Chancellor of France. But his lofty functions had also their inconveniences. It would sometimes happen that they would imprison the Chief Magistrate of a *bonne ville* because the municipal exchequer did not pay its debts, or because the citizens under his charge were late in paying their taxes. The Mayor of Auxerre was put in prison in 1637 on the application of certain financiers to whom the city owed 9,500 *livres ;* in 1651 it was the turn of the *échevins* to be imprisoned on the application of a creditor of the town ; and in 1643 the Mayor of Châtellerault was locked up for the same reason. In 1695 bailiffs were installed in the houses of the *échevins* of Mâcon, and their furniture was seized on the

---

[1] *Mais :* a green tree flowering in leaf and decorated with ribbons, which was placed on the 1st of May before the gates of anyone to whom it was desired to show honour. (H. W.)

application of the tax gatherers to whom the town was in arrears ;
for up till then we still find that solidarity, that family " solidity "
which was one of the essential elements of society in olden times,
which we have such difficulty in understanding nowadays. The
eighteenth century, on the high road towards fresh ideas, cast
aside this responsibility.

VII.—*The General Assemblies*

In addition to the town corporation (Mayor and Echevins),
urban communities had General Assemblies, originally composed
of the heads of families which, grouped together, made the town,
and existed in this form for several centuries.

Trumpeters in their gorgeous costume would go through the
streets, where the inhabitants used to pass a good part of their
lives, and call the citizens to the Assembly. This summons was
also made by the bell in the town *beffroi*, or by the Curé in his
discourse on the previous Sunday. The Assembly would meet
on the public square, or at the Town Hall, in the space within
the cloister of a monastery, in the large market hall, in the church,
or even in the cemetery round the church " in so far as it was
capable of holding them all." When the people of Nîmes abandoned the city, in 1649, on account of the plague, the town corporation convened the Assembly in the fields. Attendance was
obligatory, and down to the close of the Ancien Régime defaulters
were fined.

The municipal officers took their seats on a raised stand round
the Mayor or the King's official judge. The Town clerk would
act as secretary. One matter only was, as a rule, submitted to
the deliberations of the Assembly—a loan to contract, fresh taxes
to be imposed, a law-suit to be entered upon, suitable methods
of providing against any scarcity or of combating an epidemic.
Matters connected with public works, such as the construction of
a new road, or the closing up of some alley were also discussed,
or it might be about installing a congregation of nursing sisters
in a hospital. Albert Babeau mentions the deliberations of an
Assembly held in 1652 in the refectory of the Dominicans at Marseilles, as a consequence of which eight hundred citizens of the
ancient Phocean city decided to replace the election of the Town
Corporation by drawing lots for it " so as to sever the roots of
enmities and quarrels . . . as was the practice, and still is, in
the best cities of Christendom."

The Prince de Condé, Governor of Burgundy, once convoked
the inhabitants of Châlon-sur-Saône to a General Assembly. He

attended in person and spoke. He desired the people of Châlons to allow the Jesuits to establish themselves in the town : " Such is the King's wish," he said. He then retired in order to allow the Assembly full liberty of discussion. Condé was at table when they came to inform him that his request had been refused, and the noble prince thereupon fell into a great rage. The bourgeois, in their General Assembly, more than once gave proofs of their independent spirit, at a time when the constellation of Louis XIV was shining with its greatest brilliancy.

But we can well imagine the trouble, disorder and tumult which frequently arose at these meetings. Government of the people by the people in a public assembly of the people is theoretically the finest institution in the world—but in practice ?

" These Assemblies," writes an Intendant in the eighteenth century, " to which everybody is admitted and where the least docile citizens put to silence the more reasonable ones, can only be a source of disorder." The town of Bar-sur-Seine proposed to make the General Assembly consist of two delegates from each of the ten jurisdictions of the town, and from each of the twenty-two corporations : " thus everybody could meet in the hall, and give his opinion without trouble or confusion." Admirable to relate—this plan was adopted and carried out throughout the whole province.

When these General Assemblies had become too unwieldy owing to the growth that had taken place in many towns, recourse was had to representative General Assemblies which were presided over by the King's judge in the seventeenth century, and by the Mayor in the eighteenth. They were composed of delegates from the different Wards, or parishes, and representatives of the merchant corporations and guilds. Certain members of the legal profession, the Town Council, the municipal officers, and often the officers of the Town Militia also took part *ex officio*. The delegates from the parishes, and the representatives of the merchant corporations attended with precise instructions dictated by those who had chosen them at meetings whereat the question to be discussed had been already examined. Thus at these representative General Assemblies there could be no discussions or deliberations ; all they did was to vote. And the reason for this can be easily understood ; in theory it was always the General Assembly of all the citizens that met, but practically, inasmuch as it was impossible to hold a session of them all, they met in the person of a certain number of delegates who only had the power to give expression to the will of those who had sent them.

The town corporation emanated from the General Assembly,

but so great was the diversity of the customs in olden France
that it is impossible to fix any general rule.

" Down to the end of the seventeenth century," writes de Tocqueville, " we find towns still continuing to form, as it were, small
democratic republics, in which the officials were chosen freely by
the people to whom they were responsible, where municipal and
public life were active, and where the city showed itself proud of
its rights and very jealous of its independence." Then came the
reform of 1696 by which Louis XIV enacted that the municipal
offices should be subject to purchase and that the office of Mayor
should become a civil function purchased by the holder. De
Tocqueville studied the Ancien Régime from the archives of the
time ; Albert Babeau replies very justly : " One cannot obtain
an exact idea of the Ancien Régime from studying its laws." Active
life, customs, privileges, the spirit of independence as well as the
difficulty and slowness of communications, and the incompetence
of the administrative *personnel*, everywhere created obstacles
against which decrees, meant to be of universal application, came
to grief. " On first approaching the subject," writes Babeau,
" one might think that elections had been everywhere long forbidden ; but one would be wrong. Although from the year 1697
to 1789 elections had been suppressed by legal enactment, they
did not cease to be held in certain towns, and in the majority of
cases they were only suppressed for a few years."

What interfered most grievously with the freedom of the
municipal elections was the control assumed by a kind of local
aristocracy over the administration of a town, often of a very
stringent character, which made them its master. In a large
number of towns there existed a situation like that described by
M. Normand in the case of Saint-Quentin, where " thirty families,
at the most, rendered powerful by their wealth," had taken possession of the administrative authority. In conformity with the
spirit of olden times they had united themselves together by inter-
marriage, and had thus succeeded in forming a solid block into
which new blood had no chance of entering. Retif de la Bretonne,
with his vivid pen, describes the same state of affairs as obtaining
in humble isolated little market-towns :

" I know of no place wherein the dignity of man is more abased
than in the small provincial towns ; five or six well-to-do inhabitants
look upon themselves as owning it. It would appear that only by
their grace are they kind enough to tolerate the meritorious population
who cultivate the land, exercise their calling and make trade thrive.
I have sometimes seen in the public thoroughfares revolting examples
of these would-be proprietors, who, possessed of the chief offices in

the magistrature (town council and municipal offices), retain all the power in their own hands."

Endeavours were made, however, sometimes by most energetic measures, to ensure liberty in the elections. The Parliament of Dijon erected the gallows-tree before the voting hall, on which those who entered upon unseasonable canvassing, monopolies, and law-proceedings were to be "hanged and strangled." But canvassing continued " by means of money, gifts of casks of wine, banquets and popular gatherings at *cabarets* and in the gardens— the luxuriant growth ever springing forth on electoral soil.

As regards the systems of voting, they were so numerous, so varied, and sometimes so complicated, that to enumerate them and give their details would be an interminable task. The following system was practised at Marseilles where it had been decided to choose by lot. Albert Babeau gives us the details for the year 1717, in the case of the election of an *échevin*.

A pedestal was placed in the municipal hall, and on the pedestal a vase, and in the vase were placed six white and six blue balls. The acting Councillors drew out a ball one after the other. The "blues" then named eight notables and submitted this list to the Town Council, who chose four out of them. These four names were written on slips of paper which were inclosed in hollow silver balls and the balls placed in a silver-gilt coffer, from which finally the town clerk drew out one containing the name of the happy man to be elected.

This roundabout way was called "*la voie du Saint-Esprit*," for the Holy Spirit could not fail to guide, in such drawings by lot, a destiny submitted to its prescience. In other places the procedure was quite the opposite, and elections were made by public suffrage in the most open way. All the electors would assemble in a great hall where the moment the ballot began every one would start to shout at the top of his voice, and as distinctly as he could, the name of the candidate he preferred. In one of these assemblies, held at Rheims, an artisan who was a ventriloquist shouted out the name of a candidate in so many different tones of voice that his favourite appeared to have acquired the largest number of votes. A disagreement arose, and finally they had recourse to a secret ballot from which it transpired that the ventriloquist's candidate had only received one vote, to the great stupefaction of all present who were taken by surprise that one man "had been able to make so much noise." The practice of secret voting, however, became generally established during the eighteenth century. Formerly the ballot used to take place in two stages;

the electors of the second stage were called "*portant voix*," because they represented in their own person the votes of those who had chosen them.

At Rethel, at the close of the seventeenth century, the six quarters of the town nominated 72 citizens, a dozen for each quarter ; of these, two-thirds were subsequently eliminated by drawing lots ; the 24 still remaining named 72 others who chose 36 out of them, six for each quarter, and out of these the three *échevins* to be elected were chosen by lot. These manifold precautions were taken to guard against canvassing, and especially against the undue predominance of a few important families. It was better still at Puy, where every year on the 25th November each of the 23 guilds in the town named 3 of their masters, making a total of 69 who repaired to the Town Hall, where two-thirds were eliminated by drawing lots. The 23 electors remaining then joined forces with the 6 retiring Consuls who were to be replaced by others, for the purpose of naming 80 citizens suitable to occupy the six vacant offices. These 80 were summoned to the Hall where the ballot was to take place, where 80 tickets were ready, on six of which the word "Consul" was inscribed. The tickets were then handed to a child who folded them up, put each one inside " a little white hollow ball," and then threw the balls into a bag from which the 80 candidates each drew out the ball and the ticket which was to decide his fate.

In some towns, however, at every election the municipality left it to the citizens to choose the method of balloting they wished to adopt. The president of the electoral body at Limoges announced at the meeting the three courses open to them : " The *scruptine* (ballot), the *compromis* (arbitration), and the *via santi spiritus* (drawing by lot)." This time they decided on the *compromis*, which was a form of election in two stages, but the second stage was very limited, and in the present case consisted of only three bourgeois, who appointed the members of the magistracy themselves.

We can well imagine the *fêtes*, rejoicings, and solemnities these municipal elections occasioned, among which religious ceremonies, Mass and the blessing given by the priest, took the first place. A singular custom was in vogue in certain towns in the south, possibly a distant survival, as it would seem, of the Roman triumphs. The newly-elected Consuls, after taking the oath in the Town Hall, were led back to their houses by bands of small boys who pelted them with "insults" as a foretaste of what was in store for them in case they should be guilty of a betrayal of trust in their administration.

We thus come to the Edict of 1765, which, under the impulse leading France towards political and administrative unity, endeavoured to introduce a little order into this picturesque chaos. The Edict provided each community with two councils, the first representing the old Town Council, and the second composed of the Town Council plus the municipal officers and fourteen notables in places of more than 4,500 inhabitants, a proportionally less number where the population was not so large.

The members of these councils had to be chosen from among the different classes, and from the corporations; in this way the clergy, nobility, the officials, finance, merchant corporations and guilds were all equally represented.

VIII.—*Internal Dissensions and Financial Disorder*

In his study on *Les Pouvoirs des Intendants sous Louis XIV*, M. Charles Godard expresses this opinion, the accuracy of which is confirmed by M. Marion: "The deplorable thing is not that the Intendants have placed the communities under their control, but that the bad use of their municipal liberties has rendered this necessary." With the exception of writers like Albert Babeau, Marcel Marion, and several others, who have made a profound study of urban constitutions, historians are wellnigh unanimous in deploring the progressive encroachment on the liberties of the towns made by the royal authority. As stated by de Tocqueville, this intervention by the Government of the King had often been clamoured for and suggested by the towns themselves, and, on the other hand, it would be a mistake to think that the Intendants on principle constituted themselves into agents of centralization. Very many of them thought what one of them wrote in 1692: "It is indispensable that a Governor (of a province in the King's name) should have a counterpoise in the authority of the *échevins.*"

We have already spoken of the formation of a kind of municipal aristocracy which came to weigh more heavily on their fellow citizens than the seigneurs did on their vassals in the country. Even in this patriciate a selection took place, and the judicial and administrative positions became the patrimony of certain families, the "*nous les ferons*" as they were called at Rheims, to show that these bourgeois, who were masters of the elections, indicated beforehand the names of those they would make into Councillors. In Provence they were called the "*mange-communes,*" for sometimes our magistrates did not lose the opportunity of dabbling in the municipal funds. The inhabitants of La Rochelle complained that these dignitaries sold their offices when they did not give them to their children. "Certain families," writes de

Tocqueville, "conducted all the public business in private, far from the eye of the public, and with no responsibility towards it; it is a disease affecting the administration throughout the whole of France." The Intendant of Auvergne notes : "It is a dangerous thing to give this prerogative (drawing up the roll of those subject to the *taille*) to the Mayors, who exempt their friends and relations."

In former times, disputes between rival families—Montagues and Capulets—led to divisions in the population, and to fierce combats. At Nîmes there were the "Petites Croix" against the "Grandes Croix"; and at Auxerre the "Grecs" against the "Latins." A citizen of Rheims writes : "For forty years I have seen nothing but the town versus the clergy, the town versus the *échevins*, the drapers versus the mercers, and nearly all the guilds of workers versus each other."

The question arose at Nancy in 1769 of raising the subordinate parish of Trois-Maisons into a Rectorship. Everybody was in agreement over the matter and the scheme seemed likely to be realized without any difficulties, when the rivalry existing between the gardeners and vine-dressers blazed up. The former desired to have their patron saint, St. Fiacre, as the celestial guardian of the new parish, while the latter wished it to be under the patronage of St. Vincent, *their* patron saint. A law-suit began. The gardeners opposed the creation of the new parish which had been asked for by the vine-dressers, and attacked the Bishop's motion in the Parliament. The case went on for twelve years, accompanied by all the complications, incidents, and expense which we can readily imagine.

At La Flèche, the wig-makers were at loggerheads with the bakers, and the bourgeois refused to take their seats with the artisans in the Town Corporations. "The Intendant and the tribunals were deafened with the noise of these quarrels" (De Tocqueville).

We should bear in mind that municipal administration was a more difficult and complicated matter in olden France than it is at the present day, precisely because of the liberties with which the towns were endowed. Even at the time when royal authority kept the tightest hand over them, it did not go nearly so far as it does now. The champagne merchants nowadays draw attention to the incapacity of the working men who find places on the Town Council; in former times it was the advocates and lawyers who proved unfitted to administer the affairs of industrial and commercial cities. "Take one of these old pedants," writes Pierre Charron in his treatise on *La Sagesse* (1656), "and conduct him

to the Town Council . . . you would never see any man more
flabbergasted. Listen to a merchant, a bourgeois, who has never
heard the name of Aristotle, and he will give the best advice to
this Council. . . ." Colbert complained that among the municipal
authorities one could never find a Councillor well versed in commerce or manufactures.

We now come to the lack of order in municipal finance, which
decided Colbert to draw up the regulations contained in the Edict
of 1683 first introducing royal control into the affairs of urban
communities, a work completed by the subsequent Edicts of 1703,
1764 and 1765 already mentioned. At the end of the seventeenth
century there were Town Councils, such as those of Auxerre, Tours
and Pont-Audemer, which had not rendered their accounts for
seventeen, twenty-five, and forty years respectively. The financial
disorder, as at Montpellier, was sometimes so great, that " very
large " sums lay doing nothing in the town coffers, while the authorities would resort to burdensome loans instead of using what they
had. The waste was so great at Bordeaux that the workmen
refused to work for the municipality unless the members of the
Council personally undertook to pay them out of their own money.
The inhabitants of Orchies complained that the authorities arbitrarily disposed of the public funds. " The abuses only go on
increasing," writes the Intendant of Languedoc in 1782, " and
there is no longer any order."

We know the ending of La Fontaine's fable of the dog carrying
his master's dinner :

> Je crois voir en ceci l'image d'une ville
> Où l'on met les deniers à la merci des gens.
> Echevins, prévôt des marchands,
> Tout fait sa main, le plus habile
> Donne aux autres l'exemple, et c'est un passe-temps
> De leur voir nettoyer un monceau de pistoles. . . .

This worthy man was exaggerating, but he expressed the general
opinion based no doubt on the fact that the Town Councils too
often neglected to go into the matter of rendering the public
accounts.

IX.—*Civic Development and Industrial Progress*

Dating from the middle of the eighteenth century we see appearing over the whole of France a transforming movement which
developed so surely that, as we said at the beginning of this work,
it is almost a question whether the reign of Louis XVI should still
be ranked under the Ancien Régime. From this point of view we

may say that the year 1750 almost marks a new era, just as the year 1830 in the succeeding century. A new orientation set in, particularly noticeable in the material transformation of France. Baron Grimm writes about it to his noble friends in his *Correspondance :* "Large buildings are being multiplied in France on every side. There is hardly a town of any size which does not wish to have a public square, a bronze statue of the King, a Town Hall or a fountain." In the arrangement of buildings, as in society itself, more regularity was sought after, broader avenues in straighter lines, more space and air. To effect this a portion of the *octroi* was set aside. Picturesqueness, so dear to the tourist and archæologist, certainly lost in the process, but at what gain to hygiene, to the conveniences of life, and to moving about, for people themselves were also tending to withdraw from their former immobility.

In the history of nations everything holds together and is in harmony. Look at the mediæval city as it existed down to the Renaissance, with its round towers and turrets, its bell towers, its steeples, pinnacles, belfries, loopholes and battlements; it represents the history of a society bristling with manifold and diverse customs, usages, privileges, liberties, rights and duties. The modern age sets in, and demands more uniformity : symmetrical streets where hanging signs no longer menace the head of the passer-by, and houses lined up with military precision. Albert Babeau is careful to note that under the Ancien Régime twenty spires were the admiration of Troyes, each surmounted with its golden pinnacle, its cock, its crockets, and its vane ; only one of these remains at the present day. The bourgeois in the Middle Ages did nothing for the ornamentation of their city, but were nevertheless very proud of possessing the most glorious Cathedral and the most imposing belfry tower. Camille Jullian makes the very interesting statement that the idea of creating public promenades and walks in the towns, called *cours*—from the *corso* to be found in Italian cities—and places of amusement for the townspeople, came from the Bourbon monarchy, that is from the French Ancien Régime. Henri IV appears to have taken the initiative by laying out the Place Royale on the site of the former Palais de Tournelles which had been pulled down.

A town under the Ancien Régime, according to Camille Jullian, recognized three kinds of public places : those belonging to commerce, destined for the business of holding fairs and markets ; those set apart by custom for official announcements and proclamations, such as royal or municipal orders, police regulations or those connected with the public thoroughfares ; and *places royales* or public squares for the beautifying of the town and the

enjoyment and benefit of the inhabitants, and very often adorned
with a statue of the King.   From this period also date the broad
avenues or alley-ways planted with trees, with which the Intendants
took pains to endow the towns within their jurisdiction.   They
are to be found in large numbers in Paris, Marseilles, Rennes,
Toulouse and Moulins.   In these efforts the Intendant Foucault
greatly distinguished himself, and his successive sojourns in different
towns can be followed up by the public walks he left behind him
planted with four rows of trees.   Then there were the parks, like
the one laid out by Lenôtre at Dijon.   The sites of the ramparts
surrounding the towns, which were demolished at about this time,
gave the land required for the creation of *boulevards* in large numbers.   Stendhal noted that the French Prefects who went to Italy
after her conquest by Napoleon, never failed to plant a great
quantity of trees in the towns within their jurisdictions, in which
practice, following the romantic tendency then setting in, he discovered " an instinct peculiar to a race of men who had been born
in the woods."   It would have been simpler to see in it a tradition
of the Bourbon Intendants.

The erection of statues of royal personages in the towns of
France became general with the growing intensity of monarchical
sentiments marking the century approximately included between
the years 1650 and 1750.   In this connection the Duc de la Feuillade
appears to have been a forerunner with the statue of Louis XIV
which he erected on a square laid out by him to serve as a setting
to it.   All the provincial towns soon after desired to have their
Place Royale, with a statue of the monarch erected in an open
space and surrounded with buildings on harmonious and regular
lines.   The Government had to moderate this zeal, as they could
not be allowed to overload their municipal finances, already in
debt.   The Controller of Finance annotated the petition presented
by the municipality of Issoire, which had already chosen a sculptor
to model the statue of the King, with the words, " Praise their
zeal and reject the whole scheme."   Statues of Louis XV were
raised at Bordeaux, Rennes, Valenciennes, Nancy, Rheims, and
Paris (Place de la Concorde), and in each case they were erected
in large open spaces, with magnificent borders, which served to
give air and light to the town.

Churches too were beginning to be built in a new style, no longer
with high vaulted roofs rising up like a prayer to God in an impulse
of faith, nor on the Gothic and over-decorated lines of the Renaissance style.   Spacious, airy, bright and elegant, the churches
became like large halls, responsive to a new conception of society,
similar to the transformations taking place in the streets, and in

the laws. The church of Saint-Louis-en-l'Ile in Paris can give us an idea of this on Feast Days, when the House of God is decorated, and bright hangings of velvet and silk descend between the pillars from the arches. The conception of the mediæval church possesses a moving beauty in its exalted faith ; but the conception of the church in Bourbon times was a fine one too, the idea of an elegant House of God prepared and decorated for His guests and children to come there and render their duty to Him.

A similar transformation, in perfect keeping, took place in the Town Halls. No more bell towers, or overhanging pepper-box turrets, spiral staircases, or tall chimneys sumptuously rising over the roofs ; no more overhanging parapets from which the *échevins* used to address the people, no more stone tribunes on which Mass was said, with the people, packed below in the open square, devoutly assisting ; no more niches for statues of the Virgin, or picturesque, gaily decorated, and entertaining clocks ; but in place of these came vast regular buildings, symmetrically built, well proportioned ; a great hall for their deliberations, another for banquets, a concert hall, and a place of meeting for learned societies. The great hall was adorned with glistening crystal chandeliers and hung with tapestry ; it served numerous purposes, even that of public balls for which people paid to enter. It contained statues of the King, the Dauphin, the Governor of the Province, and members who had adorned the Council. The armorial bearings of Nîmes contained a crocodile, and so stuffed crocodiles were to be seen hanging from the ceiling of the council chamber.

The public thoroughfares were improved ; the sides of the streets were raised so as to form pavements, and the number of fountains was increased.

As regards hygiene and cleanliness, the society that issued from the Renaissance was terribly behind that of the Middle Ages. In those days people used often to have baths, and Michelet's cry " A thousand years without a bath ! " is heresy. But in the seventeenth and eighteenth centuries . . . ! Where were to be found those establishments of vapour baths and their guilds ? It is true that in some towns one could still have come across streets named " *Rue des Bains*," but as far as actual baths were concerned the matter stopped there.

On this point too a reaction set in during the second half of the eighteenth century, not only in Paris, but in a few provincial towns, notably at Troyes, Angers and Caen, where establishments for baths were inaugurated, sometimes with much pomp and solemnity.

In other respects also the towns were generally very dirty, and here too the Intendants made useful and efficacious efforts. The Sub-delegate of Pont-l'Abbé, in Brittany, has given us this little sketch of the town where he resided : " Stagnant pools of water, stinking heaps of refuse, and tottering houses half sunken under the ground." In several of even the most important towns the streets were swept only once a week ; in others not at all ; in those they swept the refuse was carefully piled up into little heaps, but as these were never removed all the refuse became scattered again, to be piled up once more into little heaps the following week.

Arthur Young describes Clermont-Ferrand as being

" one of the worst built, dirtiest, and most stinking places I have met with. There are many streets that can, for blackness, dirt, and ill scent, only be represented by narrow channels cut in a night dunghill. The contention of nauseous savours, with which the air is impregnated, when brisk mountain gales do not ventilate these excrementitious lanes, made me envy the nerves of the good people who, for what I know, may be happy in them."

The Paris streets were hardly any cleaner. Retif de la Bretonne speaks of them as follows :

" A torrent of filth inundates the streets when there is even a little rain, and at all times a man on foot is splashed with greasy black slime thrown up by the horses' feet and the carriage wheels. The houses have no gutters to carry off the rain, and a spout sticking out from the roofs pours a flood of water on to the passers-by and drenches them, long after the rain has ceased."

Arthur Young too describes in vigorous language the mud and filth of the great city, for which it had been famous since the Middle Ages, and had not belied its ancient reputation.

But the beauty of her buildings and the incomparable charm of the surrounding neighbourhood had already rendered Paris celebrated throughout all Europe. Let us listen to what Helen Williams, an Englishwoman, says at the time of the outbreak of the Revolution :

" The entrancing surroundings of Paris, unlike those of London, are not encumbered by houses and buildings ; it is not necessary, as when leaving London, to have to cross ten or twelve miles before arriving in the country ; the moment one has passed through the barrier one sees before one a charming variety of vine-clad hills, field, woods, and green meadows. . . . From our house in Paris we can prolong our drive in a short while to the beautiful park of Saint-Cloud, to the tangled woods of Meudon, or to the elegant gardens of Bellevue. . . . Nearer to the town lies pasture land, with scat-

tered hamlets so little frequented that all we can hear are the sheep
bells and the song of the nightingale, and the only human figure to
be seen is that of an old white-bearded peasant watching over his
flock with a great black dog. . . ."

Paris was renowned for the elegance of its public walks and
above all for the beauty of its gardens. The Parisians did not
call each other " cousin " as was the case in a very great number
of French towns—yet another legacy from their family beginnings
—but society life at the Palais Royal, at the Célestins, in the Cours-
la-Reine, and the Gardens of the Tuileries and the Luxembourg,
possessed the charm of unconstrained urbanity in the highest
degree. At the Palais Royal people would group themselves
under the trees in their most elegant costumes, forming little
societies to themselves, although elsewhere they did not know
each other. *Habitués* would meet there, after leaving the Opera,
and the evening would be prolonged till far into the night, and
under the pale light of the stars the voices of the most famous
artistes would be heard. Garat would sing " Bouton de Rose,"
and Saint-Georges the most exquisite airs of Rameau.

The Tuileries was a vast open-air *salon*, where people would
converse without knowing each other, just as at home when some one
is introduced to the family. " A woman of the highest rank," says
Sébastien Mercier, " if she happened to be there, would willingly
enter into conversation with a stranger." One could not be admitted if badly dressed, for at the gates there was a rigorous control. Rich financiers might be seen strutting about, proud of
having recently married their children into the *haute noblesse*.
Foreigners would secure the company of their Paris acquaint-
ances in order to have the notabilities pointed out to them as
they passed by. Poets would read their verses to groups of people
they did not know, but who would readily listen to them ; they
would approach the first-comer, draw out a few sheets from their
pocket, and begin to declaim.

The mud and filth to be found at that time in Paris, or Clermont-
Ferrand, while shocking our sensibility, should not lead us to
think that there was any decadence in French towns in the eighteenth century. The reader will remember the insupportable filth
and stinks at the Louvre and Versailles in their days of splendour.
The ideas of mankind differ according to the times they live in.
The Ancien Régime saw the realization by the towns of France
of the greatest progress in industry and wealth, to which the transformation in their streets and buildings, indicated above, bears
testimony. The eighteenth century in France was a period we
admire in our times for its charming brilliancy in the arts, the

sparkling imagination of its writers, its marvellous perfection in decorative industries, its furniture, silks, binding and printing ; we forget the profound transformations in harmony with a new age which took place, to which neither the monarchy nor its government were strangers :

" Industry is increasing day by day," writes Voltaire ; " to see the luxury of individuals, the prodigious number of pleasing houses built in Paris and the provinces, the quantity of carriages, conveniences, and contrivances which go by the name of ' luxe ' one would think that opulence was twenty times greater than formerly. All this is the fruit of ingenious toil far more than of wealth. . . . The middle classes have become rich through industry. . . . The returns from trade have increased. Less opulence than formerly is to be found among the great, and more in the middle classes, and this has lessened the distance between men. In former days there was no other resource for the little but to serve the great ; to-day industry has opened a thousand roads unknown to us a hundred years ago."

Proof of this growing prosperity is also to be found in the constantly progressive revenue from the excise taxes. If we may believe Arthur Young who, moreover, never missed an opportunity of exalting his own country, the trade of Bordeaux in 1788 exceeded that of Liverpool. In that year the English traveller wrote : " In recent years the progress made in commerce has been more rapid in France than in England, and has doubled in the last twenty years."

BIBLIOGRAPHY

Ardascheff (Paul), Les Intendants de province sous Louis XVI, transl. L. Jousserandot, 1909.—Babeau (Albert), La Ville sous l'Ancien Régime, 1880. —Babeau (Albert), Les anciennes tourelles des maisons de Troyes, from l'Annuaire de l'Aube, 1885.—Babeau (Albert), Paris en 1789, 1889.—Babeau (Albert), La Province sous l'Ancien Régime, 1894, 2 vols.—Boislisle (Arthur de), Correspondance des contrôleurs généraux, 1874–1897, 3 vols.—Boulainvilliers, Etat de la France, 1727, 3 vols.—Busquet (Raoul), Hist. des institutions de la Provence de 1482 à 1790, 1920.—Depping (G.-Bern.), Correspondance administrative de Louis XIV, 1850–1855, 4 vols.—Dupuy (Antoine), Etudes sur l'administration municipale en Bretagne, 1891.—Fage (René), La Vie à Tulle au dix-huitième siècle, 1902.—Gallier (A. de), La Vie de province au dix-huitième siècle, 1877.—Godard (Charles), Les pouvoirs des intendants au dix-huitième siècle, 1901.—Loyseau (Charles), Œuvres, 4th ed., 1701.—Marion (Marcel), Dictionnaire des institutions de la France aux dix-septième et dix-huitième siècles, 1923.—Mathieu (Cardinal), L'Ancien Régime en Lorraine et en Barrois, 4th ed., 1907.—Mercier (Sébastien), Tableau de Paris, 1781, 2 vols.—Monin (H.), Etat de Paris en 1789, 1889.—Normand, Saint-Quentin et la royauté, 1881.—Tocqueville, L'Ancien Régime et la Révolution, 5th ed., 1866.—Young (Arthur), Travels in France, 1794, 3 vols.

CHAPTER X

PUBLIC OPINION

I.—*The Power of Public Opinion*

WE can no longer imagine the power wielded by public opinion in the eighteenth century, nor the intensity of its expression, the stir it created and its influence in the towns of which we have just read a rapid description. Ministers, even the King, bowed to public opinion. We find Secretaries of State and Lieutenants of Police overthrown by it—Ravot d'Ombreval in 1725, Sartine and Montbarey in 1780, and Calonne in 1787. "It is I who appoint my Ministers," said Louis XV; "it is the nation who turns them out." On the accession of Louis XVI to the throne the voice of the public brought Turgot and Malesherbes into the Ministry, against the wishes of Maurepas who enjoyed the King's confidence; but, said Mme. de Stael, " public rumour pointed them out for distinguished employment, and public opinion was once again obeyed."

Its choice was not always so happy; it imposed Loménie de Brienne [1] upon the Ministry, but shortly afterwards, it is true, compelled the King to recall Necker. " Once again," observes Sénac de Meilhan, " the will of the sovereign bowed to public opinion, and the King was compelled to receive again a Minister whom he had exiled a short time before."

Necker declared in 1784 : " Most foreigners can hardly form an idea of the authority exercised by public opinion in France ; it is difficult for them to understand that an invisible power, with no money at its back, no guards and no army, dictates laws to the town, the Court, and even within the King's palace. It

---

[1] Loménie de Brienne: Cardinal, Minister of Finance under Louis XVI, whose tenure of office was marked by a series of expedients, whereas the Treasury required a radical reform (1727–1794). (H. W.)

is so, nevertheless." The voice of the nation in 1778 demanded war on behalf of America, and imposed it. "Public opinion declared itself more and more for the war, and rendered it inevitable . . ." wrote the Comte de Ségur.

After the battle of Rosbach [1] Bernis wrote : " The public cannot reconcile itself to the disgrace of this battle ; where should we have been to-day if I had not caused Parliament to reassemble ? We should have had to bolt."

In the struggle between royal authority and the members of Parliament it was public opinion which intervened and gained the victory.

" The King has sometimes deprived Parliament of its right to protest (remontrances)," writes Besenval in his *Mémoires*, " but public outcry has always made him give it back to them " ; and the people even went so far as to dictate to Parliament itself. We know with what frenzied obstinacy the Parliaments unceasingly opposed allowing Protestants in France to resume their entire rights ; but from the middle of the eighteenth century, the period when the evolution we have alluded to was most marked, the nation became more and more favourable towards them, and the Parliaments gradually capitulated—" under the pressure of public opinion," as contemporary writers did not fail to emphasize.

This pressure had very unexpected consequences. De Tocqueville writes : " France had not yet become the mute country we are now living in ; on the contrary, although political liberty did not .exist, she knew how to make her voice heard, and it was sufficient to raise it to be heard far and wide."

But in what way did France make her voice heard ? The Press did not exist. It is true there was the *Gazette*, founded by Renaudot in 1631, which issued every week what could now be contained in a half page of one of our dailies, and what news ! The *Gazette* certainly had correspondents at the Sublime Porte and in the States of the Great Mogul, but was not so well provided for as concerned France. The week's information consisted in reporting that such and such a nobleman had left for his house in the country, or that Madame Deuxième had acted as godmother to the granddaughter of the Duchesse de Créquy at her baptism. Of any other news to interest the reader there was no sign. Let us open one at random—the *Gazette de France* of the 15th January, 1709. One learns therein that on the 2nd January the Duc d'Enghien received the Collar of the Order of the Saint Esprit, and that on the same day the Court heard Vespers sung in the chapel at

---

[1] Rosbach : a village in Saxony where Frederick II defeated in 1757 the French and their German auxiliaries. (H. W.)

Versailles. Nothing more. Such was the news which had to last
a Frenchman for a whole week, for the *Gazette de France*, provided
with an exclusive licence by Richelieu, did not permit any other
similar publication. The *Mercure* was only a literary review.

II.—*The Nouvellistes*

In place of any printed newspaper a huge and many-sided
spoken journal was spread over the whole of France in which
everything of interest to the nation was said, repeated, carried
to and fro, and commented upon. It was journalism with a
hundred mouths, in which everybody collaborated ; it possessed
its own organization, sometimes in the most definite forms. The
newsmongers, the *nouvellistes* as they were called, met in Paris
at the Palais Royal, the Tuileries, the Luxembourg, the benches
on the Pont Neuf, the cloisters of the Cordeliers, the cloister of
the Célestins and in the public squares, the walks and *cafés* of
almost every provincial town. How did it happen that on one
and the same day, at the time of the American war, the whole
of France found that she was on the side of the insurgents ? It
was brought about by the *nouvellistes*. Their activity, which made
itself felt from the time of the Wars of Religion, continued to
exercise its influence right down to the height of the Revolution ;
the *nouvellistes* of the Palais Royal, the Feuillants and the Cordeliers,
among whom Camille Desmoulins and Marat were the most heeded,
gave the signal of revolt.

But who were these *nouvellistes* ? Every one. Since from its
very nature it was a gratuitous rôle it could not be composed of
professionals, apart from a few men of leisure possessing private
means, or old country gentlemen, or officers on half-pay.

The *nouvellistes* were not content with merely diffusing items
of news, they discussed and commented on them. Just as with
the press of the present day, some made politics more particularly
their department, others foreign affairs, others literary and
dramatic criticism, and others made a speciality of personal
gossip.

We will mention first those who interested themselves only in
great affairs, namely the State *nouvellistes*. These were more
particularly called by the name of " *Les Politiques*," which we find
in the *Mercure* in 1673. Inasmuch as they constituted the most
important and most turbulent section, and were those who talked
most and loudest, " Les Politiques " came to be the name by
which the *nouvellistes* were generally designated in the course of
the eighteenth century.

The brow of the State *nouvelliste* was clouded in mist; he carried the destinies of the country in his mind:

> Aux affaires d'Etat tout entier il s'applique,
> Et d'être très grand politique
> En tous lieux il a le renom;
> Il pourrait gouverner lui seul mille provinces,
> Et nous n'avons point aujourd'hui
> De personne qui mieux que lui
> Sache les intérêts des princes.

Of quite another kind were the *nouvellistes* of Parnassus, as the literary chroniclers were named. They were smart and lively, going about with their pockets bulging with productions in verse and prose, of which they prided themselves on giving the first notice. They did more than provide themselves with the varied information out of which they composed their *chronique des lettres*; they appraised and commented on clever productions and were literary critics. Some of them acquired real authority as critics; Molière's *Précieuses* proclaim them as "the sovereign arbiters of fine writing."

"In Paris they can make the reputation of anyone," says Magdelon, "and you know that it is only necessary to frequent the company of such and such a man to give you a reputation for ability, if you have no other claim."

Molière gives a full-length portrait in his *Précieuses* of the *nouvelliste* of Parnassus:

"Through him one can learn every day the little titbits of *nouvelles galantes*, the dainty interchange of prose and verse. We know the exact details; so-and-so has written the most dainty piece in the world on such and such a subject; another has written words for such and such an air; so-and-so has composed a madrigal for some happy occasion, another, stanzas on an infidelity. Yesterday evening Monsieur wrote a stanza of ten lines to Mlle. —— to which she sent a reply at 8 o'clock this morning. So-and-so has made a certain sketch, this one is writing the third portion of his romance, the other is sending his work to the press."

Among the literary *nouvellistes* were the dramatic critics, called in the eighteenth century by the nickname of "*chenilles de théâtre*." [1]

To the *nouvellistes* of Parnassus should be added the musical news-writers, who went by the name of "*coureurs de chansons*." For new melodies and airs they occupied the same place as their

---

[1] *Chenilles de théâtre*: grubs in theatre-land, like our "Grub Street." (H. W.)

confrères did for political news and literary productions. " All
they did was to ask for and to give out the latest airs of the
moment," said Donneau de Vizé.

Then there were the art critics. They took the greatest interest
in the royal buildings and in the work being carried out for the
embellishment of the city, which they appraised as *connoisseurs.*
They would be seen planted before the work-yard, watching the
coming and going of the workmen and contractors, and discoursing to a crowd of gaping sight-seers, inquisitive people, and
passers-by, who would form groups round them and would come
up " to listen to them rather than to look at the buildings."

The " *nouvelliste galant* " represented a press to itself. Smartly
dressed and perfumed, he would glide along the narrow streets.
" It is not only war that produces *nouvellistes,*" states the Editor
of the *Mercure.* " We may see the *nouvellistes galants* in the side
streets, and they are even more occupied, because Love has more
subjects than Mars."

There was also the *Journal pour Rire.* This consisted of the
facetious *nouvellistes.* We must recognize that in the century of
Corneille and Racine, they were great favourites because " the
manner in which they told their news amused all those who
listened to them. Thus their news, whether false or true, pleased
everybody, because they were pleasing in themselves."

In 1782, the French fleet was besieging Gibraltar, then in the
occupation of the English. Great importance was attached to
taking this stronghold :

" And how goes the siege of Gibraltar ? "

" Hey ! why fairly well ; *il commence à se lever !* "

The essential thing was to have the information quite fresh and
to be the first to announce it. " They would give anything you
like in order to have some piece of news that no one yet knew."
To use the expression of d'Ardène's hero in his comedy *Le Nouvelliste,* " Each tries to be the first to cluck."

" Some of them," says La Bruyère, " would be willing to see
enemies once more at the gates of Dijon or Corbie, and watch
them stretching out chains and putting up barricades, for the sole
pleasure of being able to tell the news."

Political *nouvellistes,* like those of Parnassus, or the *galant* news-
writers, were, however, at one on this point—up-to-dateness ; and
one of the characteristic features of this kind of journalism consisting of conversation only which spread everywhere and was
soon forgotten, was its concentration on the question of the day,
l'affaire en règne, to use the expression current at the time.
" *L'affaire qui est en règne* always forms the principal subject of

their conversations," says Donneau de Vizé, " and they tell each other the news every day."

> Leurs emplois sont fort beaux sur la terre et sur l'onde,
> Ils gouvernent seuls tout le monde,
> Ils prennent les villes d'assaut ;
> Sans leur avis jamais rien n'est fait comme il faut,
> El leur prudence est sans seconde.
> Ils jugent souverainement. . . .
>
> *Mercure galant.*

This craving to collect and spread news became a passion, a mania, as is noted by Du Camp d'Orgas in his *Réflexions sur les Nouvellistes* :

> Une inquiète ardeur d'apprendre des nouvelles
> Agite mille gens, trouble mille cervelles
> Et cause tous les jours des effets si plaisants
> Qu'il semble que le monde ait perdu le bon sens.

A wife thought her husband would be more wisely occupied at home in attending to his own affairs ; she exclaims distractedly :

> Ce métier où l'on perd son temps
> N'est pas le fait d'un homme sage
> Qui doit songer à son ménage,
> C'est affaire de fainéants.
>
> Donneau de Vizé.

She complains to her neighbours that her husband is quite useless :

> Quand chez un procureur il va pour ses affaires,
> Il oublie en causant ce qui l'y fait aller ;
> Pourvu qu'il nouvellise, il n'y songe plus guères,
> Et s'en revient sans en parler.

Montesquieu, who hated them, draws this somewhat unflattering portrait :

" There is a certain tribe which assembles in magnificent gardens where their leisure finds perpetual occupation. They are very useless to the State, and their harangues for the past fifty years have had no different effect from what would have been produced by a silence for the same length of time. Notwithstanding, they esteem themselves of considerable importance, because they discuss magnificent projects and treat of high matters."

Donneau de Vizé, who knew the *nouvellistes* intimately, appreciated their value more justly :

" At first you will find it hard to believe, among the false news which creeps into what they have to say, how very much of it is really true, is even curious and witty. I had difficulty in believing this for a long time, before becoming a member of these celebrated bodies, but at last I have discovered the reasons. They arise from the diversity in the people of merit, wit, and birth, who frequent them from all parts ; and you can easily understand that among the news brought by people of so many different occupations in the world there may be much that is curious and true. Some bring letters from their friends, others from their relations. Some have dealings with certain underlings of the Ministers, or with people in the service of Princes, whose confidence they sometimes enjoy. Others too have relations in the *entourage* of the King's Ambassadors in foreign countries, and some even know those of other sovereigns appointed to His Majesty's Court, and learn from them many things it would be difficult to know from other sources. During the campaign of 1673 I saw *nouvellistes* who had letters twice a week from bankers in Holland and so learnt of very curious matters which could not have come to hand from the army until long afterwards, because the bankers' couriers were not obliged to turn out of their way as was the case with those who came from the King's armies ; and by these letters the *nouvellistes* knew of the crossing of Tolhuys three or four days before there was any letter in Paris from the Court mentioning this fine action embodying so many other memorable feats."

So great was the position occupied by these open-air *nouvellistes* among their contemporaries at the height of their popularity, that a very large number of writers took note of their personality for the purpose of describing their attitudes at those moments when they might be seen perorating with animation, or, as often as not, listening with rapt attention to those discoursing before them. " They never look at those who salute them, and hardly ever greet anyone, so attentive are they to listen to everything that is said. Those of their friends who are *nouvellistes* too come and mingle with them without any greeting of ' good-day,' and without even uttering a word ; this custom they observe so as not to interrupt the man who is speaking."

They would group themselves in a circle, and those behind would almost climb on the shoulders of those in front so as to hear better what was being said :

> Tels étaient ces amas d'avides nouvellistes
> Qu'une nouvelle fait grossir ;
> Et qu'une autre plus loin, dite par leurs copistes
> Fait en un instant éclaircir :
> Je m'imagine voir des têtes avancées,
> Sur des épaules entassées. . . .

In this way were formed organizations for the purpose of bringing, concentrating, and discussing news, which, as time went on, assumed cohesion and solidity. These groups of *nouvellistes*, occupied over the day's events, to be seen meeting in this way in the public walks, were called "*pelotons*," and the groups who had reached the stage of appearing to possess some sort of stable and regular institution were called associations, companies, and, more definitely, *bureaux*. They were *bureaux* constituted like some deliberative assembly, and that, really, is the name most characteristic of these open-air meetings, for even thus early, in 1690, Du Camp d'Orgas specifies one of these *bureaux* deliberating under the green shade of the walnut trees in the Tuileries, by the name of "*La Chambre.*"

> . . . La Chambre se sépare.
> La Chambre, dites-vous ? oui,—c'est un corps entier. . . .

Beside the president and registrar—nowadays we should call him the secretary—the "*questionneur*" played an important part. If a battle was concerned he would write down in his notebook while following the account being given by those present the losses and gains and the number of dead and wounded on both sides. "It is from this notebook," he would say—after the man who had described the naval battle had ceased speaking—"that one should be in a position to know accurately which side has won the battle ; and I shall examine it when I go to bed as I cannot make it clear without counters."

At the time appointed the president would open the "session." Those who arrived later would mingle with the group without any greeting in order not to interrupt the speaker, contenting themselves with a slight nod to their friends who would return it in the same manner.

> Si quelqu'un d'entre eux vient trop tard,
> Il dit d'une âme un peu dolente
> Qu'il en aura pourtant sa part
> Quoiqu'il ne soit venu qu'à nouvelle expirante.

When all the news had been given to the meeting—*mises sur le bureau* as this was called—an interval for reflection over it ensued, that is, for summing it up, and this was the most important part of it all :

> L'heure où les politiques
> Font, en parlant des affaires publiques,
> Redoubler les attentions.

All the news received was, therefore, passed through the sieve, and only after this had been done was it considered to be reliable. In addition, it had to receive the approval of those *nouvellistes*, who, from their connections and the authority they had gradually acquired, were privileged to invalidate or confirm the news under discussion. For there were *nouvellistes* in the position of the newspapers of to-day ; some had acquired the reputation, not only of being generally well-informed, but of giving their views with prudence and in a critical spirit.

To these *bureaux* holding their sessions on the benches in the public walks would come those Parisians desirous of providing themselves with news to send to their relations and friends in the country, together with the current ideas and events of the day. There too repaired for information those compilers of " *gazettes secrètes*," also called " *nouvelles à la main*," which were distributed so widely. From the same source also the printed gazettes, beginning with the *Mercure* and the *Gazette*, and the different news-letters drew their chief inspiration.

> Dessus nos bancs
> On fait les courriers allemands,
> Ceux qu'on appelle polonais,
> Et tous les courriers français.
>
> *Mercure galant.*

Thus we can see how far and wide their influence extended beyond the frontiers over all Europe.

But who is this man sitting on a bench beneath the flowering chestnut-trees, and in a loud voice calling out :

" Let me tell you that I have it personally from my brother-in-law—from the King, I say, or my brother-in-law, it is the same thing ! "

Of swarthy countenance, and stout, squat build, he is Comte Charles d'Aubigné, brother of the Marquise de Maintenon—Charles d'Aubigné, whose quick and unassuming intelligence, as much as his connections at the Court, had transformed into a *nouvelliste* who was always surrounded and applauded on the public promenades.

" He was a spendthrift," says Saint Simon, " and mad enough to be locked up, but an amusing man, possessed of wit and an unexpected power of making sallies and repartees ; in addition, he was a good, honest fellow, polished, and with none of the vanity or impertinence that his sister's position might have given occasion to." Consequently people elbowed each other for the first places in the circle of chroniclers of which he was the orator.

The most famous *nouvelliste* in the reign of Louis XIV was Comte Joachim de Lionne, cousin of the celebrated Foreign Minister, Hugue de Lionne. A retired officer, who had earlier distinguished himself in Flanders, he lived in Paris devoting his fortune, his time, and connections to presiding over the *nouvellistes* of " Petite Provence " in the Tuileries Gardens, the oldest of whom looked up to him as their chief and " star." He had friends at Court, in the army, and in the Diplomatic service, by means of whom he could provide them with information. The celebrated Saint-Evremont from his place of exile sent him news of what was happening in England and the Low Countries, and great was the despair which reigned among the *habitués* of the circle when Lionne had the gout ! They would even go as far as his house to inquire, at least . . . news of his health !

When the fortune of war was turning strong hearts were to be found among the military *nouvellistes*, who revived men's courage, toned down reverses, and showed that victory was approaching. Such a one was Louis de Mérode-Montmorency, Prince d'Isenghien, and a Maréchal de France, who thought it no derogation from his rank to walk in the public *promenades* at the time of the disastrous Bohemian campaign and thus inspire vigorous hope in men's hearts.

" He would stir up warlike ardour by relating a victory every week, and the news-lovers loaded him with affectionate attentions, while the politically-minded showed their respect for him." Grown old and white in his soldier's uniform, he used good round military expressions ; he feared nothing, and fine old soldier that he was, one day in his capacity as President of the Marshals of France, he handed over to the police those two scamps, Marmontel and Fréron,[1] who had dared to presume to fight a duel just as though they were of noble birth !

In order the better to follow the military operations, some would bring maps which they spread out on the benches or on their knees. If there happened to be no map, some one with a skilful hand would trace by means of his cane the course of the rivers on the sanded paths, mark the position of the besieged towns, and picture great strategic evolutions. " If our armies were on a campaign they would trace out and direct their march with the end of a cane. They would mark out the spot where they should camp, the movements they should make, the position and strength of the enemy, and the operations of either side."

[1] *Marmontel :* author of the *Incas, Bélisaire* and *Contes Moraux* (1723–1799). *Fréron :* a celebrated critic, and one of Voltaire's enemies (1718–1776). (H. W.)

From speaking about marches and counter-marches, equipment and artillery, these strategists of the public gardens came to consider themselves in all good faith as great captains, and in all sincerity exclaimed :

> Oui, si le Roi voulait me donner un armée,
> Je connais le terrain . . .

Naturally these specialists were for the most part old soldiers, who would come to these meetings in times of wars that were for ever being renewed, in order to add their quota of knowledge acquired in their campaigns. But the Abbés too—who would have thought it ?—displayed particularly bellicose dispositions ; after the old soldiers it was they who followed the manœuvres of our generals with the greatest interest.

The anonymous author of the *Grand Théâtre des Nouvellistes*, who missed no opportunity of making fun of these tacticians of the thoroughfare, writes in this connection :

> Et vous, abbés du temps, dont le cœur est tout braise
> Pour enflammer la guerre assis tout à votre aise,
> Et qui, dans le transport de cette passion,
> Faites du Luxembourg un second Illion,
> Parlez, abbé, parlez, est-ce-que vos bréviaires,
> Pour bien décrire un camp vous donnent des lumières ?

A citizen of the Rue des Cordeliers used to listen assiduously to an Abbé who was a great enemy of the English, and was delighted with his vehement dissertations. This formula was always on the Abbé's lips : " We must raise 30,000 men ; we must embark 30,000 men ; it will possibly cost 30,000 men to seize London ; but we shall do it."

The citizen fell ill, and thought of his cherished Abbé whom he would no longer hear in the Allée des Carmes, and who had always promised him the approaching destruction of England with his 30,000 men. As a mark of his gratitude this patriotic citizen left him a legacy and put in his will : " I bequeath to M. l'Abbé ' *Trente Mille Hommes*,' an annuity of 12,000 *livres*. I do not know him under any other name, but he is a good citizen who has proved to me in the Luxembourg gardens that the English will shortly be destroyed."

Armed with this will the notary betook himself to the Luxembourg and inquired for a certain Abbé " *Trente Mille Hommes*."

" What ! Why there he is ! "

The notary then went up to the worthy Abbé who was at that very moment engaged in demonstrating to a circle of attentive listeners the approaching ruin of England, thanks to his 30,000 men. This sketch is taken from Sébastien Mercier's *Tableaux de Paris*.

III.—*Bonhomme Métra*

Of all the *nouvellistes* in the Ancien Régime the most celebrated was Métra, *le bonhomme Métra*, as he was called. Many of his contemporaries have left sketches of him; let us take that by Norvins in his *Mémorial* :

" I continually saw Métra, the *nouvelliste*, clad in an ample long coat of greenish material slightly ornamented with a little gold braid, which was repeated on the brim of a very small and crushed down three-cornered hat, the three sides of which were turned up and held back by gold cords. His hat hermetically covered a small unkempt wig of one row of round curls, and the whole was completed by a little taffeta silk bag which confined his hair. In addition, Métra carried negligently under his arm a fine gold-topped cane, and held in his hand a great snuff-box of old lacquer. The rest of his costume consisted of a scarlet waistcoat, also braided, black velvet breeches, two watch chains, *chiné* silk stockings, and buckled shoes of beaver skin."

Bonhomme Métra was of a very high colour, his face was as red as a tomato, and he had an enormous, formidable, and colossal nose—" a monstrous nose, purple, bulbous, ridged in folds, fortified by nature, like three noses one above the other," was the description given by the pretty little Marquise de Villeneuve-Arifat. "Métra's nose was of such huge proportions," writes Salabery, " that without looking a fool, he could not see much further than it."

In spite of this, the worthy man was not particularly ugly. He was always very neat, and had a refined expression, and eyes sparkling with mischief.

Regularly, every day, Métra would go at the same hour to take up his position on the terrace of the Feuillants, the terrace in the Tuileries which, as we know, looks over the Rue de Rivoli to-day. He would take his seat under a great chestnut tree which was growing there at the time. All around was arranged a vast circle of chairs, many rows deep, for the privileged ones admitted by the *nouvelliste* to his discourses. An hour or two beforehand the titled occupants of the finest houses in Paris would send their servants to keep seats for them in the first rows, but no intruder would have dared to take possession of one of those chairs, neither would the park-keepers have allowed it. These places belonged to subscribers to this spoken gazette, the amount being left to each man's generosity.

As soon as the *nouvelliste* began to speak a great silence fell. Métra would tell them the day's news, which he had received from his correspondents, or through the relations he maintained with the Court, even among the domestic servants, to the exclusion, however, of any indiscreet spying, and from the friends he could count by the hundred who sent him information from all parts.

Métra generally spoke seated. He leant one hand on his gold-headed cane, while in the other he held his old lacquer snuff-box. When he spoke standing up he always held his hands behind his back. His head already had a shaky movement, although he was not yet very old, and this made the black silk bag confining the ends of his hair quiver also.

The Spanish Ambassador, Comte d'Aranda, who lived in the vicinity of the Tuileries and used to pass through the gardens daily, having stopped to listen to Métra, noticed the care he took in repeating the news he had learnt and the justice and moderation of the comments with which he accompanied it.

So much was he impressed that, during the naval war which Spain was waging with England, he hastened to communicate to Métra any news he wished to be made public. The English Ambassador, not to be beaten by his Spanish *confrère*, did not hesitate to transmit in the same way the news he too desired to become known, and he was soon imitated by the other Ambassadors and foreign Ministers, even by our own Foreign Minister himself, who began to depute regularly his " third assistant " to interview the *nouvelliste*. To such an extent was this carried that Métra became a " clearing house " for news concerning foreign affairs, the channel by which the public received any information that the French Minister and foreign Courts wished them to have.

From the beginning of the reign of Louis XVI the *Bonhomme* fulfilled, as it were, the functions of an unofficial agency, similar to the Havas, and in a manner we should nowadays think unusual.

The comments with which Métra accompanied the items of news he transmitted to his audience likewise appear to have possessed great importance. He had much good sense, and judged men and matters with plain straightforwardness and perspicuity. Of very bourgeois mentality in other respects, he was the interpreter of the middle classes, restrained, far-seeing, and trusty, so much so that at each new event that came to his ears Louis XVI never failed to ask his courtiers :

" And what has *Bonhomme* Métra got to say about it ? "

IV.—*The Public Gardens of Paris*

Nevertheless these numerous *nouvellistes*, whether political or of Parnassus, military or art critics, were not indiscriminately mixed up together. Each group and special division had its own place of meeting tacitly fixed in each public walk. The public knew that on the edge of the bowling green the talk would be more particularly concerned with the marches and counter marches of Turenne's army, while in the precincts of the round pond the subject discussed would be foreign affairs, and that under the lime trees in the broad walk the literary claims of new Academicians, and the last piece presented at the Hôtel de Bourgogne, would be competently debated. Soon even the large public gardens acquired their speciality, and those of the Luxembourg became the meeting place of the *nouvellistes* of Parnassus.

Those most qualified to speak grouped themselves around a tree to which they gave great celebrity, a yew conspicuous for its beauty and form. This yew tree consequently became known as *the* yew, *par excellence*, the *great* yew, or simply—*the yew*. When people in the republic of letters talked of "the yew," every one knew that the yew tree of literary criticism was meant.

Lesage speaks of it in his *Mariages du Canada* :

> Grand juge, consul du Permesse,
> Vous savez notre différend
> De grâce, réglez notre rang,
> Par un arrêt plein de sagesse,
> Par un arrêt définitif,
> Tel que vous en rendez à l'if.

The organization and effect of those "cabals," which were so much written about at the time, may be explained by these literary *nouvellistes*. In our days a piece that meets with a "bad press" runs a strong risk of being a failure after the first presentation. This same procedure had its effect in the times of Racine, Molière, Marivaux and Beaumarchais. When a piece had become known before its production it sometimes encountered absolute hostility from the moment the curtain was raised ; it had been considered bad in the circles of the literary *nouvellistes*, and they lost no time in making their judgment felt. On another occasion the hostile movement would take shape after a first night which had not been a success. We can therefore understand how, in the absence of journalism, the arguments and appreciations of authorized critics and duly qualified *nouvellistes* carried weight with the public.

"The talk going the round after the first presentation of a

piece is always the factor which decides its fate," writes Donneau de Vizé, " and this talk can never be favourable, even though the piece may be good, when it has been ill received at the readings that have previously taken place."

The daily record of society events and foreign affairs was given more particularly in the Tuileries Gardens, where the best dressed and best shod *nouvellistes* assembled and chatted in the Broad Walk over the chronicle of the latest *salons*, while on the terrace of the Feuillants external politics were discussed.

In the parallel walk by the side of the river learned men assembled to make their observations on the weather and give forth their predictions, thus giving rise to the " weather forecast."

Internal politics, properly so-called, formed the speciality of the Palais Royal, where also stood a tree rendered famous by the *nouvellistes*. It was a large chestnut known as " the Cracovie tree," a name given to it at the time of the Polish war on account of the analogy between the Polish city (Cracow) and the word " craquer," to tell " crackers."

Lastly—and this fact should be noted—in the cloisters of the Cordeliers assembled the *nouvellistes* of advanced opinions to discuss their views. From the year 1725 the police reports made mention of the most violent discourses against the Government, accompanied by cries of " *Vive la République*," as taking place there.

As the eighteenth century pursued its course the *nouvellistes* went on increasing in importance, and likewise in number. Their groups began to overflow from the public gardens into the streets.

" These groups," writes Sébastien Mercier in his *Tableau de Paris*, " have received permission to hold their discussions on the streets, with their feet in the gutter, amid the din of passing coaches which interrupt the orator's zeal and eloquence, for wheels would crush this new Demosthenes just as they would any other. What is most astonishing is to see poor devils in tatters so eager for fresh news, and devouring it as though it were bread." And he adds, " It was no use their trying to stifle this indiscreet babbling . . . from a Minister's head down to a dancer's legs the Parisian must have his say about everything ; but his cackle is as inconstant as his ideas. Wait a week and all this noisy cackle which seems bound to overthrow everything . . ."

These lines were written in 1781 ; we have in fact only to wait *eight years*, and this " noisy cackle " *was* in reality to overthrow everything.

Among the *nouvellistes* at the close of the Ancien Régime we find the names of Turgot, Raynal, d'Holbach, Diderot, and most of the encyclopædists. Marat and Desmoulins were *nouvellistes*. The chief centres where they met were the Terrace of the Feuillants in the Tuileries, the Cloître des Cordeliers, and the Palais Royal. The *nouvellistes* of the last named set on foot the movement which led to the taking of the Bastille and the march on Versailles. In 1790 the author of the *Dictionnaire Inutile* [1] wrote : " The Palais Royal continues to be a pleasure resort, a public forum, and a school of liberty. Political orators who dine on *bavaroises* [2] and earn their supper at billiards, hound together night and morning all the shoe-blacks, hawkers, hair dressers and market porters to retail to them, as at a market, the news of the day and the reflexions of Marat."

V.—*Private Correspondence*

Our friends had collaborators who wielded the pen. Private letters were real news-gazettes ; there was Mme. de Sévigné, Mme. de Grignan, Mlle. de Scudéry, Mme. d'Huxelles, Mme. de Maintenon, and many others. " There is no greater pleasure to me than having a chat with you," writes Mlle. Aissé to Mme. Calandrini. " I tell you the news I am well acquainted with. I should not care to relate to you all that is said in Paris. You know, Madame, that I hate untruths and exaggeration, and so all I am going to write to you will certainly be true."

Gaston Boissier says :

" Mme. de Sévigné tells everything she knows, and since she has great connections and moves in good circles she is aware of almost everything that is going on, or is to take place. There is no item of domestic intrigue, no political or military event that she does not touch upon in passing, so that if we wanted to follow her through all her letters we should be forced to relate the entire history of that period."

It was a social duty to insert news in the letters one wrote, and to share with friends the incidents with which one might be acquainted that were taking place at Court and in town. A letter was looked forward to, and was much prized, and moreover it might not be kept to oneself. It was passed from hand to hand ; copies were made of it which went the round of the town or countryside, and passed from one château to another. This explains the form taken by this correspondence, the turn of phrase, style, and the details contained. It explains also the frequent

[1] Gallais.
[2] *Bavaroises :* a drink consisting of a mixture of tea, syrup and milk. (H. W.)

note "*Lisez bas,*" generally written on the margin of letters of former days, which meant "keep to yourself what follows, and pass it over when you are reading my letter aloud."

Madame de Sévigné wrote for a circle of listeners.

In order to furnish news for their correspondence they organized a regular service for obtaining information. That set on foot at the beginning of the eighteenth century by the Marquise de Balleroy may be quoted as an example. Her brothers, nephews (among whom were the two d'Argensons), family friends and even servants, were laid under contribution ; the last-mentioned were among the most zealous providers of news ; one can imagine what their spelling was like :

"*Sé seulement pour vous dire que l'on disoy ier au Tuilery que les ennemis marchè du côté de Namur* . . ." ("This is only to tell you that they say at the Tuileries that the enemy are marching by Namur . . .") Domestic seekers after news, reformers in braided liveries who found their way everywhere. They could be met with at *cafés*, in the public walks, in the ante-chamber of Ministers, in the pit at the Comédie theatre. They would sum up the acting and the merits of a piece. Their information might be drawn from the highest sources ; one of these liveried gazetteers wrote on the 28th October, 1706, to his noble correspondent :

"No more news is to be obtained, Madame ; the channels have been cut by order of M. de Torcy (Minister for Foreign Affairs), who has had thirty clerks arrested for having taken pains to spread news among the public in spite of the express prohibition he had given them *novissime.*" Note the "*novissime,*" the Latin of the ante-chamber, not of the servants' quarters.

On the 6th January, 1721, the Marquis de Balleroy wrote to his wife from Paris, "I have just arrested a *nouvelliste,* at which news, I am assured, you will be very pleased." Relatives, friends and servants did not suffice ; recourse was had to specialists from whom one could have a right to demand punctuality and accuracy in return for a definite fee. People of rank were soon to have their salaried informers whose duty it would be to collect and transmit the echo of the hour, one who would form part of their household, just like their hall-porter or *chef.*

VI.—*Paid Nouvellistes*

"There is no frequented town house without its *nouvelliste,*" we read in the *Entretiens du Palais-Royal,* "and since, as a rule, he is a being who goes and searches every remote corner in order to fulfil his task, he gives a hazy report of all that is told him, and will often even imagine it . . ." just such another as the *nouvel-*

liste of Plautus who " knew everything," and " related everything," even the intimate conversations between Jupiter and Juno.

Thus no great house was without its news-service. The heads of this class of agency would send out their written sheets at regular dates. In one of these written news-letters we find the following, dated 10th July, 1664 :

" No one in Paris is talking of anything else but the *rentes de l'Hôtel de Ville* " (the town corporation annuities), about which the following song was composed :

> Dans l'empire d'amour le désordre s'est mis,
> Dorize, Climène et Phylis
> En sont dans l'épouvante ;
> Beaucoup n'ont plus déjà que mépris pour leurs lois,
> Et chacun crie à haute voix :
> Ah ! ma rente !

The climax of the famous madrigal, *Femmes Savantes* :

> Ne dis plus qu'il est amarante,
> Dis plutôt qu'il est " de ma rente,"—

was an echo of a song then in vogue.

These salaried hunters after news were for the most part poor, needy fellows. One should read the entreaties they used to send to their noble patrons for the writing paper they were in want of, imploring them to provide them with the necessary money.

This service of information became more varied. To stories of the Court and town these correspondents were not long in adding matters of interest in the " Republic of Letters," descriptions of public shows, analyses of new books, academic intrigues, etc. Sometimes the books mentioned were sent too : the new publications, plays, pamphlets, and the latest romance the leaves of which were " still wet with the kiss of the printing press." This was the service of " *Parnasserie.*" It was mixed up with packages containing olive oil, oranges, Marseilles soap and candles, and the consignment all went together in the domestic hamper.

VII.—*Written News-Letters*

A step further and we are in presence of news-providers who not only furnished one, but several clients, from all of whom they drew fees. Their labours grew in extent, they found themselves obliged to obtain collaborators, and this led them to form a central office, a *bureau* of *nouvellistes*—an editor's room. These were the *nouvellistes à la main*, active and important collaborators with the *nouvellistes de place* in the public gardens of whom we have been speaking. The manuscript news-letters were far more severely forbidden than the printed gazettes.

It was Figaro over again : " I still trim my pen and ask every-one what people are talking about."

These news-sheets were real letters written by a *nouvelliste à la main* for several subscribers.

" The news-letter," wrote the Goncourts, "is to be found everywhere, it lifts off every roof, it knows who is behind the mask, what is under the cards, the insides of alcoves . . . ; it is a power, it will become the press."

The *nouvellistes* would meet, a good many at a time, to draw up their reports. They would parcel themselves into " branches," to use their own expression, or into " *bureaux*," as they more commonly designated them, hence the present term " *bureau de rédaction*," or editorial office.

At the head of the *bureau* was the Editor-in-Chief who called himself " *le chef de nouvelles*." Then came the secretary, who put together the news that had come to hand, and had it trans-cribed by copyists. He also kept a register of the subscribers and would himself see the sheets despatched after they had been placed in envelopes bearing the name and address of each sub-scriber. To each *bureau* reporters were attached, for the *nouvellistes* understood about reporting from the beginning of the seventeenth century.

Under this heading the liveried throng rendered the greatest service. Lackeys would keep their ears open as they served at table, or when showing in visitors to Monsieur le Comte or to Monsignor the Intendant ; the hall-porter would take note of those who went in. And what was the result ? During his mission to London in 1717, the Abbé Dubois wrote thus to the Regent, the Duc d'Orléans :

" Is not the furious opposition they are showing to the matter on hand at the present moment a monstrous thing (an alliance with England and a rupture with Spain) ? I am more than astonished to find that they hold meetings over such a negotiation just as in the case of the Bull *Unigenitus* (relating to Jansenism), that they read news-letters in their houses, publish the news in the streets and entrust a matter of this importance to the tittle-tattle of everybody. Of a truth the affairs of His Royal Highness are overmuch betrayed ; everything I write in my despatches to you leaks out to such an extent that everything that may be prejudicial to his affairs goes the round in Paris and then travels as far as Madrid."

The *nouvellistes* had correspondents in the provinces and abroad. Chevrier announced in 1762 " a system of correspondence established in all the capital cities, and the other chief towns in Europe. Seventy-two people are entrusted with the gathering and sending of news to the *bureau*."

How many journals at the present day could boast of so many correspondents ? True, the subscription to Chevrier's manuscript news-letter cost 240 *livres*, nearly 3,000 francs at the present value.

As regards their social position the *nouvellistes* were, for the most part, poor needy fellows, outcasts, the flotsam and jetsam of the great city. Marchand, the advocate, depicts them " in tattered black coats, brown waistcoats, holes in their stockings, nailed shoes, dirty linen and russet brown wigs." Among them was Nicolas Mahudel, a member of the *Académie des Inscriptions*, but he was a hopeless fellow upon whom women fastened like leeches ; others were law clerks who had been dismissed by their employers, unfrocked priests, officers on half-pay, students in search of funds wherewith to satisfy Lisette—one must live and trick out one's little friend with finery. And lastly, there were the servants ; Figaro was a true type of the times.

But ridiculed and despised though they were, how great was the influence these needy folk exercised from the depths of their poverty upon their contemporaries ! They wielded active and untiring pens, and had thousands of readers in France and throughout Europe. They possessed a greater power than the philosophers of stirring public opinion, and were more faithful interpreters of it. The time was approaching when these " scribblers," as Voltaire called them, were to enrol names, such as that of the Abbé Prévost, Grimm, Raynal, Diderot, Favart, Mirabeau and Marat.

Their *clientèle* was recruited among the different classes of society, but more especially among the higher ranks. " I addressed my sheets twice a week to certain distinguished persons for whom I executed literary commissions," said one Gautier by name, and he was not exaggerating. Among his subscribers in Paris he numbered the Comtes de Lamarcq and de Tessin ; the Duc de Valentinois ; the Princess Lichtenstein, Campo-Florido, and Grimberghen ; the Marquis de Fontanges, and M. de Joinville ; in the provinces he had the Duc d'Agenois at Montpellier ; M. de Spon at Lyons ; and the Marquis de Choiseul at Lunéville ; at Florence, M. de Richecourt ; at Brussels M. de Bucquoy ; and at Amsterdam M. de Medina. Gautier also sent his Thursday and Saturday news-letters to M. de Chambrier, the Prussian Minister, Princesse de la Tour, and the Prince de Ligne, President de Brosses, the Chevalier de Launey, M. de Romigny, the Abbé de Chevreuse and Comte de Loc Maria.

Séchelles, the Intendant of Lille, stated that the news-letters (*nouvelles à la main*) found their way into every château. The subscription was very costly, averaging 144 *livres* a year, or nearly 1,500 francs at present value. Some were lower, but others reached an annual sum of 600 *livres*, or 6,000 *francs* at the present day.

The number of subscribers varied ; some *nouvellistes* had only four or five, others as many as two hundred and over.

When the news-letter was completed, distributors would take it ,to the Paris *clientèle*, a proceeding necessitating endless precautions. Women were chosen by preference for this dangerous task. In some cases the *chef de nouvelles* would go in person to the house of an important subscriber in the morning, at the hour devoted to his *toilette*, and would hand him the newly-written sheets.

" The dressing room of a man of fashion resembles a perfumer's shop by reason of the different scents. It is adorned like an open show-case, and embellished with pomades of frangipane and parsley, amber, vanilla, tuberose, jasmine, roses and pinks. The different powders are matched with the colour of his garments, and as far as possible, have the same scent as the pomades. There are some that are yellow, green, red, rose, black and white.

During the dressing hour there would come along spruce Abbés, *nouvellistes* and literary hangers-on to bring to his notice any works deserving of encouragement."

Citizens who evinced any curiosity about public affairs, and had not the necessary means to subscribe to these secret newsletters, were able to find them at certain cafés, near to Renaudat's Gazette and the news-sheets from Holland. Foreigners would resort [thither to read them. In other cafés the waiters would secretly sell little written items of news to their clients. In the provinces the *nouvelles à la main* would be sent in an envelope, like letters by the ordinary post, and possibly the use of an envelope may have taken its rise from the despatch of these newsletters, for, as is well known, the name and address was inscribed on the back of a letter in former days, after it had been folded and sealed. In the case of the news-letter, should it fall into the hands of the police, it was important that it should not betray the secret of such a trade, and a news-letter with no address on it, or an envelope with no news-letter within, were not likely to arouse suspicion.

VIII.—*The Dangers of News-letters*

The public authorities were, as a matter of fact, very severe on the " *gazetiers à la main.*" Figaro was put into the Bastille, and furiously exclaims :

" How I should like to get hold of one of those four-days-old authorities—so casual in the harmful orders they issue—after a good round disgrace has subdued their insolent pride! I would tell him . . . that only little men fear these little manuscripts."

That is all very well, but these little manuscripts were clandestine, backbiting, defamatory and calumnious—we remember the couplet in the *Barbier de Séville*—and were circulated under sealed cover. How was it possible to make any reply? More often than not a young wife, whose reputation was being attacked, was unaware of the source of the scandal with which people hoped to wound her. Her family would tell her about it, but through what channel and to what people could the real truth be made known? And supposing the story was really true, was it lawful that mercenary correspondents should be allowed to divulge and spread abroad secrets of the alcove, or to throw out some love affair like a choice morsel for the chatter of worldlings?

The same considerations applied to public life, commercial transactions, operations on the Bourse, matters relating to the defence of the nation, and to the King's secrets. " Every one complains about it," we read in a report to the Lieutenant of Police, " because they attack people unsparingly and spread false and defamatory facts about them, without any consideration."

In the provinces the evil raged, and with a greater intensity, because there were less means available of combating it. The author of *Ménagiana* remarks : " Should not the distribution of *gazettes à la main*, which are crammed with falsehoods, be stopped ? They do not do nearly so much harm in Paris as in the provinces, where they sometimes cause people great distress."

We read in the reports presented to the Lieutenant of Police, dated 10th February, 1732 :

" Louis XIV never permitted the *petites nouvelles à la main*, and throughout his life he caused all who wrote and sold them to be arrested, because he knew their danger, on account of his enemies to whom they were sent." Mazarin and Hugue de Lionne likewise discovered their danger. The *gazetiers* to whom Louis XIV, Mazarin, and Lionne alluded, were those who went by the name of " *nouvellistes pour l'étranger*," or " news-writers for abroad." The English, Prussian and Spanish Ambassadors attached to France took care to cultivate them. In this connection we cannot give too much importance to the declaration made by Lord Taaffe, a former member of the English Parliament who was arrested in France as an agent of the British Government at the time of the Seven Years War. Taaffe collaborated with some *nouvellistes* in Paris, some of whom must have been unconscious of the part

they were being made to play. Taaffe said that the King of
England spent annually up to a sum of £60,000—equivalent to
15 million francs at the present value—on remunerating Frenchmen, and even pensioning them, in order to serve his policy in
their own country. In such cases the *nouvellistes* were not only
of use to the foreigner in providing information he wanted, but in
spreading throughout France and Europe reports he might wish
to be circulated.

IX.—*What the Nouvellistes Accomplished*

But these news-writers for abroad formed a very small minority.
The greater portion of our *gazetiers* carried out their task like good
Frenchmen, often as patriots devoted to the public welfare ; hence
their success.

" It is pleasing in the provinces," observes Racine ; " there everyone is a *nouvelliste* from the cradle."

In his *Comtesse d'Ercarbagnas* Molière makes the Vicomte speak
in a way that would be sure to please Louis XIV, who held
nouvellistes in horror :

" I should have been here an hour ago had there been no tiresome
people in the world, but I was stopped on the road by a troublesome
old aristocrat who asked me the news of the Court expressly to make
an opening to tell me the most extravagant things anyone could
utter ; and this, as you know, is the scourge of small towns, I mean
those great *nouvellistes* who seek everywhere for channels whereby
to spread abroad the stories they pick up.

This one started by showing me two sheets of paper (*nouvelles à la
main*) filled to the very edges with a great jumble of rubbish, coming
—as he told me—from the most trustworthy source in the world.
. . . To listen to him one might imagine he knows the secrets of
the cabinet better than those who hold them. State policy lets him
see all its plans, and it cannot take a single step without his being
able to see through its intentions. He can tell us the hidden springs
of all that is going on, can discover the farseeing views of our neighbours, and moulds to his liking all European affairs. His sources
of information extend as far as Africa and Asia, and he is posted up
in everything that is agitating the High Council of Prester John and
the Great Mogul."

However, the news-sheets for abroad and for the provinces
were sent under sealed cover.

After he had reached the stage of having regular subscribers,
the *nouvelliste à la main* had in fact accomplished his task, whether
good or bad, serviceable or harmful, but one which was necessary
to society at the time, just as it would have been to-day if the

press did not exist. He had accomplished his task to the best of his ability, often in poverty, and always under the agonizing fear of a *lettre de cachet*. Just think of the terrible silhouette of the police official in his black felt hat and armed with his red *baton*, and the still more sinister appearance of the Bicêtre, " which made my limbs tremble and my teeth chatter," said the *nouvelliste* Fouilhoux. Sometimes he had introduced much talent, something of his real soul, into these fugitive leaves ; under disguised forms he—the unfortunate, the reprobate, and eternally outcast—had insinuated the sentiments of revolt rumbling within him, until the day came when he was to succeed in letting loose the anger of the people against that wealthy, brilliant and frivolous society, which, while despising him, had made him work for it, and while making use of him had suffered him to lead a proscribed life—that society which was to be finally overthrown, crushed beneath the ruins of that edifice the foundations of which he had sapped with his feverish hands.

His work had thus completed, more secretly but possibly more efficaciously, that of his first cousin, the *nouvelliste* who proclaimed his news in the public gardens. These two sections were the organs of public opinion at a time when, in the words of Mercier de la Rivière, public opinion was " the queen of the world."

" In other countries," writes the Comte de Ségur, " people did not confine themselves to bending under the yoke of ministerial despotism ; not only did they grovel in servitude but they preserved a shameful silence. In France, on the contrary, it was never possible to chain up our minds. . . . "

BIBLIOGRAPHY

Aubertin (Ch.), *L'esprit public au dix-huitième siècle*, 1873.—Babeau (Albert), *La publicité à Troyes il y a cent ans*, 1882.—Babeau (Albert), *Les préambules des Ordonnances royales et l'Opinion publique*, 1896.—Besenval (Baron de), *Mémoires*, 1805, 3 vols.—Boissier (Gaston), *Madame de Sévigné*, 5th ed., 1901.—Donneau de Vizé, in *Le Mercure Galant*, 1672.—Du Camp d'Orgas, *Réflexions sur les nouvellistes*, 1690.—Fr. F. B. et Paul d'Estrée, *Les Nouvellistes*, 1905.—Fr. F. B. et Paul d'Estrée, *Figaro et ses devanciers*, 1909.—(Gallais), *Extrait d'un dictionnaire inutile*, 1790.—*La Gazette de France*.—La Bruyère, *Caractères*, various eds.—Mercier (Sébastien), *Tableau de Paris*, 1781, 2 vols.—*Le Mercure*.—Molière, *Les Précieuses ridicules, la Comtesse d'Escarbagnas*, various eds.—Montesquieu, *Lettres persanes*, various eds.—Ségur (Comte de), *Mémoires*, illust. ed., librairie Fayard, collection of *Mémoires illustrés*.—Sénac de Meilhan, *Le Gouvernement, les Mœurs et les Conditions en France avant la Révolution*, ed. Lescure, 1862.—Sévigné (Marquise de), *Correspondance*, various eds.—Tocqueville (Alexis de), *l'Ancien Régime et la Révolution*, 1866.

CHAPTER XI

FRANCHISES AND LIBERTIES

I. The Royal Authority assured Liberty.—II. Social Hierarchies.—III. The Independence of the Provinces.—IV. The Independence of the Parliaments.—V. *Ordres Arbitraires.*—VI. Servitude.—VII. The Work accomplished by the Revolution.

I.—*The Royal Authority assured Liberty*

AS a heading to his *Considérations sur le Gouvernement*, written in the year 1737, the Marquis d'Argenson placed this epigraph : " Liberty is the support of the Throne." In the person of the King our forefathers respected absolute power, and that, possibly, was because absolute and uncontested authority alone assured them liberty. Sénac de Meilhan did not think he was formulating a paradox when he wrote : " The nation owed to its sovereigns the liberty it enjoyed." It is the same view as that of the Councillor of the Besançon Parliament quoted by Gallais in his charming *Dictionnaire Inutile* (1790) : " I maintain that liberty in perfection, its real goal, and final resting place, is authority fixed in the hands of a chief, like that of a ship in the pilot's helm." Foreigners made no mistake about that. Dallington went so far as to define France under the government of its Princes as " a vast democracy."

" Order renders liberty legitimate," to quote d'Argenson again. Now to maintain this order giving freedom to liberty there existed only the authority of the King.

In France the King's authority was, in itself, order. It represented justice. " Liberty," observes Ségur, " is at bottom only justice "—a deep saying and admirably true. Order, liberty, sovereign authority, and justice thus issued from a common source, blending together in their course. For if we imagine for a moment the King's authority restricted, France would have fallen back into anarchy destructive of all liberty.

It is always necessary to go back to the origins of these institutions in order to understand their character at the period we are considering. M. Dognon describes France of the thirteenth century as "a collectivity of *seigneuries* in the hands of private individuals who escaped the direct control of the Kings." The *bonnes villes* (towns possessing feudal rights) were *seigneuries* in themselves, and these conditions had hardly changed in the sixteenth century. The following lines by Montaigne were quoted on a former page:

"There is nothing more royal than the suite, the subjects, the officers, the occupations, the attendance and ceremony of a seigneur living in his own home among his serving-men; he hears mention of his master (the King) once a year, just as he might of the King of Persia, and only recognizes him on account of some old distant cousinship which his secretary keeps in his register. In truth our laws are fairly liberal, and the weight of sovereignty barely touches a French gentleman twice in his life. Essential and effective subjection is of no concern to us except for those who care to obtain honour and riches for themselves by such service; for the man who likes to sit crouched by his own hearth and knows how to rule his house without disputes and lawsuits is as free as the Duke of Venice."

The local liberties enjoyed by France of old have remained justly celebrated. She was bristling with liberties. They swarmed innumerable, active, varying, tangled, and often overlapping each other in a moving confused mass. Each was inspired by special powers, and these too were of infinite variety—active but ill-defined local authorities in countless numbers, often encroaching on and thwarting each other. "However," in the words of De Tocqueville, "it ended in the establishment of some regular order which worked fairly smoothly."

"Each village in France is a capital," said Richelieu, and the Parliament of Provence declared that "Among us each community is self-governing, making its own laws, and guarding its own interests." There was no provincial Parliament which could not have said the same thing about itself.

We have seen on a former page how each parish constituted an autonomous group. Whence came all these liberties? They came from that source from which everything issued: "Local liberties are nothing but the ordering of families organized into societies" (Ch. de Ribbe).

Jean Jacques Rousseau, who was anything but a "vile tool of despotism," was brought to acknowledge the fact: "The King is obeyed without soldiers and without threats." He compares monarchical government in France to a "tyranny" to which, in his own words, he was entirely opposed. And this was also the conclusion of that Jacobin, Retif de la Bretonne.

II.—*Social Hierarchies*

These liberties were further strengthened by what modern historians have called the " social hierarchies." Montesquieu and Saint-Just regarded them as the ramparts of liberty, and to these we must add those other protecting strands of the fabric spoken of by Montesquieu as forming *corps intermédiaires*, namely, the nobility, the clergy, the magistracy, and the different district Assemblies. The royal authority found both a support and a limitation in the hierarchy of the different classes, each armed with its privileges, and these offered to its arbitrary exercise a " more effective resistance than that afforded by the laws," as Ségur remarked.

Men of most discerning vision, like Governor Morris during the Revolution, and subsequently De Tocqueville, have defined in a succinct manner the part played by these different authorities in maintaining the liberties of the public. On the 13th July, 1789, the American Ambassador (Morris) was dining with La Fayette :

" We conversed on politics, and I adjured him (La Fayette) to preserve, if possible, some constitutional authority in the hands of the nobility as the sole means of preserving some liberty to the people."

This again is something we have much difficulty in understanding to-day, when we live under the care of the Administration, which, like the royal authority in the France of old, is the chief preserver of liberty—but holding us in leash with far more stringent and numerous bonds. The Kings of old left their subjects to govern themselves under the shelter of their sovereign authority ; they left them to govern themselves through the agency of numerous jurisdictions, which, as far as the general balance was concerned, acted mutually as counterpoises—" the system of counterpoise favoured during the past two centuries," as Albert Babeau notes. Nothing is more true : that constituted government.

" The division of authority," wrote Sénac de Meilhan, " provided an opposition to the abuse of authority in France ; the Parliaments embraced among their prerogatives the control of military power ; the Intendants watched over the use made of its powers by judicial authority, and checked its encroachments into their own . . . the result was a division of power and influence from which sprang a happy balance."

" People are too much inclined to think," says Albert Babeau again, " that there is no other liberty but political freedom, and that where the former is not guaranteed, there can be no other. There can, however, exist governments, absolute in theory, which allow to their subjects liberties not possessed by the citizens of a State calling itself free." And De Tocqueville states : " We should be very wrong in thinking that the Ancien Régime was an epoch of servility and dependence ; under its rule there was more liberty than we possess in our own times."

III.—*The Independence of the Provinces*

The social hierarchies were further strengthened by the independent condition of the provinces wherein they were set up. The majority of the provinces had the appearance of forming separate States. People commonly talked of the "*nation*" of Artois, the Picardy *nation*, the Normandy, Brittany, Franche-Comté or the Béarn *nation*. The Bretons used to declare that their province was quite their own ; they had a Breton constitution, and if they were French, it was only because the King was Duke of Brittany. The Normans too only regarded themselves as French because the King was Duke of Normandy, and there was also a Norman constitution. Provence and Dauphiné had their constitutions, and it was only a happy coincidence that the King was Comte de Provence and Dauphin of the Province of Vienne. The Boulonnais had their own constitution, and their own army distinct from the King's, composed of " soldiers belonging to the province," commanded by " nobles of the province," charged with the duty of " guarding the province." In fact they formed a State.

Provence boldly proclaimed itself an " *Etat Principal* " united to, but not under the Crown ; Béarn and Artois did likewise. There existed "*provinces françaises*" and provinces "*réputées étrangères*," such as Brittany, Angoumois, Périgord, Auvergne, Languedoc, Guyenne, Provence, Dauphiné, Flanders, Artois, and Franche-Comté ; and those provinces called "*l'étranger effectif*" were Lorraine, Alsace and Roussillon. Dunkerque and Gravelines were administered under what was called the custom of Bruges, inherited from the old *communes* of Flanders.

These different provinces were not united together ; they were only in juxtaposition. "France," said M. Sagnac, "was an unorganized aggregation of separate peoples," and in these provinces separated by economic barriers, " the towns and villages," said Turgot, " had no relationship with each other any more than the departmental districts to which they were assigned ; they could not even come to an understanding with a view to taking in hand the public works which they required."

Even in the same province the diversity of customs, laws of succession, weights and measures, were almost inconceivable.

The same measure, the "*boisseau*," [1] for instance, would vary in quantity from town to town and even between neighbouring villages of the same province, as stated by Vauban. In 1787 the Provincial Assembly of Alsace stated that its constitution "is difficult to understand by reason of the labyrinth of local rights and usages."

When Henri IV took in hand the draining of the marshlands the provinces withstood the operations that had been undertaken. Sully encountered the same obstacles in making the Languedoc canal, and Louis XIV and Colbert were reduced to the necessity of appealing to the personal influence of Richet.

In 1621 Louis XIII and Richelieu planned the setting up of certain customs on merchandise on the Spanish frontier ; there was an immediate protest from Languedoc before which the King and his Ministers had to bow, and by declaration made at Cognac, in 1622, Louis XIII had to allow to the people of Languedoc the free exchange of their merchandise with Spain, but he set up customs offices where Languedoc bordered on Auvergne. "When my subjects of Languedoc," said the King, "shall authorize me to place customs officers on the Spanish frontier, I will withdraw those I am compelled to place within the Kingdom." We can well understand that Louis XIII, so truly French at heart, had a horror of these provincial privileges. "He fell into a rage," said Boulainvilliers, "as soon as he heard the word mentioned." Provence agreed to having "*bureaux de traites*" (customs offices) on the frontier, but also wished to establish them on her French borders so as to form economically a separate State. As regards Burgundy, Dauphiné, Aunis, Guyenne, Brittany and Maine, some of these provinces decided to have customs on the foreign border, and some on the French side. As late as 1789, when drawing up a report, Lorraine declared that the establishment of customs on her frontiers would be a disaster ; she meant to remain a "*province étrangère*." Alsace too resisted the withdrawal of her barriers, and at the beginning of the Revolution declared her determination to remain a "*province étrangère effective*." Marseilles was a free city, holding herself aloof both from the Kingdom and even from Provence. She was a separate State, like Bayonne and Dunkerque. In 1788 the Parliament of Pau declared that the Béarnais occupied a country "*étranger à la France, indépendant et souverain*."

In each of these provinces the inhabitants had the right to be governed by men of their own district and to be judged in their own province by the local law officers. The same held good in

[1] *Boisseau :* a former measure of capacity in France of about 13 *litres*, for grain, etc. (H. W.)

Artois, Burgundy and Languedoc. They were not provinces *of* the Kingdom, but provinces *in* the Kingdom. Speaking of these districts, and of Guyenne, Imbart de la Tour wrote: "their autonomy was complete," and each of them "formed a ring-fence round their public liberties."

The Dombes district constituted an independent principality, as well as the principalities of Sedan and of Orange, at least down to 1714. The Prince Bishops of the House of Lorraine handed down to each other the suzerainty of Verdun. Here and there, even as late as the seventeenth century, there existed *franc-alleus*,[1] such as the *seigneurie* of Henrichemont, and the famous "*royaume*" of Yvetot.

People spoke of the legislative power resting in the hands of the French Kings. On what a strange soil was it exercised! It makes one think of a bed of thorns over which one would have to spread a white cloth before sitting down to regale oneself there.

At the beginning of the war with England, Richelieu thought it would be wise to have ships built in the port of Saint-Malo; but these fine gentlemen of Saint-Malo asserted that such a proceeding was contrary to their franchises, and the imperious Minister had to expend much ink and eloquence in persuading the citizens to yield to the general interest, with a promise of adding still further to these same franchises of which he had had to complain!

France was divided up into 364 different legislatures. How often had attempts been made to introduce a little more uniformity! D'Aguesseau imagined he would be able to work usefully in this direction, and made a start with the Norman institutions in which he proposed a few modifications. What a storm arose in the Rouen Parliament! He had to run to earth!

Everywhere the same spirit of independence existed, even in the most remote corners of society.

"The Savoyards in Paris," wrote Mercier, "are chimney-sweeps, and errand-runners, and form a kind of confederation possessing their own laws. The elders have the right to exercise *surveillance* over the young, and can punish those who go astray. They have been known to mete out justice on one of their number convicted of theft; they instituted their own prosecution and then hanged him."

Can we imagine the chimney-sweeps in Paris to-day setting up their own tribunal, condemning one of their number to death, and erecting a guillotine to cut his head off?

[1] *Francs-alleus :* hereditary properties exempt from any equivalent service, unlike the fiefs the tenure of which was held on certain compulsory services. (H. W.)

Voltaire, in order to show the diversity, the picturesque and chaotic complication of these innumerable forms of authority, the inextricable entanglements of which formed the constitution of the Kingdom, made as they were at haphazard and with no order, described them with his witty pen as follows :

"See how the quarter of the Halles in Paris, of Saint-Pierre-aux-Bœufs, the Rue Brise-Miche, and the Rue Pet-au-Diable, contrast with the Louvre and the Tuileries : therein we have the image of our laws."

IV.—*The Independence of the Parliaments*

In his Edict of 1770, Louis XV expressed himself as follows : "Our Parliaments exalt their authority to the same level as our own and even above it, since they reduce our legislative power to a simple faculty of proposing our wishes to them, while reserving to themselves the right to hinder their execution."

The Parliaments were neither related to, nor in subordination to each other. The Paris Parliament would accept an Edict which that of Toulouse would refuse, and of which Rouen, while adopting it, would modify the application. La Roche-Flavin said that he had seen more than eighty Edicts, accepted by the Paris Parliament, which had been rejected by the Parliament of Toulouse notwithstanding the royal *lettres de jussions* (royal orders to register them). "The Parliament of Paris having ordered by decree that the Jesuits shall quit France . . . we (at Toulouse) prohibit the carrying out of the said decree . . . thereby maintaining the Jesuits in the whole of our province of Languedoc and in the portion of Guyenne within our jurisdiction."

The Government had to transmit to the Parliament concerned the nominations it made to the majority of the public offices ; and more than once we find these Assemblies refusing to register them, in other words, cancelling the King's appointments.

Treaties concluded by the monarch with foreign powers had to be submitted to them, and it sometimes happened that the Parliaments refused their ratification.

With a view to bending this independent magistracy, whose resistance nullified their authority, the Kings could have recourse to the *lits de justice* by means of which they had the power to compel a Parliament to register a given edict ; but this procedure entailed ceremonies of a complicated nature, and it was only possible to have recourse to it on rare occasions, all the more so because this method of constraint, cumbersome as it was, often proved illusory. After liberty to have their say had been restored to them, the Councillors would think out fresh methods of resistance ; in the administration of justice they would put on one side the law which they had registered against their wish, or else they would all send in their resignations, in the certainty that they could not be accepted ; in the last resort they would suspend the administration of justice, a procedure which would introduce the greatest disorder within the limits of their jurisdiction.

On other occasions the Kings would resort to sending *lettres de jussion* in order to ensure the registration of their edicts ; but to these the various legislative bodies would reply by renewing their refusal to approve the royal edict, whereat the King would despatch further *lettres de jussion*, to be again met with a further refusal ; the months would pass to years ; the King would be taken up with other matters, and the last word remained with the Parliaments.

It is well known that in the reign of Louis XIV Parliament caused the withdrawal of the Edict establishing the Inquisition in France. Even in matters which would seem to be the exclusive prerogative of royal authority the Parliaments did not fail to intervene and to speak in the tone of a master. On more than one occasion we find the Paris Parliament refusing to register the creation of fresh Dukes and Peers without giving any other reason than " the fear of rendering this dignity too common."

In the event of any Parliament at last feeling that it was incumbent upon it to give way by registering an edict of which it did not approve, mention of this fact was made in the register, wherein it was stated by way of protest that the order had only been transcribed by the express will of the King, " which was an indication," according to Guy Coquille, " that the Court had not found the Edict to be reasonable." Furthermore, *remontrances* (formal protests) were sent in each year to the King asking him to revoke his edict. What force could the edict retain, more especially as each Parliament, by issuing instructions regulating its application, so arranged that it became in point of fact of no effect within their jurisdiction ?

As the Chancelier de l'Hospital reminds the Rouen Exchequer :

" You bend the regulations just as you please, as if they were made of wax. And worse still, you assert that you are above them, and are not bound thereby if they do not please you . . . you say you are supreme."

" If we were to examine the mass of regulations, declarations, and other decisions issued by the King," notes M. d'Avenel, " and see how they had been changed in practice, we should discover that the Parliaments were in the habit of amending, abrogating and interpreting them to their liking, without any interference from the central power."

The reports drawn up in 1789 by the Third Estate of Nemours, present all the facts in a happy nutshell :

"The King would propose laws ; they would be rejected by the Parliament. He would hold a *lit de justice* ; sometimes this ceremony would end the matter ; sometimes too the Parliaments would protest again ; in that case anyone could obey who wished. Some provinces would submit ; others would refuse ; they were in fact left to do as they liked. No one as yet had conceived the idea that there was only one State, one King, and one country, and that everything should be subordinated to their interest ; or if anybody did venture to suggest this he was at once considered to be a dreamer or a philosopher."

Here we have the language of the men of the Revolution.

What modern government would put up with these *remontrances*, even in a mitigated form, which the Parliaments and the different supreme courts, as well as the Assemblies of the Clergy and all the great bodies of the State, were in the habit of addressing to the King under the most varying circumstances—protests which were cleverly drawn up, sometimes insinuating, sometimes violent : going so far as to refer to the Royal Government, as in the case of the Parliament of Franche-Comté, as "an administration odious at any time, and now fallen into universal discredit." These *remontrances*, now collected and tabulated in a series of volumes, were printed and circulated by the thousand. Renewed on every pretext and on every occasion, they were drawn up with pomp and display and then repeated in a thousand echoes of protest emanating from the constitutional bodies who presided over the judicial and financial administration of the country.

V.—" *Ordres Arbitraires* "

" I have proved," wrote Sénac de Meilhan in the concluding words of his *Considérations sur le Gouvernement*, " that far from being oppressive the Government was moderate and weak." Napoleon said : " The permanent weakness of the Government, even under Louis XIV, under Louis XV and Louis XVI, should inspire the need to uphold the work newly accomplished, and to maintain the preponderance now acquired by the central power." And Chancellor Pasquier : " Apart from a few persons whose actions were a source of special irritation to the Government, the remainder of the citizens, in point of fact, enjoyed the most complete liberty. They could speak, write, and act with the greatest independence ; they could even brave authority with impunity."

People will point to the existence of "*ordres arbitraires*," by which is meant *lettres de cachet* dealt with on an earlier page. These were divided into three categories :

1. Family *lettres de cachet*, in which the King's Government had no personal interest in any way, and which were so firmly anchored in the sentiments of the time that even the municipalities issued them.

2. *Lettres de cachet* issued by the Police, which were like the warrants to arrest, issued by our judges of to-day.

3. *Lettres de cachet* issued in connection with State matters in which the Government did have a direct interest ; but these were very rare, only two or three out of every thousand issued ; and in those cases where they were enforced, the regular tribunals more often than not—notably in the famous Latude [1] case—would have acted far more severely than the King. In this connection the following statement will possibly appear conclusive : in the space of three years the Revolution issued more *lettres de cachet* for State affairs—the great majority of which had tragic consequences—than the Royal Government had issued during eight centuries.

Furthermore—and we have already given an indication of our view—the royal authority, by reason of its very existence, was the essential condition of liberty in France, and the *lettre de cachet* was the sole means possessed by the King to exert this authority. Thanks to this latent power, which existed in every place without necessarily manifesting itself in tangible acts, the thousands of local authorities were maintained in equilibrium, and, in the fear of abusing their power, were preserved from that anarchy with which their disputes and entanglements threatened them. We therefore come to this conclusion—certainly a most unexpected one—that the *lettres de cachet* formed the framework of liberty in France of old. This idea, to all appearance so paradoxical, has already been ventilated by us, and has been violently combated. We think it is our duty to stand by it.

VI.—*Servitude*

At the close of the Ancien Régime a great number of Frenchmen were seized with an irresistible *anglo-mania*. Horse-racing—which had been imported from England—was becoming the fashion in France and may possibly have contributed to this. Everything became English, from the public gardens to philosophy, sociology,

---

[1] *Latude* (1725–1805) : an adventurer who, on account of disputes with Mme. de Pompadour, was imprisoned successively in the Bastille, Vincennes, Châtelet and Charenton, and was kept a prisoner for thirty-five years. (H. W.)

and politics. Voltaire, Montesquieu and Sébastien Mercier got quite out of breath with it all, just like a runner hastening up a hill in order to see the sun rise. And of all the marvellous products of England the most marvellous was that of liberty, from which, after more than a century, we have hardly recovered.

A few less positive minds who saw facts in their reality showed less enthusiasm. Retif de la Bretonne, the Jacobin, had the courage during the Reign of Terror to remind people in his *Nuits de Paris* how frail were these English liberties in comparison with the real liberty enjoyed in Paris under the Government of their Kings. At the time when Frenchmen, taken with the idea of free air under the beautiful blue sky, were celebrating the freedom enjoyed by England, servitude still existed among our neighbours across the Channel, and in quite another form than in our good old land of France. Hewers of coal and workers in salt mines were still serfs, bound to their toil throughout their lives, and were not finally made free till June, 1799. The Scottish writer, Robert Chambers, speaks of an old Lancashire miner, still living in 1820, who had been exchanged by his master for a pony. Hugh Miller mentions villages he visited in 1834 where the women working in the mines still bore the marks on their bodies of the servitude to which they had been bound. Archibald Geikie, too, in his *Scottish Reminiscences* published in 1904, talks of serfs working at the bottom of the mines, whom he had known in his childhood.

In France the last remnants of serfdom had disappeared before the Revolution, save in a few districts in Alsace and Franche-Comté, which remained " *provinces étrangères,*" and were not truly in a condition of serfdom but of " *colonat,*" [1] which entailed the sole obligation of living on cultivated land. In 1778 Louis XVI abolished the last traces of servitude on the royal domains, and the few seigneurs on whose lands it still existed were not long in following his example. The last French serfs were enfranchised in 1789. These had been subject to the Abbey of Saint-Claude in the Jura. M. Pierre Laborderie, who had made a study of their history, asks himself this question : how did it happen that the last serfs to be enfranchised belonged to ecclesiastical lands ? It was because, he says, those still subject to mortmain on ecclesiastical lands showed themselves little disposed to shake off the yoke.

" Their legal status was already of a higher order and the clergy understood how to make their material conditions more favourable than anywhere else. Well acquainted with the difficulties and uncer-

---

[1] *Colonat :* a *colon* was an independent farmer living on the land of his seigneur, not subject to seigneurial dues. (H. W.)

tainties of agricultural toil, which formed one of the largest sources
of its revenues, the Church rendered a considerable rural population
secure against the general anxieties of mankind. In the peace surrounding them these people felt less desire of changing their special
conditions, and the idea of the deprivation of actual freedom being
a hindrance or a tyranny entered their minds far more slowly than
elsewhere."

VII.—*The Work accomplished by the Revolution*

The Revolution came upon the scenes, and the " patriots," as
we know, declared war against the " federalists," that is the partisans of the old local liberties and franchises. The Kings had
succumbed on several points in the struggle waged against these
liberties, since the days of Louis XIII and Richelieu ; the " patriots " guillotined, shot, and drowned people with such energy
that they ended in triumph.

In 1790, Mirabeau had pointed out to Louis XVI the value of
the work undertaken :

" Is it nothing gained to be without a Parliament, a country, clerical
corporations, privileged bodies and the nobility ? The idea of constituting one single class of citizens would have pleased Richelieu :
this levelled surface facilitates the exercise of authority. Several
reigns of absolute power would not have accomplished as much for
royal authority as this one year of revolution."

" That was to understand the Revolution as a man capable of
leading it," adds De Tocqueville.

As a conclusion to this chapter devoted to the liberties of ancient
France, we will quote from this same author the following page,
one of the finest and truest he ever wrote :

" We should be very careful not to appraise the debased condition
of men by the degree of their submission to the sovereign power.
However subservient to the King's will the men of the Ancien Régime
may have been, there was one kind of obedience to which they were
strangers ; they never knew what it meant to bend beneath any
unlawful or disputed power, one held in little honour, often despised,
but submitted to voluntarily because it could be useful or inimical.
To this degrading form of servitude they had always been strangers.
The King inspired in their minds sentiments which none of the very
despotic princes who have appeared since, have been able to arouse
—sentiments which have by now become well-nigh incomprehensible
to us, so radically has the Revolution extirpated them from our hearts.
They felt for him both the affection which a man has for his father,
and the respect due to God alone. In submitting to his most arbitrary
commands they yielded less to constraint than to love, and thus it
often happened that they were able to preserve complete freedom of

soul in the midst of the most extreme dependence. For them the greatest evil in obedience was constraint ; for us it is the least. The greatest evil resides in a servile sentiment which compels obedience. Let us not despise our forefathers, for we have no right to do so. Would to God we might recover, with all their prejudices and faults, a little of their greatness ! "

BIBLIOGRAPHY

Argenson (Marquis d'), *Considérations sur le gouvernement ancien et présent de la France*, 1767.—Avenel (Vicomte d'), *La Noblesse Française sous Richelieu*, 1901.—Babeau (Albert), *La Province sous l'Ancien Régime*, 1894, 2 vols.— Babeau (Albert), *La Ville sous l'Ancien Régime*, 1880.—Babeau (Albert), *Le Village sous l'Ancien Régime*, 1891.—Boiteau, *Etat de la France en 1789*, 2nd ed., 1889.—Boulainvilliers, *Etat de la France*, 1727, 3 vols.—Busquet (Raoul), *Histoire des institutions de la Provence*, 1920.—Champion (Edme), *La France d'après les cahiers de 1789*, 1889.—Esmein, *Cours d'histoire du droit français*, 3rd ed., 1898.—Esmein, *Gouverneur Morris*, 1906.—Funck-Brentano (Théophile), *Histoire du pays de France*, introduction to *Traité de l'économie politique d'A. de Montchrestien*, 1889.—(Gallais), *Extrait d'un dictionnaire inutile*, 1790 —Imbart de la Tour, *Les Origines de la Réforme*, 1905–1914, 3 vols.—Laborderie (Pierre), *Le Procès des serfs du Mont-Jura (1767–1777)*, in *Feuilles d'histoire*, 1st Aug., 1919.—Marion (Marcel), *Dictionnaire des institutions de la France aux dix-septième et dix-huitième siècles*, 1923.—Mathieu (Cardinal), *l'Ancien Régime en Lorraine*, 1879.—Montaigne, *Essais*, various eds.—Retif de la Bretonne, *Les Nuits révolutionnaires*, Fayard, in their collection of *Mémoires illustrés*.—Reuss (R.), *L'Alsace au dix-huitième siècle*, 1890, 2 vols. —Ch. de Ribbe, *La Famille et la Société en France avant la Révolution*, 1879, 2 vols.—Sénac de Meilhan, *Le Gouvernement, les mœurs et les conditions . . .*, ed. Lescure, 1862.—Tocqueville (Alexis de), *L'Ancien Régime et la Révolution*, 5th ed., 1866.—Vauban, *Projet d'une dixme royale*, 1707.—Voltaire, *Histoire du Parlement*, in *Œuvres*, various eds.

CHAPTER XII

THE REIGN OF LOUIS XVI

I. The Accession of Louis XVI.—II. The Progress Realized.—III. His Reforms.—IV. Conclusion.

I.—*The Accession of Louis XVI*

LOUIS XVI came to the throne on the 10th May, 1774, at the age of nineteen. The young King fully appreciated the responsibilities with which he was to be overwhelmed. A contemporary depicts him seated with his elbows resting on his knees and his hands over his eyes, repeating: "What a load! . . . at my age . . . and they have taught me nothing!"

Henry of Prussia, the brother of Frederick the Great, who saw Louis XVI at Versailles, has left us this sketch of him:

"The King surprised me : I had formed quite another idea of him. People had told me that his education had been neglected, that he knew nothing, and had little natural ability. I was astonished when talking to him to notice that he had a very good knowledge of history and geography, and that his ideas on politics were very accurate, that the welfare of his people occupied him entirely, and that he was full of good sense, which is worth more to a Prince than wit ; but he distrusted himself too much, though of all his Council it is he who should be the most often consulted."

That is a very true portrait.

But he was clumsy, and heavy in appearance, *brusque* and occasionally rough in his manner ; he was moreover short-sighted, which fact increased his awkwardness. People said, "You must close your eyes to do him justice." His lack of self-confidence made him shy and hesitating. Many repartees are quoted of his giving evidence of his clearness of mind and balance.

Louis XVI understood English and German. He had read *Clarendon's Memoirs* in the original, and was greatly struck by the account of the death of Charles I on the scaffold in Whitehall. It obsessed him, and he made a resolve never to do violence to the wishes of his subjects.

At the very outset of his reign he showed his great kindness of heart. He cut down the expenses of his Court in every possible way, to the extent of giving annoyance to his courtiers who got something out of a feast and its leavings. His first act as King, on the very day of his accession, was to send word to the Controller of Finance to distribute 200,000 *livres* among the poor in Paris. " If, in view of the needs of the State, you find this to be too much, you will deduct this from my State allowance. . . ."

Public opinion demanded the return of the Parliaments : they were immediately called together again—a first mistake. The triumvirate of Maupeou, Terray and d'Aiguillon, was dismissed— mistake number two. They were men of energy and action, and the men required at the moment. Louis XVI chose Turgot, nominated by public opinion ; shortly afterwards he chose Males- herbes, likewise put forward by public opinion. They were men of great intelligence, uprightness, and imbued with new ideas, but the reforms they endeavoured to introduce, conformable to the needs of a society in process of transformation, were not under- stood by the general public, nor even by the higher ranks, such as the Parliaments ; and they wounded the interests of the privi- leged classes. By proclaiming the free circulation of cereals Turgot let loose a storm of protests, and aroused public disturbances. He was perhaps the most liberal-minded of all the Ministers of the Ancien Régime, and yet it was he who signed the most *lettres de cachet* in proportion to the length of his administration. In deference to public opinion, Louis XVI engaged France in the war for American Independence. The heavy liabilities resulting there- from increased the embarrassments of the Treasury, and these embarrassments opened a breach for the Revolution.

Cardinal Mathieu gave expression to the following luminous views on the Government of Louis XVI :

" It was necessary to satisfy public opinion, which demanded reforms, and to find money to fill up the deficit. How were they to obtain these two results at one and the same time ? The great reforms were costing at first more money than they brought in. . . . Ministers endeavoured to solve the two parts of the problem together, the one by the other, and to procure money by means of reforms . . . ; but the same decree, while abolishing a privilege, increased a tax. The public were less charmed by the useful measure than they were irritated by the odious one, and joined hands with the privileged classes who had been despoiled in attacking the Ministry, and in cases where these holders of privileges were members of Parliament, the latter became popular, because by resisting, or refusing to register the edicts, they coloured their own personal spite with a seeming love for the general welfare. . . ."

II.—*The Progress realized*

A very potent movement was bearing France on to new destinies. It started at about the middle of the eighteenth century and had developed its greatest proportions at the period corresponding to the accession of Louis XVI.

Foreign historians, such as Wahl, the German, and Ardascheff, the Russian, who approached their study of these last years of the Ancien Régime without any preconceived notions due to French influence, both arrived at the same conclusions. At the end of his account of the prosperity which spread over France from the end of the reign of Louis XV down to the Revolution, Ardascheff wrote :

"The present chapter was written before M. Wahl's work had appeared ; now the investigations we have made independently of each other, and from different sources, have led us both to practically the same conclusions, and both of them are equally at variance with the prevalent ideas on the subject."

M. Wahl concluded his book as follows :

"Without any doubt we are in presence of a period of tremendous progress (*in der Zeit eines gewaltigen Aufschwungs*), manifested chiefly in the towns, but in many points likewise visible in the country districts. This expansion, already noticeable at the end of the reign of Louis XV, is being continued under his successor, and in many places the rise is very rapid."

"Progress in agriculture," wrote E. Levasseur, "appears to be one of the characteristic features of the general economic conditions in France during the second half of the eighteenth century." The labours of numerous agricultural societies, the example given by the great scientific agriculturists, among whom shone the names of the highest nobility, and the encouragement afforded by the Government, had borne fruit. Cultivation still followed the old triennial rotation, the land being left fallow every third year. The agricultural societies recommended : "Vary your crops, sow your fallow land with clover, vetch, peas, broad-beans, turnips, carrots and maize . . ." and their advice was followed.

The Intendants provided the peasants with seed for their sowing ; they organized committees of growers which met every week at the Sub-delegate's house to discuss the best measures to be taken, and medals were awarded to the most meritorious growers. The extension of the system of growing foodstuffs for cattle enabled them to utilize unprofitable barren land to the great benefit of their stock. Prosperity increased rapidly. A Curé in Maine wrote in 1783 : " To-day the women servants are better dressed than the daughters of the family were twenty years ago." Doctor Rigby, who visited France in the summer of 1789, at the very time that the Bastille was stormed, utters repeated exclamations at the prevailing prosperity, as he went through France from Normandy to Burgundy :

" We have journeyed from five to six hundred miles and have hardly seen a single uncultivated acre, with the exception of the forests of Chantilly and Fontainebleau ; practically every inch of ground has been ploughed, and seems at this moment to be loaded with crops."

When in the neighbourhood of Lyons he exclaimed : " What a country ! What fertile soil, what industrious people ! " Throughout the length of the Rhône valley, even in fissures of the rocks, the land was made use of, thanks to manures. Fresh exclamations are called forth when approaching Toulon. On leaving France, Rigby passed through the district of Cleves and finally arrived in Holland. " How greatly do the districts and populations we have seen since leaving France lose by comparison with that land so full of life ! "

The progress realized in industry during this same period was possibly greater than that in agriculture. Notwithstanding the frequent opposition of guilds and masters fresh methods were being introduced, tools were improved, and steam engines were imported from England. The weaving of stuffs spread among the villages. There was a general rise in prices, testifying to the influx of money, " a certain sign," in the words of Arthur Young, " that money had considerably increased in bulk through the undoubted expansion of the industry of the country." Inflation of artificial values was then still unknown.

Those were incredible times ; the price of wheat became lower, while wages rose.

In his *Recherches sur le prix du Blé*, Messance states : " Every educated person agrees that trade has achieved surprising progress during the past forty years, that the factories in the Kingdom are at the present time much more fully occupied than ever before, and that, in spite of the progress made in the old workshops and factories, a large number of new ones have been introduced." He goes on to say, " The price of wheat has diminished, but the wages paid are on a constantly increasing scale, as well as the rents and the population."

" The progress realized in manufactures has considerably increased the cultivation of basic products, such as flax, hemp, colza, swedes, woad, reseda, saffron, mulberries. . . ."

The figures of our foreign trade had doubled since the Seven Years War (1763), and quadrupled since the death of Louis XIV. Even our maritime trade, as acknowledged by the English, had developed in a greater degree in France than in England. Our ports of Bordeaux, Dieppe, Havre, La Rochelle, etc., had increased in size. When speaking of the work in progress for improving the port of Cherbourg, Arthur Young described it as " prodigious."

Rivers and streams were rendered navigable, and a huge system, combining with the admirable net-work of roads constructed by the Intendants, realized a gigantic accomplishment, which, even at the present day, contributes to our prosperity, in regard to which we still continue to display the most serene and the most human ingratitude. It has been calculated that between the years 1737 and 1787 France was presented with between forty to fifty thousand kilometres of new roads, more than half of which were constructed in the latter five-and-twenty years.

" One sees our industry greatly thriving," writes Sénac de Meilhan, "and trade daily growing more flourishing. The ports of Nantes, Marseilles, Bordeaux, and Rouen are full of ships ; the Atlantic Ocean is joined to the Mediterranean and the treasures of the two worlds flow into every province of the Kingdom ; the city of Lyons, the centre of our national industries, subjects three-quarters of the world to our modes, and in the smallest towns the appearance of more convenient and more tasteful houses attests to the prosperity of the lowest classes of society."

Necker said one could reckon that the revenue from excise was increasing by two millions a year.

Add to all this the indisputable superiority we had by then acquired in the domain of literature, science and art. Lavoisier, Guyton-Morveau, Berthollet, Monge, Laplace, Lagrange, Dauben-ton, Lamarck, Jussieu—was there ever seen in any nation or at any period such a cluster of luminous minds ? Long before the labours of Fulton,[1] Jouffroy-d'Abbans' steam paddle boat was navigating the Doubs (1776) ; the brothers Montgolfier invented the balloon (1783), and Philippe Lebon discovered gas for lighting purposes (1786). The world was set on new roads. That was the period when the greatest French sculptors, Houdon, and the charming Clodion, rendered themselves illustrious ; Fragonard with enchanting grace was covering his canvases with warmer tints than those of the Venetians ; Hubert Robert was making

[1] *Fulton :* the American engineer who first applied steam to propel ships (1763–1815). (H. W.)

old monuments live again with his fantastic art, while Vien and Louis David, returning to the ancient methods, were re-discovering possibilities that had been long neglected.

Industrial arts arrived at a perfection never before attained, and doubtless never again to be reached. The Louis XVI furniture —the pearls of our collections—and the silks of the same period woven from the designs of men like Philippe de la Salle, Berjon, Ranson, and Bony, were incomparable marvels. The Berlin Academy did not dispute the superiority of the French language ; it endeavoured to discover reasons for this fact. People spoke of a French Europe. Baron de Trenck, celebrated for his marvellous escapes from captivity, emphasized the jealousy inspired by our country in the minds of the whole of Europe.

Gribeauval made our artillery the foremost of the time ; our infantry was unrivalled for its accuracy in aiming, and the rise of our navy seemed like a miracle. " In 1776 we did not possess thirty ships in good condition," wrote Kerguélen, " and in 1779 we had balanced the naval forces of England." The Bailli de Suffren triumphed over the English fleets wherever he was able to meet them ; the victory of the *Belle Poule*—a charming name and so French—over the English ship *Arethusa* (17th July, 1778), made every heart beat. The Treaty of 1783 gave us Tobago in the Antilles, installed us in Canada, re-established us in India, and freed the port of Dunkerque from the bonds in which English jealousy had enslaved it. The Treaty of 1763 was blotted out.

The progress effected in public education had been marked, as stated in the report on his district drawn up by Dupont de Nemours in 1789.

The reign of Louis XVI was one of the greatest epochs in our history, a glorious twilight to the setting sun of old France.

III.—*His Reforms*

Reforms both rapid and energetic, and vibrating with goodwill, were instituted in every direction. Turgot decreed free trade in cereals (15th September, 1774) ; he suppressed forced labour (*corvée*) on the high-roads, and in connection with military convoys (February, 1776) ; and at the same time abolished the outworn system of trade corporations and their masters. The royal edict ran : " The right to work is the most sacred of all individual possessions, and any law in restraint of this violates a natural right." The purchase of grades in the army was abrogated ; the Protestants acquired all the rights of French citizens ; the

Jews were set free of the tolls to which they had been subject (January, 1784).

Freedom in matters of religion was proclaimed in November, 1787.

" Our sense of justice," said Louis XVI, " does not allow us to exclude any longer from civil rights those of our subjects, or foreigners domiciled within our Empire, who do not profess the Catholic religion. . . . The regulations have gone so far as to suppose that there were no longer any but Catholics within our States . . . principles which are hurtful to the tranquillity of our Realm and would have aroused continual family conflicts if we had not utilized the legal assistance of our tribunals to warn off greedy collaterals who were disputing with the children the inheritance of their father. The natural law does not permit the refusal to non-Catholics of the right to establish their births, marriages and deaths with a view to enjoying the resulting civil rights in common with all our other subjects."

As might be expected Parliament opposed this.

Louis XVI insisted : " My will is that my Parliament shall proceed to the registering of this edict *without delay*," wrote the King to the Chief President. " You will account to me on Wednesday."

Torture was abolished in judicial proceedings on the 1st May, 1788, in spite of the opposition from these same Parliaments. The abolition of *lettres de cachet* was taken in hand by Malesherbes, and achieved by Breteuil in 1784. The former had directed an investigation of the reasons which had caused prisoners to be incarcerated by *lettres de cachet*, and determined the duration and circumstances of their detention. All who had established just claims to be set at liberty were released without delay. As we saw on a former page only two such claims were established. The donjon of Vincennes, a State prison, was closed, and the demolition of the Bastille was officially decided upon.

The King brought it about that the secrecy of letters entrusted to the post should be respected in the most absolute manner, even by the officers of justice—a reform which later on the men of the Revolution did not feel bound to uphold. The Government forbade the burial of private individuals under the flagstones of the churches, and decided that the cemeteries should be removed outside the limits of inhabited areas (March, 1776) ; it established the Mont-de-Piété (official pawn offices) at a most moderate rate of interest (3 per cent.) in December, 1777 ; mortmain was suppressed in April, 1779.

In 1787, through the institution of Provincial Assemblies, the King's Government sought to realize self-administration by the country itself—a liberal and enlightened conception which might have borne fruit. Each province was placed under the administration of a local assembly which was to exercise its authority through a kind of executive directorate composed of a few members—generally three—who were called the " executive commission." Needless to say the Parliaments declared implacable war on this new creation. The Dauphiné Parliament squarely forbade the assembly to meet ; its opposition was insurmountable, as well as that of the Parliaments of Bordeaux and Besançon. The Parliament of Rouen fined the village syndics who carried out the instructions of the Assembly, and coldly reproached the members of the executive commission for obeying the King's decrees rather than their own.

The idea of this institution goes back to that amazing Marquis de Mirabeau who clamoured for it in 1730 in a pamphlet which was reprinted in 1758, and made a great stir at the time. A first attempt was made between the years 1778 and 1781, but the hostility of the Parliaments and the diatribes of the press had clipped its wings. We now see it realized in 1787.

In these measures we see the justification of the opinion we expressed at the beginning of this book, an opinion which other historians (notably Semichon, in his studies on the reign of Louis XVI) had already expressed before us, namely, that Louis XVI created a new era, differing far more from the periods that had preceded him, than from those which came after.

" If these reforms had been continued," says Semichon, " they would have completely realized a peaceful revolution in the constitution of France."

Mistakes, the result of inexperience, were certainly committed. The Provincial Assemblies, with their administration by " executive commissions," engendered some confusion. In the long run everything would have been put into shape by practical experience, but the Parliaments, with their immense authority, systematically, blindly, and obstinately thwarted everything, and in this they were noisily seconded by the press, then unfolding its wings. Here we see plainly the work of the *nouvellistes* and pamphleteers of whom we have spoken.

IV.—*Conclusion*

The transforming movement which took possession of France from the middle of the eighteenth century and became accentuated in 1774, was not only concerned with forms of administration and different branches of national activity ; it had to do with the people themselves and all classes of the nation. The population was increasing rapidly. Arthur Young was astonished; it was active, energetic and industrious, and another Englishman, Doctor Rigby, was no less surprised at it. That vigorous and magnificent French nation was developing which was to give birth to the Revolution—a nation whose volunteer formations, commanded by officers trained under the Ancien Régime, equipped with unrivalled armament and having the advantage of original methods of warfare, were to be victorious over the armies of Europe. To incorporate the ideas of the Duc de la Rochefoucauld-Liancourt in the Declaration of the Rights of Man even with the addition of the storming of the Bastille, the burning down of a few dozen châteaux, and the massacre of a certain number of aristocrats, was not enough, we imagine, to cause a nation like the French of 1792 to spring from the ground, armed head to foot, like a Minerva issuing from the head of Jove : those Frenchmen were formed on the sound and vigorous principles of the eighteenth century.

To the above we must add the social transformation that took place. The basis of former society, namely the family, with its special character, manners and traditions, had been modified in the course of the eighteenth century. The first work of the Revolution, its essential and fundamental work, which will not be shaken, and against which no reaction will take place because it corresponded to the transformation that had been accomplished in the very heart of the nation itself, was the destruction of the old French family. There was to be no more absolute paternal authority—listen to Mirabeau's long, his interminable bellowing against it—no more eldest son's rights, but only a very circumscribed right to make a will, no more inheritances transmitted in their entirety from generation to generation, no more family communities, no more *maisons de village*, no more of that family solidarity and one-ness. The time-honoured basis, on which ancient France had been built up, was laid in ruins, for the sentiments which had formed the mortar binding it together had decayed, had disappeared. In his *Mémoires de deux jeunes Mariées*, a marvel of historical perspicuity, Balzac wrote incomparable pages on this great historical fact. The real cause of the French Revolution lies therein, namely, in the transformation of the family which had made ancient France. And when the Restoration came, no one thought of modifying the work of the revolutionists on this point, because the family of olden times, whether under Louis XVIII and Charles X, under Napoleon as Consul or Emperor, or under Robespierre and Marat, existed no longer.

A second cause of the Revolution—for historic events rarely

have one sole cause—lay in the very progress which France had realized in the eighteenth century. She had been built up by those thousands and thousands of family groups which had increased in importance on the spots where they were rooted, and had developed in the course of centuries their local strength, along with their particular customs, ideas, and traditions. Hence arose those local groups, that "federalism," which Louis XIII and Richelieu had long ago detested, and which the revolutionists of 1793 persecuted with bloodthirsty hatred. Each family had been a closed cell shut up within another cell, either a village or town, —in a large number of towns each quarter even formed a private cell; each province, corporation, class, every division of the State was a closed cell, from which fact arose barriers between provinces and jurisdictions, and divergences in customs and legislation; then there were the many and varied privileges, the tolls on the roads and watercourses, all forming a State composed of hundreds of different States in juxtaposition. But a vast movement, arising from the progress we have sketched above, set in. Space was needed for self-development, for the widening out of social relations, the extension of trade and industry, the new-born national sentiment, and the transformation of habits resulting from these new circumstances. The cry was, "Break down the barriers between provinces, towns, wards, classes and families! Unite together!" In the course of their development those thousands and thousands of diverse groups had got nearer to each other and had clashed. A fusion, a national one-ness had become necessary, together with uniformity in the laws and administration. But each of these local forces had been fashioned after its particular traditions, each had its own habits, ideas, and past, which engendered a resistance to the very movement which was drawing it on. The King at the summit of the edifice, and the people at the bottom, were alone in their ability to come to terms in the general evolution, and to be in harmony with it; but the intermediate bodies, the most powerful, the most active in existence, armed with their privileges, their wealth, their past history, and their rights . . . !

The Kings, from the days of Louis XIII and Richelieu to Louis XIV and Colbert, and the Intendants under Louis XV, had striven to realize the unity that had become necessary to the national organization. The Ministers of Louis XVI worked at it with feverish energy. We have alluded to the resistance they encountered, a resistance all the stronger from France being then in a better condition to resist. Then came the Revolution, brutal, terrible, with the splendour of its pools of blood. In hundreds and thousands the "federalists" were guillotined in Paris, shot at Lyons, drowned at Nantes, and a certain number of throats were cut practically everywhere. France was flattened out and levelled; the old provinces, with their particular traditions and authorities, were pulled to pieces and cut up into departments. The first idea had been to call these departments, not by the names of their mountains and rivers, which would have left them too much local colour, but by numbers, which would have completely robbed France of her variegated physiognomy. When the Revolution had ended its career, after it had accomplished its task, the number of officials had increased tenfold. The France of patronal and feudal traditions, that picturesque, energetic France with her fruitful beginnings, her tangled offshoots teeming with life and colour—the old " family " France was dead : we were in presence of an administrative France.

The Revolution destroyed the old French family, and, by means of administration, gave to centralization the form suited to it. Neither was this second effect of its work touched by the Restoration. " We prefer the departments to the provinces," said a Minister of Louis XVIII.

The reform of the family, the reform of the administration : in these two essential characteristics which distinguished it well-nigh throughout, the work of the Revolution has lived on, for they were in accordance with the transformation in manners and customs that had taken place, and with new economic needs. Had Louis XVI remained on the throne, he and his successors, his Ministers or their successors, in spite of themselves, would have been brought to realize them.

BIBLIOGRAPHY

Ardascheff, trans. Jousserandot, *Les Intendants de province sous Louis XVI*, 1909.—Balzac (Honoré de), *Mémoires de deux jeunes mariées*, various eds.— Boiteau, *Etat de la France en 1789*, 2nd ed., 1889.—Busquet, *Hist. des Institutions de la Provence de 1483 à 1790*, 1920.—Carré (Henri), *La Noblesse en France et l'Opinion publique au dix-huitième siècle*, 1920.—Dreyfus (Ferdinand), *Un Philanthrope d'autrefois : La Rochefoucauld-Liancourt*, 1903.—Jobez (Alphonse), *La France sous Louis XVI*, 1877–1893, 3 vols.—Kovalewsky, *La France économique et sociale à la veille de la Révolution*, 1909.—Lavergne (Léonce de), *Les Assemblées provinciales sous Louis XVI*, 2nd ed., 1879.— Legrand d'Aussy, *Voyage fait en 1787–1788 dans ci-devant Auvergne*, an III, 3 vols.—Levasseur, *Des progrès de l'agriculture dans la seconde moitié du dix-huitième siècle*, in *Acad. des Sciences morales et politiques, Séances et travaux*, 1898.—Masson (E.), *La Puissance Paternelle et la Famille sous la Révolution*, 1910.—Mathieu (Cardinal), *L'Ancien Régime en Lorraine et en Barrois*, 4th ed., 1907.—Messance, *Nouvelles recherches sur la population de la France*, 1788. —Pradel de Lamase, *Une famille Française sous la Révolution*, 1912.—Ségur

(Comte de), *Mémoires*, Fayard, collection of *Mémoires Illustrés*.—Ségur (Marquis de), *Au couchant de la monarchie*, undated.—Semichon (Ernest), *Les Réformes de Louis XVI*, 1876.—Sépet (Marius), *Les Préliminaires de la Révolution*, 1890.—Tocqueville (Alexis de), *L'Ancien Régime et la Révolution*, 5th ed., 1866.—Wahl (Adalbert), *Vorgeschichte der franzosischen Revolution*, 1905–1907.—Young (Arthur), *Travels in France, 1787–1790*, 3 vols.

THE END

INDEX

Abbans, Jouffroy d', 360
Adalbéron, Archbishop of Rheims, 144
Aguesseau, H. F. d', and Bull *Unigenitus*, 233; as Chancellor, 254; and the Rouen Parliament, 348
Aigues-Mortes, 299
Aiguillon, Duc d', his "consolation" money, 110; Arthur Young on, 118; Parliament of Brittany's lawsuit against, 244; dismissal from office, 357
Aissé, Mlle, 334
Aix (Provence), magistrates of, 253; town clock of, 298; cannon of, 300
Albi, trumpeter of, 296
Alincourt, Mlle d', 62
Allier, village communities in, 50, 52
Alsace, customs of succession in, 44, 46; peasant dues in, 274; as a province *étrangère effective*, 346–7; *colonat* system in, 353
America, European consequences of discovery of, 77, 88; War of Independence, 320, 321, 357
Andilly, Robert Arnaud d', 24
Angers, seigneurial courts at, 130; public baths at, 315
Angoumois, customs of succession in, 45
Anjou, and House of Laval, 21; succession rights in, 43
Anville, Duchesse d', 119
Aranda, Comte d', and Métra, 331
Arc, Chevalier d', 108
Arc, Joan of, 7
Ardascheff, 358
Ardène's *Nouvelliste*, 30, 323
Ardres, Arnoul d', 75
Argenson, Comte d', exiled to his own property, 118, 189; and a *lettre de cachet*, 209
— Comtesse d', speculations of, 107
Argenson, Marquis d', his marriage, 29; on his family's solidarity, 46–7; on the Court, 168; on separation actions, 219–20; on agricultural distress, 269; on liberty, 343
Argentré, *Avis sur le Partage des Nobles*, 45
Arles, customs of succession in, 46
Aubigné, Charles d', as *nouvelliste*, 327
Auch, 101
Audrans, the, 67
Auguste III, King of Poland, 117
Aumale, Duc d', 110
Aunis, and customs duties, 347
Aussy, Legrand d', 275

Auvergne, abduction in, 38; customs of succession in, 45; village communities in, 48, 51, 52; election of the *Maître* in, 49; oppression of peasants in, 98; Intendant of, 311
Auxerre, municipal debts of, 304; municipal quarrels in, 311; finances of, 312
Avenel, Vicomte d', on marriage, 24; on family honour, 58; poverty of nobility, 91, 108; on Parliamentary families, 250; on rise in land values, 284; on Parliamentary alterations of Edicts, 350

Babeau, Albert, on respect for the past, 2; scenes at Besançon, 244; on village assemblies, 261; on education in the Dept. of Aube, 277; on the mediæval town, 292; the streets of France, 297; on Epernay, 300; on a General Assembly at Marseilles, 305; on the suppression of municipal elections, 307; on an Election at Marseilles, 308; as a historian, 310; on mediæval Troyes, 313; on liberty, 345
Bachaumont, President de, 255
Badonviller, feudal rights of, 299
Bailli, the office of, 133–5
Baillivy, Chevalier de, on *lettres de cachet*, 208
Bakery, Seigneurial, 20; see *Banalités*
Balzac, 25, 58, 96, 364
Banalités, 124–5
Barberino, Francesco da, 154
Barbezieux, 61–2
Barbier, description of a *lit de justice*, 240–1; on electing a Mayor, 303–4
Barbier de Séville, 340
Barine, Arvède, quoted, 24
Barnave, Antoine, 140
Barry, Comtesse du, 56, 188, 191, 193
Bastille, and the *nouvellistes*, 334; Louis XVI's decision to demolish, 362
Baudrillart, 24
Baume, House of, 21
Bayonne, the Mayor's robes, 295; the city as a god-parent, 296; militia of, 300; an independent State, 347
Beaubruns, the, 66–7
Beauce, payment of Bailli in, 134
Beaumarchais, *Mariage de Figaro*, 118; as Lt.-Gen. of Preserves, 128; and the Goezmann case, 248
Beaune, town clock of, 298

Beauvais, and seigneurial courts, 133
Belle-Isle, Maréchal de, 118
Benjamin, René, 70
Bernard, on peasant food, 275
Bernis, Cardinal de, 189
Berry, Province of, family laws in, 21 ;
and village communities, 54 ;
poverty of nobility in, 102
Berryer, 204 *et seq.*
Bertin, Comptroller General, 246
Besançon, Intendant of (1750), 102
Besançon, Parliament of, 243–4, 246
Besenval, on the Maupeou reform, 247 ;
on magistracy, 257 ; on public
opinion, 320
Bettoncourt, 129
Beugnot, Comte, on feudal rights, 122 ;
on the Duc de Penthièvre, 142 ; on
the magistracy, 252
Bèze, Théodore de, 90
Bignon (Advocate General), 37
Blainville (Lorraine), costs of justice, 136
Blois, Mlle de, marriage of, 32 ; her
bib, 147
Blois, Robert de, quoted, 4
Bodin, J., on the family's organization,
11, 12 ; on the father's authority,
14 ; on "family laws," 21 ; on
the Monarchy, 147 ; on the King
and his Parliament, 234 ; on
family origin of institutions, 291
Boissier, Gaston, on Mme de Sévigné, 334
Bonald, on conception of royalty, 153
Bordeaux, magisterial robes of, 295 ;
seigneurial obligations of, 299 ;
privileges of, 302 ; municipal finance
of, 312 ; trade in 1788, 318
Bort (Dept. of Corrèze), 265
Bossuet, 25
Boucher, François, 67
Bouhier, President, 255
Bouillon family, 24
Boulainvilliers, Henri de, quoted, 2, 347
Boulle, Charles, 68
Boulonnais, poverty of nobility in, 101 ;
independent constitution of, 346
Bourbon, Henri de, 25
Bourbon, House of, 19
Bourbonnais, customs of succession in,
45 ; village communities in, 52 ;
during Revolution, 286
Bourdaloue, 18, 34, 65, 181
Bourges, marriage custom in, 38 ;
magisterial robes, 295
Brantôme, 89–90, 92
Breteuil, as a Minister of reform, 249 ;
and *lettres de cachet*, 362
Brienne, Cardinal Loménie de, 249, 319
Brionne, Mme de, 64
Brissot, 105
Brittany, united to France, 18 ; and
House of Laval, 21 ; customs of
succession in, 43 ; rural nobility of,
78–9 ; staff of coastguards in, 94 ;
poverty of nobility, 101 ; Parliament's lawsuit against D'Aiguillon,
244 ; aristocratic magistracy of, 252 ;
peasant dress in, 274 ; as an independent province, 346, 347

Broc, Vicomte de, on feudal rights, 122
Broglie, Duc de, 190
Brosses, President de, 115, 255
Bruges, the "custom" of, 346
Burgundy, peasants in, 17 ; customs of
succession in, 45 ; purchase of
mairies, 303 ; as an independent
State, 347–8
Bussy-Rabutin, 32, 34, 156

Cadenet de Charleval, César de, 84
Caen, proposed destruction of the Tower
at, 229 ; public baths at, 315
Calonne, grants made by, 110 ; fall of,
319
Calonne, A. de, on gentlemen farmers, 119
Campan, Mme, on Louis XV, 158 ; on
Marie Antoinette, 194, 198
Candide, 9, 123
Caffiéri family, 68
Capet, Hugh, 144, 147
Capet Monarchy, customs of succession
under, 41
Capitaineries, the, 128
Carcassonne, 299
Carignan, Duc de, 107
Carré, M., quoted, 113, 248
Cartouche, 57
Caulaincourt, Marquis de, 119
Caumont La Force, Anne de, marriage
of, 39
Cens, the, 124
Cernon, 283
Chaffault, Admiral du, 121-2
Chalabre, Marquis de, 186
Challerenge, President Rolland de, 256
Châlon-sur-Saône, 305
Chambers, Robert, 353
Chamfort, 141
Chamillart, 31
Champagne, customs of succession in,
41, 44
Champfort, quoted, 113
Champion, Edme, 9
Champs (Auxerre), 133
Chanteloup, Château of, 117
Charles V, dispensing justice, 148
Charost, Duc de, services to agriculture,
119, 120
Charron, Pierre, *La Sagesse*, quoted, 311
Chartres, purchase of *mairie* in, 303
Chateaubriand, on his father, 14, 102–3 ;
on rural nobility, 96 ; story of his
poor cousin's pride, 139–40
Châtelet, Madame du, 140
Châtellerault : Militia of, 301 ; im-
prisonment of Mayor, 304
Chaulieu, Louise de, 25
Chaussée, Nivelle de la, 34, 35
Chevreuses, the, 19
Chevrier, 337–8
Choiseul, Duc de, at his château of
Chanteloup, 117 ; at a *lit de justice*
in Lorraine, 241–2
Clermont-Ferrand, its lack of cleanliness,
316, 317
Clermont-Tonnerre, family of, 64
Cognac, Declaration at (1622), 347
Coislin, Duc de, 66